A Critique of William Lane Craig's *In Quest of the Historical Adam*

A Critique of
William Lane Craig's
In Quest of the Historical Adam

Thomas A. Howe

WIPF & STOCK · Eugene, Oregon

A CRITIQUE OF WILLIAM LANE CRAIG'S *IN QUEST OF THE HISTORICAL ADAM*

Copyright © 2022 Thomas A. Howe. All rights reserved. Except for brief quotations in critical publications or reviews, no part of this book may be reproduced in any manner without prior written permission from the publisher. Write: Permissions, Wipf and Stock Publishers, 199 W. 8th Ave., Suite 3, Eugene, OR 97401.

Wipf & Stock
An Imprint of Wipf and Stock Publishers
199 W. 8th Ave., Suite 3
Eugene, OR 97401

www.wipfandstock.com

PAPERBACK ISBN: 978-1-6667-9756-5
HARDCOVER ISBN: 978-1-6667-9755-8
EBOOK ISBN: 978-1-6667-9754-1

05/19/22

Contents

List of Figures | vii
List of Tables | ix
Acknowledgements | xi
Abbreviations | xiii
Introduction | xv

1. What Is At Stake? | 1
2. The Nature of Myth | 34
3. Are the Primaeval Narratives of Genesis 1–11 Myth? (Part 1) | 47
4. Are the Primaeval Narratives of Genesis 1–11 Myth? (Part 2) | 67
5. Is Genesis 1–11 Mytho History? | 116
6. Are Myths Believed To Be True? | 129
7. Adam in the New Testament | 162
8. Scientific and Philosophical Preliminaries | 223
9. Locating the Historical Adam | 232
10. Putting It All Together | 235

Bibliography | 251
Index | 257

List of Figures

Figure 1: Pentateuch Basic Structure | 16

Figure 2: Flood Chiasm | 21

Figure 3: Comparison of Language in Exodus-Numbers | 24

Figure 4: Exodus-Numbers | 25

Figure 5: Assumption of Movement | 28

Figure 6: Family Resemblances | 34

Figure 7: Genealogy of Genesis 5 | 48

Figure 8: Adam Genealogy | 50

Figure 9: Creation Week | 83

Figure 10: The Serpent | 87

Figure 11: Death Mask | 89

Figure 12: The Saraswati Palaeochannel | 94

Figure 13: Genesis Genealogies | 119

Figure 14: Waters Above and Below | 139

Figure 15: Thematic Structure of Isaiah | 145

Figure 16: Plate 163 | 150

Figure 17: Plate 165 | 151

Figure 18: Flow in Genesis 1–7 | 158

Figure 19: Claims about Claims | 163

Figure 20: Verbs and Verbals in 2 Peter 2 | 178

Figure 21: Adam and Christ Parallel | 198

Figure 22: Rom. 5:12 Diagram: Greek | 208

Figure 23: Rom. 5:12 Diagram: English | 209

Figure 24: Eph. 2:8 Diagram | 210

List of Tables

Table #1: Repetition of Creation Imagery | 17
Table #2: The Four Adams | 20
Table #3: Japheth, Ham, and Shem Genealogies | 24
Table #4: Comparison of Pharaoh and Balak | 26
Table #5: Genesis 1 and Genesis 2 Creation Order | 79

Acknowledgements

A SPECIAL THANK YOU to Dr. Doug Potter for his input and editing of the manuscript. Thank you to Aimee Cassada for reading the manuscript, making suggestions, and correcting errors.

Abbreviations

BDAG Arndt, William, Frederick W. Danker, Walter Bauer, and F. Wilbur Gingrich. *A Greek-English Lexicon of the New Testament and Other Early Christian Literature*, 3d ed. Chicago: University of Chicago Press, 2000.

CSD Smith, R. Payne. Edited by J. Payne Smith. *A Compendious Syriac Dictionary: Founded upon the Thesaurus Syriacus of R. Payne Smith.* Oxford: Oxford University Press, 1902.

HAL Koehler, Ludwig, and Walter Baumgartner. *The Hebrew & Aramaic Lexicon of the Old Testament.* Leiden: Brill, 2001.

LXX Rahlfs, Alfred. *Septuaginta*. Stuttgart: Deutsche Bibelgesellschaft, 1979.

SSL Sokoloff, Michael. *A Syriac Lexicon*. Winona Lake, Indiana: Eisenbrauns, 2009.

ZE Ziegler, Joseph. *Ezechiel*. Vol. XVI, 1. *Vetus Testamentum Graecum. Auctoritate Academiae Scientiarum Gottingensis Editum.* Göttingen: Vandenhoeck & Ruprecht, 2006.

ZJ Joseph, Ziegler, ed. *Iob*. Vol. XI, 4, *Vetus Testamentum Graecum. Auctoritate Academiae Scientiarum Gottingensis Editum.* Göttingen: Vandenhoeck & Ruprecht, 1982.

Introduction

FOR EVANGELICAL CHRISTIANS THERE can be no argument that Dr. William Lane Craig has had an important and beneficial impact. For many, he is considered to be a Christian scholar's scholar. Even attempting to list the books, articles, debates, lectures, etc., would not do justice to his importance for Christian apologetics, theology, and philosophy. He has defended the historic Christian faith against countless attacks and has demonstrated that Christian thinkers are a force that cannot be brushed aside or ignored.

His latest book, *In Quest for the Historical Adam*, is generating as much if not more attention than any of his previous publications. This text is controversial, but the controversy is not primarily from those outside the faith. His claims in this book have penetrated to the very foundations of classical orthodox theology, and many Christians are alarmed at his conclusions. Dr. Craig has set out on a quest to discover, by philosophical argument, an analysis of the biblical text, appeal to contemporary evolutionary theory, and arguments from an array of disciplines, whether the Adam depicted in the Genesis account was an actual historical person.

Dr. Craig attempts to show that the narratives of Gen 1–11 should be understood in the literary context of Ancient Near Eastern (ANE) myths. According to Craig, the narratives of Gen 1–11 should be thematically separated from the rest of the Pentateuch as containing the primaeval history. Craig classifies these narratives as mytho-history. According to Craig, mytho-history is a genre in which these narratives contain some or all of the characteristics of a myth but also contain an historical interest. In the biblical narratives, the historical interest is found in the genealogies that depict a generally chronological progression. Craig is not proposing that the biblical authors borrowed from ANE myths. Rather, he argues that the Genesis narratives compare to ANE myths by containing fantastic elements that Craig argues are "palpably false" if taken literally. For Craig, fantastic elements are not troubled by logical contradiction or inconsistencies in the narrative. For example, Craig argues that the story of a world wide flood is a fantastic element that should not be taken literally and should not be interpreted as recounting actual historical events. As mytho-history the author(s) of the narratives of Gen 1–11 did not mean for them to be taken literally. Rather, these narratives function as the foundation myths for the nation of Israel. Ultimately Craig believes that it cannot be known with certainty whether the Adam of Genesis was an actual historical figure.

Following the structure of his book, this essay is a critical evaluation and response to Dr. Craig's arguments and conclusions about the historical Adam. This essay will propose that Craig's separation of Gen 1–11 violates the literary strategy of the biblical author, that Craig's adoption of Wittgenstein's notion of family resemblances is illegitimate both in Wittgenstein's project and Craig's application of it to biblical narratives, and that Craig's lack of facility in the biblical languages has repeatedly led him to interpretive conclusions that cannot be supported by the text. Ultimately the goal is to demonstrate that Craig's claim that the narratives of Gen 1–11 are mytho-history are not only not convincing, but that they are philosophically, biblically, and theologically erroneous.

For the sake of informing the reader about this author's qualifications, for thirty years I have been Professor of Bible and Biblical Languages at Southern Evangelical Seminary in Charlotte, North Carolina. I have been both a formal and an independent student of biblical Hebrew, Aramaic, and Greek for more than forty years. I have taught introductory and advanced courses in grammar, syntax, and exegesis of Hebrew, Aramaic, and Greek, and I have personally translated the entire Bible from Hebrew, Aramaic, and Greek.

Throughout this essay there will be frequent references to Dr. Craig's lack of facility in biblical Hebrew and koine Greek; not just in the lexicology, but in the grammar and syntax of the languages. It must be emphasized that this is not an intent to mount an *ad hominem* abusive argument against Dr. Craig. Many people misunderstand an *ad hominem* argument as a logical fallacy. Not every *ad hominem* argument is a fallacy, as Howard Kahane explains: "The question of when an *ad hominem* argument is fallacious, and when not, is quite complex. In general, it can be said that such an argument is *not* fallacious when the man argued against is or claims to be an *expert* on the question at issue."[1] Dr. Craig consistently presents his arguments as if his rendering of the text is accurate, and yet in almost every case Dr. Craig has misunderstood and misrepresented the words, grammar, and/or syntax of the texts. Nevertheless, this is about his arguments and claims, not about the person.

1. Kahane, *Logic and Philosophy*, 240.

1

What Is At Stake?

What Is At Stake?

CRAIG IS CERTAINLY NOT one to shy away from the difficult questions. He faces them head on, and this book is no different. Chapter 1 of his book is titled, "What Is At Stake."

> The attempt to make the doctrine of original sin a necessary condition of the doctrine of the atonement is, however, an overreach. Nowhere in the New Testament (NT) is Christ said to have died for original sin. Rather, the gospel proclaimed by the apostles was, in the words of the traditional kerygmatic formulation quoted by Paul, that "Christ died for our sins in accordance with the scriptures" (1 Cor 15:3). Never mind Adam's sin; ours alone are quite sufficient to require the atoning death of Christ for salvation! Interpreting Adam as a purely symbolic figure, a sort of Everyman, that expresses the universality of human sin and fallenness would not undercut the gospel of salvation through Christ's atoning death. Therefore, denial of the doctrine of original sin does not undermine the doctrine of the atonement.[1]

There are, of course, many things that the New Testament does not express in the way we might. To say, "Nowhere in the New Testament is Christ said to have died for original sin," does not make any substantive claim about whether it is true that he did or whether the New Testament

---

1. Craig, *Adam*, 5.

teaches this as truth. Nowhere in the New Testament is Christ said to have died for William Lane Craig, but I believe that the NT teaches this as truth. Christ did indeed die for William Lane Craig because the NT declares that Christ died for all of us. The truth is taught even though it is not expressed in so many terms. By the same token, nowhere does the NT say that Christ *did not* die for original sin. Of course, Craig is not necessarily arguing that this particular expression is not asserted in the NT. He is saying that since the NT does not say that he did die for original sin, then this doctrine may not be taught in the NT, although it seems as if Craig is making a stronger statement than that the doctrine "may not" be taught. He rather seems to be declaring that the doctrine *is not* taught in the NT regardless of how it might be expressed.

The appeal to 1 Cor 15:3 does not necessarily support the claim that Jesus did not die for original sin. The text states, "For I delivered to you as of first importance what I also received, that Christ died for our sins according to the Scriptures" (1 Cor 15:3).[2] I suspect Craig would not deny that if Adam was an actual historical person, that Christ died also for Adam's sin. To claim that our sins are sufficient to require the atoning death of Christ says nothing about whether there was an historical Adam as the one through whom sin entered the world. Nor does it even imply that Christ did not die for original sin.

As early as the writings of Tertullian (AD 160–220) the doctrine of original sin was a Christian conviction:

> You pronounce Satan in all aversion, disdain, and detestation, whom we call the angel of malice, the craftsman of all error, the corrupter of the entire world, by whom man from the beginning was deceived to transgress the command of God, and for this reason he was given to death, and afterward made the whole race of his own semen infected with the transmission of his own condemnation.[3]

Augustine argued that the death of infants demonstrated the fact of original sin:

---

2. Παρέδωκα γὰρ ὑμῖν ἐν πρώτοις, ἃ καὶ παρέλαβον, ὅτι Χριστὸς ἀπέθανεν ὑπὲρ τῶν ἁμαρτιῶν ὑμῶν κατὰ τὰς γραφάς (1 Cor 15:3).

3. Tertullian, "De Testimonio Animae," 3.181. "Satanan denique in omni aversatione et aspernatione et detestatione pronuntias, quem nos dicimus malitiae angelum, totius erroris artificem, totius seculi interpolatorem, per quem homo a primordio circumventus, ut praeceptum dei excederet, et propterea in mortem datus, exinde totum genus de suo semine infectum suae etiam damnationis traducem fecit."

> However, everyone—including even children—have broken God's covenant, not, indeed, in virtue of any personal action, but in virtue of mankind's common origin in that single ancestor in whom all have sinned... Yet, what is said in the Psalm is true: "I have reckoned as transgressors all the sinners of the earth" [Ps 119:119]. We must take this to mean that all who are held responsible for any sin are guilty of the transgression of some law. That is why even children are born in sin, not, as the true faith teaches us, in actual personal sin, but in original sin, and hence need the grace, as we say in the Creed, of the forgiveness of sins.[4]

As we will demonstrate below, the fact that death reigned from Adam to Moses even over those who had not sinned in the same way Adam sinned testifies to the fact of original sin.

It is difficult, however, to pass up the observation that Craig has prejudiced the reader before making his case. He simply declares, "Therefore, denial of the doctrine of original sin does not undermine the doctrine of the atonement." In fact, denial of the doctrine of original sin may indeed undermine the doctrine of the atonement, but should such a statement at the beginning be expressed as a fact without any support having yet been presented? If there was no original sin, then how did sin enter the world? Did sin enter the world by the actions of distinct individuals? Did a group of people sin together by which sin entered the world? And if sin entered the world by way of each individual sinning, does this not constitute an original sin? Or does sin "enter" the world when each human being becomes old enough to sin? And if each individual falls when he first sins, why would each human inevitably sin? But perhaps we are getting ahead of ourselves and ahead of Craig's arguments. Perhaps he will address the questions in due course.

---

4. Augustine, *City of God*, Books VIII–XVI, 537–38. "nisi quia etiam parvuli, non secundum suæ vitæ proprietatem, sed secundum communem generis humani originem, omnes in illo uno testamentum Dei dissipaverunt, in quo omnes peccaverunt... quo pacto quod legitur in Psalmo verum est, *Prævaricatores æstimavi omnes peccatores terræ* [Ps 119:119]; nisi quia omnes legis alicujus prævaricatæ sunt rei, qui aliquo peccato tenetur obstricti? Quamobrem si etiam parvuli, quod vera fides habet, nascuntur non proprie, sed originaliter peccatores, unde illis gratiam remissionis peccatorum necessariam confitemur;" Sancti Aurelii Augustini, *Civitate Dei*, XVI.27.700.

Craig goes on to assert, "It is, however, dubious that the doctrine of original sin is essential to the Christian faith."[5] Craig adds a footnote to this statement:

> For the opposite view, see the treatment of Matthew Levering, *Engaging the Doctrine of Creation; Cosmos, Creatures, and the Wise and Good Creator* (Grand Rapids: Baker Academic, 2017), chap. 6. As a Catholic theologian, Levering is guided in his theologizing principally by the teaching of the magisterium rather than Scripture, which takes a decidedly subordinate role in his discussion. By contrast, for me as an evangelical Protestant, the teaching of Scripture is paramount; hence, our strikingly different treatments of the importance of the historical Adam.[6]

It is curious that Craig does not reference any Protestant theologians, for example, Francis Turretin, Herman Bavinck, Charles Hodge, Herman Hoeksema, John Murray, Robert Duncan Culver, etc., who were committed to the doctrine of original sin. It is also curious that Craig does not allow the possibility that Levering depends upon the teaching of the magisterium because he, Levering, believes that the magisterium depends upon Scripture. Craig depends on other theologians whom he, Craig, believes depend upon Scripture. In fact, he does this with David Clines' claims about the structure of the Pentateuch. And to imply that the reason for the "strikingly different treatments" is because Levering is a Catholic and Craig is a Protestant seems to be designed to present Craig's view as a Protestant view while the contrary view is a Catholic view. This seems to be disingenuous treatment. It is certainly true that Protestants and Catholics have many contrary views, but it is also true that they have many views that are consistent; the Trinity, the deity of Christ, et al.

In support of his claim that the doctrine of original sin is dubious, he argues,

> Paul does not teach clearly that either (1) Adam's sin is imputed to every one of his descendants or (2) Adam's sin resulted in a corruption of human nature or a privation of original righteousness that is transmitted to all of his descendants. That Christianity can get along without (1) is evident from the example of the Orthodox Church, whose doctrine of original sin affirms only (2). Even (2) can hardly be said to be essential: not only

---

5. Craig, *Adam*, 5.
6. Craig, *Adam*, n4.

is it not clearly taught in Rom 5, but the mere universality of sin among human beings is sufficient to require Christ's atoning death for our salvation. "Since all have sinned and fall short of the glory of God, they are justified by his grace as a gift, through the redemption which is in Christ Jesus" (Rom 3:23–24). The attempt to explain the universality of human sin by postulating a corruption or wounding of human nature inherited from Adam is a theological add-on to which the Christian theologian need not be committed.[7]

There are a number of problems with his argument. First, who decides what Paul "clearly" taught? Just because it might not be clear to Craig does not show that it is not clear in itself. Something can be clear in itself and to us, and something can be clear in itself and not to us. That a whole is greater than any one of its parts is clear in itself, but for someone who does not know the meaning of the words "whole" and "part," it would not be clear. What Paul teaches may be clear in itself but not to Craig because Craig either has misinterpreted the text, or because he does not understand the terms, in this case Greek terms, used by Paul, or because Craig has imposed his prior assumptions on the texts. Again by way of prejudicing his reader without having given any supporting evidence, Craig simply declares *ex cathedra* that Paul's statements are not clear. Isn't it interesting that Craig claims that certain of Paul's teaching is not clear—when Craig disagrees with Paul's teaching—while he quotes from Rom 3:23–24 as if this is clear—when it benefits Craig's cause? Are there not also conflicting interpretations of these verses? Craig has clearly set himself as the authority on what is and what is not clear.

Second, to claim that Christianity can "get along" without point 1 because the "Orthodox Church"—Craig's designation—affirms only point 2 is predicated on a variety of unstated assumptions. First, what does it mean for the Orthodox Church to "get along"? Does it mean that they continue to function as a church? Atheists seem to "get along" with their denial that God exists, but that does not make their denial true. All this proves is that this particular church "gets along" without point 1. It does not in the least show that Christianity *qua* Christianity can "get along" without it. Many Arminian theologians "get along" with the belief that a person can lose his salvation. Second, Craig assumes that what the Orthodox Church can "get along" without is sufficient to show what Christianity can "get along" without. Craig assumes that churches who

---

7 Craig, *Adam*, 6.

cannot "get along" without point 1 are in error. Isn't it possible that "getting along" without point 1 is simply an error of the Orthodox Church? Third, Craig assumes that the Orthodox Church is coincident with Christianity. There are other churches and denominations that cannot "get along" without point 1. Is Craig implying that these churches are therefore not Christian or are not part of Christianity? Fourth, Craig assumes that what he thinks Christianity can "get along" without is in fact what Christianity can "get along" without. But isn't this the very point at issue? To state this up front before making his case begs the question and prejudices the reader.

Third, Craig, again *ex cathedra*, declares, "The attempt to explain the universality of human sin by postulating a corruption or wounding of human nature inherited from Adam is a theological add-on to which the Christian theologian need not be committed." In fact, isn't this the very question? Isn't this the point of contention? Craig has assumed his conclusion before presenting any evidence for his conclusion. Craig seems to function as a one-man magisterium.

It is disappointing that such an accomplished scholar as William Lane Craig would engage in such derogatory characterizations as the following:

> Ironically, perhaps, they [revisionist theologians] are thus hermeneutical bed fellows with traditional literalists, who argue that the plain interpretation of Scripture is that the world is a recent creation by God in six consecutive days, that there was an original human pair living in the Garden of Eden who sinned by eating the fruit of the tree of the knowledge of good and evil, that there was a worldwide flood that destroyed all terrestrial life save that aboard the ark built by Noah, that the world's languages resulted from the confusion of tongues at the Tower of Babel, and so on.[8]

First, "traditional literalists" do not constitute a monolithic conglomerate of interpreters as Craig presents it. There certainly have been interpreters who have taken each statement in Scripture in a strictly literal sense. Finis Jennings Dake taught that God has a literal, spiritual body with arms, legs, a mouth, etc., and that God lives on a planet called "Heaven." The expression "traditional literalists" is an ambiguous and unjustly prejudicial characterization.

---

8. Craig, *Adam*, 9.

Second, Craig misrepresents "traditional literalists" as holding to a "plain interpretation," whatever that is. Most Evangelical interpreters who might be characterized as "traditional literalists" hold to an essentially literal interpretation, which takes into account figurative expressions, the use of round numbers, literary features of the text, etc. In fact, Craig acknowledges this later when he says, "Such a straightforward interpretation of the text does not exclude the use of figures of speech like 'the eyes of both were opened' (Gen 3:7), but it does affirm that the [creation] accounts are basically nonfigurative."[9] To identify traditional literalists as he does seems to be calculated to stigmatize literal interpretation.

Third, to claim that "traditional literalists" hold that "the world is a recent creation" is calculated to put literal interpretation into the camp of Bishop Ussher. What does it even mean to say "a recent creation"? Considering the billions of years proposed by many evolutionists, to claim that the earth was created one hundred thousand years ago could qualify as a "recent creation." Even to propose that the earth was created one million years ago would be "recent" in relation even to one billion years. Assuming that a stack of one hundred dollar bills six inches tall would amount to one million dollars, a stack of one hundred dollar bills amounting to one billion dollars would be six thousand inches or five hundred feet tall. There is an enormous distance between one million and one billion. I am not aware of any young earth creationist who believes that the earth was created one million years ago, but the characterization of young earth creationists as holding to "a recent creation" can only be prejudicial.

Fourth, to believe that the earth was created in six literal days does not necessarily mean that such an interpreter holds that the world was "a recent creation." Someone could hold that the world was created in six literal days one million years ago. In fact, John Sailhamer made this very kind of argument:

> There is no textual reason why "the beginning" in Genesis 1:1 could not have lasted millions, or even billions, of years. However, the word does not *require* vast time periods; it leaves the duration an open question.
>
> I contend that two distinct time periods are mentioned in Genesis 1. In the first period (the "beginning," Genesis 1:1), God created the universe; no time limitations are placed on that period. In the second period (Genesis 1:2—2:4a), God prepared

---

9. Craig, *Adam*, 13.

the garden of Eden for man's dwelling; that activity occurred in one week.[10]

Additionally, how likely is it that the author of the Pentateuch, whom I assume to have been Moses, could have expected his audience at that time in history to think of the beginning of the world as having occurred billions of years ago? There certainly were ancient cultures who held the belief in an ancient creation. Some ancient Hindu texts describe an ongoing cyclic process of creation and destruction spanning trillions of years or even involving an infinite cycle. However, there is no evidence that the people in the time of Moses held such views. Also, there is no reason to think that when Moses referred to "evening and morning," that he would have expected his audience to understand this expression in any other terms than a single, literal day. Although the word "day" (יוֹם, yôm) can be used to refer to an indefinite period, this does not show that it must be so understood in the enumeration of the creation days. Also, if an interpreter takes the word "day" in the creation account to refer to an indefinite period of time, what does he then do with the word "night" (לַיְלָה, lâlāh)? Are we to conclude that the nights were also undetermined periods? Again Craig's statements seem to be calculated to place the essentially literal approach in an unfavorable light in order to prejudice the reader.

Fifth, there are some serious problems with the way Craig renders the biblical text. For example, the text does not say that Adam and Eve were "living in the Garden of Eden." The text states, "And planted YHWH God a garden in Eden [גַּן־בְּעֵדֶן, gan bĕʿēḏen] toward east, and there He put the man whom He formed" (Gen 2:8).[11] God put the man in Eden. It does not say that he put the man in the garden to live there. Now this might seem rather nitpicking, but it may also indicate a lack of familiarity with Hebrew syntax and grammar. We perhaps see this emerging in his rendering, "tree of the knowledge of good and evil." In fact, the text refers to the tree as "the tree of the knowledge, good and evil" (הַדַּעַת טוֹב, haddaʿat ṭôḇ wārāʿ). The word הַדַּעַת (haddaʿat, "the knowledge") has the definite article and therefore cannot be in a construct relation to the words טוֹב וָרָע (ṭôḇ wārāʿ, "good and evil"). A construct relation is the juxtaposition of two or more nouns that indicate a genitive relation between the words. So, for example, the word דַּעַת (daʿat) in the absolute state

---

10. Sailhamer, *Genesis Unbound*, 33.
11. (Gen 2:8) וַיִּטַּע יְהוָה אֱלֹהִים גַּן־בְּעֵדֶן מִקֶּדֶם וַיָּשֶׂם שָׁם אֶת־הָאָדָם אֲשֶׁר יָצָר

means "knowledge."[12] In the construct state, the word means "knowledge of," as in דַּעַת אֱלֹהִים (daʿat ʾĕlōhîm), meaning "the knowledge of God," in which the word translated "God" is in the absolute state. However, a word in the construct state can never take a definite article. The word in the construct state gets its definiteness from the word in the absolute state. As in the example, the word translated "the knowledge of" does not have a definite article, but it gets its definiteness from the word translated "God," since it is a definite name. In the text, the word הַדַּעַת (haddaʿat) has the definite article, so it cannot be in a construct relation, therefore it cannot be translated "the knowledge of good and evil." It must have the sense of "the knowledge, good and evil" such that the words "good and evil" qualify the word "the knowledge." Not being familiar with Hebrew syntax, Craig is thinking that the text is talking about eating the fruit as transmitting some content of the knowledge.

We will begin to see a pattern in Craig's rendering of various passages of the OT that reveal a lack of facility in Hebrew lexicology, grammar, and syntax. For example, we see this in his rendering of Gen 12:3: "... and by you all the families of the earth shall bless themselves."[13] The text actually states, וְנִבְרְכוּ בְךָ כֹּל מִשְׁפְּחֹת הָאֲדָמָה (wĕnibrĕkû bĕkā kō mišpĕḥōt hāʾădāmāh). The word that Craig renders "shall bless themselves" is a Niphal verb. As Waltke and O'Connor point out, the Niphahl verb in this instance is passive, not reciprocal:

> 1a. "And through your offspring all nations of the earth *will be blessed* [וְהִתְבָּרֲכוּ, wĕhitbārăkû]" (*Hithpael*). Gen 22:18
>
> 1b. "And through you all peoples on earth *will be blessed* [וְנִבְרְכוּ, wĕnibrĕkû]" (*Niphal*). Gen 12:3
>
> The passive import of both verbs is clear from the context: it is God who blesses (Gen 12:3a, 22:17), that is, who fills the potency for life, albeit through an agent. With some verbs the *Niphal* suffix conjugation and the *Hithpael* prefix conjugation supplement or complement one another, forming one paradigm;[14]

No doubt Craig gets this rendering from Clines who characteristically renders the verb as reciprocal—22:18, 26:4; 28:14. Since each one of these instances follows the pattern of the statement in Gen 12:3, rendering these as reciprocal is contrary to the context of each and is contrary

---

12. See HAL, s.v. "דַּעַת."
13. Craig, *Adam*, 21.
14. Waltke and O'Connor, *Introduction to Biblical Hebrew*, 395.

to Hebrew syntax. What seem to be minor points begin to reveal a lack of facility in the original language.

Again Craig misrepresents the case. He says, "On the other hand, young earth creationism's scientific claim is wildly implausible. By its proponents' own admission, young earth creationism places Genesis into massive conflict with mainstream science, not to mention history and linguistics."[15] By "mainstream science" Craig seems to be referring to some form of evolutionary theory. Of course, on the basis of his interpretation of the evidence, Craig thinks that the claims of young earth creationists are "wildly implausible." But many scientists reject, on scientific grounds, the claims of evolution. One might say that many scientists "get along" without accepting naturalistic evolution. And to claim that young earth creationism is "wildly implausible" on the basis of linguistics is wildly implausible. To whose notion of language would one appeal—Aristotle,[16] Ockham, Locke, Kant, Condillac, Humboldt, Frege, Marx, Wittgenstein, Heidegger, Derrida, Quine, etc.? If Craig is using the word "linguistics" in a strict sense, he is faced with the same situation. Linguistics is not a monolithic discipline. Whose linguistics—Peter Ramus, the Port-Royal Grammarians, Saussure, Sapir, Whorf, Skinner, Jacobson, Hjelmslev, Bloomfield, Chomsky, Harris, Evans, McWhorter, et al.? But one has the same problem with reference to history. Whose interpretation—realist historians, speculative historians, positivist historians, Marxist historians, postmodern historians, historical determinists, etc.? To claim that young earth creationism is "wildly implausible" on the basis of history and linguistics is wildly simplistic and disingenuous. And truth is not determined by the "mainstream." At one time mainstream science held that the earth was the center of the solar system.

Craig goes on to assert, "In defense of their view, creation scientists tend to focus on anomalies within the current scientific paradigm, failing to appreciate that the presence of anomalies serves neither to overturn the overwhelming weight of the evidence nor to establish a credible alternative paradigm."[17] One wonders if Craig has actually read any of the creation scientists. There can be no doubt that he has, since in their book, *Philosophical Foundations for a Christian Worldview*, both Craig

---

15. Craig, *Adam*, 13.

16. Many scholars have denied that Aristotle had a theory of language, but Deborah Modrak has shown that in fact he did: see Modrak, *Aristotle's Theory of Language and Meaning*.

17. Craig, *Adam*, 13–14.

and Moreland argue that Intelligent Design (ID) creation scientists do in fact offer a credible alternative paradigm to naturalistic evolutionism. For example, they argue, "According to ID advocates, one can use science to discover the products of intelligent design without having any idea how those products came about. Critics who raise a 'god-of-the-gaps' objection against theistic science fail to take into account ID theory."[18]

In another place Moreland asserts,

> the ID movement not only exemplifies the value of objective reason, but also supports it.
>
> (2) An ID approach to science does not take place in an intellectual vacuum. Rather, it is an expression a realist view of science. Scientific realism may be taken to countenance these propositions:
>
> SR 1: The central observational and theoretical subject terms in a mature science refer to entities the world (referential realism).
>
> SR 2: Scientific theories (in mature, developed sciences) are true or approximately true (truth realism).
>
> SR 3: Scientific rivals are commensurable and scientific rationality is epistemically objective (epistemic objectivity).[19]

ID creationists are not necessarily young earth creationists, but many are. Craig and Moreland do not necessarily subscribe to the ID approach, but one must wonder why Craig has seemed to backpedal on his earlier more favorable account of ID creationism.[20] There is no doubt that Craig has entered his "quest" assuming an evolutionary perspective and presenting it as if it is *the* measure of the validity of an approach to cosmogony.

Structure of the Pentateuch

In this section Craig wants to justify his belief that Gen 1–11 should be treated as thematically distinct from the rest of the Pentateuch. Beginning on page 21, he briefly discusses the theme of the Pentateuch. It is curious that he takes David J. A. Clines' notion of the theme rather than any other OT scholar; for example, John H. Sailhamer,[21] or O. T. Allis,[22] or R.

18. Moreland and Craig, *Philosophical Foundations*, 364.
19. Moreland, "Postmodernism and the Intelligent Design Movement," 99.
20. See Moreland and Craig, *Philosophical Foundations*, 356–58, 484.
21. Sailhamer, *Meaning of the Pentateuch*; Sailhamer, *Pentateuch as Narrative*.
22. Allis, *Five Books of Moses*.

Norman Whybray,[23] or the myriad of other OT scholars. Not that Clines is necessarily incorrect, but Craig's presentation is extremely one-sided, and yet he presents this as if Clines' proposal in fact captures the theme of the Pentateuch. It is clearly Clines' thematic separation of Gen 1–11 from the rest of the Pentateuch that is of significance for Craig.

It is also curious that Craig would adopt Clines' position since Clines has identified himself as a postmodernist. Clines asserts,

> So the postmodern is where I am at now, whatever that means, and whatever postmodern means. In the essay called 'The Pyramid and the Net: The Postmodern Adventure in Biblical Studies' (pp. 138–57 below), I have developed the image of the net as symbol of the postmodern, decentred and flexible and polymorphous and multifunctional. It is different in so many ways from the pyramid, which for me has been the symbol of the modern, stable and unitary and totalizing and impressive, like the structure of Western intellectual thought. I try to stress in that essay that I do not see the postmodern as displacing the modern, nor yet as being only a supplement to it. I see the postmodern as a quizzical re-evaluation of the values of the modern, and I suggest how the practice of biblical studies in the coming century could be transformed by a series of postmodern reappraisals.[24]

Clines has adopted the postmodern rejection of metanarratives, *à la* Lyotard, and company. Jean-François Lyotard (1924–98), a French philosopher, sociologist, and literary theorist, has been characterized as one of the leading strategists in the development and propagation of postmodernism. For Lyotard, postmodernism is the disbelief or rejection of metanarratives:

> To oversimplify, the disbelief in the meta-narratives is "postmodern." This is undoubtedly an effect of the progress of the sciences; but this progress in its turn presupposes it. To the obsolescence of the metanarrative device of legitimation corresponds in particular the crisis of metaphysical philosophy, and that of the university institution which depended on it. The narrative function loses its functors, the great hero, the great perils, the great perils, the great journeys and the great goal.[25]

23. Whybray, *Introduction to the Pentateuch*.

24. Clines, "On the Way to the Postmodern," xvi.

25. Lyotard, *La Condition Postmoderne: Rapport Sur Le Savoir*, 7–8. "En simplifiant à l'extrême, on tient pour « postmoderne » l'incrédulité à l'égard des métarécits. Celleoci est sans doute un effet du progrès des sciences; mais ce progrès à son tour la

A metanarrative is a second order explanation that is designed to encompass and account for everything. The example Lyotard uses is the legitimation of the rules of science by an appeal to philosophy. In this instance, philosophy would be the metanarrative designed to legitimate the rules of science. The ultimate metanarrative would be a grand narrative that is designed to legitimate or explain life, the world, and reality. Of course the Bible is one of those metanarratives with its "stable and unitary and totalizing" narrative that explains, accounts for, and gives value to everything.

Pointing out that Clines has adopted a postmodernist perspective may seem to be an *ad hominem* fallacy, but such arguments are not necessarily fallacies. Only when the *ad hominem* is abusive is it a fallacy. But being a postmodernist speaks to Clines' very worldview, how he views the text, his interpretive grid. Clines' rejection of "modern, stable and unitary and totalizing" structures, i.e., metanarratives, speaks to the way he interprets the biblical text. Either he must reject the Bible as a metanarrative, or he must treat the Bible as simply one among a multitude of narratives having equal validity and truth, or he must reject postmodernism. He certainly did not opt for the rejection of postmodernism.

J. P. Moreland explains,

> As a philosophical standpoint, postmodernism is primarily a reinterpretation of what knowledge is and what counts as knowledge. More broadly, it represents a form of cultural relativism about such things as reality, truth, reason, value, linguistic meaning, the self, and other notions. On a postmodernist view, there is no such thing as objective reality, truth, value, reason, and so forth. All these are social constructions, creations of linguistic practices, and as such are relative not to individuals, but to social groups that share a narrative.[26]

According to Moreland and Craig, from a postmodernist perspective there is no objective meaning in a text:

> According to postmodernism, an item of language, such as a literary text, does not have an authorial meaning, at least one that is accessible to interpreters. Thus the author is in no privileged

---

suppose. À la désuétude du dispositif métanarratif de légitimation correspond notamment la crise de la philosophie métaphysique, et celle de l'institution universitaire qui dépendait d'elle. La fonction narrative perd ses foncteurs, le grand héros, les grands périls, les grands périls, les grands périples et le grand but."

26. Moreland, "Truth, Contemporary Philosophy and the Postmodern Turn," 79.

position to interpret his own work. In fact, the meaning of a text is created by and resides in the community of readers who share an interpretation of the text. Thus there is not such thing as a book of Romans. Rather, there is a Lutheran, Catholic and Marxist book of Romans.[27]

For the postmodernist there is no objective truth. Rather "truth" is culturally determined or determined by one's own perspective. It seems to follow from Clines' commitment to the rejection of metanarratives and the relativity of truth that Clines' claims about the structure of the Pentateuch are not about the structure of the Pentateuch at all. Rather it is Clines' own socially and arbitrarily constructed belief about this text, which has no determinate meaning since there is no stable, unitary, and totalizing meaning because meaning is always deferred. Craig's reliance on Clines' "reading" of the Pentateuch, particularly his separation of Gen 1–11 as constituting a separate theme from the remainder of the Pentateuch, seems misplaced at best.

In their construction of a theme of the Pentateuch, both Clines and Craig have also completely ignored or overlooked the literary features of these chapters of Genesis that would indicate a completely different structure. Commentators have a history of proposing structure based on what the commentator takes to be important or significant in the text, which is what Clines does. Such an approach is decidedly subjective. However, the structure of the Pentateuch is indicated by certain literary indicators that are objectively discoverable.

At certain points in the text are large poetic sections the theme of which is repeated in each instance. There is an introduction to each poetic section that ties it to the preceding narrative. In Gen 49:1 we find that Jacob gathers his sons and announces that he is going to instruct them about "what shall befall you in the days to come" (בְּאַחֲרִית הַיָּמִים, bĕ'aḥărît hâyāmîm, lit. "in the after the days"). In Num 24:14 Balaam calls Balak in order to tell him "what this people will do to your people in the days to come" using exactly the same terminology (בְּאַחֲרִית הַיָּמִים, bĕ'aḥărît hâyāmîm). In Deut 31:28–29, Moses gathers the people in order to warn them of their apostasy "in the latter days," again using the same terminology (בְּאַחֲרִית הַיָּמִים, bĕ'aḥărît hâyāmîm). In fact, there is only one other place in the entire Pentateuch in which this terminology appears, and this is in Deut 4:30 which can be accounted for on the basis of the

---

27. Moreland and Craig, *Philosophical Foundations*, 147.

context of the passage and the fact that there is no large poetic section following the statement. Assuming this is indicative of the author's compositional technique, this fits into the author's narrative style.

At the close of each major narrative section there is a poetic section that looks forward to the end of days. Each one of these statements in the Pentateuch is predictive prophecy. The capacity to tell what will happen in the future is a capacity that belongs only to God. In Isa 41 God challenges the false gods whom the people of Israel have begun to worship:

> 21 "Present your case," the LORD says. "Bring forward your strong arguments," The King of Jacob says. 22 "Let them bring forth and declare to us what is going to take place; as for the former events, declare what they were, that we may consider them and know their outcome. Or announce to us what is coming; 23 Declare the things that are going to come afterward, that we may know that you are gods; indeed, bdo good or evil, that we may anxiously look about us and fear together" (Isa 41:21–23).[28]

God challenges the false gods to tell the future, and by predicting the future "we may know that you are gods (וְנֵדְעָה כִּי אֱלֹהִים אַתֶּם, wĕnēdʿāh kî ʾĕlōhîm ʾatem.) God announces that he has declared the end from the beginning: "9 Remember the former things long past, for I am God, and there is no other; I am God, and there is no one like Me, 10 Declaring the end from the beginning, and from ancient times things which have not been done, saying, 'My purpose will be established, and I will accomplish all My good pleasure';" (Isa 46:9–10).[29] God is not simply saying that he knows the difference. Rather, God is saying that in the beginning he has declared the end. God is telling us that there is an inherent relationship between the past, the present, and the future. That is why the author concludes each major section of the Pentateuch with prophecy about "the last days." The chart in **Figure 1** sets out the structure of the Pentateuch based on the literary characteristics.

---

28. 21 קָרְבוּ רִיבְכֶם יֹאמַר יְהוָה הַגִּישׁוּ עֲצֻמוֹתֵיכֶם יֹאמַר מֶלֶךְ יַעֲקֹב 22 יַגִּישׁוּ וְיַגִּידוּ לָנוּ אֵת אֲשֶׁר תִּקְרֶינָההָרִאשֹׁנוֹת מָה הֵנָּה הַגִּידוּ וְנָשִׂימָה לִבֵּנוּ וְנֵדְעָה אַחֲרִיתָן אוֹ הַבָּאוֹת הַשְׁמִיעֻנוּ: 23 הַגִּידוּ הָאֹתִיּוֹת לְאָחוֹר וְנֵדְעָה כִּי אֱלֹהִים אַתֶּם אַף־תֵּיטִיבוּ וְתָרֵעוּ וְנִשְׁתָּעָה וְנִרְאֶה יַחְדָּו:(Isa 41:21–23)

29. 9 זִכְרוּ רִאשֹׁנוֹת מֵעוֹלָם כִּי אָנֹכִי אֵל וְאֵין עוֹד אֱלֹהִים וְאֶפֶס כָּמוֹנִי: 10 מַגִּיד מֵרֵאשִׁית אַחֲרִית וּמִקֶּדֶם אֲשֶׁר לֹא־נַעֲשׂוּ אֹמֵר עֲצָתִי תָקוּם וְכָל־חֶפְצִי אֶעֱשֶׂה:(Isa 46:9–10)

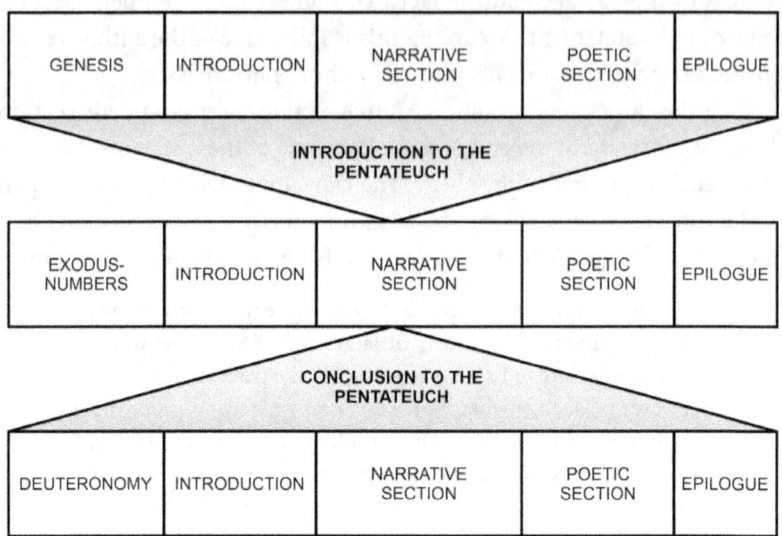

Figure 1: Pentateuch Basic Structure

Clines' proposal about the structure of the Pentateuch is not *the* structure, and Clines has either ignored or overlooked these very literary devices that the author employed to signal the structure and to lead the reader through his material. It is beyond the scope of this book to delve into the details of these literary devices and how they are picked up by subsequent biblical authors, but we can perhaps consider some examples.

As in the creation account, the waters of the flood are divided and the dry land [יַבָּשָׁה, yābbāšāh] appears. This is the same word used in Gen 1:9ff to refer to the appearance of the dry land after God had commanded the waters to divide. In Deut 32:11, Moses recounts the superintending care of God at the creation of the nation of Israel by pointing out that, "Like an eagle that stirs up its nest, that hovers [רָחַף, raḥaph] . . ."[30] This imagery corresponds to the description in Gen 1:2 of the Spirit of God hovering (מְרַחֶפֶת, měraḥephet, from the root רחף rḥph) over the waters. The following Table gives only some of these repeating words, phrases, and imagery connecting the creation account, the flood, and the exodus.

30. (Deut 32:11): כְּנֶשֶׁר יָעִיר קִנּוֹ עַל־גּוֹזָלָיו יְרַחֵף יִפְרֹשׂ כְּנָפָיו יִקָּחֵהוּ יִשָּׂאֵהוּ עַל־אֶבְרָתוֹ

Creation	Flood	Exodus
Empty and uninhabitable Gen 1:2	Sinful and uninhabitable Gen 6:5	Oppressed and uninhabitable Exod 1:11–14
Darkness on the face of the deep Gen 1:2	Only evil continually Gen 6:5	Cry out to God because of oppression Exod 2:23–25
Waters cover the land Gen 1:2	Waters cover the land Gen 7:24	Waters cover the land Exod 14:1–22
Spirit (רוּחַ) hovers over the waters Gen 1:2	Wind (רוּחַ) blows over the water/ Dove hovers over the water Gen 8:1; 8–12	Wind (רוּחַ) blows over the waters/ God hovers over Israel Exod 14:21; Deut 32:11
Let there be light (Light in the Darkness) Gen 1:3	God remembered Noah (Light in the Darkness) Gen 8:1	Light of the glory of God (Light in the Darkness)' Exod 13:21; 14:21
Let there be a division Gen 1:6	Abating of the waters Gen 6:11	Waters divide Exod 14:21
Let the dry land appear Gen 1:9	Dry land appears Gen 8:14	Dry ground appears Exod 14:22
Let the plants grow Gen 1:11	Plants grow (mouth of the Dove) Gen 8:11	Land flowing with milk and honey Exod 13:5
Ten times God says (establishes cosmic order) Gen 1:3–29	Ten men with whom God dwelt (establishes godly line) Gen 5	Ten words of commandments (establishes national order) Exod 19
God plants a garden Gen 2:8	Noah plants a garden Gen 9:20	Israel is planted in the Land Isa 5:2
God rests Adam in the garden Gen 2:15	Noah offers sacrifice of rest Gen 8:20	Israel enters land of rest Deut 12:10

Table #1: Repetition of Creation Imagery

These connections hardly indicate that the opening chapters of Genesis should be treated as outside the theme of the remainder of the Pentateuch.

The repetition of the creation imagery is found even in the NT. In John 3:5 Jesus explains to Nicodemus what he meant when he referred to being born again: "Truly, truly I say to you, unless one is born out of water and breath [ὕδατος καὶ πνεύματος, hudatos kai pneumatos], he is not able to enter into the kingdom of God."[31] When Jesus refers to water he cannot be referring to physical birth, since a person cannot be commanded to be physically born. Jesus cannot be referring to baptism, since there was no Christian baptism when Jesus is commanding Nicodemus to be born of water and breath. The word that in almost every English translation is rendered "the Spirit" (πνεύματος, pneumatos) does not have the definite article.[32] The earliest NT manuscripts were written in majuscule script. Majuscule script did not have upper and lower case letters, nor were there spaces between the words. Jesus is explaining to Nicodemus that being born again means being born of water and breath, not water and "the Spirit."

Yet in John 3:10 Jesus says to Nicodemus, "Are you the teacher of Israel and you do not understand these things?" Here Jesus uses the definite article identifying Nicodemus as "the teacher" of Israel (ὁ διδάσκαλος τοῦ, ho didaskalos tou Israēl). If being born again is a NT concept, how would Nicodemus have been expected to know these things? In fact, being born again is an OT concept emphatically depicted in Ezekiel. In Ezekiel's prophecy, God promises to wash the people with water and make them clean (Ezek 36:25). And in 37:5, God instructs Ezekiel to prophecy to the wind to blow on the bones, and God would breath into the bones, and God says, "Thus says the Lord GOD to these bones, 'Behold, I will cause breath [רוּחַ, rûaḥ] to enter you that you may come to live'" (Ezek 37:5).[33] As with the word πνεῦμα (pneuma), the word רוּחַ (rûaḥ) can be used to mean "spirit," or "wind," or "breath." This is creation imagery when God spoke and the world was born out of water, and God breathed into man the breath of life. The new creation is patterned after the first creation. In fact, not only are the opening chapters of Genesis intimately tied to the

---

31. Ἀμὴν ἀμὴν λέγω σοι, ἐὰν μή τις γεννηθῇ ἐξ ὕδατος καὶ πνεύματος, οὐ δύναται εἰελθεῖν εἰς τὴν βασιλείαν τοῦ θεοῦ (John 3:5).

32. There is no textual variant here.

33. (Ezek 37:5): כֹּה אָמַר אֲדֹנָי יְהוִה לָעֲצָמוֹת הָאֵלֶּה הִנֵּה אֲנִי מֵבִיא בָכֶם רוּחַ וִחְיִיתֶם

What Is At Stake?

overall theme of the Pentateuch, these chapters are the foundation upon which the rest of the Bible is based.

The creation account follows the pattern of subduing and filling. Verse two of chapter 1 characterizes the earth as "empty and uninhabitable" (וְתֹהוּ וָבֹהוּ, tōhû wāḇōhû). In the first three days God subdues creation and makes the earth habitable; light, waters above and below, dry ground. In the second three days he fills it up; light giving bodies, sea creatures, land creatures, and man. In Gen 1:28 God commands the couple to fill the earth and subdue it. This is the same command God gives to Israel; to fill the earth with proselytes and to subdue it by teaching Torah. This is the same command God gives to the church: fill the earth with disciples and subdue it by teaching them what Jesus has commanded. The creation account forms the pattern of mission for Adam and Eve, for Israel, and ultimately for the church.

The flood imagery is employed by Jesus in Matthew 24:

> **37** For the coming of the Son of Man will be just like the days of Noah. **38** For as in those days before the flood they were eating and drinking, marrying and giving in marriage, until the day that Noah entered the ark, **39** and they did not understand until the flood came and took them all away; so will the coming of the Son of Man be. **40** Then there will be two men in the field; one will be taken and one will be left. **41** Two women will be grinding at the mill; one will be taken and one will be left (Matt 24:37–41).[34]

This is not referring to the rapture as many have claimed. This is referring to the second coming when Jesus returns to judge. In the Genesis flood, Noah was not taken. The wicked were taken in judgment. Noah and his family were left to repopulate the earth. So at the second coming, some will be taken in judgment, others will be left to repopulate the earth in the Millennial kingdom.

Additionally, Adam is connected through the Pentateuch and into the NT. Paul refers to Jesus as the "last Adam" (ἔσχατος Ἀδάμ, *eschatos*

---

34. **37** ὥσπερ γὰρ αἱ ἡμέραι τοῦ Νῶε, οὕτως ἔσται ἡ παρουσία τοῦ υἱοῦ τοῦ ἀνθρώπου. **38** ὡς γὰρ ἦσαν ἐν ταῖς ἡμέραις [ἐκείναις] ταῖς πρὸ τοῦ κατακλυσμοῦ τρώγοντες καὶ πίνοντες, γαμοῦντες καὶ γαμίζοντες, ἄχρι ἧς ἡμέρας εἰσῆλθεν Νῶε εἰς τὴν κιωτόν, **39** καὶ οὐκ ἔγνωσαν ἕως ἦλθεν ὁ κατακλυσμὸς καὶ ἦρεν ἅπαντας, οὕτως ἔσται [καὶ] ἡ παρουσία τοῦ υἱοῦ τοῦ ἀνθρώπου. **40** τότε δύο ἔσονται ἐν τῷ ἀγρῷ, εἷς παραλαμβάνεται καὶ εἷς ἀφίεται **41** δύο ἀλήθουσαι ἐν τῷ μύλῳ, μία παραλαμβάνεται καὶ μία ἀφίεται (Matt 24:37–41).

Adam) not the second Adam as is so frequently claimed. And there were three Adams prior to Jesus, as the chart below indicates.

ADAM The First Adam	NOAH The Second Adam	ISRAEL The Third Adam	JESUS The Last Adam
created by God	found favor with God	chosen by God	was God
cause to rest in the garden	offered a sacrifice of rest	entered the land of rest	brought us into God's rest
sinned	sinned	sinned	became sin
in the garden	in his tent	in the land	tented among us arrested in a garden crucified in the land
ate the fruit of the tree	drank the fruit of the vine	was the vine of God who bore bad fruit	is the true vine who bears good fruit and was hanged on a tree
became aware of his nakedness	exposed his nakedness	nakedness was exposed by God	was hanged in nakedness
incurred a curse	pronounced a curse	was cursed by God	became cursed
worked the ground	worked a garden	worked for salvation	completed the work
Sword Cain against Abel	Sword Babel against Zion	Sword Israel against Judah	Sword Unbelievers against believers
precipitated the flood	preserved from the flood	judged by a flood	saved us from the flood

Table #2: The Four Adams

Jesus is the last Adam because he perfectly embodies the image of God, and he accomplishes what the prior Adams could not. Paul refers to Jesus as the "second man" (ὁ δευτερος ἄνθρωπος, *ho deuteros anthrōpos*) because he is the progenitor of the new humanity by the new birth, the new creation.

The first Adam was commissioned by God to expand the boarders of Eden ultimately to cover the entire earth with the glory of God. In Dan 2, Nebuchadnezzar has a vision of a stone cut out of the mountain not by hands. The stone strikes the statue on the feet, pulverizes the statue, and grows into a mountain that covers the entire earth. What the first Adam failed to do, the Last Adam will accomplish in establishing the kingdom of God on earth to cover the earth with the glory of God. To treat Gen 1–11 as distinct from the rest of the Pentateuch violates the literary strategy of the author and the biblical imagery that is carried through into the NT.

Genesis 1–11 does not even form the "Primaeval history" as Clines and Craig propose. The literary devices determine the initial unit as Gen 1:1–7:24. The flood account that begins in Gen 6:10 forms a large chiasm, only a portion of which is illustrated in **Figure 2**. The focal point of the chiasm is the statement in 8:1, "And God remembered Noah" (וַיִּזְכֹּר אֱלֹהִים אֶת־נֹחַ, wâyizkōr ʾĕlōhîm ʾet Nōaḥ). At this point the creation imagery repeats (see Table #1 above).

```
A   Noah..................................................6:10
 B   Schem, Ham, Japheth..............................6:10
  C   Announcing the Flood...........................6:17
   D   Covenant with Noah..........................6:18–20
    E   Command to Enter the Ark................7:1–3
     F   Mountains Covered.......................7:19–20
      G   Waters Prevail 150 days..............7:21–24
       H   GOD REMEMBERED NOAH...8:1
      G'  Waters Abate 150 days................8:3
     F'  Mountains Revealed......................8:4–5
    E'  Command to Leave the Ark.................8:15–17
   D'  Covenant with All Flesh....................9:8–10
  C'  Renouncing the Flood.........................9:11–17
 B'  Schem, Ham, Japheth............................9:18
A'  Noah..................................................9:19
```

Figure 2: Flood Chiasm

Genesis 1 describes the original creation of the world and the bringing of the dry land (יַבָּשָׁה, yābbāšāh) out of the waters of chaos. This is paralleled by the narrative of Noah and the bringing of dry land (Gen

8:7, יָבֵשׁ, yāḇēš], this is the verb form of the word in Gen 1:9) out of the waters that covered the earth. The parallel nature of these narrative accounts suggests that as the waters covered the entire earth in the original creation, so the waters of Noah covered the entire earth, not simply a local area as some have proposed.

The movement is from God's work to God's rest. In the creation account God works for six days and rests on the seventh. In Gen 8:20 Noah (נֹחַ Nôaḥ, which comes from the word נוּחַ, nûaḥ, which means "he rested" and has implications for the notion of salvation) builds an altar to YHWH (יהוה) and offers a burnt offering upon it. In verse 21 the passage states, "and Yehwah smelled the aroma of rest."[35] The word smell (יָרַח, yāraḥ) is from the word translated by our English words, 'spirit,' or 'breath,' or 'wind' (רוּחַ, rûaḥ). The word used in Genesis for the 'rest' of God is a different Hebrew word, שָׁבַת (šāḇbaṯ), which means "to bring to completion" or "to finish." But, in Exod 20:11 the word נוּחַ (nûaḥ) is used to describe God resting on the seventh day: "For in six days the Lord made the heavens and the earth, the sea and all that is in them, and rested [וַיָּנַח, wâyānaḥ] on the seventh day; therefore the Lord blessed the Sabbath (הַשַּׁבָּת, haššabbāṯ) day and made it holy."[36] The depiction of God being at rest is referred to by both words נוּחַ, (nûaḥ) and שָׁבַת, (šāḇbaṯ). The movement from work to rest sets the pattern for the Sabbath day. The command was to cease from one's work, and rest in God's completed work. This is a depiction of salvation by grace through faith. God does the work, and we rest in God's completed work.

In the creation account the Spirit (רוּחַ, rûaḥ "breath" or "wind") of God hovered מְרַחֶפֶת , měraḥepheṯ) over the waters. In fact, the Piel form of the verb רָחַף (rāḥaph) occurs only twice in the entire Hebrew Bible: Gen 1:2 in which the Spirit hovered over the waters to bring the earth out of the chaos, and in Deut 32:11 in which God hovered over Israel to bring the people out of the chaos of the wilderness and bring them into the land of rest. In Gen 8:1 God remembered Noah and caused a wind (רוּחַ, rûaḥ) to pass over the waters of the flood. As an indication of the emergence of dry land, God brings forth vegetation upon the land. As an indication that the waters of the flood have abated from off the earth, the dove returns with an olive branch—that is, vegetation. The association of the

---

35. (Gen 8:21a) וַיָּרַח יְהוָה אֶת־רֵיחַ הַנִּיחֹחַ

36. כִּי שֵׁשֶׁת־יָמִים עָשָׂה יְהוָה אֶת־הַשָּׁמַיִם וְאֶת־הָאָרֶץ אֶת־הַיָּם וְאֶת־כָּל־אֲשֶׁר־בָּם וַיָּנַח בַּיּוֹם הַשְּׁבִיעִי עַל־כֵּן בֵּרַךְ יְהוָה אֶת־יוֹם הַשַּׁבָּת וַיְקַדְּשֵׁהוּ׃
(Exod. 20:11)

dove with the Spirit of God in Matt 3:16 may be traceable to this association between the Spirit of God hovering over the waters and the dove that Noah sent out from the ark. In Deut 32:11 the text states, "Like an eagle that stirs up its nest, that hovers (יְרַחֵף, yĕraḥēph) over its young . . ." In this verse the verb form of "hovering" is used, while in Gen 1:2 the participial form is used. As the Spirit of God hovered over the waters so as to bring about the habitable land, so God hovers over his people to bring about a nation that will inhabit the land that God has made habitable by driving out the darkness of the inhabitants. In fact, Isaiah uses this very imagery in Isa 5. The repetition of the creation imagery shows that a new section of the Pentateuch begins at Gen 8:1.

Another factor that indicates the structure are the references to the sons of Noah. From the first time the sons of Noah are named, the list follows the same order; Shem, Ham, and Japheth. However, with the beginning of the genealogy in Gen 10, the order is reversed, beginning with Japheth, then Ham, then Shem. Shem's genealogy is interrupted at the beginning of Gen 11 with the Tower of Babel incident. The name translated "Babel" (בָּבֶל, Bāḇel) is the same name that is translated "Babylon" elsewhere in the Pentateuch. This becomes extremely significant as ones moves through the rest of the OT.

The name translated "Shem" is שֵׁם (Šēm), which is the same word that is translated "name" (שֵׁם, šēm). This word ties the genealogy of Shem with the tower incident in which the people seek to make a name (שֵׁם, šēm) for themselves. The tower narrative is designed to contrast the efforts of men to make a name for themselves with the fact that God is going to make Abram's name (שֵׁם, šēm) great. This also connects the account of Abram, who calls upon the Name of the Lord (וַיִּקְרָא בְּשֵׁם יְהוָה, wâyiqrā', Gen 12:8). This harks back to the concluding statement in Gen 4:26, "then was begun to call on the Name of the Lord" (בְּשֵׁם יְהוָה אָז הוּחַל לִקְרֹא, bĕšēm YHWH 'āz hûḥal liqrō'). Consequently, the literary indicators show that the Primaeval history does not end in chapter 11, but rather in chapter 7, and the Babel narrative is an integral part of the genealogy of Shem leading up to Abram. Dividing the Genesis narrative at the end of chapter 11 ignores the literary connection of Shem's genealogy with the call of Abram.

Japheth Genealogy	10:2–19	
Ham Genealogy	10:20–30	
Shem Genealogy	10:31–32	"Name"
Tower of Babel	11:1–9	Make a Name for Themselves
Shem Genealogy	11:10–32	"Name"
Abram Descendant of Shem	12:1ff	Make Your Name Great

Table #3: Japheth, Ham, and Shem Genealogies

1. הִנֵּה עַם בְּנֵי יִשְׂרָאֵל רַב וְעָצוּם מִמֶּנּוּ Exod. 1:9 "Behold, the people of the sons of Israel are many and mightier then we."	Exodus-Numbers Wilderness Experience (Exodus 16–Numbers 21) וְאִכָּבְדָה בְּפַרְעֹה וּבְכָל־חֵילוֹ וְיָדְעוּ מִצְרַיִם כִּי־אֲנִי יְהוָה "And I will be honored upon Pharaoh and all his army, and Egypt will know that I am the LORD."	1. וַיָּגָר מוֹאָב מִפְּנֵי הָעָם מְאֹד כִּי רַב־הוּא לְכָה־נָּא אָרָה־לִּי אֶת־הָעָם הַזֶּה כִּי־עָצוּם הוּא מִמֶּנִּי Num. 22:3, 6 "And feared exceedingly from before the people, for they were many . . . place a curse on these people for they are mightier than we."
2. וַיִּכְבַּד לֵב פַּרְעֹה Exod. 9:7 "And Pharaoh's heart became hard."		2. כִּי־כַבֵּד אֲכַבֶּדְךָ מְאֹד Num. 22:17 "For I will indeed honor you exceedingly . . ."

Figure 3: Comparison of Language in Exodus-Numbers

Another factor that indicates the structure of the Pentateuch as argued for above is the structure of the Exodus-Numbers narratives. The Exodus-Numbers narrative section is divided into four parts; an introduction, the redemption and sanctification narratives forming the major portion, the poetic conclusion, and the epilogue. **Figure 3** above gives the repeating words and phrases that mark out the beginning, middle, and ending of the Exodus-Numbers narrative structure. An important aspect of this parallelism is the repeated use of the word כָּבֵד (kāḇēḏ) in Exod 9:7 and Num 22:17. This parallelism is not immediately evident to the English reader since the translation is different in the two verses. The word כָּבֵד (kāḇēḏ) is translated "make hard" in Exod 9:7 and is translated "honor" in Num 22:17. The basic meaning is "heavy." In Exod 9:7 Pharaoh's heart is made heavy against letting the people go. The notion of "heavy" can also indicate honor, as in Num 22:17. This figure is evident in modern English when someone is said to be a "heavy weight," that is, worthy of honor. Table #4 below compares the material concerning Pharaoh and Balak showing the parallelism that supports the literary structure.

As illustrated in **Figure 4** below, the main part of the narrative is punctuated by the repeating events that form a chiastic structure focusing on Sinai.

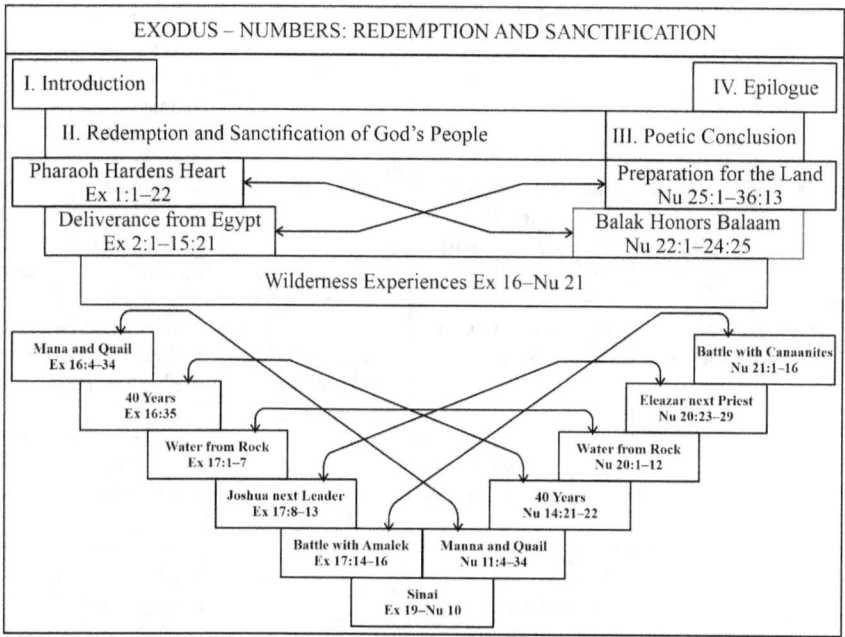

Figure 4: Exodus-Numbers

PHARAOH		BALAK	
Exod 1:9	"See, the people of the sons of Israel..."	Num 22:2	"Now Balak the son of Zippor saw all that Israel had done to the Amorites."
Exod 1:9	"Behold, the people of the sons of Israel are many and mightier than we."	Num 22:3, 6	"And feared exceedingly from before the people, for they were many... place a curse on these people for they are mightier than we"
Exod 1:10	"Come, let us deal wisely with them, lest they... depart from the land."	Num 22:6	"...curse this people... and drive them out of the land."
Exod 1:11–22 Three attempts to condemn Israel	11–14 Slave masters to oppress them	Num 22:41—24:25 Three attempts to curse Israel	22:41—23:12 At Kiriath-huzoth to the high places of Baal
	15–21 midwives to kill male children		23:13–26 At Zophim to the top of Mt. Pisgah
	22 command to throw male children into Nile		23:27—24:25 To the top of Mt. Peor.

Table #4: Comparison of Pharaoh and Balak

By ignoring the literary features of the text, Clines and Craig have violated the structure of the text as Moses has constructed it.

In Relation to ANE Mythology

In a section titled "Ancient Near Eastern Mythology," Craig spends several pages discussing the myths of the ancient Near East. Much of this material is very informative and written in a style that makes it easily accessible to the reader. Early in this discussion, Craig asserts, "Not only should the primaeval narratives of Gen 1–11 be read within the context of Genesis and the Pentateuch, but they should also be read within the wider context of the literature of the ancient Near East (ANE)."[37]

In what seems to be an effort to justify the claim that Gen 1–11 ought to be read in the context of ANE mythology, Craig points out, "OT scholars have been aware for centuries of the resemblance of the primaeval narratives of Gen 1–11 to ancient Mesopotamian myths on the basis of the Babylonian priest Berossus's account of Mesopotamian religion for Greek readers of the third century BC."[38] At the conclusion of this section he asserts,

> We have seen that in order to understand the narratives of Adam and Eve, we must read them within the context of the primaeval history of Gen 1–11, and the primaeval history in turn within the context of Genesis as a whole, and Genesis within the context of the Pentateuch. Moreover, we should read the primaeval history within its ANE cultural context. To understand that cultural context, we shall consider the myths of the abovementioned Mesopotamian and Egyptian deities more closely. But as a preliminary to our discussion it will be necessary to say something about the nature of myth itself.[39]

Between these two points, Craig offers no other reason why one should understand Gen 1–11 in the context of ANE mythology other than what have been seen to be resemblances. Of course, similarity of design does not necessarily indicate identity of origin, nor do resemblances necessarily mean literary context. What the resemblances show is resemblances. Of course one would expect resemblances since ANE myths and the biblical narratives are about the perennial questions of the origin of the world, origin of mankind, etc.

In two instances Craig refers to ANE myths as the oldest literary remains—"from ancient Sumer and Babylon has augmented our knowledge of the literature of the ANE, the earliest literary remains of mankind"[40]—and—"Sumerian literature, the oldest in the world . . ."[41] If by these remarks Craig is simply saying that the artifacts and manuscripts of ANE myths predate the oldest existing manuscripts of the Hebrew

37. Craig, *Adam*, 22.
38. Craig, *Adam*, 22.
39. Craig, *Adam*, 31.
40. Craig, *Adam*, 23.
41. Craig, *Adam*, 25.

Bible, then there is certainly no issue with these observations. However, if Craig is implying that because the artifacts are older it must mean that the content—the myths and the stories—predate the biblical accounts, then this is an assumption that has never been demonstrated. Among contemporary OT scholars, the similarities between ANE myths and the biblical narratives have always been taken to indicate that the biblical authors have adapted, or adopted, or copied, or composed their narratives against this literary background. But why should anyone think that the ANE myths *qua* myths are necessarily older or even contemporary with the events that are narrated in Gen 1–11? Is it not at least as reasonable to suppose that the ANE myths developed out of the events that the Bible reports? Based on artifacts, OT scholars assume the movement is always from ANE myths to biblical narrative. However, based on content, it is just as reasonable to assume a movement from biblical narrative to ANE myths (see **Figure 5**).

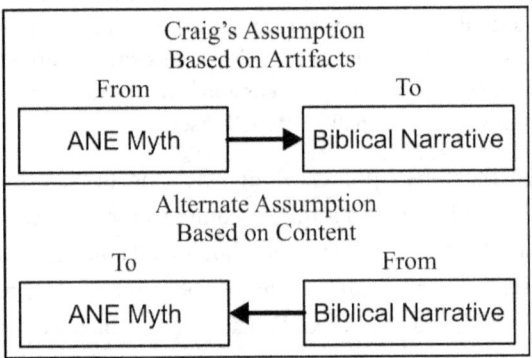

Figure 5: Assumption of Movement

Demonstrating literary dependency is extremely difficult, and sometimes it is literally impossible. OT scholars assume that the similarities necessarily indicate some literary context, and that these similarities necessarily indicate that the biblical authors adopted, or adapted, or borrowed from ANE literature. Yet these same scholars have never been able to substantiate the claims of either literary dependency or that the content of biblical narratives find their origin within the temporal context of ANE mythologies. For all the scholarly rhetoric, the assertions of OT scholars is so much subjective speculation. Where in the biblical narrative does any author claim that he has adapted, or adopted, or borrowed, or employed the literature of a story from ANE myth? The only reason for thinking this are the apparent similarities. But similarity of design does not necessarily mean identity of origin, nor do resemblances necessarily indicate literary context.

In fact, Craig acknowledges,

> The structural similarities can be exaggerated, however. The *Atrahasis* and *Gilgamesh* epics contain no creation account, and the Eridu Genesis, a hypothetical narrative compiled of texts of different dates, is merely presumed to have included an account of creation, now missing. None of these myths has anything similar to the story of Adam and Eve, their temptation and fall, so pivotal to Gen 1–11, prior to the flood, nor do we read of anything like the ensuing story of the Tower of Babel.[42]

But it is not simply the structural dissimilarities. There are critical differences in content. That ANE myths do not contain the content that Craig identifies are what make the difference between ANE myths and the biblical narratives.

So, if there are these differences between the biblical narratives and ANE myths, does this deter OT scholars in trying to establish some connection between these accounts? As Craig goes on to say, "More important than the structure of the narratives of Gen 1–11, then, are the similar themes that these chapters and ANE myths treat."[43] In other words, the only basis for thinking that the content of the biblical narratives must be understood in the context of ANE literature is the perceived similarities. There is no other basis upon which to propose a connection. But, again, similarity of design does not necessarily mean identity of origin. Craig makes the same mistake here that OT scholars made with reference to the wisdom material of Proverbs. The authors of the various proverbs did not adopt, adapt, or borrow from Egyptian or Mesopotamian wisdom literature. The similarities are accounted for by the fact that they are writing about the same subject matter, that is, wisdom. If Craig and OT scholars are going to substantiate such a literary connection, then there needs to be a great deal more evidence than simply the fact the stories seem to deal with "similar themes."

And why would not ancient writings deal with similar themes—origin of the world, origin of mankind, etc. Authors have attempted to deal with these kind of questions throughout history, but the similarity

---

42. Craig, *Adam*, 23.
43. Craig, *Adam*, 23.

of themes between the writings of the Greeks, Romans, Germans, philosophers, sociologists, theologians, etc., does not show that there is necessarily a literary context in which each one of these groups should be understood, much less does it show literary dependence. And temporal proximity, assuming there is such, does not show literary connection, nor does geographical proximity.

It seems reasonable to consider the similarities of practice, cultural imagery, literary style, etc., between ANE myths and biblical narrative, but this does not justify the claim that Gen 1–11 must be understood in this literary context. Is it not just as reasonable to suppose that the events recorded in biblical narrative formed the literary context in which ANE myths grew up, that the authors of ANE myths adopted, adapted, and/or borrowed from the stories of the persons and events that the Bible reports? Why do OT scholars assume that the movement is always from ANE to biblical narrative rather than from the historical events and persons which the biblical narrative records to ANE mythology? They do this on the basis of prior assumptions and prejudice.

Craig and many OT scholars make the same mistake committed by those who claim that early Christianity borrowed from Hellenistic mystery religions. Ronald Nash points out that similarities prove nothing except similarity.

> The mere fact that Christianity had a sacred meal and a baptism is supposed to prove that it borrowed these ceremonies from similar meals and washings in the pagan cults. By itself, of course, such outward similarity would really prove nothing. After all, religious rituals can assume only a limited number of forms, and they will naturally relate to important or common aspects of human life. Alleged similarities might reflect only common features of a time or culture, rather than genetic dependence. Consequently, we need to dig below the surface of apparent similarities and ask the more basic question. *What did the pagan practices mean?*[44]

The crucial difference between the meaning of biblical narratives and the meaning of ANE myths makes all the difference. Later Nash points out that similarities do not prove dependence: "Granted, there is a similarity between Paul's writings and Hellenistic thought on the human need for redemption. But does the mere presence of this similarity prove

---

44. Nash, *Christianity and the Hellenistic*, 150.

Paul's dependence?"⁴⁵ And J. Gresham Machen makes the same point: "Why should similarity of language between Hermes and Paul, supposing that it exists, be regarded as proving dependence of Paul upon a type of paganism like that of Hermes, rather than dependence of Hermes upon Paul?"⁴⁶ Why should similarity between the narratives of ANE mythology prove dependence, or even literary context? The similarity of themes can be accounted for without having to claim dependency or literary context. In order to show dependency one would need to show much more than resemblances. In order to show that ANE myth constitutes the literary context in which the biblical narratives should be understood, more than similarity must be demonstrated. There would need to be a significant amount of identical statements, as one would need in order to show plagiarism. But even in the case of plagiarism the judgment can be subjective. The only definitive way to show dependency is for one author to state that his material is taken from, borrowed from, or adapted from an external source. Since this cannot be done with ANE and biblical narratives, the claim for dependency and/or literary context is a subjective judgment based on the prior assumptions of the one making the judgment.

The supposed similarity of themes between ANE myth and biblical narrative are not decisive since the principal themes of biblical narrative are not present in ANE myth. Although it is not within the scope of this essay to present a full-fledged argument for the theme of the Pentateuch, suffice it to suggest that the theme of the Pentateuch could be seen to be a contrast between the lives of Moses and Abraham. By faith Abraham fulfilled the righteousness of the law. Moses' faith was weakened under the law. In Gen 26:4 God declares to Isaac that he will fulfill the covenant that he established with Abraham, and in verse 5 God says, "because Abraham obeyed Me and kept My charge, My commandments, My statutes, and My laws" (Gen 26:5).⁴⁷ But at this time God had not given the commandments, statutes, and laws. It was by faith that Abraham kept God's commandments, statutes, and laws. Yet Moses is forbidden from leading the people into the land of rest: "Because you have not believed in Me [לֹא־הֶאֱמַנְתֶּם בִּי, lō' he'ĕmantem bî], to treat Me as holy in the sight of the sons of Israel, therefore you shall not bring this assembly into the

---

45. Nash, *Christianity and the Hellenistic*, 179
46. Machen, *Origin of Paul's Religion*, 248.
47. (Gen 26:5): עֵקֶב אֲשֶׁר־שָׁמַע אַבְרָהָם בְּקֹלִי וַיִּשְׁמֹר מִשְׁמַרְתִּי מִצְוֹתַי חֻקּוֹתַי וְתוֹרֹתָי

land which I have given them" (Num 20:12).[48] Abraham fulfilled the law by faith. Moses' faith was weakened under the law.

Before the giving of the law the Patriarchs, headed by Abraham, exhibited a life of faith, and by faith fulfilled the righteousness of the law. Abraham lived by faith (Gen 15:6), in Egypt the Israelites lived by faith (Exod 4:31), and when the people came to Mount Sinai they believed (Exod 14:31). However, after the giving of the law the people of God, headed by Moses, exhibit a life of sin and failure, and lack of faith. After the giving of the law, the text no longer refers to the people believing. Rather, the text refers to the fact that the people did not believe in God:

> Num 14:11 "And the Lord said to Moses, 'How long will this people spurn Me? And how long will they not believe in me, despite all the signs which I have performed in their midst?'"[49]

> Deut 1:32 "But for all this, you did not trust the Lord your God."[50]

> Deut 9:23–24 "**23** When the LORD sent you from Kadesh-barnea, saying, 'Go up and possess the land which I have given you,' then you rebelled against the command of the LORD your God; you neither believed Him nor listened to His voice. **24** You have been rebellious against the LORD from the day I knew you."[51]

The people are defeated and eventually dispossessed of the land. The law was not given to Israel in order for the people to establish a relationship with God by keeping the law. The law was given in order to instruct the people on how to live in the kingdom that God would establish by bringing them into the promised land, the land of rest. The relationship of Israel to God was established in Egypt by the shedding of the blood of the Passover lamb, by the sacrifice of the first-born of Egypt, and by the act of faith on the part of the people to apply the blood. In other words, God bought the people with the sacrifice and the shedding of blood, and the people responded in faith. The theme of the Pentateuch is that there is only one way to have a relationship with God, and that is salvation by

---

48. יַעַן לֹא־הֶאֱמַנְתֶּם בִּי לְהַקְדִּישֵׁנִי לְעֵינֵי בְּנֵי יִשְׂרָאֵל לָכֵן לֹא תָבִיאוּ אֶת־הַקָּהָל הַזֶּה אֶל־הָאָרֶץ אֲשֶׁר־נָתַתִּי לָהֶם׃(Num 20:12)

49. וַיֹּאמֶר יְהוָה אֶל־מֹשֶׁה עַד־אָנָה יְנַאֲצֻנִי הָעָם הַזֶּה וְעַד־אָנָה לֹא־יַאֲמִינוּ בִי בְּכֹל הָאֹתוֹת אֲשֶׁר עָשִׂיתִי בְּקִרְבּוֹ׃(Num 14:11)

50. וּבַדָּבָר הַזֶּה אֵינְכֶם מַאֲמִינִם בַּיהוָה אֱלֹהֵיכֶם׃ (Deut 1:32)

51. **23** וּבִשְׁלֹחַ יְהוָה אֶתְכֶם מִקָּדֵשׁ בַּרְנֵעַ לֵאמֹר עֲלוּ וּרְשׁוּ אֶת־הָאָרֶץ אֲשֶׁר נָתַתִּי לָכֶם וַתַּמְרוּ אֶת־פִּי יְהוָה אֱלֹהֵיכֶם וְלֹא הֶאֱמַנְתֶּם לוֹ וְלֹא שְׁמַעְתֶּם בְּקֹלוֹ׃ **24** מַמְרִים הֱיִיתֶם עִם־יְהוָה מִיּוֹם דַּעְתִּי אֶתְכֶם׃(Deut 9:23–24)

grace through faith based on the shedding of the blood of our Passover Lamb, God's only begotten Son. No such theme can be found in the all the writings of ANE mythology. It is the differences that make all the difference.

2

The Nature of Myth

Family Resemblances

IN THIS CHAPTER, CRAIG discusses the nature of myth for the purpose of showing that Gen 1–11 fits into the literary category of myth. His discussion of myths is very interesting and contains enlightening and helpful information. In the section titled, "Family Resemblances Among Myths," Craig employs Wittgenstein's notion of "language games" as a way of relating Gen 1–11 to ANE myth:

> Using the illustration of games, Wittgenstein observed that given the diversity of games—board games, card games, athletic games, guessing games, and so on—it is impossible to lay down necessary and sufficient conditions for what it is to be a game. Rather, games exhibit family resemblances, features that are shared by different games with no feature sufficient for being a game common to all.[1]

0_1	0_2	0_3	0_4	0_5	0_6
A	B	C	D	E	F
B	C	D	E	F	A
C	D	E	F	A	B
D	E	F	A	B	C

Figure 6: Family Resemblances

---

1. Craig, *Adam*, 43.

Robert Fogelin provides the diagram in **Figure 6** to illustrate the notion of family resemblances.[2] "O_1 through O_2 represent a set of objects; the letters represent properties they possess. Here each object shares three features with two others in the group, but there is no single feature that runs through the lot."[3] According to Wittgenstein, language is not a single monolithic structure that operates according to a rigid calculus. Rather, as Hacker describes it, "language is a motley of language-games" loosely governed by the rules that apply to the specific game in which one is involved.[4] Wittgenstein characterizes language as a relation of family resemblances, and he illustrates his point by reference to actual games. Wittgenstein argues that when one considers all the games that one knows, one realizes that there is no single common characteristic that can be identified as the essence of all games: "Consider for example the proceedings that we call 'games.' I mean board-games, card-games, ball-games, Olympic games, and so on. What is common to them all?"[5] But Wittgenstein does not want us to think about it: "don't think, but look! [*denk nicht, sondern schau!*]"[6] What he means by this is, don't start with the supposition that because all these activities are designated "games" that they must have some common essence or nature. Rather, set aside this assumption and just look at the games themselves. Wittgenstein believes that if you look at all the games you will inevitably conclude that instead of a single characterizing essence or nature, you will "see a complicated network of similarities overlapping and criss-crossing: sometimes overall similarities, sometimes similarities of detail."[7]

However, at what are we supposed to look? At all activities that take place in life? At certain activities? Who decides at what we should look? On what basis are the activities at which we are supposed to look grouped or selected? Some might claim that a game is a competition in which there is a winner and a loser. However, take, for example, throwing a ball

---

2. Fogelin, *Wittgenstein*, 133.
3. Fogelin, *Wittgenstein*, 133.
4. Hacker, *Wittgenstein's Place in Twentieth-century Analytic Philosophy*, 125.
5. Wittgensetin, *Philosophical Investigations*, §66. "Betrachte z.B. einmal die Vorgänge, die wir 'Spiele' nennen. Ich meine Brettspiele, Kartenspiele, Ballspiele, Kampfspiele, u.s.w . Was ist allen diesen gemeinsam?"
6. Wittgenstein, *Philosophical Investigations*, §66.
7. Wittgenstein, *Philosophical Investigations*, §66. "Wir sehen ein kompliziertes Netz von Ähnlichkeiten, die einander übergreifen und kreuzen. Ähnlichkeiten im Großen und Kleinen."

against a wall and catching it. There does not seem to be a competition or a winner or loser, yet this kind of activity is usually referred to as a game. What Wittgenstein wants us to look at are the activities that he has already grouped together and identified as games, which is the very thing he wants his reader *not* to do. By demanding that we look at what he thinks we should look at, he has already imposed his assumption in order to tell us what to look at. He is saying, "Don't just look at activities in which there is a winner and a looser. Don't just look at activities that have a common nature. Look at all kinds of activities that I think you should look at." But this approach stacks the deck; it begs the question.

Wittgenstein's characterization of "games" is arbitrary and serves to define his position into existence. Wittgenstein's claim that there are no characteristics that can be found in all games is true only if one defines a game in Wittgenstein's terms. However, one can easily define what constitutes a game in such a manner as to capture one or more characteristics that are the same, and argue that the term "game" is predicated of other activities analogically. In the case of throwing a ball against a wall, one could argue that in fact there is a competition, a winner, and a loser. The competition involves one's own skill to anticipate the speed and trajectory of the ball so as to catch it on its return. If the thrower catches the ball, he wins. If he does not catch the ball, he loses. Even if this characterization of throwing the ball is not convincing, one could simply say that throwing a ball against a wall is called a game analogically. When Wittgenstein says that we should look and not think, he simply assumes that we should look at all the activities that he calls games. However, if I look at all the activities that I call games, I discover that all games involve a competition in which there is a winner and a loser, and Wittgenstein's effort falls flat. Why should anyone think a game is what Wittgenstein thinks a game is? Without a decisive argument for defining games the way Wittgenstein does, his argument merely begs the question.

When Craig takes Wittgenstein's characterization of games and applies it to myths, he must necessarily encounter the same question-begging problem. Craig has already decided what myths are, and he constructs his argument on this assumption. This applies to Craig's appeal to Richard Burridge's study of the Gospels. According to Craig, "Burridge was able to identify a considerable number of family resemblances among ancient biographies that were also shared by the Gospels, including both external

The Nature of Myth

features of form and structure and internal features of content."[8] Craig claims that although there may be aspects that are missing, this does not present a problem. He then quotes Burridge: "It does not matter if a particular work does not have all the features or fit the genre exactly. What is important is that it has sufficient features for the family resemblance to be recognized."[9] But this is the same problem encountered in Wittgenstein's characterization of games. For Burridge and Craig, it does not matter if there are missing aspects because Burridge and Craig have simply defined their position into existence. They have already decided what we should look at, and then they demand that we abide by their definitions.

The claim that the Gospels are a category of Greco-Roman biography brings with it insurmountable problems. Lydia McGrew has shown that such associations misrepresent the case.[10] Concerning McGrew's book, *Mirror or the Mask*, J. P. Moreland says,

> As Thomas Kuhn pointed out long ago, it is often someone from a different discipline who has the epistemic distance and objectivity to evaluate a widely accepted paradigm methodology in another discipline, because practitioners in the latter tend to look at things the way they were trained and, thus, cannot see things accurately. Kuhn's remarks are right on target when it comes to philosopher Lydia McGrew's critique of widespread methodological practices in New Testament studies. While *The Mirror or the Mask* is very easy to read, it is also a massive piece of first-rate, rigorous scholarship that leaves no stone unturned. Replete with very careful distinctions. *The Mirror or the Mask* offers a precise analysis of the contemporary practice of employing "fictionalization" to exegete various Gospel texts. McGrew's careful analysis finds such a practice wanting and dangerous and replaces this practice with an approach that treats the Gospels as honest historical reports based on eyewitness testimony. This book is a must read for all who are interested in the historical accuracy of our portraits of Jesus. I highly recommend it.[11]

McGrew convincingly argues that Burridge's position is untenable. For example, she points out,

---

8. Craig, *Adam*, 43–44.
9. Burridge, *What Are the Gospels?* 42; quoted in Craig, *Adam*, 44.
10. McGrew, *Review of Michael Licona's Why Are There Differences in the Gospels?* and *Mirror or the Mask*.
11. From the recommendation pages of McGrew's book.

Burridge's work is also noteworthy for the extent to which he overlooks evidence for the traditional authorship of the Gospels. This is relevant to his thesis because traditional authorship would mean that at least three out of four Gospels—Matthew, Mark, and John—were written by Jews who were likely not educated in a Hellenistic fashion. Then too there is the probability that Peter, a Galilean Jew, was a major oral source for Mark's Gospel (the latter point noted by Stein). The evidence that Matthew, Mark, and John were written by their traditionally ascribed authors tends to disconfirm the thesis that they were influenced by Greco-Roman literature. How likely is it that Matthew the tax collector, John Mark, Peter, or even John the son of Zebedee would have read or heard the earlier writers of biography discussed by Burridge such as Xenophon, Isocrates, Satyrus, and Nepos and that they would have desired to emulate a specific Greco-Roman genre?—It would require, at least, direct positive evidence for the Hellenistic education of these authors to begin to reply to this point, and simply ignoring the debate about authorship will not do. Burridge gives little evidence of taking traditional authorship of Matthew and Mark or Peter's probable influence on Mark with any seriousness whatsoever. In the case of John, he ascribes it briefly to a "Johannine community" operating within the "syncretistic milieu of the eastern Mediterranean toward the close of the first century AD."[12]

Earlier in her book McGrew warns that if the Gospels are Greco-Roman biography then like Greco-Roman biography there must be unhistorical elements such that, "if the Gospels belong to the genre of Greco-Roman biography, that in and of itself means that we will find it difficult to determine whether their reports have an historical intention and where history ends and legend begins."[13] In fact, Mike Licona makes this very point:

> Authorial intent often eludes us, and the motives behind the reports are often difficult to determine. This is a challenge when we consider the four earliest extant biographies of Jesus, known as the canonical Gospels. There is somewhat of a consensus ... that the Gospels belong to the genre of Greco-Roman biography (*bios*) ... Because *bios* was a flexible genre, it is often difficult to determine where history ends and legend begins.[14]

12. McGrew, *Mirror or the Mask*, 103–4.
13. McGrew, *Mirror or the Mask*, 95.
14. Licona, *Resurrection of Jesus*, 34; quoted in McGrew, *Mirror or the Mask*, 95.

The Nature of Myth

In other words, in order to maintain the classification of Gospels as Greco-Roman biography one must jettison the doctrine of inerrancy.[15] Having done that, then one can simply stipulate what counts as history and what counts as legend. So, one can simply relegate the accounts of the resurrection of Jesus to legend, or myth.

Craig goes on to argue,

> Similarly, we can examine myths to determine what family resemblances exist among them. It might be objected that this approach suffers from vicious circularity because to determine family resemblances among myths one must have already settled on a class of myths. But this sort of problem will attend any inductive, as opposed to a merely stipulative, approach to determining genre and may be resolved, as James Barr advises, by beginning with paradigmatic examples of myths and then looking for family resemblances among the paradigms in order to then determine further instances. We have in ancient Mesopotamia, Egypt, and Greece just such paradigmatic examples of myths.[16]

But this does not resolve the problem. Who decides what counts as "paradigmatic examples of myths"? In order to identify what constitutes a paradigmatic example "one must have already settled on a class of myths" as paradigmatic. Why should anyone think that the myths from ancient Mesopotamia, Egypt, and Greece are paradigmatic examples? Craig simply stipulates which myths should be considered paradigmatic and then he works from this stipulation as if this justifies his stipulation. This is both circular and begging the question.

In fact, Hans-Johann Glock identifies the notion of central paradigmatic cases as a problem that undermines the whole notion of language games and family resemblances. Although he is discussing the notion of family resemblance as a possible characterization of analytic philosophy, his point applies to the very notion of what constitutes a family resemblance: "Furthermore, like an essentially contested concept, a family resemblance concept requires some central paradigmatic cases around which other cases are clustered."[17] What this reveals is that the central paradigmatic cases that serve as the core around which other terms cluster as belonging to a particular language game cannot be determined by the language game itself lest it be involved in a vicious circle. So, who and

---

15. By inerrancy is meant that the Bible is true in everything that it affirms.
16. Craig, *Adam*, 44.
17. Glock, *What Is Analytic Philosophy?* 205.

how are these central paradigmatic cases determined? Ostensibly, these cases would be determined outside the game itself which undermines the very notion of language games and the fact that they cannot be judged by the rules of some other language game.

Also, Glock noted that a central paradigmatic case would be characterized as "an essentially contested concept." As Glock goes on to describe, "Essentially contested concepts are notions like art, democracy, justice, or repression."[18] By whom would a central paradigmatic concept be contested? It would perforce be contested by those not necessarily engaged in the language game concerning these very concepts. Again, this undermines the very notion of language games as games that cannot be "contested" by the rules of other language games. This, along with the very notion of central paradigmatic concepts, forms weaknesses that are fatal to the whole concept of family resemblance and language games.

What this means for Craig's use of family resemblances in relation to myths is that the central paradigmatic cases are determined not by the myths themselves, but by Craig's decision of what constitutes a myth, and this means that Craig's notion of the central paradigmatic cases can be contested since they are simply stipulated by Craig from outside the actual myths. Craig arbitrarily selects the characteristics that he holds to be core paradigmatic cases and then builds his argument on the basis of his predetermined notion of what constitutes myths. But this begs the question and serves to define his position into existence.

And in fact this problem does not necessarily attend any inductive approach as Craig claims it does. It is only a problem for an inductive approach that assumes the problem of induction, which is founded on a form of nominalism.[19] If in fact there are natures and essences, induction can make true statements about anything that has that same nature or essence. Craig's approach assumes a form of nominalism, yet he has neither stated this assumption nor defended it in this book.[20]

---

18. Glock, *What Is Analytic Philosophy?* 206.

19. There are many versions of nominalism. According to E. J. Lowe, "Nominalism, traditionally understood, is a doctrine which denies the real existence of universals, conceived as the supposed referents of general terms like 'red' and 'table.'" E. J. Lowe, "Nominalism," *Oxford Companion to Philosophy*, 624. Nominalism holds that the extra-mental world is composed of bare particulars. Universals are simply names—hence, nominal-ism—that are applied to entities that are grouped by the mind on the basis of similarities. For example, the name "tree" is a universal term applied to entities that are grouped together on the basis of perceived similarities among these entities.

20. In his article "Anti-Platonism," Craig identifies two distinct positions that are

Ten Characteristics of Myths

Craig concludes his chapter on myths by enumerating ten "family resemblances among myths." The most troubling is the tenth resemblance: "Myths exhibit fantastic elements and are not troubled by logical contradiction or incoherence."[21] Of course, working with Craig's notion of family resemblances one could simply say that the biblical text does not include this particular aspect. However, on what basis can one simply declare that the biblical text does not include resemblance 10? On the basis of the notion of family resemblance, one would simply have to stipulate that resemblance 10 does not occur in the biblical text, and this stipulation would need to be based on some assumption that is outside the notion of the "family resemblance" paradigm. But since that is the case, why should anyone employ the notion of family resemblance in the first place? McGrew has convincingly demonstrated that the classification of the Gospels as Greco-Roman is wrong. On the basis of some assumption(s) cannot one simply stipulate that the biblical text does not resemble myths *tout court*? What this indicates is that the whole notion of family resemblance between the biblical text, whether Gospel or OT narrative, and ancient myths is built on some prior assumption(s) by Craig, and the real question is, what are these assumptions and why should anyone adopt them?

Craig gives the following list of characteristics that identify a myth:

1. Myths are narratives, whether oral or literary.

2. Myths are traditional stories handed down from generation to generation.

3. Myths are sacred for the society that embraces them.

4. Myths are objects of belief by members of the society that embraces them.

---

indicated by the designation "nominalism": "The first is the age-old dispute over universals, nominalism being the position that there are no universals. The second concerns a very recent debate, centered in the philosophy of mathematics, which has arisen only since Gottlob Frege's *Foundations of Arithmetic* (1884). In this debate nominalism is the position that abstract objects like numbers do not exist. A nominalist in the context of the first debate is not necessarily a nominalist in the context of the second, and *vice versa*." William Lane Craig, "Anti-Platonism," *Beyond the Control of God?* 116. Craig seems to favor the second nominalist position. However, the problem of induction arises in the context of the first position, "the age-old dispute over universals."

21. Craig, *Adam*, 46.

5. Myths are set in a primaeval age or another realm.
6. Myths are stories in which deities are important characters.
7. Myths seek to anchor present realities such as the world, mankind, natural phenomena, cultural practices, and the prevailing cult in a primordial time.
8. Myths are associated with rituals.
9. Myths express correspondences between the deities and nature.
10. Myths exhibit fantastic elements and are not troubled by logical contradiction or incoherence.[22]

Since we have already shown that the notion of family resemblances is arbitrarily constructed by Craig, why should anyone take these ten characteristics as constituting the core characteristics of myths? Each one of these characteristics is an essentially contested concept. Why cannot someone simply add an eleventh characteristic? The eleventh: *All* myths are false. It can be rationally demonstrated that the so-called paradigmatic cases of myths cannot possibly be true. That being the case, the biblical narratives are summarily eliminated as falling into the category of myth and cannot be evaluated in terms of myth.

Xenophanes of Kolophon (c. 570 BC) is famous for his statements:

> 5. But mortals suppose that the gods are born (as they themselves are), and that they wear man's clothing and have human voice and body.
>
> 6 But if cattle or lions had hands, so as to paint with their hands and produce works of art as men do, they would paint their gods and give them bodies in form like their own—horses like horses, cattle like cattle.[23]

What is not usually reported, however, are his statements leading up to the above:

> 170 One god, greatest among gods and men, in no way similar to mortals either in body or in thought.
>
> 171 Always he remains in the same place, moving not at all; nor is it fitting for him to go different places at different times but without toil he shakes all things by the thought of his mind.
>
> 172 All of him sees, all thinks, and all hears.[24]

---

22. Craig, *Adam*, 45–46.
23. Xenophanes, *Fragments of Xenophanes*, 66–67.
24. Kirk, et al., *Presocratic Philosophers*, 169–70.

Referring to Xenophanes as "representative of the critical stream of thought in Greek philosophy," Deirdre Carabine asserts,

> his ideas have an important bearing on the development of the concept of transcendent divinity. Xenophanes showed himself strongly opposed to the *muthoi* in his criticism of the prevalent notions of the gods accepted by popular cults. The myths, he said, are nothing but useless old tales which make the gods too much like the society they are supposed to govern, and mortals consider the gods to have been born like themselves. According to Xenophanes, it is not fitting for the human mind to think of the gods in this way, rather we should conceive of: 'one god, greatest among gods and men, in no way similar to mortals either in body or in thought.' Whatever the underlying reasons of Xenophanes in positing the idea of one, supreme god, he can be regarded as the first Greek thinker to have conceived of the gods as existing in a realm different from the realm of mortal nature. Xenophanes, like Protagoras, also insisted that human nature cannot know the truth about the gods: 'No man knows, or ever will know, the truth about the gods and about everything I speak of.' This attitude of diffidence concerning knowledge of the gods is one which was to have a long history in Greek thought and may perhaps be linked to Plato's famous remark about knowledge of the father and maker from the *Timaeus*.[25]

According to Xenophanes, myths are useless old tales that make the gods like men. Perhaps this should be the twelfth characteristic in Craig's list. It is just as legitimate to add the eleventh and twelfth characteristics to Craig's list as is his construction of the list itself.

We have already considered the problems with point ten, but point two also introduces problems related to the biblical text. Other than the written text, there do not exist any extra-biblical Hebrew stories coincident with the time of the writing of the Pentateuch. There is no historical evidence that the content of the Pentateuch, from the time it was composed, was ever anything other than the written text that we currently possess. The claims about sources have been unable to identify any sources beyond what has been proposed in the speculations and conjectures of scholars. To claim that the biblical narratives are myths that are "traditional stories handed down from generation to generation" is to assert what has not been proved. Critical scholarship is not universally accepted among OT scholars, as Craig would have us believe, and the

---

25. Carabine, *Unknown God*, 15–16.

claims and methodology of critical scholarship have been shown to be wildly speculative at best and unsupportable at worst.

As we will see below, point five does not apply either since the narratives of Gen 1–11 do not in fact constitute a thematically separate unit. Also, as will be argued, point six is not applicable to biblical narrative since the Bible does not claim that God is "a deity." Rather, the Bible, both OT and NT, declare that there is *only one God*. There are no "deities" of which God can be included as in a class. Point nine does not apply to the Bible since the Bible does not claim that there is a correspondence between "deities and nature." Rather, the Bible repeatedly declares that there is only one God who created nature. Of course the rest of Craig's book will be an attempt to show that the biblical narratives contain all or most of these characteristics. But how many of the characteristics must the biblical narrative have to be enough to claim that biblical narratives are myths? One? Two? Three? Half? More than half? And who sets this quantity? Yet, even if it can be shown that biblical narratives contain all or most of these characteristics, this still does not prove either literary dependency, literary correspondence, or even literary context except in the sense of there being similarities, and similarity of design does not necessarily mean identify of origin. Craig's entire "family resemblances" approach is illegitimate.

Let us consider each of the characteristics of Craig's list:

1. That a myth is a narrative is such a wide open characteristic that modern books on the history of the Ancient Near East could be classified as myths. This characteristic is not specific enough to distinguish myths from any narrative in any culture at any point in the history of mankind.

2. That a myth is a traditional story handed down from generation to generation is also a wide open characteristics. Even the stories handed down from generation to generation about one's own ancestors could be classified as myth. However, there is no historical or documentary evidence that the biblical narratives were handed down from generation to generation. If one believes in God, one could legitimately claim that the content of Gen 1–11 was supernaturally revealed to the author. This characteristic is not specific enough to distinguish myths from any story that is handed down by any generation to any other generation in the history of mankind.

3. That myths are sacred for the society that embraces them is a characteristic of any belief that is considered sacred to any society that embraces them. This characteristic is not specific enough to distinguish a myth from anything that a given society might embrace as sacred.

4. That myths are objects of belief by members of the society that embraces them likewise can apply to any beliefs that members of any society believe. It is not specific enough to distinguish myths from religions or from superstitions.

5. That myths are set in a primaeval age or another realm is not specific enough to distinguish myths from other kinds of narrative. What constitutes a "primaeval age"? If by this Craig simply means that myths are set in the earliest age or ages of the world, then this could apply to novels, or religions, or other kinds of literature, or even to evolutionary theory. This characteristic is not specific enough to distinguish Craig's paradigmatic myths from virtually all kinds of literature from all cultures throughout human history.

6. That myths are stories in which deities are important characters is not specific enough to distinguish myths from world religions. Deities are important characters in all kinds of literature.

7. That myths seek to anchor present reality in primordial time is not specific enough to distinguish myths from religions, or novels, or histories, or evolutionary theory.

8. That myths are associated with rituals is not specific enough to distinguish myths from religions, or social groups such as the Freemasons.

9. That myths express correspondences between the deities and nature does not explain what constitutes a correspondence. Does this mean that myths set forth a relationship that a god has to nature? Again, it is not specific enough to make a distinction between myths and religions, or any belief system in the history of mankind that sets forth such a relationship.

10. That myths exhibit fantastic elements and are not troubled by logical contradiction or incoherence may be specific enough to distinguish myths from religions, or speculations, or philosophies. Of course Craig will argue that the Bible does contain such fantastic elements, but we will show that Craig argues this on the basis of his failure to

understand the language of text and the literary characteristics of the biblical narratives.

Nine of the characteristics given by Craig are not sufficiently specific enough to distinguish myths from virtually any kind of literature that anyone has ever composed or handed down throughout the history of mankind, and we will show that characteristic 10 simply does not apply. Even if Gen 1–11 could be said to have some similarity with several of these characteristics, the characteristics are not specific enough to qualify the Genesis narratives as mytho-history. Of course, Craig will attempt to specify and compare these characteristics with the biblical narratives in subsequent chapters, and each attempt will be considered.

3

Are the Primaeval Narratives of Genesis 1–11 Myth? (Part 1)

CRAIG BEGINS THE NEXT chapter with the following observations:

> In our last chapter we observed ten family resemblances among myths. Many of these family resemblances among myths will be shared by folk-tales and legends as well as other kinds of literature, and so the presence of one of these characteristics will not be very helpful in classifying Gen 1–11. On the other hand, the absence of one of these characteristics would count against taking Gen 1–11 as myth, even if not decisively. Consider, then, our list in numerical order.

Narrative

Craig begins this section with a discussion of Gen 1–11 as narrative: "These chapters tell the story of primaeval events in roughly chronological succession."[1] He refers to the genealogies as constituting a "timeline on which the individual stories are ordered." He then asserts, "The primaeval narrative thus encompasses the entire sweep of prehistoric events from the creation until the call of Abraham, a period of at least 1,948 years according to the given life spans of pre-Abrahamic ancestors."[2]

1. Craig, *Adam*, 47.
2. Craig, *Adam*, 47–48.

Here again Craig indicates a lack of facility in the biblical language. The mistaken assumption is the belief that each father was the immediate, biological father of the son named. For example, Gen 5:6–8 states,

> ⁶ When Seth had lived 105 years, and he brought forth Enosh. ⁷ Seth lived 807 years after he brought Enosh, and he had other sons and daughters. ⁸ The entire lifetime of Seth was 912 years, and then he died.[3]

In fact, the text does not say, "he became the father of." The word אָב ('āḇ, "father") does not occur in Gen 5. Rather, the text states, "and he brought forth [וַיּוֹלֶד, wâyôleḏ]." However, even this verb does not necessarily require that Seth be the immediate, biological parent of Enosh. These statements can be understood differently. At age of one hundred and five years, Seth became the immediate, biological father of a son whose name is not given. This son brought forth sons and daughters who became the ancestors of Enosh (see **Figure 7**). So, at age one hundred and five, Seth became the ancestor of Enosh through his immediate son and through sons who were born to Seth's descendants leading up to Enosh.

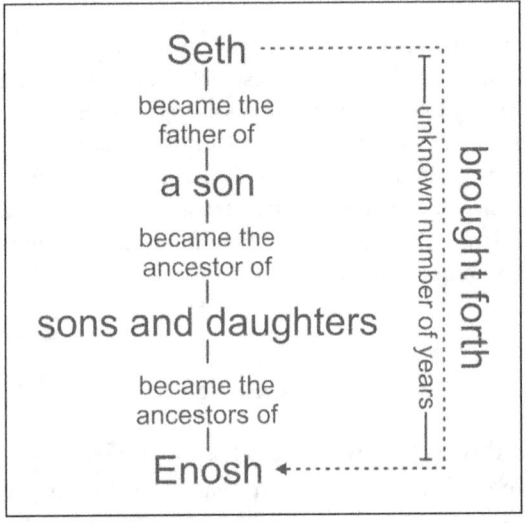

Figure 7: Genealogy of Genesis 5

3. וַיְחִי־שֵׁת חָמֵשׁ שָׁנִים וּמְאַת שָׁנָה וַיּוֹלֶד אֶת־אֱנוֹשׁ: ⁷ וַיְחִי־שֵׁת אַחֲרֵי הוֹלִידוֹ אֶת־אֱנוֹשׁ שֶׁבַע שָׁנִים וּשְׁמֹנֶה מֵאוֹת שָׁנָה וַיּוֹלֶד בָּנִים וּבָנוֹת: ⁸ וַיִּהְיוּ כָּל־יְמֵי־שֵׁת שְׁתֵּים עֶשְׂרֵה שָׁנָה וּתְשַׁע מֵאוֹת שָׁנָה וַיָּמֹת:
(Gen 5:6–8)

Even if we take the text to be saying that Seth "became the father of," the Hebrew Bible did not use a word for "grandfather" or "grandparent." Even if the Hebrew language did have such words in its lexical structure, the Hebrew Bible does not use these words, and there is no evidence that such words existed at the time. So, for the text to say that X became the father of Y does not necessarily mean that X was the immediate biological parent of Y. Rather, it could be saying that at age a, X became the ancestor of Y. The word אָב ('āḇ, "father") does occur twice in Genesis chapter 4: "20 Adah gave birth to Jabal; he was the father of [אֲבִי, 'ăḇî] those who dwell in tents and have livestock. 21 His brother's name was Jubal; he was the father of all those who play the lyre and pipe" (Gen 4:20–21).[4] In these two uses it is clear that neither Jabal nor Jubal were the immediate biological parents of those who developed these lifestyles and skills. Here the word 'father' is used to refer to Jabal and Jubal being the progenitors or ancestors of those who developed the lifestyles and skills.

The text does not provide any indication of the number of years between Seth and Enosh, so calculating the "entire sweep of prehistoric events" based on the genealogy of Genesis 5 cannot be done. To conclude that "a period of at least 1,948 years according to the given life spans of pre-Abrahamic ancestors" is simply a misreading and a misunderstanding of the underlying language. Indeed, Craig has made the same mistake made by James Ussher (1581–1656) in his book, *The Annals of the World*, who set the date of creation at 4004 BC according to the Julian Calendar.[5]

Why would Moses have named the specific individuals that appear in the genealogy of chapter 5? The aim is to lead the reader to compare and contrast the descendants of Cain and the descendants of Seth. The chart in **Figure 8** below shows these comparisons and contrasts. The Hebrew names correspond and contrast on several levels. This structure culminates in the replacing of the descendants of Cain with the descendants of Noah. By ignoring the literary features of the text. Clines and Craig have missed the structure of the text as well as the function of the genealogy in the flow of the text.

---

4. ‏20 וַתֵּלֶד עָדָה אֶת־יָבָל הוּא הָיָה אֲבִי יֹשֵׁב אֹהֶל וּמִקְנֶה: 21 וְשֵׁם אָחִיו יוּבָל הוּא הָיָה אֲבִי כָּל־תֹּפֵשׂ כִּנּוֹר וְעוּגָב:
(Gen 4:20–21)

5. Ussher, *Annals of the World*, 1.

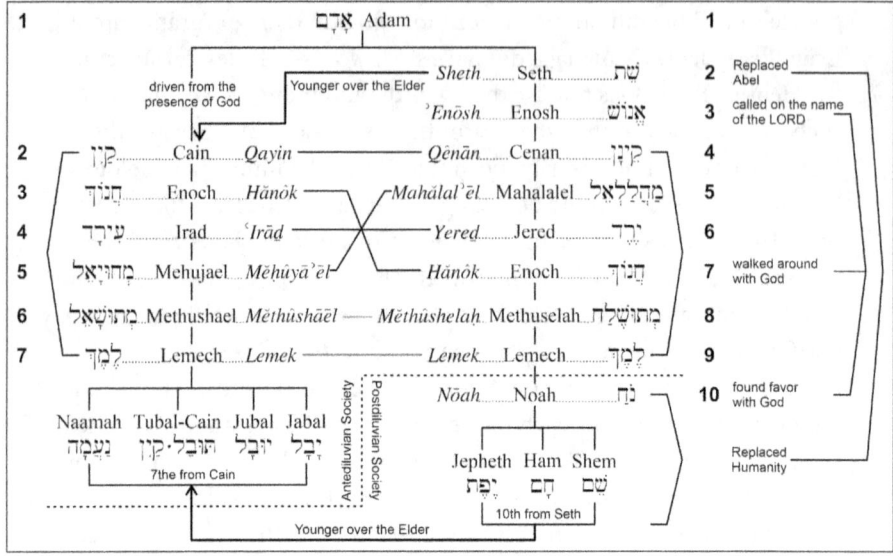

Figure 8: Adam Genealogy

So, is Gen 1–11 composed of narratives? Undoubtedly much of the material is composed of narratives. Does this equate to Craig's first characteristic of myths? Yes it does. But it also equates with any narrative material that has been produced or handed down by any person or group in any culture throughout the history of mankind. Craig has not sufficiently specified the first characteristic so as to qualify Gen 1–11 as falling into the category of myth. The narrative of Gen 1–11 also equates with narratives that compose most of the material from Genesis to Esther. Craig has identified a characteristic without a difference. Basically all Craig has done is to show that biblical narrative and ANE myth fall into the category of narrative.

Traditional Narratives

In this section Craig discusses various forms of higher criticism, but Craig makes sweeping assertions that do not accurately characterize either the history or the current state of these various approaches. The philosophical climate at the beginning of the modern age and the Enlightenment fueled by the social and intellectual Renaissance set the stage for the rise of modern biblical criticism. Of course, critical assessments of the Bible

Are the Primaeval Narratives of Genesis 1–11 Myth? (Part 1)

were not new with the dawn of the modern age. In his *Adversus Octoginta Hæreses*, Epiphanius (c. AD 310–320–403), bishop of Salamis, Cyprus at the end of the fourth century, briefly described the Gnostics' rejection of the law and the prophets: "And from this, we call them the Gnostics, the origin of error. But the law was not of God, but they believed by a kind of left hand of power: the prophets did not proceed out of the good God, but a different one and another power."[6] Critical assessment of the Bible has been around a long time.

As R. K. Harrison points out,

> An attack upon the Mosaic authorship of the Pentateuch was made by Andreas Rudolf Rodenstein (1480–541), a contemporary and rival of Martin Luther. Arguing from the fact that Moses could not possibly have written the account of his own death, he proceeded to reject the Mosaic authorship of the entire Pentateuch, since it seemed to him to be composed in the same general style as the obituary passage.[7]

However, Jean Astruc (1684–1766), a professor of medicine at Montpellier, France, is acknowledged by many scholars as the father of the documentary hypothesis in particular and modern biblical criticism in general. Briefly, the documentary hypothesis is a critical approach to the biblical text that seeks to explain the origin of the Pentateuch, particularly focusing on Genesis, as a compilation of four primary sources dubbed the J-Jehovist, E-Elohist, D-Deuteronomist, and P-Priestly documents. In 1753 Astruc anonymously published a small book that played a fundamental role in the development of the modern documentary hypothesis—*Conjectures sur les mémoires originauz dont il paroit que Moyse s'est servi pour composer le livre de la Génèse. Avec des remarques qui appuient ou qui éclaircissent ces conjectures* (*Conjectures on the Original Documents That Moses Appears to Have Used in Composing the Book of Genesis. With Remarks That Support or Throw Light upon These Conjectures*).[8] He applied to the study of Genesis the techniques of criticism that had been used in the analysis of Homer's *Illiad* arguing that Genesis was composed of several sources or manuscript traditions.

---

6. Epiphanii, *Adversus Octoginta Hæreses*, I.2.292.

7. Harrison, *Introduction to the Old Testament*, 8.

8. Astruc, *Conjectures sur les mémoires originauz dont il paroit que Moyse s'est servi pour composer le livre de la Génèse*.

The foundation of Astruc's argument was the use of two names to identify God:

> II. In the Hebrew text of Genesis, God is primarily designated by two different names. The first, which presents itself, is the one *Elohim*, אלהים. Although this word has several meanings in Hebrew, or at least has been used to signify many things, it is certain that it is particularly used to designate the Supreme Being, and in this sense all Versions have it rendered the same, that of the Septuagint by qeoV, the Vulgate by *Deus*, and all the French Versions, made on the Vulgate, by the word *Dieu*, which the Version of Geneve followed.
>
> The other name of God is that of *Jehovah*, יהוה, and it is, by the admission of all Commentators, the great name of God, the name which expresses his essence. The Jews did not pronounce this name out of respect, and instead read that of *Adonai*, אדני, and for this reason the Massoretes have placed, under the consonants of this name, the vowel points of *Adonai*. It is this name *Adonai*, which signifies in Hebrew *Dominus, Lord*, that the Septuagint, and the Author of the Vulgate, have read the example of the Jews, and that is why they have constantly translated *Jehovah*, the Septuagint by κύριος, the Vulgate by *Dominus*, and all the French Versions, which follow the Vulgate, by the *Lord*. But the Translation of Geneva, made on the Hebrew, read *Jehovah*, and translated this name by that of *Jehovah*, the Eternal, which expresses the truth exactly.[9]

---

9. Astruc, *Conjectures sur les mémoires originauz dont il paroit que Moyse s'est servi pour composer le livre de la Génèse*, II.10–12. "Dans le texte Hebreu de la Genese, Dieu est principalement designé par deux noms differents. Le premier, qui s'y présente, est celui d'*Elohim*, אלהים. Quoique ce mot ait plusieurs significations en Hebreu, ou qu'on s'en soit du moins servi pour signifier plusieurs choses, il est certain qu'il y est particulierement emploié à designer l'Etre Supreme, & dans ce sens toutes les Versions l'ont rendu de mesme, celle des Septante par QeoV, la Vulgate par *Deus*, & toutes les Versions Françoises, faites sur la Vulgate, par le mot de Dieu, ce que la Version de Geneve a suivi.

L'autre nom de Dieu est celui de *Jehovah*, יהוה, & c'est, de l'aveu de tous les Commentateurs, le grand nom de Dieu, le nom qui en exprime l'essence. Les Juifs ne prononçoient pas ce nom par respect, & ils lisoient à la place celui d' *Adonai*, אדני, & pour cette raison les Massorethes ont mis, sous les consonantes de ce nom, les points voielles d'*Adonai*. C'est ce nom d'*Adonai*, qui signisie en Hebreu *Dominus, Seigneur*, que les Septante, & l'Auteur de la Vulgate ont lu à l'exemple des Juifs, & c'est pour cela qu'ils ont constamment traduit *Jehovah*, les Septante par, kuvrioV, la Vulgate par *Dominus*, & toutes les Versions Françoises, qui suivent la Vulgate, par le *Seigneur*. Mais la Traduction de Geneve, faite sur l'Hebrew, a lu *Jehovah*, & a traduit ce nom par celui de l'*Eternel*, qui en exprime affez exactement la valeur. The translation of this text is not a translation by this author."

Astruc set out the text of Genesis in parallel columns assigning the first column to A and the second to B.

> On these reflections it was natural to attempt to decompose Genesis, to separate all the different pieces which are concentrated there, to unite those which are of the same kind, and which appear to have belonged to the same memoirs, and by this means of reestablishing these original memoirs, which I believe Moses had. The enterprise was not so difficult, as one might have thought. I only had to join together all the places, where God is constantly called *Elohim*: I put them on a column, which I named A, and I looked at them like so many pieces, or if you want, from fragments of a first original memoir, that I signify by the letter A. I placed on another column, that I call B, all the other places, where one does not give to God another name, than that of *Jehovah*, and I have gathered all the pieces, or at least, all the fragments of a second memoir B. In making this distribution I have had no regard to that of the chapters in verses, because it is certain that these divisions are new and arbitrary.[10]

By the time Astruc published his conclusions about Mosaic authorship of the Pentateuch, there already existed a tradition of scholarship in which the figure of Moses was analyzed and examined from many different perspectives. Moses had been presented as the originator of Israelite religion, the founder of the nation, and the victim of assassination at the hands of Joshua and Caleb.

However, at the time of the writing of Astruc's book, and even after the treatments of Briggs, and Carpenter and Harford-Battersby,[11] the na-

---

10. Astruc, *Conjectures sur les mémoires originauz dont il paroit que Moyse s'est servi pour composer le livre de la Génèse*, Sur ces réflexions il estoit naturel de tenter de décomposer la Genese, de séparer tous les différents morceaux qui y sont consondus, de réunir ceux qui sont d'une mesme espece, & qui paroissent avoir appartenu aux mesmes mémoires, & par ce moien de rétablir ces mémoires originaux, que je crois que Moyse a eus. L'entreprise n'estoit pas aussi difficile, qu'on auroit pu le croire. Je n'ai eu qu'à joindre ensemble tous les endroits, où Dieu est constamment appellé *Elohim*: je les ai placez sur une colomne, que j'ai nommée A, & je les ai regardez comme autant de morceaux, ou si l'on veut, de fragmens d'un premier mémoire original, que je devsigne par la lettre A. J'ai placé à costé sur une autre colomne, que j'appelle B, tous les autres endroits, où l'on ne donne point à Dieu d'autre nom, que celui de *Jehovah*, & j'ai rassemblé par là tous les morceaux, ou du moins, tous les fragmens d'un second mémoire B. En faisant cette distribution, je n'ai point eu d'égard ni à celle des chapitres en verset, parce qu'il est certain que ces divisions sont nouvelles & arbitraires.

11. See for example Carpenter and Harford-Battersby, *Introduction and Tabular Appendices*.

ture of literary productions by persons in the time and cultural context of the composition of the Pentateuch were not known. Much information about the cultures and literary productions of ancient societies has surfaced since the time of Astruc's writing. For example, discoveries of ancient writings have shown that the use of different names for a god or gods was not only employed by single authors but was expected. As Umberto Cassuto asserts, "There is no reason, therefore, to feel surprise that the use of these Names varies in the Torah. On the contrary, we should be surprised if they were not changed about."[12] Nevertheless, the claims of Astruc and subsequent scholars even up to today dismiss the discoveries that call this approach into question, and scholars persist in employing the same basic methodologies that were set forth by Astruc.

Following upon Astruc's initial proposals concerning the names of God, Julius Wellhausen (1844–1918), a German biblical scholar and orientalist, set forth what many hold to be the definitive, systematic expression of the documentary hypothesis. Craig briefly discusses Wellhausen's theories, but he fails to point out that Wellhausen's theories were predicated on an evolutionary development of the religion of Israel. It did not matter that there was no religion in the history of mankind to which Wellhausen could appeal to show that such a development ever occurred, and since Wellhausen's day such an assumption has been almost universally abandoned. Yet the assumption of an evolutionary development is at the very foundation of Wellhausen's documentary hypothesis and the dating of the various books.

Craig declares, "The Documentary Hypothesis has been subjected to much criticism and has continued to evolve since the time of Wellhausen, but no scholar seems prepared to give it up entirely."[13] If by "entirely" Craig means that no scholar has denied the possibility of the use of sources in the production of the Pentateuch, then this is certainly true. But there are many OT scholars, such as Umberto Cassuto, O. T. Allis, R. K. Harrison, Gleason Archer, etc., who have repudiated the claims of the documentary hypothesis. Additionally, there are no conclusions of the various critical approaches that have produced a consensus among proponents. The criticisms and modifications have produced a cacophony of voices that conflict and often contradict one another.

---

12. Cassuto, *Documentary Hypothesis and the Composition of the Pentateuch*, 41.
13. Craig, *Adam*, 49.

Are the Primaeval Narratives of Genesis 1–11 Myth? (Part 1)

The Achilles heel of the dating of the books of the Pentateuch is the dating of Deuteronomy. The dating of the book of Deuteronomy is the cornerstone of the documentary hypothesis. Although there are disagreements and conflicts concerning various aspects of the critical approach, the dating of Deuteronomy is the most significant and the most widely assumed claim of the critical approach. As Gordon Wenham points out, "It is well-nigh universally assumed by mainstream scholarship that Deuteronomy was written in the late seventh century and should be associated with Josiah's reform c. 622 BC."[14] In their analysis we can see the following assumptions:

1. Rejection or modification of divine inspiration
2. Acceptance of pseudonymous works in ancient cultures
3. Centralization of worship in Jerusalem

It is argued that the centralization of worship in Jerusalem during the reforms of Josiah was the occasion of the production of Deuteronomy in order to give divine sanction to Josiah's reforms. The argument asserts, the anonymous author of Deuteronomy, recognizing that it would be anachronistic to include the name "Jerusalem" in a text supposedly written by Moses, employed a code expression: "the place which the LORD will choose." Perhaps the best example of this is found in Deut 12:5–14:

> 5 But you must seek only the place he chooses from all your tribes to establish his name as his place of residence, and you must go there. 6 And there you must take your burnt offerings, your sacrifices, your tithes, the personal offerings you have prepared, your votive offerings, your freewill offerings, and the firstborn of your herds and flocks. 7 Both you and your families must feast there before the LORD your God and rejoice in all the output of your labor with which he has blessed you. 8 You must not do like we are doing here today, with everyone doing what seems best to him, 9 for you have not yet come to the final stop and inheritance the LORD your God is giving you. 10 When you do go across the Jordan River and settle in the land he is granting you as an inheritance and you find relief from all the enemies who surround you, you will live in safety. 11 Then you must come to *the place the LORD your God chooses* [הַמָּקוֹם אֲשֶׁר־יִבְחַר יְהוָה אֱלֹהֵיכֶם] for his name to reside, bringing everything I am commanding you—your burnt offerings, sacrifices,

---

14. Wenham, "Date of Deuteronomy," 15.

tithes, the personal offerings you have prepared, and all your choice votive offerings which you devote to him. ¹² You shall rejoice in the presence of the LORD your God, along with your sons, daughters, male and female servants, and the Levites in your villages (since they have no allotment or inheritance with you). ¹³ Make sure you do not offer burnt offerings in any place you wish, ¹⁴ for you may do so only in the place the LORD chooses in one of your tribal areas—there you may do everything I am commanding you.¹⁵

Speculation that the book of Deuteronomy was actually produced during the time of Josiah's reforms was perhaps first made by Samuel Parvish, an English theologian whose book, *An Enquiry into the Jewish and Christian Revelation*, was first published in 1739:

> He [*Hilkiah*] must have been very antient, to have seen the Book of the Law, which it is probable had then been lost seventy four Years; and we know how Marks of Antiquity may be imitated, as by Medals, &c. I have known a Person impose on a very ingenious Attorney, by a Copy of an original Deed, imitating the old Writing, and by smoking the Parchment, deceived him in a Mortgage, though he had before sold the Estate, and delivered the original Deed to another Person. And you Notion of there being many authentick Hands of Idolaters, it is probable they would have destroyed them; and if they had been in the Hands of those that worshiped the Lord, they would have delivered them to the Priests for their Direction, at the Beginning of the Reformation under *Josiah*; which seems to have been made by Tradition only, to confirm which, observe but the Behaviour of the King when he heard the Law read, he then rent his Clothes, and set to a Prophetess to know what would be the Consequence of their Disobedience to the Law; though indeed they were only

15. ⁵ כִּי אִם־אֶל־הַמָּקוֹם אֲשֶׁר־יִבְחַר יְהוָה אֱלֹהֵיכֶם מִכָּל־שִׁבְטֵיכֶם לָשׂוּם אֶת־שְׁמוֹ שָׁם לְשִׁכְנוֹ תִדְרְשׁוּ וּבָאתָ שָׁמָּה: ⁶ וַהֲבֵאתֶם שָׁמָּה עֹלֹתֵיכֶם וְזִבְחֵיכֶם וְאֵת מַעְשְׂרֹתֵיכֶם וְאֵת תְּרוּמַת יֶדְכֶם וְנִדְרֵיכֶם וְנִדְבֹתֵיכֶם וּבְכֹרֹת בְּקַרְכֶם וְצֹאנְכֶם: ⁷ וַאֲכַלְתֶּם־שָׁם לִפְנֵי יְהוָה אֱלֹהֵיכֶם וּשְׂמַחְתֶּם בְּכֹל מִשְׁלַח יֶדְכֶם אַתֶּם וּבָתֵּיכֶם אֲשֶׁר בֵּרַכְךָ יְהוָה אֱלֹהֶיךָ: ⁸ לֹא תַעֲשׂוּן כְּכֹל אֲשֶׁר אֲנַחְנוּ עֹשִׂים פֹּה הַיּוֹם אִישׁ כָּל־הַיָּשָׁר בְּעֵינָיו: ⁹ כִּי לֹא־בָּאתֶם עַד־עָתָּה אֶל־הַמְּנוּחָה וְאֶל־הַנַּחֲלָה אֲשֶׁר־יְהוָה אֱלֹהֶיךָ נֹתֵן לָךְ: ¹⁰ וַעֲבַרְתֶּם אֶת־הַיַּרְדֵּן וִישַׁבְתֶּם בָּאָרֶץ אֲשֶׁר־יְהוָה אֱלֹהֵיכֶם מַנְחִיל אֶתְכֶם וְהֵנִיחַ לָכֶם מִכָּל־אֹיְבֵיכֶם מִסָּבִיב וִישַׁבְתֶּם־בֶּטַח: ¹¹ וְהָיָה הַמָּקוֹם אֲשֶׁר־יִבְחַר יְהוָה אֱלֹהֵיכֶם בּוֹ לְשַׁכֵּן שְׁמוֹ שָׁם שָׁמָּה תָבִיאוּ אֵת כָּל־אֲשֶׁר אָנֹכִי מְצַוֶּה אֶתְכֶם עוֹלֹתֵיכֶם וְזִבְחֵיכֶם מַעְשְׂרֹתֵיכֶם וּתְרֻמַת יֶדְכֶם וְכֹל מִבְחַר נִדְרֵיכֶם אֲשֶׁר תִּדְּרוּ לַיהוָה: ¹² וּשְׂמַחְתֶּם לִפְנֵי יְהוָה אֱלֹהֵיכֶם אַתֶּם וּבְנֵיכֶם וּבְנֹתֵיכֶם וְעַבְדֵיכֶם וְאַמְהֹתֵיכֶם וְהַלֵּוִי בְּשַׁעֲרֵיכֶם כִּי אֵין לוֹ חֵלֶק וְנַחֲלָה אִתְּכֶם: ¹³ הִשָּׁמֶר לְךָ פֶּן־תַּעֲלֶה עֹלֹתֶיךָ בְּכָל־מָקוֹם אֲשֶׁר תִּרְאֶה: ¹⁴ כִּי אִם־בַּמָּקוֹם אֲשֶׁר־יִבְחַר יְהוָה בְּאַחַד שְׁבָטֶיךָ שָׁם תַּעֲלֶה עֹלֹתֶיךָ וְשָׁם תַּעֲשֶׂה כֹּל אֲשֶׁר אָנֹכִי מְצַוֶּךָּ:

(Deut 12:5–14)

> Sins of Ignorance: Whereas, if there had been any Copy, they could as well have known the Words of the Law by that Copy. So that if there were any Copies, they were false and imperfect; from which I yet conclude that the Whole depends only on *Hilkiah*: Of whose Ability and Honesty we know nothing; but whose Interest it was to have a Law, either genuine or spurious; and beyond whose Time, you cannot date any Thing with any Certainty.[16]

Wenham sets out the two key arguments for the late dating of Deuteronomy:

> There are essentially two key arguments: the language of Deuteronomy and its demand for the centralization of worship. The style of Deuteronomy, a rhetorical or preaching style with various characteristic words or phrases, markedly resembles other works which must date from the late seventh or early sixth centuries BC. The most obvious parallels are found in the prophets Jeremiah and Ezekiel and in 2 Kings. An elaboration of this theory is Noth's theory of a Deuteronomic history. This holds that Deuteronomy is not so much the last book of the Pentateuch, but the first volume in a history comprising Deuteronomy, Joshua, Judges, Samuel and Kings. It is, I think, undeniable that the language and style of Deuteronomy have close affinities with some books undoubtedly written about 600 BC. Whether this is sufficient grounds for holding that Deuteronomy must also have been written then, we shall return to later.
>
> The second and historically more important reason for holding that Deuteronomy is a seventh-century work is its attitude to the central sanctuary. Until the time of King Josiah people worshipped, whether legally or not is unclear, at the temple in Jerusalem and at high places, village shrines scattered up and down the land. But then Josiah, perhaps following the earlier attempt of Hezekiah, abolished all the local high places and insisted that sacrifice be offered only in the Jerusalem temple. An English equivalent would be the destruction of all the English parish churches and the limitation of worship to Westminster Abbey. Josiah's innovations are described in 2 Kings 23.[17]

Wenham says, "Until the time of King Josiah people worshiped, whether legally or not is unclear, at the temple in Jerusalem and at high places, village shrines scattered up and down the land." To say that it is

---

16. Parvish, *Enquiry into the Jewish and Christian Revelation*, 324.
17. Wenham, "Date of Deuteronomy," 17.

unclear whether worshiping at the high places was legal or not ignores the commands in other portions of the Pentateuch and assumes that one cannot appeal to the declaration in Deuteronomy as a stipulation against worshiping in the high places. As recorded in Numbers, God commanded the people to destroy the high places: "you must drive out all the inhabitants of the land before you. Destroy all their carved images, all their molten images, and demolish their high places" (Num 33:52).[18] God commanded the people to "exterminate" (שמד, *sûmḏ*) the high places. In Deut 12:13–14 God commanded the people not to worship in just any place: "**13** Make sure you do not offer burnt offerings in any place you wish, **14** for you may do so only in the place the LORD chooses in one of your tribal areas—there you may do everything I am commanding you" (Deut 12:13–14).[19] The command in Deuteronomy is in perfect accord with the earlier commands of God to destroy the high places and not to worship in just any place. The statement in Deuteronomy is not anachronistic or unique to the Pentateuch. Indeed, the exclusivity of worship is theologically significant. For anyone to come to God he must come according to God's stipulations. No one worships God apart from the way God prescribes. To separate the Deuteronomic stipulations from the theological context of worship and to treat these stipulations as merely historical records is to take the commands of God out of the theological context of salvation. Worshiping at the high places was contrary to God's stipulations and his revelation of himself from the very beginning.

Of course, the problem among many critical scholars is the fact that they do not consider the texts to be divinely inspired. Paul Enns provides a succinct definition of divine inspiration: "Inspiration may be defined as the Holy Spirit's superintending over the writers so that while writing according to their own styles and personalities, the result was God's Word written—authoritative, trustworthy, and free from error in the original autographs."[20] For many critical scholars, divine inspiration does not play a part in their efforts to explain the origin of the biblical text, as Wenham also points out:

---

18. וְהוֹרַשְׁתֶּם אֶת־כָּל־יֹשְׁבֵי הָאָרֶץ מִפְּנֵיכֶם וְאִבַּדְתֶּם אֵת כָּל־מַשְׂכִּיֹּתָם וְאֵת כָּל־צַלְמֵי מַסֵּכֹתָם תְּאַבֵּדוּ וְאֵת כָּל־בָּמֹתָם תַּשְׁמִידוּ׃
(Num 33:52)

19. הִשָּׁמֶר לְךָ פֶּן־תַּעֲלֶה עֹלֹתֶיךָ בְּכָל־מָקוֹם אֲשֶׁר תִּרְאֶה׃ **14** כִּי אִם־בַּמָּקוֹם אֲשֶׁר־יִבְחַר יְהוָה בְּאַחַד שְׁבָטֶיךָ שָׁם תַּעֲלֶה עֹלֹתֶיךָ וְשָׁם תַּעֲשֶׂה כֹּל אֲשֶׁר אָנֹכִי מְצַוֶּךָּ׃
(Deut 12:13–14)

20. Enns, *Moody Handbook of Theology*, 160.

> Some scholars simply do not believe in the divine inspiration of the Bible: certainly Wellhausen fell into this camp, so it was easy for him to accept that Deuteronomy was fictitious. However the majority of biblical critics do believe that the Bible is in some sense the word of God: in the case of Deuteronomy we have an example of the inspired imagination of a later writer addressing the problem of his own generation. In order to persuade his hearers he clothed his message in the dress of Israel's greatest lawgiver and prophet. This practice of pseudonymous writing was both widespread and respectable in ancient Israel, it is maintained. Therefore it is not difficult to envisage the Spirit of God using such devices to gain acceptance of this vital message.[21]

Wenham points out that critical scholars who do believe that the Bible is "in some sense the word of God" nevertheless argue that Deuteronomy is "an example of the inspired imagination of a later writer addressing the problem of his own generation." In other words, critical scholars claim that, under inspiration, an anonymous author composed the book of Deuteronomy and presented it as if it were the work of Moses. So, we are to believe that God inspired an author to deceive the people of Israel and to misrepresent the authorship of the book. Once one allows for such "inspired" deception, one can claim any portion of Scripture to be divinely deceptive.

The significance of the dating of Deuteronomy was indicated by Wellhausen:

> The assumptions I make will find an ever-recurring justification in the course of the investigation; the two principal are, that the work of the Jehovist, so far as the nucleus of it is concerned, belongs to the course of the Assyrian period, and that Deuteronomy belongs to its close. Moreover, however strongly I am convinced that the latter is to be dated in accordance with 2 Kings xxii., I do not, like Graf, so use this position as to make it the fulcrum for my lever. Deuteronomy is the starting-point, not in the sense that without it it would be impossible to accomplish anything, but only because, when its position has been historically ascertained, we cannot decline to go on, but must demand that the position of the Priestly Code should also be fixed by reference to history. My inquiry proceeds on a broader basis than that of Graf, and comes nearer to that of Vatke, from

---

21. Wenham, "Date of Deuteronomy," 16.

whom indeed I gratefully acknowledge myself to have learnt best and most.[22]

As Wenham explains, "Put more simply: fix the date of Deuteronomy and then date the rest of the Pentateuch by comparison with it."[23] That being the case, once it has been shown that the late date of Deuteronomy is simply an unproven assumption, or a complete falsehood, one is obliged to conclude that the late dating of the rest of the Pentateuch fails, and the failure of the late dating of Deuteronomy undermines the dating of all the other books of Torah.

Deities

The tacit assumption of these scholars is that there cannot be a monotheistic myth. Logically speaking, that assumption is demonstrably false. For, logically, a story that is about a deity is a story about deities. In quantificational logic, "There is one deity" entails that there are deities. To say "Some deities exist" is just to say that at least one deity exists. If it is true that "There is some x such that x is a deity," then at least one individual, but perhaps many individuals, are values for x. Thus, if one deity exists, then deities exist. So logically, a story about one deity is a story about deities. Logically, then, a myth could be about just one deity; accordingly, there can be monotheistic myths.[24]

As true as Craig's statement about quantificational logic may be, this is certainly not relevant to the Bible. The Bible does not assert that one god

---

22. Wellhausen, *Prolegomena zur Geschichte Israels*, 13–14. "Die Voraussetzungen, die ich mache, werden im Laufe der Untersuchung immer wieder neu gerechtfertigt; die beiden vornehmsten sind, dass das jehovistische Werk, seinem Grundstocke nach, vor die assyrische Periode fällt, das Deuteronomium an den Schluss derselben. Für so sicher ich übrigens die Datirung des letzteren nach 2. Reg. 22 auch halte, benutze ich diese Position doch nicht in dem Maase wie Graf, um meine Hebel anzusetzen. Das Deuteronomium ist der Ausgangspunkt nicht in dem Sinne, dass ohne es nichts zu macher wäre, sondern nur in dem Sinne, dass seine Ansetzung nach historischen Gründen die notwendige Forderung nacht sich zieht, auch den Priesterkodex nach historischen Gründen anzusetzen. Meine Untersuchung ist breiter angelegt als die Grafs und nähert sich der Art Vatkes, von welchem letzteren ich auch das Meiste und das Beste gelernt zu haben bekenne."

23. Wenham, *Date of Deuteronomy*, 17.

24. Craig, *Adam*, 59.

exists. The Bible asserts that *only* one God exists. There are no other gods. According to the Bible, the God of Israel is the only true and living God.

> Now, O LORD our God, rescue us from his power, so that all the kingdoms of the earth will know that you, LORD, are the only God" (2 Kgs 19:19).[25]

> "Thus says the LORD, the King of Israel and his Redeemer, the LORD of hosts: 'I am the first and I am the last, and there is no God besides Me" (Isa 44:6).[26]

> "I am the LORD, and athere is no other; Besides Me there is no God. I will gird you, though you have not known Me;" (Isa 45:5).[27]

> "Now to the King eternal, immortal, invisible, the only God, be honor and glory forever and ever. Amen" (1 Tim 1:17).[28]

In John 5:44 Jesus declared, "How can you believe, when you receive glory from one another and you do not seek the glory that is from the one and only God?"[29]

Additionally, to refer to God as "a deity" is to commit a fallacy, as Richard Howe explains:

> To regard God as a deity is to talk as if God is a species (even if the only member of the species) of the genus "deity." But since God is substantial existence itself, then God cannot be a genus in as much as being cannot be a genus since, the only way to distinguish species of a genus is by its specific difference. But the specific difference (1) has to be something not prevented by the genus (as the genus "animal" cannot exclude the specific difference "rationality" otherwise humans would not be animals); and (2) has to be something outside of (i.e., not included in) the genus otherwise (for example) if rationality was part of the genus "animal" then every animal would be human. So, being cannot be a genus because there could be no specific difference

---

25. וְעַתָּה יְהוָה אֱלֹהֵינוּ הוֹשִׁיעֵנוּ נָא מִיָּדוֹ וְיֵדְעוּ כָּל־מַמְלְכוֹת הָאָרֶץ כִּי אַתָּה יְהוָה אֱלֹהִים לְבַדֶּךָ׃ (2 Kgs 19:19)

26. כֹּה־אָמַר יְהוָה מֶלֶךְ־יִשְׂרָאֵל וְגֹאֲלוֹ יְהוָה צְבָאוֹת אֲנִי רִאשׁוֹן וַאֲנִי אַחֲרוֹן וּמִבַּלְעָדַי אֵין אֱלֹהִים׃ (Isa 44:6)

27. אֲנִי יְהוָה וְאֵין עוֹד זוּלָתִי אֵין אֱלֹהִים אֲאַזֶּרְךָ וְלֹא יְדַעְתָּנִי׃ (Isa 45:5)

28. τῷ δὲ βασιλεῖ τῶν αἰώνων, ἀφθάρτῳ, ἀοράτῳ, μόνῳ θεῷ, τιμὴ καὶ δόξα εἰς τοὺς αἰῶνας τῶν αἰώνων· ἀμήν (1 Tim 1:17).

29. πῶς δύνασθε ὑμεῖς πιστεῦσαι, δόξαν παρ' ἀλλήλων λαμβάνοντες, καὶ τὴν δόξαν τὴν παρὰ τοῦ μόνου θεοῦ οὐ ζητεῖτε; (John 5:44).

> to constitute any species (and consequently, any real member of the kind) since to be something outside of being (#2 above) would be non-being. But to be non-being is to be nothing and nothing cannot be a difference.[30]

Craig's appeal to quantificational logic in this instance is misplaced and irrelevant because he does not accurately depict the biblical claim that there is only one God. Yet Craig goes on to argue,

> Now these OT scholars might be averse to this sort of "logic chopping," insisting that myths are inherently stories of a plurality of gods and that therefore there cannot be monotheistic myths. But such a contention seems highly implausible. How could the literary function of a narrative depend on the numerosity of the gods featured in it? If the number of gods in a myth that serves to explain some present feature of the world in terms of divine activity in the primaeval past were reduced from, say, seven to three, would its mythic character be diluted? Presumably not! And if the number were reduced from three to one, why would its mythic character suddenly disappear? Would it not still function to ground present realities in the primaeval past for members of the society that embraces it?[31]

But what this amounts to is, ANE mythologies are narratives that have a certain function in that culture with reference to the deities in which they believed, and biblical narratives are narratives that have a certain function for Israel with reference to God in whom they believed. In other words, so what? Does the fact that these narratives have functions in their own contexts indicate a literary relation between these narratives other than the fact that they are narratives? No matter how one wants to justify a literary connection, the fact of the matter is, ANE myths refer to many gods, whereas the biblical narrative declares that *there is only one God*. This is a critical distinction that Craig seems to want to bypass or remove or ignore in order to make a literary connection he has already assumed there must be.

Craig continues,

> In the Sumerian myth *Enki and Ninmah* 24–37 we read that Enki enjoins the mother goddess Namma to knead clay so that the birth-goddesses could nip off pieces with which she could fashion human beings. How is the story of God's forming man

---

30. Howe, email message to author, 10/18/2021.
31. Craig, *Adam*, 59.

from the dust of the earth in Gen 2 functionally distinct from such a story simply in virtue of the fact that Yahweh is the sole deity? It is easy to understand why the presence of at least one deity is crucial for a story's being a myth, but it is hard to see why the number of deities assumed in a story is determinative for its being a myth.[32]

Whether these stories are "functionally distinct" is not the question. The question is, how does this show any literary relation between these stories? The differences are what make all the difference. Neither Enki nor Ninmah are depicted as eternal deities since they are distinct entities, they move, they are located in various places, they are temporal, and neither Enki nor Ninmah are said to have created the clay out of which they are formed. Neither Enki nor Ninmah created anything by the words of their mouths. Enki was the eldest son of King Anu. Ninmah was a daughter to King Anu. Each one had a beginning.

Elohim exists apart from the creation, and he is the one who created all that has come into being. The God of Israel is eternal. God had no beginning. God created the dust from which he formed the man. There is no other god than YHWH Elohim. By his word God created all that has come to exist. There is no comparison between the ANE deities and the God of Israel. Isaiah declares, "To whom then will you liken God? Or what likeness will you compare with Him?" (Isa 40:18).[33] And God also declares, "To whom would you liken Me and make Me equal and compare Me, that we would be alike?" (Isa 46:5).[34] The gods of ANE myth simply do not compare to the God of Israel, the creator of all that has come to be.

The function of the biblical narratives cannot be confined to what Craig stipulates is the function of myths. The function of the biblical narrative is not simply to describe or tell the story of creation, but to depict the God of Israel as the eternal creator of all that has come to be. A function of the biblical creation account is to depict God as the only God. The argument that there is a literary relation between the biblical narrative and the ANE myths in terms of claims about gods simply fails.

In his effort to find some relation between biblical narrative and myths he refers to an African myth: "Indeed, there are pagan myths in

---

32. Craig, *Adam*, 60
33. (Isa 40:18): וְאֶל־מִי תְּדַמְּיוּן אֵל וּמַה־דְּמוּת תַּעַרְכוּ לוֹ
34. (Isa 46:5): לְמִי תְדַמְיוּנִי וְתַשְׁווּ וְתַמְשִׁלוּנִי וְנִדְמֶה

which only a single deity is a character in the story. For example, the African Bushongo have a creation story that describes Bumba, the creator, as a gigantic white being in human form who existed alone in the beginning, in a universe where there was nothing but water."[35] But the Bumba was a product of the Kuba Kingdom, a pre-colonial kingdom in Central Africa in a region south-east of the modern-day Democratic Republic of the Congo that flourished between the seventeenth and nineteenth centuries. Yet Bumba did not create the universe. The universe already existed when Bumba appears in the darkness.

Craig is certainly not referring to the Bumba myth as a source for biblical narratives. He is trying to show that myths do not necessarily require multiple deities. But this fact does not demonstrate that the biblical narratives fall into the category of myths. Bumba comes to be, whereas the God of Israel is self-existing. Bumba is a temporal being, but the God of Israel is eternal. Bumba is sick to his stomach and vomits out creation, but God creates by the word of his mouth, and God does not have a stomach that might get sick. These are critical distinctions that make the difference between Bumba and God. All this similarity shows is that this myth did not require multiple deities. Bumba is not like the God of Israel, and Craig's appeal to the Bumba myth shows that the biblical narratives are not like this African myth.

In fact, Craig's reference to Bumba actually works against his claim. The similarity between Bumba myth and the biblical creation story certainly does not demonstrate or even imply literary context since the Bumba myth was produced many centuries later than the Genesis narratives. Of course what Craig is arguing is that the Bumba myth is an example of a myth concerning a single deity rather than multiple deities, and that the multiple deities of ANE myths should not count against the claim that the biblical narratives are myths. However, the claim is not that the biblical narratives should be understood in the literary context of an African myth composed several thousand years after the writing of the Pentateuch. Craig's claim is that the biblical narratives should be understood in the literary context of ANE myths, all of which contain stories of multiple deities. Having to appeal to the Bumba myth concerning a single deity actually serves to accentuate the literary distinction between the biblical narratives and ANE myths and counts against the claim of literary context. ANE myths always involve multiple deities, which is why

35. Craig, *Adam*, 60.

Craig must appeal to Bumba. In fact, what Craig's argument shows is that not even the Bumba myth should be classed among the ANE myths.

Why should similarities between ANE myths and the biblical narratives imply literary context? The only basis for an assumption between ANE myths and the biblical narratives is temporal proximity. The ANE myths as compositions pre-date the writing of the Pentateuch even if we take an early date of the Exodus at 1400 BC. Yet the events that the creation account reports took place before any ANE existed. The temporal relation does not prove literary context. It simply shows that Craig believes there are thematic similarities. And why would there not be thematic similarities since they contain narratives about the creation of the world, the creation of man, etc. Yet authors have been writing about these same themes throughout history, but it would be impossible to show that there is a literary context that spans the centuries, cultures, religions, and peoples of the world.

Primaeval Narratives

Craig begins this section with the assertion, "The stories of Gen 1–11 are *set in a primaeval age*." If by "primaeval age" Craig simply means that these narratives recount the beginning of the world, then there is no argument. However, Craig seems to be using the term "primaeval" to indicate more than its bare definition. Depending on what Craig means by the term, what might be identified as a primaeval history encompasses only Gen 1:1–7:24. Chapter 8 begins the creation imagery anew, and the material beginning with 8:1 is integrally connected with the following chapters. Craig has either ignored or is unaware of the literary structure of the text.

Craig's criticisms of Brevard Childs' claims are to the point and decisive. However, to dispense with Childs is not to establish the biblical narratives as myths. Once again, the differences make all the difference. In ANE myths, the place where gods come to be, are born, or simply exist, is already present in some form. The gods are temporal beings existing or coming to exist in some place. In the case of Bumba, the universe already existed as water and darkness. In the case of *Enuma Elish*, the text begins, "When the heaven (-gods) above were as yet uncreated, the earth (-gods) below not yet brought into being, alone there existed primordial Apsu who engendered them, only Mummmu, and Tiamat who brought them forth."³⁶ Even in the case of Enki and Ninmah, the text begins, "In those days, in the days when heaven and earth were created; in those nights, in the nights when heaven and earth were created; in those years, in the years when the fates were determined;" This indicates that there was heaven and earth before "the Anuna gods were born." The text states that the heaven and the earth were created in the days and nights, but not that day and night themselves were created. In the biblical creation narrative, only God exists prior to the creation, and God creates out of nothing all that comes to be.

What Craig is trying to do is to show, assuming the characteristics of myths that he enumerates, that the biblical primaeval narratives have family resemblances to ANE myths and should therefore fall into the category of myths. Besides the fact that we have already demonstrated that Craig's characterization as family resemblance is faulty, family resemblances, assuming there are such things, still do not show literary context or literary dependence. If there are family resemblances, all this shows is that there are family resemblances. One can show similar family resemblances between Hellenistic mystery religions and early Christianity, but this does not show either literary context or dependence. Craig seems to be trying to paint a picture of myths so as to argue that the biblical narratives can be so classified. But either the definition of myth must be so broad as to be meaningless, or the differences between the ANE and African myths on the one hand, and the biblical narratives on the other are so radically different that they simply do not fall into the same category. He is making an unjustified leap from family resemblances to literary context, and his argument simply does not show this.

---

36. Thomas, ed., "Epic of Creation," 5.

4

Are the Primaeval Narratives of Genesis 1–11 Myth? (Part 2)

Etiology

AS WE HAVE ARGUED repeatedly, similarities between OT narratives and ANE narratives do not show literary dependency or literary context. Of course Craig is not arguing for literary dependency. Rather, he is arguing that ANE myths form the literary context in which the narratives of Gen 1–11 should be understood. Up to this point, his efforts have been unsuccessful. In this chapter Craig will deal with the remaining characteristics that he gave in chapter 2.

Craig begins his fourth chapter by arguing the same point: "The claim here is not that the narratives of Gen 1–11 are derived from ANE myths. Hermann Gunkel and the pan-Babylonian school that followed in his train made such a claim, but few scholars defend the dependence thesis today."[1] Craig's arguments soundly refute the claim that the biblical authors borrowed from ANE myths. Craig goes on to identify two pitfalls in the efforts to establish some kind of borrowing, the first pitfall being "*neglecting context*."[2] Craig provides an excellent example of neglecting the context in attempting to make connections:

---

1. Craig, *Adam*, 65.
2. Craig, *Adam*, 65.

Focusing on isolated elements in a text while ignoring context courts the danger of "cherry-picking." To illustrate, we all know about the tragic disaster that occurred when a large airliner, on its way from Massachusetts to New York, crashed into one of New York's tallest office buildings between the seventy-seventh and eighty-fifth floors shortly after 9:00 a.m., setting it afire and resulting in the loss of everyone on board and many office workers. The terrorist attack of 9/11? No, the crash of a B-25 into the Empire State Building on July 28, 1945? By cherry-picking details and ignoring context, one can create the illusion of parallelism where in fact none exists. A full story of the events in this illustration makes it evident that the points of similarity are coincidental.[3]

The problem with this example, however, is that neglecting context is precisely what Craig has done by not taking into account the literary characteristics, techniques, and devices by which Moses constructed his narrative. Craig "cherry-picked" a single author to establish his thematic separation of Gen 1–11 from the rest of the Pentateuch. By neglecting the literary context, Craig has attempted to make a case for a literary context of these chapters with ANE myths. And contrary to his opening claim in this chapter—"We have seen that the stories of Gen 1–11 exemplify the first six such family resemblances"[4]—Craig has not shown either that the notion of family resemblances is even a reasonable method or that Gen 1–11 has exemplified the first six characteristics, except in such a broad since that any kind of literature from any culture or religious group throughout the history of mankind can be said to "exemplify" the first six family resemblances.

Craig identifies the second pitfall: "The second pitfall in establishing parallelism is the fallacy of *overgeneralization* or *abstraction*. OT scholars engaged in comparative studies very frequently resort to a high degree of descriptive generalization or abstraction in order to make two elements appear parallel."[5] Again his arguments against those who engage in comparative studies are decisive. However, Craig then employs this very method in comparing biblical narratives with ANE myths. He says, "Genesis 1–11 shares with myths in general and the ANE myths in particular the grand etiological themes of *the origins of the world, of mankind, of certain natural phenomena, of cultural practices,* and *of the*

---

3. Craig, *Adam*, 66.
4. Craig, *Adam*, 65.
5. Craig, *Adam*, 70.

prevailing cult."⁶ But the creation as set forth in Genesis 1 is not simply the creation of the world, and actually Craig points out the radical differences between the biblical account and the ANE myths:

> As such it is spectacularly different from the cosmic etiologies of Israel's neighbors. In contrast to Babylonian and Egyptian myths, there is neither theogony nor theomachy in Genesis; rather, "In the beginning God created the heavens and the earth" (Gen 1:1). All of physical reality is brought into being by an unoriginate and transcendent Deity. Over the ensuing six days the world is filled out by God's effortless creation of day and night, of the sky with waters above and below, of dry land and seas, of vegetation, of the heavenly luminaries, of marine life and birds, of terrestrial animals, and finally of humans. "Thus the heavens and the earth were finished, and all the host of them" (Gen 2:4). The creation narrative grounds the world with its various familiar creatures and phenomena in the primordial creative work of God.⁷

Considering the "spectacularly different" accounts, on what basis then is there a comparison? Is it simply the case that the biblical account and ANE myths both talk about the beginning of the world? But this is surely overgeneralization and/or abstraction. As Craig says, the biblical account is about all of physical reality that is brought into being "by an unoriginate and trancendent Deity." The comparison is so general that one could make a comparison with almost any story that exists.

Origin of the World

Again Craig ignores the literary aspects of the text. Genesis 1 begins, "In *the* beginning God created the heavens and the earth" (Gen 1:1).⁸ The italicized word 'the' indicates that there is no definite article present in the Hebrew word בְּרֵאשִׁית (bĕrēʾšîṯ), although definite articles are regularly omitted in prepositional phrases. An important literary consideration is the author's use of the word אֶרֶץ (ʾereṣ), translated "earth." There is another Hebrew word that is regularly translated "world"; תֵּבֵל (tēḇēl). This word does not occur in the Pentateuch, which has led most scholars to conclude that the word did not exist at the time of the composition of

---

6. Craig, *Adam*, 87.
7. Craig, *Adam*, 88.
8. (Gen 1:1) בְּרֵאשִׁית בָּרָא אֱלֹהִים אֵת הַשָּׁמַיִם וְאֵת הָאָרֶץ׃

the Pentateuch. Of course there is no evidence that this was the case. The simple fact that it is not used does not show that it did not exist. Assuming Moses to have been the author of the Pentateuch, it is important that Ps 90, which has been traditionally attributed to Moses, does use this word in parallelism with אֶרֶץ (ʾereṣ). "Before the mountains were born, even You brought forth earth [אֶרֶץ, ʾereṣ] and world [וְתֵבֵל, wĕṯēḇēl], and from everlasting to everlasting, You are God" (Ps. 90:2).[9] In the composition of his text, an author selects the words he wants to use in order to express his meaning. Assuming that Moses could have used תֵּבֵל (tēḇēl) instead of אֶרֶץ (ʾereṣ), one must wonder why he chose the latter. As one goes through the Pentateuch, one discovers that the word אֶרֶץ (ʾereṣ) becomes more significant as a reference to "the land which the LORD our God is giving to us" (Deut 2:29).[10] In the creation account, God overcomes the darkness and the deep to make the land habitable and to fill it up. What Moses is doing by using אֶרֶץ (ʾereṣ) is connecting the Creator who has overcome the darkness and the deep to make the land habitable to the God of Israel who is going to overcome the darkness and the enemy in the land, to make the land habitable for his people whom he will plant in the land. The biblical account is not simply a grounding of the world or a background for Israel's worldview. The creation account is the basis of Israel's trust that God will bring them into the promised land that they may inherit it and prosper there, and from there to fill and subdue the world. It is the differences that make the difference.

Origin of Humanity

In this section Craig makes a convincing case that the account in Gen 2 focuses upon the creation of the man and the woman that is given in summary form in chapter 1. Chapter 2 is not a separate or contrary account. The account in chapter 2 is much more than simply a supplement to the description in chapter 1. Beginning at 2:18, the description takes on a more important significance than simply the origin of humanity.

The text states, "Then the LORD God said, 'It is not good for the man to be alone; I will make him a helper suitable for him'" (Gen 2:18).[11] The word translated "good" is טוֹב (ṭôḇ). Although it can be used in a moral

9. (Ps 90:2): בְּטֶרֶם הָרִים יֻלָּדוּ וַתְּחוֹלֵל אֶרֶץ וְתֵבֵל וּמֵעוֹלָם עַד־עוֹלָם אַתָּה אֵל

10. (Deut 2:29): הָאָרֶץ אֲשֶׁר־יְהוָה אֱלֹהֵינוּ נֹתֵן לָנוּ

11. (Gen 2:18): וַיֹּאמֶר יְהוָה אֱלֹהִים לֹא־טוֹב הֱיוֹת הָאָדָם לְבַדּוֹ אֶעֱשֶׂה־לּוֹ עֵזֶר כְּנֶגְדּוֹ

sense, its principal significance is to indicate completeness or wholeness. Man is not complete, so God will make a one suitable for him. However, verses 19–20 give the account of Adam naming the animals, and the text points out, "but for Adam there was not found a helper suitable for him" (Gen 2:20).[12] In other words, by searching, Adam was not able to find the good that he lacked.

God caused a deep sleep to fall upon Adam. The word תַּרְדֵּמָה (tardēmāh), translated "deep sleep" indicates a state or condition in which the individual is unable to do anything, unable to participate, unable to contribute. This is very important. It is used to describe Abram when God establishes the covenant with him. The covenant is an unconditional covenant. Abram is not able to pass through the pieces with God, so the covenant rests only upon God's faithfulness, not the faithfulness of God *and* Abram. In this state, Adam is not able to search for or contribute to the creation of the good that he lacks. The good is provided only by God's act.

The text then states, "then He took one of his ribs and closed up the flesh at that place" (Gen 2:21).[13] One has to wonder why God would cut the man open in order to get out one of his ribs. Could not God simply have taken the rib from the man without surgery? The imagery employed here ought to cause the Christian to connect this description with the description of Jesus whose side is pierced and out of his side is born his bride. Now it is certainly the case that Moses' audience would not have connected this imagery to Jesus who had not even come into this world at the time that the people are on the plains of Moab preparing to enter the promised land, but, as Paul declared, "For whatever was written in earlier times was written for our instruction, so that through perseverance and the encouragement of the Scriptures we might have hope" (Rom 15:4).[14] What instruction might a Christian gain from this imagery? That one cannot find the good on one's own but must trust God to supply the good that makes us whole. The account in Genesis 2 is not simply about the creation of mankind. It is about depicting God as the one who provides the good that makes us whole. By overgeneralizing the text, Craig has ignored the literary features and the imagery that the biblical author employed. Craig has reduced the biblical account to bare enough bones to propose a literary context.

12. (Gen 2:20) וּלְאָדָם לֹא־מָצָא עֵזֶר כְּנֶגְדּוֹ
13. (Gen 2:21) וַיִּקַּח אַחַת מִצַּלְעֹתָיו וַיִּסְגֹּר בָּשָׂר תַּחְתֶּנָּה
14. ὅσα γὰρ προεγράφη, εἰς τὴν ἡμετέραν διδασκαλίαν ἐγράφη, ἵνα διὰ τῆς ὑπομονῆς καὶ διὰ τῆς παρακλήσεως τῶν γραφῶν τὴν ἐλπίδα ἔχωμεν (Rom 15:4).

Natural Phenomena

In this section Craig attempts to make the judgment of God recounted in Gen 3 a case of similarity with ANE myths. However, Craig has actually misrepresented the account. Craig asserts, "Etiological motifs concerning *natural phenomena* are also evident in Gen 1–11. Such motifs are especially obvious in the account in Gen 3 of the primordial couple's disobedience to God as a result of their seduction by the serpent."[15] Later he says, "Whatever one thinks of the enmity established between the serpent and the woman and their respective offspring, the serpent's slithering on the ground is clearly said to be the consequence of God's judgment for its seduction of the couple."[16] First of all, the serpent did not seduce the couple. Rather Eve says, "the serpent deceived me and I ate." The word translated "deceived me" indicates giving someone false hopes.[17] What "false hope" could the serpent have given Eve? The false hope is that she could be an independent being on par with God having the right and freedom to decide for herself what is good, to be "as God" (כֵּאלֹהִים, kēʾlōhîm). But Adam was not deceived. Rather Eve simply gave the fruit to her husband, and he ate. Nowhere does the text state that Adam was seduced by the serpent. In fact, God's judgement upon Adam was because "you obeyed the voice of your wife" (Gen 3:17).[18] The word translated "listened to" is the word שָׁמַע (šāmaʿ), which indicates to harken to in the sense of to obey.[19]

Second, Craig refers to the serpent "slithering on the ground," which he takes literally. However, in this same passage the text states, "and dust you will eat all the days of your life" (Gen 3:14).[20] However, serpents do not literally eat dust. Why take the first part of the judgement literally and yet not take the second part literally? Both of these judgments depict defeat, not necessarily natural phenomena. The fact that the judgment also includes, "Cursed are you more than all cattle, and more than every beast of the field" (Gen 3:14),[21] does not depict the נָחָשׁ (nāḥāš, translated "serpent") as an animal, but is a sign of his humiliation below even the beasts of the field. In fact the נָחָשׁ (nāḥāš) is a depiction of Satan, the deceiver,

---

15. Craig, *Adam*, 93.
16. Craig, *Adam*, 94.
17. HAL, s.v. "נשא."
18. (Gen 3:17) כִּי־שָׁמַעְתָּ לְקוֹל אִשְׁתֶּךָ
19. See HAL, s.v. "שמע."
20. (Gen 3:14) וְעָפָר תֹּאכַל כָּל־יְמֵי חַיֶּיךָ
21. (Gen 3:14) אָרוּר אַתָּה מִכָּל־הַבְּהֵמָה וּמִכֹּל חַיַּת הַשָּׂדֶה

who, by the seed of the woman, will be utterly defeated. Rev 12:9 refers to Satan as "the serpent": "And the great dragon was thrown down, the serpent of old who is called the devil and Satan, who deceives the whole world" (Rev 12:9).[22] The word translated "serpent" is ὄφις (ophis), which is used in Gen 3 to translate the Hebrew word נָחָשׁ (nāḥāš). This is not talking about natural phenomena. In other words, this text is not talking about the נָחָשׁ (nāḥāš) actually going on its belly or eating dust. This is talking about the spiritual realm. The curse to go on its belly and eat dust are figures expressing the ultimate defeat of the נָחָשׁ (nāḥāš), and literal serpents serve as symbols of the poisonous influence and ultimate defeat of Satan. Once again Craig has so overgeneralized the text that the comparison is without significance.

Craig concludes, "Though the story of the fall does not contemplate the later dogma of original sin, still it does portray the disobedience of the first couple as the floodgate through which sin entered into the paradisiacal world created for them by God, leading to their expulsion from the garden to eke out a living from the cursed soil, cut off from the tree of life and so doomed to death."[23] Of course Craig has not presented any evidence that the fall does not "contemplate the later dogma of original sin," since from what other source could Paul have concluded, "Therefore, just as through one man sin entered into the world, and death through sin, and so death spread to all men, because of which all sinned—" (Rom 5:12).[24] However one wants to deal with the fact that death spread to all because of which all have sinned, Paul simply states that sin entered the into the world by the one man. What other man could that have been than Adam. And what other narrative depicts the fall of Adam. On what basis does Craig think that the story of the fall "does not contemplate the later dogma of original sin"?

Craig concludes this section with the following assertions:

> It is evident, then, that Gen 1–11 is brimming with etiological motifs concerning the origins of the world, of mankind, of certain natural phenomena, of cultural practices, and of the prevailing cult. Even if attempts to show direct borrowing of

---

22. καὶ ἐβλήθη ὁ δράκων ὁ μέγας, ὁ ὄφις ὁ ἀρχαῖος, ὁ καλούμενος Διάβολος καὶ ὁ Σατανᾶς, ὁ πλανῶν τὴ οἰκουμένη ὅλην (Rev 12:9).

23. Craig, *Adam*, 95.

24. διὰ τοῦτο ὥσπερ δι' ἑνὸς ἀθρώπου ἡ ἁμαρτία εἰς τὸν κόσμον εἰσῆλθεν καὶ διὰ τῆς ἁμαρτίας ὁ θάνατος, καὶ οὕτως εἰς πάντας ἀνθρώπους ὁ θάνατος διῆλθεν ἐφ' ᾧ πάντες ἥμαρτον (Rev 5:12).

Gen 1–11 from ANE myths are fraught with conjecture and uncertainty, it cannot be plausibly denied that these chapters treat many of the same themes as ANE myths and seek to ground present realities in events of the primordial past. Even if some of the examples here identified are disputable, the multiplicity and variety of etiological motifs in Gen 1–11 make it difficult to deny that these chapters exemplify this central family resemblance of myths.[25]

It is certainly accurate that the accounts to which Craig refers are "brimming with etiological motifs," but, again, this does not prove that these accounts fall into the category of ANE myths. Notwithstanding Craig's mishandling of several of these passages, it is the difference that makes the difference. That both the Genesis accounts and the ANE myths "treat many of the same themes" can be accounted for by the fact that they both are addressing the perennial questions that humanity has addressed throughout history. Of course they deal with the same themes, but that still does not show literary context or dependence. Since Craig's appeal to family resemblances is faulty, as was shown in chapter 2 above, and since Craig's list of characteristics is so broad that almost any kind of literature could fit into his notion of myth, Craig's arguments fail.

Fantastic and Inconsistent Elements

Anthropomorphisms

In this section Craig argues that there are inconsistencies in the biblical account. He first deals with what he labels "anthropomorphisms." Craig claims, "Despite God's transcendence so dramatically declared in Gen 1, God is portrayed in the story of man's creation in Gen 2 as a humanoid deity worthy of polytheistic myths, as he forms man from the dirt and breathes the breath of life into his nostrils."[26] These anthropomorphic depictions do not present God as a "humanoid deity worth of polytheistic myths." This is eisegesis. They are anthropomorphisms, not literal depictions. The creation account is depicted as God speaking things into existence. Are we to suppose that this depicts God as having a mouth, or a tongue? In Ruth 2:12 Boaz refers to the wings of God of Israel: "May the LORD reward your work, and your wages be full from the LORD, the

---

25. Craig, *Adam*, 100.
26. Craig, *Adam*, 102.

God of Israel, under whose wings you have come to seek refuge" (Ruth 2:12).[27] Should we supposed that Boaz is depicting God as a being with wings? Of course not. These are figures of speech.

Craig next appeals to Gen 3: "The same is true of the story of the fall in Gen 3, where God strolls in the cool of the day and searches for the man and woman hiding among the trees;"[28] Once again Craig's apparent lack of facility in the language surfaces. The appearance of God on Mt. Sinai in the thunder and lightening and the cloud is not the first of such instances. The first instance is in fact Gen 3:8. The NASB translates this verse as follows: "And they heard the voice of Jehovah God walking in the garden in the cool of the day: and the man and his wife hid themselves from the presence of Jehovah God amongst the trees of the garden."[29] The phrase "in the cool of the day" (לְרוּחַ הַיּוֹם, lĕrûaḥ hâyôm) has for centuries puzzled translators due to its peculiarity. The fact that the word translated "cool" is the word רוּחַ (rûaḥ), and is never used to mean "cool," the rendering "cool of the day" is very problematic. This word is often used for "wind" or "breath."

Another problem arises from the understanding of the meaning of the term הַיּוֹם (hâyôm), universally translated "the day" in this verse. Jeffrey Niehaus makes a convincing argument that in this instance the word yôm is not the more commonly occurring word for "day." Rather, this is an Akkadian loan word, *ūmu* meaning "storm." This corresponds with the use of the word רוּחַ (rûaḥ). Neihaus argues, "Akkadian *ūmu* is often used with theophanic overtones. What if the same were true of the Hebrew יוֹם, 'storm'? Such an interpretation understands the enigmatic phrase לְרוּחַ הַיּוֹם to mean not 'in the cool of the day,' but 'in the wind of the storm.'"[30] The picture here is not of God casually meandering through the garden on a cool afternoon keeping an eye out in case He happens to run into Adam. The word translated "walking" (וַיִּתְהַלֵּךְ, wâyiṯhalēk) is a Hithpael stem implying the notion that God was *walking back and forth* as if searching. The picture is of God coming in the storm of divine

---

27. יְשַׁלֵּם יְהוָה פָּעֳלֵךְ וּתְהִי מַשְׂכֻּרְתֵּךְ שְׁלֵמָה מֵעִם יְהוָה אֱלֹהֵי יִשְׂרָאֵל אֲשֶׁר־בָּאת לַחֲסוֹת תַּחַת־כְּנָפָיו׃
(Ruth 2:12)

28. Craig, *Adam*, 102.

29. וַיִּשְׁמְעוּ אֶת־קוֹל יְהוָה אֱלֹהִים מִתְהַלֵּךְ בַּגָּן לְרוּחַ הַיּוֹם וַיִּתְחַבֵּא הָאָדָם וְאִשְׁתּוֹ מִפְּנֵי יְהוָה אֱלֹהִים בְּתוֹךְ עֵץ הַגָּן׃
(Gen 3:8)

30. Niehaus, *God at Sinai*, 157.

judgment. This interpretation, as Niehaus goes on to point out, changes the understanding of this entire event: "This understanding of יוֹם affects the translation of other terms in the passage. For example, in the context of such a theophany, the קוֹל [qôl, 'voice'] of Yehwah that the man and woman hear is no longer merely Yehwah's 'voice.' It is the 'thunder' of his stormy presence. It is the same theophanic 'thunder' that later atop Horeb/Sinai struck terror into the Israelites."[31] God is not searching for Adam as if he does not know where Adam is. Rather the notion of God moving back and forth in search of Adam is a figure of speech designed to emphasize that Adam is now separated from God. Adam and Eve are frightened because they realize that God is coming in the storm of judgment. Craig has misunderstood and misrepresented the text. Again this indicates a lack of facility in the language.

Craig concludes,

> Such anthropomorphic descriptions of God, if interpreted literally, are incompatible with the transcendent God described at the beginning of creation. Such incoherence could not possibly have escaped the notice of the pentateuchal author, for it is so patent, and yet he felt no need to expunge the anthropomorphic elements. He doubtless assumed that his readers would have understood such anthropomorphic descriptions of God to be just part of the storyteller's art, not serious theology.[32]

But why should anyone think that these should or would have been interpreted literally? They are figures of speech. Just like the expressions "sun rise" and "sun set" should not be taken literally. There is no reason to think that the "pentateuchal author" would assume that his reader would have understood these expressions in any other way that figures of speech that should not be taken literally. These simply are not inconsistencies in the text. They are rather Craig's misunderstandings. Later Craig charges Gunkel with conflating anthropomorphisms with miracles, which Craig identifies as "a simple category mistake."[33] But Craig has done the same thing with anthropomorphisms and inconsistencies.

---

31. Niehaus, *God at Sinai*, 158.
32. Craig, *Adam*, 102.
33. Craig, *Adam*, 105.

Narrative Inconsistencies

Craig appeals to Genesis 2 as an example of narrative inconsistencies: "It would have been easy for him to bring the account of the creation of man in Gen 2 into accord with Gen 1, rather than leave the apparent inconsistencies concerning the order of creation of man, the vegetation, and the animals."[34] But again Craig has not dealt with the underlying language. Craig is unaware of some very basic principles of Hebrew grammar and syntax. In verses 5–6, the text says, "Now no shrub of the field was yet in the earth, and no plant of the field had yet sprouted, for the Lord God had not sent rain upon the earth; and there was no man to cultivate the ground. But a mist used to rise from the earth and water the whole surface of the ground."[35] The text does not say that plants had not yet been created. Rather, it simply points out that no shrub of the field had begun to appear or to sprout. The mist would go up from the ground to water the land so that the shrubs would begin to grow. The reason for these observations is to focus the attention of the reader upon those aspects of the creation that will be affected by the fall. At this point, the land is unaffected by the fall, and these verses prepare the reader for later events.

As Craig had pointed out earlier, the text continues in verse 6 to describe in more detail what was described in more general terms in chapter 1, the creation of the man and woman. Verse 19 is almost universally translated, "And out of the ground the Lord God formed every beast of the field and every bird of the sky, and brought to the man to see what he would call them; and whatever the man called a living creature, that was its name."[36] The primary reason to think that the chronology of the creation accounts is contrary is due to the translation of the word וַיִּצֶר (wâyiṣer), "and he formed." Since there are only two tenses in Hebrew—the perfect, indicating completed action, and the imperfect, indicating incomplete action—a past perfect idea must be expressed by one of these tenses. In biblical Hebrew, there is no morphologically indicated past perfect tense. The past perfect indicates an action in the past that was completed before

---

34. Craig, *Adam*, 102.

35. וְכֹל שִׂיחַ הַשָּׂדֶה טֶרֶם יִהְיֶה בָאָרֶץ וְכָל־עֵשֶׂב הַשָּׂדֶה טֶרֶם יִצְמָח כִּי לֹא הִמְטִיר יְהוָה אֱלֹהִים ⁵ עַל־הָאָרֶץ וְאָדָם אַיִן לַעֲבֹד אֶת־הָאֲדָמָה: ⁶ וְאֵד יַעֲלֶה מִן־הָאָרֶץ וְהִשְׁקָה אֶת־כָּל־פְּנֵי־הָאֲדָמָה:
(Gen 2:5–6)

36. וַיִּצֶר יְהוָה אֱלֹהִים מִן־הָאֲדָמָה כָּל־חַיַּת הַשָּׂדֶה וְאֵת כָּל־עוֹף הַשָּׁמַיִם וַיָּבֵא אֶל־הָאָדָם לִרְאוֹת מַה־יִּקְרָא־לוֹ וְכֹל אֲשֶׁר יִקְרָא־לוֹ הָאָדָם נֶפֶשׁ חַיָּה הוּא שְׁמוֹ:
(Gen 2:19)

some other past action. So, one might say, "By the time I got to the store [simple past action], it had already closed [past perfect action]." The store had closed before I got there. The form that appears in the biblical text in this instance is called a *Wayyiqtol* (pronounced *va-yik*-tōl). A *Wayyiqtol* is an imperfect form of the verb with a *waw* (pronounced *vav*) consecutive (ו, wa), translated "and." In this form, a *waw* is prefixed to the verb form. Though it is an imperfect form morphologically, as a *Wayyiqtol*, its sense is perfect. As a perfect verb, it can be translated as a past perfect, "had formed," or as a simple perfect, "formed."

Morphologically and syntactically, there is nothing in the text that would commend a past perfect translation ("the Lord God *had formed* . . .") of this verb over a simple perfect translation ("the Lord God *formed* . . ."), and yet neither are there any morphological or syntactical features that would require a simple perfect translation over a past perfect translation. Since the translation is not decided morphologically or syntactically, there must be some other criteria that help the translator and commentator to decide which translation is preferred. These criteria would principally be the context. In this instance, the context would be the previous material including the previous chapter in which the chronology is set forth. But the problem here turns out to be the already assumed theological or philosophical position of the interpreter. Contextually, the sense is capable of being understood to be past perfect, "He had formed," unless one presupposes an inconsistency or contradiction in the two accounts rather than giving the author the benefit of the doubt.

If one gives to the text the benefit of the doubt, which is the way a critic would treat any other book, then a past perfect translation is preferable since it fits into the context and complements the general creation account as depicted in chapter 1. Craig assumes a discontinuity between the accounts, and his prior assumption directs him to the translation that fits that assumption. Other interpreters assume a continuity between the accounts, and their prior assumption directs them to translate the passage accordingly. What this indicates, then, is, contrary to Craig's rendering, the continuity and/or discontinuity is not decided by the morphology, syntax, or grammar of the passage, but by the prior assumptions of the interpreter. Craig presents the case as if it were simply a matter of correctly reading the passage. It is by no means simply a matter of a correct translation. Therefore, the correctness of the translation will involve the adjudication between the theological and philosophical commitments of the interpreters. Craig is clearly influenced by commentators who assume a discontinuity, and to present this as simply a matter of reading the text is disingenuous.

However, there is another approach to this text. The text states, "Out of the ground the LORD God formed every beast of the field and every bird of the sky and brought them to the man to see what he would call them;"[37] This need not be taken as a statement about a chronological relation. Rather, it can be taken as a reminder to the reader that God is the one who formed the beasts and the birds. It would be analogous to saying, "Bill built the house, and he carried his wife through the door on their wedding day." This is not saying that he married, then built a house, then carried his wife through the door all on their wedding day. Rather it is simply pointing out that Bill was the one who built the house through the door of which he now carries his wife. Likewise, God was the one who formed the beasts of the field and the birds of the sky, and he brought them to the man to name them in order for Adam to exercise dominion over them as God commanded.

Consequently, it is not a morphological, grammatical, or syntactical necessity to conclude that the order of creation is contrary in the two accounts.

Genesis 1	Genesis 2
plants	plants have been created, but have not yet begun to sprout
animals	man is formed from the dust
man and woman	animals had already been formed/ God was the One who formed them
	woman is formed from the man

Table #5: Genesis 1 and Genesis 2 Creation Order

One reason verse 19 points out that God formed the animals from the ground is to contrast the creation of the animals with the creation of the woman. Unlike the creation of the animals, the woman is formed from the man, not from the ground. The reason the woman is an appropriate

37. וַיִּצֶר יְהוָה אֱלֹהִים מִן־הָאֲדָמָה כָּל־חַיַּת הַשָּׂדֶה וְאֵת כָּל־עוֹף הַשָּׁמַיִם וַיָּבֵא אֶל־הָאָדָם לִרְאוֹת מַה־יִּקְרָא־לוֹ׃
(Gen 2:19)

mate is because she, unlike the animals, comes from the man. So, the text is not giving a contrary creation account, but is simply giving a more detailed account of the creation of the man and the woman.

Another supposed inconsistency is the statement in Gen 4:26. Craig says, "'At that time men began to call upon the name of the Lord' (Gen 4:26), despite his later affirmation that the name 'Yahweh' had not been previously revealed (Exod 6:3), but he could not be bothered to iron out the apparent inconsistency."[38] Again this seems to be a lack of understanding the language on Craig's part. The text does not say, "At that time men began to call upon the name of the Lord . . ." The word "men" does not occur in the text, and the word translated "began to call" is actually a Hophal verb, הוּחַל (hûḥal), which is a causal, passive verb. The translation should be, "was caused to begin," or "was begun." The text is not asserting that anyone in particular began to call on the name of the Lord. The text is pointing out that this state of affairs was enacted, that it was now necessary for anyone to call upon the name of the Lord. It was no longer the case that God would immediately interact with mankind as he had done with Adam before the fall. Man is now separated from God, and this separation is indicated by the fact that it was necessary to call upon the name of the Lord. But Moses is writing to an audience for whom the name יהוה had already become known, and he is describing this condition to his audience. This becomes significant with reference to Abram who called upon the name of the Lord: "Then he [Abram] proceeded from there to the mountain on the east of Bethel, and pitched his tent, with Bethel on the west and Ai on the east; and there he built an altar to the LORD and called upon the name of the LORD" (Gen 12:8).[39] Again Moses is telling his audience that Abram called upon God whom they now know by the name יהוה. This is analogous to saying that Bob met his wife in the summer. When he met her, she was not his wife, but she is now known to be Bob's wife. To express this fact in this manner is not an inconsistency. It is merely a manner of speaking. Craig has failed to demonstrate any actual inconsistencies in the text.

---

38. Carig, *Adam*, 104

39. וַיַּעְתֵּק מִשָּׁם הָהָרָה מִקֶּדֶם לְבֵית־אֵל וַיֵּט אָהֳלֹה בֵּית־אֵל מִיָּם וְהָעַי מִקֶּדֶם וַיִּבֶן־שָׁם מִזְבֵּחַ לַיהוָה וַיִּקְרָא בְּשֵׁם יְהוָה:
(Gen 12:8)

Fantastic Elements

In this section Craig discusses some of the elements that Gunkel identifies. One of these is the description in the creation account that there were evenings and mornings constituting the first three days although the text states that the luminaries were not made until the fourth day. Craig says,

> With respect to the luminaries, while it seems natural to read the creation of the luminaries chronologically in view of the ordinally numbered days, such an interpretation does not force itself on us. For it would have made no sense to an ancient author to affirm the existence of the cycle of day and night, of evening and morning (effectively, sunset and sunrise) on days 1–3 in the absence of the sun. The existence of days prior to the sun's existence might be deemed an incoherence in the text, indicative of a mythical genre. But another possibility is to read the creation of the luminaries nonchronologically.[40]

So, we are to believe that God created the universe out of nothing, but God cannot create directional light shining on the earth without luminaries. Apparently Moses expected his audience to believe that God created *ex nihilo*, why should we think that he would not expect his audience to believe that God could create directional light without light giving bodies? In fact, Craig completely misses the significance of this depiction. As in the beginning there was light without physical light-giving bodies, so it will be at the end: "And there will no longer be any night; and they will not have need of the light of a lamp nor the light of the sun, because the Lord God will illumine them; and they will reign forever and ever" (Rev 22:5).[41]

Craig includes a lengthy footnote in which he discusses several views of interpreters concerning the creation week. But none of these interpreters deals with the literary characteristics of the text. Verse 2 of Genesis 1 states, "The earth was empty and uninhabitable, and darkness was over the surface of the deep, and the Spirit of God was moving over the surface of the waters" (Gen 1:2).[42] The movement of the creation account is to address two characterization of the earth, "empty and uninhabitable."

---

40. Craig, *Adam*, 107.

41. καὶ νὺξ οὐκ ἔσται ἔτι, καὶ οὐκ ἔχουσιν χρείαν φωτὸς λύχνου καὶ φῶς ἡλίου, ὅτι κύριος ὁ θεὸς φωτίσει ἐπ' αὐτούς, καὶ βασιλεύσουσιν εἰς τοὺς αἰῶνας τῶν αἰώνων (Rev 22:5).

42. (Gen 1:2): וְהָאָרֶץ הָיְתָה תֹהוּ וָבֹהוּ וְחֹשֶׁךְ עַל־פְּנֵי תְהוֹם וְרוּחַ אֱלֹהִים מְרַחֶפֶת עַל־פְּנֵי הַמָּיִם

The first three days involve subduing the earth and making it a habitable place. Notice that it is only in the first three days that God names. Naming is indicative of having dominion over or subduing. That is why God brings the animals to Adam to name them. It is an act of exercising dominion over the animals as God had commanded. Over the next three days God fills up the earth. On day one God subdues the darkness and creates light. In day four God fills the firmament by creating light giving bodies. On day two God subdues the waters and divides the waters above from the waters below. On day five God fills the waters with sea creatures, and he fills the firmament with birds. On day three God subdues the waters below by dividing the waters and causing the dry ground to appear. On day six God fills the dry ground with land creatures and man. On the sixth day God commands the couple to fill the earth and subdue it. God subdued and filled, and he commands his representatives to fill and subdue.

When Adam and Eve fail in their responsibility, God calls out a people to himself, and he commands them to fill and subdue; to fill the land with proselytes and to subdue by teaching Torah. Israel also fails at this responsibility, and God calls out the church to fill and subdue; to fill the earth with disciples and subdue them by teaching them whatsoever Jesus has commanded. Ultimately the last Adam must fulfill the responsibility of filling and subduing by establishing the kingdom.

Also notice that there are ten times that the text asserts, "And God said . . ." What is almost universally referred to as the "ten commandments" are never called "ten commandments." They are actually referred to as the "ten words" (הַדְּבָרִים עֲשֶׂרֶת, haddĕḇārîm ʿăśereṯ). In ten words God creates the cosmic order, and in ten words God creates the national order.

There are seven times in the creation account in which the text states, "And God saw that it was good." In the fall, the text states that Eve "saw that the tree was good." God is the one who declares the good, but Eve sought to become independent of God by taking upon herself the right and freedom to decide what is good.

Again, not being aware of the literary characteristics and imagery by which Moses has constructed his narrative, Craig does not grasp either the structure or the function of the creation account.

Are the Primaeval Narratives of Genesis 1–11 Myth? (Part 2)

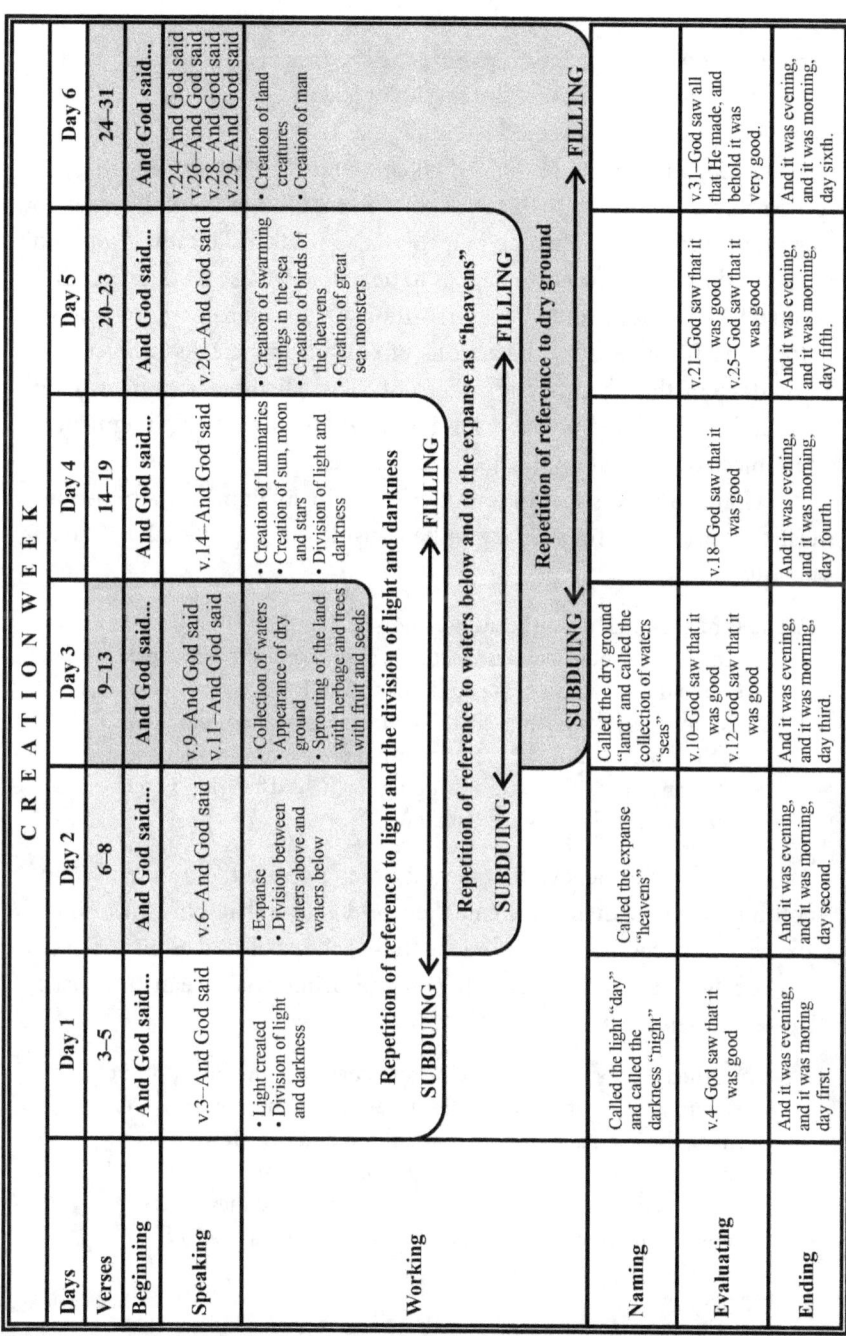

Figure 9: Creation Week

Six Creation Days

In this section Craig wants to picture the six days of creation as fantastic: "What is fantastic and therefore mythological in Gen 1 is the creation of the world over six consecutive days."[43] By "fantastic," Craig is referring to elements in an account that, "if taken literally, are so extraordinary as to be palpably false."[44] By this account, the creation of the universe is so extraordinary that it must be palpably false if taken literally. And who judges what is "so extraordinary" as to be palpably false if taken literally? And what does it mean to be "extraordinary"? Extraordinary for whom? God? The Bible is about the actions of God in this created universe. It would seem that from Craig's point of view, all these actions of God should be considered palpably false if taken literally. Craig's judgment is so subjective as to offer no objective measure.

Craig considers the notion of creation in six literal days to be fantastic; that is, so extraordinary to be considered palpably false if taken literally.

> It may be that even the author himself found creation over six literal days fantastic, for he recounts as accomplished in one day events that he well knew could not naturally have happened in twenty-four hours, but that are nonetheless nonmiraculous, such as the draining of the primordial ocean into seas on day 2 (cf. Gen 8:3) or the earth's bringing forth seed-bearing vegetation and fruit-bearing trees on day 3.[45]

So, we are to believe that God is able to create the universe out of nothing, but he is unable to create the world and all that is in it in six literal days. And why should we not take these actions of God as miraculous?

Craig refers to the "draining of the primordial ocean into seas." However, Gen 1:6–8 states:

> "**6** Then God said, 'Let there be an expanse in the midst of the waters, and let it separate the waters from the waters.' **7** God made the expanse, and separated the waters which were below the expanse from the waters which were above the expanse; and it was so. **8** God called the expanse heaven. And there was evening and there was morning, a second day" (Gen 1:6–8).[46]

---

43. Craig, *Adam*, 109.
44. Craig, *Adam*, 104–5.
45. Craig, *Adam*, 110.
46. **6** וַיֹּאמֶר אֱלֹהִים יְהִי רָקִיעַ בְּתוֹךְ הַמָּיִם וִיהִי מַבְדִּיל בֵּין מַיִם לָמָיִם: **7** וַיַּעַשׂ אֱלֹהִים אֶת־הָרָקִיעַ

Are the Primaeval Narratives of Genesis 1–11 Myth? (Part 2)

Where does the text state that there was a "draining of the primordial ocean into seas"? That description does not occur in the text of Genesis, and reading into the account what is not there is rather fantastic.

In a footnote Craig says,

> Thus, John Day is far too quick when he asserts, "Contrary to what is often said by some popular apologists, there is no reason to doubt that the original writer of Genesis 1 intended his account to be taken literally" (*From Creation to Babel*, 2). Day says nothing by way of analysis of the genre of Gen 1–11, and his expression "the original writer" is ambiguous: Is it P? Or the oral traditions enscripted in P? Or the pentateuchal author? I shall not comment on Day's characterization of OT scholars who advocate a nonliteral interpretation of Gen 1 as "popular apologists."[47]

Genre does not determine meaning.[48] How does Craig know what the genre is? It would be necessary to read the text in order to make a judgment about genre. But if genre determines meaning, one would need to know the genre before reading the text in order to grasp its meaning in order to determine the genre. In other words, one would need to know the meaning of the text before knowing the meaning of the text. Additionally, the creation account does not have any of the characteristics of Hebrew poetry. The text presents itself as narrative. So appealing to genre does not in any way call Day's assertion into question. We have already shown how Craig seems to be completely unaware of the literary aspects of the text that contribute to an understanding of genre. Also, the reference to "the original writer" is ambiguous only for those who subscribe to the Documentary Hypothesis, which has already been shown to be by no means either an established fact or even an established methodology.

Vegetarianism

Another supposedly fantastic element, according to Craig, is vegetarianism. The text does state that God gave the animals to man for food only after the flood. The statement in Gen 5:29 actually anticipates this very

---

וַיַּבְדֵּל בֵּין הַמַּיִם אֲשֶׁר מִתַּחַת לָרָקִיעַ וּבֵין הַמַּיִם אֲשֶׁר מֵעַל לָרָקִיעַ וַיְהִי־כֵן: [8] וַיִּקְרָא אֱלֹהִים לָרָקִיעַ שָׁמָיִם וַיְהִי־עֶרֶב וַיְהִי־בֹקֶר יוֹם שֵׁנִי:
(Gen 1:6–8)

47. Craig, *Adam*, 110.n99.
48. See Howe, "Does Genre Determine Meaning?" 1–19.

fact: "Now he [Lamech] called his name Noah, saying, 'This one will give us rest from our work and from the toil of our hands arising from the ground which the LORD has cursed'" (Gen 5:29).[49] The name 'Noah' (נֹחַ Nōaḥ, or נוֹחַ Nôaḥ) actually means "rest." The word translated "will give us rest" (יְנַחֲמֵנוּ, yěnaḥămēnû), is the verb form. The point of this is that God gave man rest from the toil of the cursed ground by granting the right to kill and eat. To claim, "The removal of this restriction for humans implies that a similar restriction was in place for the animals in the primordial state" does not derive from the text, and the fact that the text states the reason for the lifting of the restriction refutes any implication about animals. The restriction was lifted to give man rest from the toil of the ground. But the animals were not cursed to toil the ground. There simply is nothing in the text to support the notion that animals were vegetarians until after the flood. This is sheer speculation for the purpose of making this sound "fantastic."

The Snake

Craig's speculations get more fantastic as his text progresses. Craig continues to refer to the נָחָשׁ (nāḥāš) in Genesis 3 as a snake. It is certainly the case that this word is used in the OT to refer to a snake, but that is not its only possible use. It is used in Gen 49:17 as a figurative reference to Dan: "Dan shall be a serpent [נָחָשׁ, nāḥāš], a horned snake [שְׁפִיפֹן, šěphîphōn] in the path, that bites the horse's heels" (Gen 49:17).[50] And the text of Genesis 3 does not state that the נָחָשׁ (nāḥāš) was in fact a snake. The text simply states that the נָחָשׁ (nāḥāš) was more crafty than all the beasts of the field (מִכֹּל חַיַּת הַשָּׂדֶה, mikōl ḥāyat haśśāḏeh). Notice that the text does not state that the נָחָשׁ (nāḥāš) was more crafty "than all the *other* beasts of the field." The text does not state that the נָחָשׁ (nāḥāš) was a beast of the field.

But assuming that the נָחָשׁ (nāḥāš) was in fact a beast of the field of some sort having taken on the characteristics of a snake as a result of the curse upon it, this does not preclude the possibility that this animal was the instrument of Satan to deceive Eve. Why make reference to this if the נָחָשׁ (nāḥāš) was not a beast of the field? This observation calls attention to the command that God have given Adam and Eve to have dominion

---

49. וַיִּקְרָא אֶת־שְׁמוֹ נֹחַ לֵאמֹר זֶה יְנַחֲמֵנוּ מִמַּעֲשֵׂנוּ וּמֵעִצְּבוֹן יָדֵינוּ מִן־הָאֲדָמָה אֲשֶׁר אֵרְרָהּ יְהוָה. (Gen 5:29)

50. (Gen 49:17) יְהִי־דָן נָחָשׁ עֲלֵי־דֶרֶךְ שְׁפִיפֹן עֲלֵי־אֹרַח הַנֹּשֵׁךְ עִקְּבֵי־סוּס וַיִּפֹּל רֹכְבוֹ אָחוֹר.

Are the Primaeval Narratives of Genesis 1–11 Myth? (Part 2)

over the beasts of the field. Rather than exercising dominion over the נָחָשׁ (nāḥāš), the נָחָשׁ (nāḥāš) exercises dominion over them.

Again Craig has missed the significance of the text. The chart in **Figure 10** shows both the Hebrew and Greek words that are translated by the English word "serpent" through the OT and the Greek OT, and how these culminate in Rev 12:9 in reference to Satan.

			Satan (Rev. 12:9)	
			δράκων (*drakōn*)	ὄφις (*ophis*)
נָחָשׁ (*nāḥāš*)	Gen. 3:1	Garden Serpent	Serpent (Job 26:13; Amos 9:3)	Serpent
	Exod. 4:1	Moses' Rod		
	Num. 21:6	Fiery Serpents		
תַּנִּין (*tanîn*)	Exod. 7:9	Aaron's Rod	Serpent, Dragon	
	Ezek. 29:3	Pharaoh		
שָׂרָף (*śārāf*)	Num. 21:6	Fiery Serpents		Serpent, Fiery Serpent, Flying Fiery Serpent
	Isa. 6:2	Fiery Serpents		
	Isa. 14:39; 30:6	Flying Fiery Serpents		

Figure 10: The Serpent

When Moses confronts Pharaoh, the casting down of Aaron's rod that turned into a serpent (תַּנִּין, tannîn) was a direct attack upon Pharaoh's claim of divine power. The serpent was a significant symbol for Egyptians, especially because it symbolized the power and authority of Pharaoh whose responsibility it was to maintain life, order, and peace in Egypt. The graphic in Figure 11 below shows the serpent, particularly the cobra, adorning the death mask of Tutankamun. Living Pharaohs would wear a crown depicting the two serpents that represented Pharaoh's authority over upper and lower Egypt. The serpent was supposed to symbolize Pharaoh's power over the universe, yet Pharaoh could not control the rod of God, the rod of a shepherd. The implications of serpent imagery in Moses' confrontation with Pharaoh become very important in Ezek 29:3. Here God identifies Pharaoh as "the dragon": "Speak and say, 'Thus says the Lord God, "Behold, I am against you, Pharaoh king of Egypt, the great serpent (הַתַּנִּים, hattannîm) that lies in the midst of his rivers, that has said, 'My Nile is mine, and I myself have made [it].""'"[51] The term

51. דַּבֵּר וְאָמַרְתָּ כֹּה־אָמַר אֲדֹנָי יְהוִה הִנְנִי עָלֶיךָ פַּרְעֹה מֶלֶךְ־מִצְרַיִם הַתַּנִּים הַגָּדוֹל הָרֹבֵץ בְּתוֹךְ

'great serpent' is תַּנִּין (tannîn). The Greek word here is δράκων (drakōn). The Syriac word is ܬܢܝܢܐ (tanyn'). According to R. Payne Smith, this word means "a dragon; met. the devil."[52] The Syriac word ܬܢܝܢܐ (tanyn') occurs in Rev 12:3 as a translation of the Greek δράκων (drakōn). "Then another sign appeared in heaven: and behold, a great red dragon [δράκων drakōn, ܬܢܝܢܐ, tanyn'] having seven heads and ten horns, and on his heads were seven diadems."[53] The tannîn, which is used as a synonym for nāḥāš, is the drakōn—Pharaoh. But, in the Bible, Pharaoh himself is a symbol of an even greater serpent: "And the great dragon [δράκων, drakōn] was thrown down, the serpent [ὄφις, ophis] of old who is called the devil and Satan, who deceives the whole world; he was thrown down to the earth, and his angels were thrown down with him" (Rev. 12:9).[54] In this passage the text equates all these references: "dragon" (δράκων, drakōn), "serpent" (ὄφις, ophis), "devil" (Διάβολος, Diabolos), and "Satan" (Σατανᾶς, Satanas). The term 'serpent' in Rev 12:9 is the word ὄφις (ophis) that is used in Num 21:6 for nāḥāš. The Greek of Num 21:6 says, "So the LORD sent fiery snakes among the people, and they bit the people; many people of Israel died" (Num 21:6).[55] The LXX uses the expression τοὺς ὄφεις τοὺς θανατοῦντας (tous opheis tous qanatounatas), which means literally "the killing serpents." Also, ὄφις (ophis) is used for שָׂרָף (śārāph) in Isa 14:29. So, ultimately these several terms are used interchangeably and are symbolic of Pharaoh initially, but they ultimately point to Satan, that old serpent we first encounter in Eden.

יְאֹרַי אֲשֶׁר אָמַר לִי יְאֹרִי וַאֲנִי עֲשִׂיתִנִי׃
(Ezek 29:3)

καὶ εἶπον Τάδε λέγει κύριους Ἰδοὺ ἐγὼ ἐπὶ σὲ Φαραω τὸν δράκοντα τὸν μέγα τὸν ἐγκαθήμενον ἐν μέσῳ τοταμῶν αὐτοῦ τὸν λέγοντα Ἐμοί εἰσιν οἱ ποταμοί, καὶ ἐγὼ ἐποίησα αὐτούς (Ezek 29:3, ZE).

52. CSD, s.v. "ܬܢܝܢܐ."

53. καὶ ὤφθη ἄλλο σημεῖον ἐν τῷ οὐρανῷ, καὶ ἰδοὺ δράκων μέγας πυρρός, ἔχων κεφαλὰς ἑπτὰ καὶ κέρατα δέκα καὶ ἐπὶ τὰς κεφαλὰς αὐτοῦ ἑπτὰ διαδήματα (Rev. 12:3).

54. Καὶ ἐβλήθη ὁ δράκων ὁ μέγας, ὁ ὄφις ὁ ἀρχαῖος, ὁ καλούμενος Διάγολος καὶ ὁ Σατανᾶς, ὁ πλανῶν τὴν οἰκουμένην ὅλην, ἐβλήθη εἰς τὴν γῆν, καὶ οἱ ἄγγελοι αὐτοῦ μετ' αὐτοῦ ἐβλήθσαν (Rev 12:9).

55. (Num 21:6) וַיְשַׁלַּח יְהוָה בָּעָם אֵת הַנְּחָשִׁים הַשְּׂרָפִים וַיְנַשְּׁכוּ אֶת־הָעָם וַיָּמָת עַם־רָב מִיִּשְׂרָאֵל׃

καὶ ἀπέστειλεν κύριος εἰς τὸν λαὸν τοὺς ὄφεις τοὺς θανατοῦντας, καὶ ἔδακνον τὸν λαόν, καὶ ἀπέθανεν λαὸς πολὺς τῶν υἱῶν Ισραηλ (Num 21:6 LXX).

Figure 11: Death Mask

By treating the Genesis passage in isolation, Craig has missed the function of the term 'serpent' and how it points to Satan. By not grasping the biblical imagery Craig has misunderstood and mishandled the text. Craig simply equates the נָחָשׁ (nāḥāš) with what we think of as a snake. But before the נָחָשׁ (nāḥāš) was cursed, it did not go on its belly or eat dust, and contrary to what we know about snakes, the נָחָשׁ (nāḥāš) could talk and deceive. Whatever this being was prior to the curse, it was not what I know to be a snake. The נָחָשׁ (nāḥāš) was the instrument employed by Satan in order to deceive Eve.

The Trees of Life and of the Knowledge of Good and Evil

Concerning these so called "fantastic elements," Craig asserts, "Moreover, the trees bearing fruit that, when eaten, convey knowledge of good and evil (whatever that may mean) and immortality would have seemed fantastic to ancient Israelites, as they do to us."[56] Once again Craig's lack of facility in the language leads him to the wrong conclusions. The text does not say, "the tree of the knowledge of good and evil." The text says, "the tree of the knowledge, good and evil." This difference makes all the difference, as we have shown above. There is no sense that the tree would "convey knowledge of good and evil." By eating the fruit of the tree, their eyes would be open and they would be "as God," knowing good and evil. This is the deception of the serpent. It is not what the text says about the tree.

It is important that the serpent says, "For God knows that in the day you eat from it your eyes will be opened, and you will be like God, knowing good and evil" (Gen 3:5).[57] The serpent uses a participle translated "knowing" (יֹדְעֵי, yōḏ'ê). However, after God had cursed the couple, he says, "Behold, the man has become like one of Us, to know good and evil;"[58] (Gen 3:22). God uses an infinitive translated "to know" (לָדַעַת, lāḏa'aṯ). This difference makes all the difference. It was the serpent's deceit that by eating they would know good and evil. The actual condition, however, is that they were in a position "to know," good and evil. When Eve looked at the tree, she believed that it would make her wise: "that the tree was desirable to make wise [לְהַשְׂכִּיל, lĕhaśkîl]" (Gen 3:6). The word translated "make wise," from the verb שָׂכַל (śāḵal), is found seventy-four times in Hebrew Bible. In almost every instance it is used to indicate the capacity to reason through to a conclusion. HAL gives the following meaning: "to make wise, insightful."[59] An example of this use is found in Deut 29:9 (H8)[60] in which to understand and to practice the word is to live successfully: "So pay careful attention to the words of this covenant

---

56. Craig, *Adam*, 113.
57. (Gen 3:5) כִּי יֹדֵעַ אֱלֹהִים כִּי בְּיוֹם אֲכָלְכֶם מִמֶּנּוּ וְנִפְקְחוּ עֵינֵיכֶם וִהְיִיתֶם כֵּאלֹהִים יֹדְעֵי טוֹב וָרָע:
58. (Gen 3:22) הֵן הָאָדָם הָיָה כְּאַחַד מִמֶּנּוּ לָדַעַת טוֹב וָרָע
59. HAL, s.v. "שׂכל."
60. There are instances in which the versification of the English Bible and the Hebrew Bible is different. In these instances, it is customary to give the chapter and verse of the English Bible and then give the verse in the Hebrew Bible prefixed with the capital letter "H." In the chapter and verse from Deuteronomy, the verse in the English Bible is 9 while the verse in the Hebrew Bible is 8. There are many reasons for these differences, and these reasons cannot be discussed here.

and do them, so that you may be wise [תַּשְׂכִּילוּ, taśkîlû] in all that you do."[61] The commands, and statutes, and testimonies of God to Israel will give them the wisdom they need to be able to think correctly, to make the right choices, and to take the appropriate action; in other words, to know good and evil. This wisdom comes from the words of the covenant—the Word of God, the Torah (הַתּוֹרָה, hatôrāh). Again in Deut 32:29 the word is used to indicate wisdom to come to know and to do what is right: "If they had been wise [חָכְמוּ, ḥākmû], they would have understood [יַשְׂכִּילוּ, yaśkîlû] this, they would have been able to discern [יָבִינוּ, yāḇînû] their future" (Deut 32:29).[62] This statement comes in the warnings given to Israel through Moses. God warns the people that when they get into the land they will turn away from God and turn to idols. When they do this, God will bring disaster upon them.

In Deut 32:29 the word יַשְׂכִּילוּ [yaśkîlû] is translated "understood": "If they had been wise, they would have *understood* this." If they had been wise, that is, if they had been able to think through the events of their experience, they would have realized what was happening, they would have arrived at the conclusion that they were being judged for their sin, and they would have taken appropriate action, repentance. The text of Deut 32:28 says, "For they are a nation lacking in counsel, and there is no understanding [תְּבוּנָה, teḇûnāh] in them."[63] But, what does it mean to say they are a nation lacking in counsel? Did they lack counsel? Wasn't God's Word, the Torah (הַתּוֹרָה, hatôrāh) their counsel? God had told them, "now pay careful attention to [וּשְׁמַרְתֶּם, ûšmartem] the words of this covenant and you will be made wise [תַּשְׂכִּילוּ, taśkîlû] and successful" (Deut 29:9 H8). It was not the case that Israel did not have counsel *available* to them. Rather, they did not *give careful attention to* the counsel they had. They did not listen. God's word gives counsel and makes one wise and successful. As the writer to the Hebrew says, "**13** For everyone who partakes only of milk is not accustomed to the word of righteousness, for he is an infant. **14** But solid food is for the mature, who because of practice

---

61. וּשְׁמַרְתֶּם אֶת־דִּבְרֵי הַבְּרִית הַזֹּאת וַעֲשִׂיתֶם אֹתָם לְמַעַן תַּשְׂכִּילוּ אֵת כָּל־אֲשֶׁר תַּעֲשׂוּן׃ (Deut 29:8)

The "H8" in the citation indicates that in the Hebrew Bible this verse is 8, while in the English Bible it is verse 9.

Although the word "understood" is a verb in the Hebrew text, it is from the same root.

62. לוּ חָכְמוּ יַשְׂכִּילוּ זֹאת יָבִינוּ לְאַחֲרִיתָם׃ (Deut 32:29)

63. כִּי־גוֹי אֹבַד עֵצוֹת הֵמָּה וְאֵין בָּהֶם תְּבוּנָה׃ (Deut 32:28)

have their senses trained to discern good and evil" (Heb 5:13-14).[64] How does one have his senses exercised to discern good and evil? By paying careful attention to the word of righteousness. Why is it called the word of righteousness? Because the Word of God is designed to produce in us righteousness.

To be wise and successful is precisely what the couple in the garden were seeking. But they wanted to get it their own way, on their own terms. The counsel they needed, however, would come *from* God on God's terms! God's word is designed to make one wise and successful, but in order to get this counsel we must pay careful attention to it. It was not the case that Eve was seeking some content. Rather, it was the effort to be "as God"; free and independent decision makers, to decide for themselves what is good and evil.

But eating the fruit of the tree to become independent from God has tremendous implications for salvation. Jesus told the disciples that they must eat his flesh and drink his blood:

> [53] So Jesus said to them, "Truly, truly, I say to you, unless you eat the flesh of the Son of Man and drink His blood, you have no life in yourselves. [54] He who eats My flesh and drinks My blood has eternal life, and I will raise him up on the last day. [55] For My flesh is true food, and My blood is true drink. [56] He who eats My flesh and drinks My blood abides in Me, and I in him" (Jn. 6:53-56).[65]

By eating, Adam and Eve fell. By eating, we are restored to life. Jesus offered his flesh and shed his blood by being hanged on a tree. By eating the fruit of the tree, the first couple were separated from the life of God. By eating the fruit of the tree, we are given eternal life. By treating these passages in isolation, Craig has misunderstood and mishandled the text.

Again Craig has read into the text what it does not say. Nowhere does the text state that eating the fruit of the tree of the life would confer immortality. After the fall, God declares, "Behold, the man has become like one of Us, to know good and evil; and now, he might stretch out his hand,

---

64. [13] πᾶς γὰρ ὁ μετέχων γάλακτος ἄπειρος λόγου δικαιοσύνης, νήπιος γάρ ἐστιν· [14] τελείων δέ ἐστιν ἡ στερεὰ τροφή, τῶν διὰ τὴν ἕξιν τὰ αἰσθητήρια γεγυμνασμένα ἐχόντων πρὸς διάκρισιν καλοῦ τε καὶ κακοῦ (Heb 5:13-14).

65. [53] εἶπεν οὖν αὐτοῖς ὁ Ἰησοῦς, Ἀμὴν ἀμὴν λέγω ὑμῖν, ἐὰν μὴ φάγητε τὴν σάρκα τοῦ υἱοῦ τοῦ ἀνθρώπου καὶ πίητε αὐτοῦ τὸ αἷμα, οὐκ ἔχετε ζωὴν ἐν ἑαυτοῖς. [54] ὁ τρώγων μου τὴν σάρκα καὶ πίνων μου τὸ αἷμα ἔχει ζωὴν αἰώνιον, κἀγὼ ἀναστήσω αὐτὸν τῇ ἐσχάτῃ ἡμέρᾳ. [55] ἡ γὰρ σάρξ μου ἀληθής ἐστιν βρῶσις, καὶ τὸ αἷμά μου ἀληθής ἐστιν πόσις. [56] ὁ τρώγων μου τὴν σάρκα καὶ πίνων μου τὸ αἷμα ἐν ἐμοὶ μένε κἀγὼ ἐν αὐτῷ (Jn. 6:53-56).

and take also from the tree of life, and eat, and live forever"—(Gen 3:22).[66] There is no statement here that by eating once from the fruit confers immortality. In fact, we find a description of the tree of life in Revelation:

> "[1] Then he showed me a river of the water of life, clear as crystal, coming from the throne of God and of the Lamb, [2] in the middle of its street. On either side of the river was the tree of life [ξύλον ζωῆς, *xulon zōēs*], bearing twelve kinds of fruit, yielding its fruit every month; and the leaves of the tree were for the healing of the nations" (Rev. 22:1–2).[67]

The image here may be that one continues to eat fruit from the tree of life, not that one simply eats once and gains immortality. The tree of the life in the garden is a symbol of life that is for those who trust and obey God. The implication is that if they trusted and obeyed God, they would continue to have access to the tree of the life and live forever. That the tree can be a symbol does not mean that it was not an actual tree. By not trusting and obeying, they forfeited this access and they are condemned to spiritual and physical death. Driving them from the garden so that they could not eat from the tree of the life and live forever was both a punishment and a blessing. God prevents them from living forever in a state of separation from him, and they force mankind to face the specter of physical death, which is designed to drive man back to God for life. Craig simply does not understand the text. There is no basis to understand the text the way Craig presents it.

Craig concludes this section with the following assertions:

> Certainly magic involving incantations and ritual manipulation is foreign to Israel, but it remains the case that there is no explanation, natural or miraculous, for the effect that eating the Edenic fruit is said to have and that it is therefore in that sense magical. But we need not stand on the word *magical*; the important point is that the trees of the knowledge of good and evil and of life are fantastic and would have appeared so even to ancient Israelites.[68]

---

66. וַיֹּאמֶר יְהוָה אֱלֹהִים הֵן הָאָדָם הָיָה כְּאַחַד מִמֶּנּוּ לָדַעַת טוֹב וָרָע וְעַתָּה פֶּן־יִשְׁלַח יָדוֹ וְלָקַח גַּם מֵעֵץ הַחַיִּים וְאָכַל וָחַי לְעֹלָם׃
(Gen 3:22)

67. [1] καὶ ἔδειξέν μοι ποταμὸν ὕδατος ζωῆς λαμπρὸν ὡς κρύσταλλον, ἐκπορευόμενον ἐκ τοῦ θρόνου τοῦ θεοῦ καὶ τοῦ ἀρνίου. [2] ἐν μέσῳ τῆς πλατείας αὐτῆς καὶ τοῦ ποταμοῦ ἐντεῦθεν καὶ ἐκεῖθεν ξύλον ζωῆς ποιοῦν καρποὺς δώδεκα, κατὰ μῆνα ἕκαστον ἀποδιδοῦν τὸν καρπὸν αὐτοῦ, καὶ τὰ φύλλα τοῦ ξύλου εἰς θεραπείαν τῶν ἐθνῶν (Rev 22:1–2).

68. Craig, *Adam*, 113.

It seems uncharacteristically arrogant for Craig to think that just because he cannot come up with an explanation there cannot be one. Such an apparent assumption of omniscience is certainly fantastic. In fact, there is an explanation for these elements as we have shown. And how does Craig suppose he knows what the ancient Israelites would have thought to be fantastic? There is nothing in the Hebrew Scriptures that even hints that ancient Israelites would have thought such a thing. Craig's assertions smack of a desperate attempt to make things fit into his always, already-present assumptions.

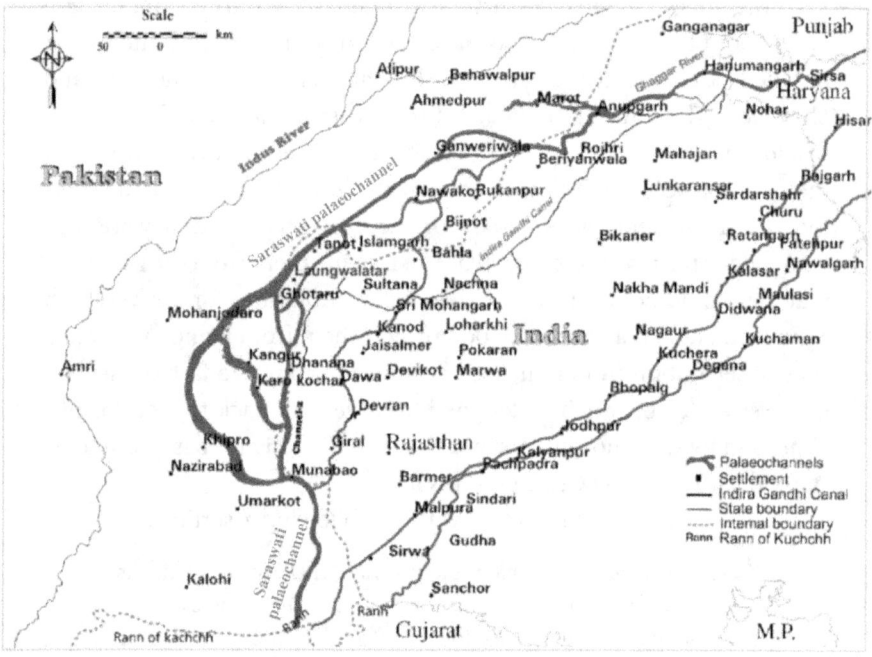

Figure 12: The Saraswati Palaeochannel

The Rivers of Eden

At this point Craig is arguing that the rivers referred to in Gen 2 are fantastic elements. The text of Genesis is given here:

> **10** Now a river flowed out of Eden to water the garden; and from there it divided and became four rivers. **11** The name of the first is Pishon; it flows around the whole land of Havilah, where there is gold. **12** The gold of that land is good; the dellium and the

onyx stone are there. 13 The name of the second river is Gihon; it flows around the whole land of Cush. 14 The name of the third river is Tigris; it flows east of Assyria. And the fourth river is the Euphrates (Gen 2:10–14).[69]

Craig argues, "The Tigris and the Euphrates would have been the rivers so known at the time of the pentateuchal author, roughly the same as the rivers so known today. Eden would have to be located in Armenia for these rivers to have a common source, which they, in any case, as Gunkel notes, do not, a fact that was long known to ancient Mesopotamians."[70] Is it reasonable to expect that the rivers described in the biblical account would have remained the same until the time of Moses? Certainly not. If we are talking hundreds of thousands of years between the events described and the time of Moses one would expect the geography and topography to have radically changed. Even if we think that the rivers in the time of Moses were the same as those described in the biblical account, is it reasonable to think, even taking a early date of the Exodus at 1400 BC, that the geological, geographical, and topographical factors would have remained the same? Again, certainly not. Digitally processed satellite images have revealed the existence of a major lost river below the sands of the Thar Desert, in the India/Pakistan region. This river, in India called the "Saraswati," had a certain course during the Vedic period (c. 1500 to 500 BC) and probably dried up around 600 BC (see **Figure 12**). These rivers were lost to contemporary knowledge until the development of the technology to find them. Yet their existence was less than five thousand years ago. Concerning the rivers referred to in the Genesis account, we could be talking about hundreds of thousands of years between their existence in Eden and the time of Moses. Some of the rivers described in Gen 2 may have simply dried up, and other parts may have been diverted and re-directed over the centuries so that the features of these rivers would not have been the same as in the time of Moses, and the familiar names may have been given to these new courses, yet still identifying the general area.

Is it necessary to think that Moses expected his audience to be familiar with these rivers the way he describes them? No! Moses described

69. וְנָהָר יֹצֵא מֵעֵדֶן לְהַשְׁקוֹת אֶת־הַגָּן וּמִשָּׁם יִפָּרֵד וְהָיָה לְאַרְבָּעָה רָאשִׁים: 10 שֵׁם הָאֶחָד פִּישׁוֹן הוּא הַסֹּבֵב אֵת כָּל־אֶרֶץ הַחֲוִילָה אֲשֶׁר־שָׁם הַזָּהָב: 12 וּזֲהַב הָאָרֶץ הַהִוא טוֹב שָׁם הַבְּדֹלַח וְאֶבֶן הַשֹּׁהַם: 13 וְשֵׁם־הַנָּהָר הַשֵּׁנִי גִּיחוֹן הוּא הַסּוֹבֵב אֵת כָּל־אֶרֶץ כּוּשׁ: 14 וְשֵׁם הַנָּהָר הַשְּׁלִישִׁי חִדֶּקֶל הוּא הַהֹלֵךְ קִדְמַת אַשּׁוּר וְהַנָּהָר הָרְבִיעִי הוּא פְרָת:
(Gen 2:10–14)

70. Craig, *Adam*, 114.

various features of Eden and the garden, but he certainly would not have expected his audience to have been familiar with these features. Moses is describing a landscape the features of which the people could not have been expected to know. However, giving this description and these names may have been designed to give the people a sense of the general area. Moses described the state of the heavens and the earth as empty and uninhabitable, but this description was supernaturally revealed to Moses, which he then described. Moses would certainly have expected his audience to be familiar with the general area of the heavens and the earth even if not the specifics of the description.

Craig goes on to declare, "... given the traditional identifications, even an ancient Israelite with some geographical knowledge would have found the rivers' description fantastic, since it would have been obvious that the Nile at least does not have the same source as the Tigris and Euphrates."[71] How much geographical knowledge would the people have had at this time? The people had been in captivity in Egypt for four hundred years. It is unlikely that he would have expected these people to be familiar with the details of the geography of ancient Mesopotamia. And again, on what basis does Craig presume to know what ancient Israelites would have thought to be fantastic? There are no statements in the biblical text indicating that these Israelites thought these descriptions to be fantastic.

For all of Craig's discussion of the speculations and claims of various scholars, none of this shows that these descriptions are "fantastic." What they show is that we simply do not know to what specifically Moses is referring, except in a very general sense, since we cannot with precision extrapolate from our present knowledge back to what was the geographical, geological, and topographical conditions that existed at the time of the establishing of Eden and its garden. This is particularly the case since the flood would have radically altered the geography, geology, and topography of the area. What is "fantastic" is to think that because we cannot presently explain or identify the state or placement of the rivers, mountains, valleys, plains, etc., or connect these with the present state of things, that the descriptions in Gen 2 cannot have been anything but mythical.

---

71. Craig, *Adam*, 114–15.

Are the Primaeval Narratives of Genesis 1–11 Myth? (Part 2)

The Cherubim

In this section Craig argues that the cherubim in Genesis are fantastic creatures. He says,

> What makes this detail fantastic is that the cherubim were not thought to be real beings but fantasies composed of a lion's body, a bird's wings, and a man's head. Nahum Sarna observes that the motif of composite human-animal-bird figures was widespread in various forms in art and religious symbolism in the Fertile Crescent, and the biblical cherubim would seem to be connected with this artistic tradition.[72]

The problem here is that nowhere in the Bible are the cherubim said to have these features. The most detailed description in the Bible of what are called "cherubim" is found in Ezekiel chapter 10. In this description, the cherubim are said to have these characteristics:

- Heads
- Standing (implying legs and feet of some kind)
- Four Wings
- Form of a Man's Hands Beneath its Wings
- Full of Eyes
- Four faces
    - Face of a Cherub
    - Face of a Man
    - Face of a Lion
    - Face of an Eagle

There is a very curious part of the description of the faces of the Cherubim. The description in verse 14 states: "And each one had four faces. *The first face was the face of a cherub*, the second face was the face of a man, the third the face of a lion, and the fourth the face of an eagle" (Ezek 10:14, emphasis added).[73] So, it is not just the case that the face of the cherub is not the same as the face of a man, or a lion, or an eagle.

---

72. Craig, *Adam*, 119.

73. וְאַרְבָּעָה פָנִים לְאֶחָד פְּנֵי הָאֶחָד פְּנֵי הַכְּרוּב וּפְנֵי הַשֵּׁנִי פְּנֵי אָדָם וְהַשְּׁלִישִׁי פְּנֵי אַרְיֵה וְהָרְבִיעִי פְּנֵי־נָשֶׁר:
(Ezek 10:14)

According to Ezekiel's description, a cherub has its own distinct face. Additionally, later Ezekiel describes carved cherubim that have only two faces: "**18** It was carved with cherubim and palm trees; and a palm tree was between cherub and cherub, and every cherub had two faces, **19** a man's face toward the palm tree on one side and a young lion's face toward the palm tree on the other side; they were carved on all the house all around" (Ezek 41:18–19).[74] In fact, the description in Ezek 10 differs in certain respects from the description in Ezek 1. In chapter 1 the beings described are not referred to as cherubim. They are simply referred to as "living creatures": "In the fire were what looked like four living beings [חַיּוֹת, ḥayôṯ]. In their appearance they had human form" (Ezek 1:5).[75] The vision described in chapter 1 took place by the river Kebar. In Ezek 10:15 Ezekiel says, "The cherubim rose up; these were the living beings I saw at the Kebar River" (Ezek 10:15).[76] So, since the faces of a man, a lion, and an eagle are identified in both chapter 1 and 10, whereas the first face in chapter 10 is said to be the face of a cherub, and the remaining face in the description of chapter 1 is that of a שׁוֹר, (šôr), translated "ox" or "bull"), this implies that the face of the cherub in chapter 10 is the face of a bull.

What this shows is that just because the word 'cherub' or 'cherubim' is used, the text may not be referring to the same kind of entity with all the same characteristics. These terms may be classes in which the individuals do not necessarily have the same characteristics. So, even if, as Craig reports, "the motif of composite human-animal-bird figures was widespread in various forms in art and religious symbolism in the Fertile Crescent," this does not correspond to what the biblical text depicts. Not all cherubim have the animal-man-bird characteristics. The description in Ezek 41 states that the cherubim had the face of a man and the face of a lion, but not the face of an eagle. In fact, the description in Ezek 41 does not even say that these carved cherubim had the face of a cherub.

And it cannot be the case that the first face in Ezek 10 is saying that the face of a cherub was composed of the three other faces since the four faces are treated as distinct faces facing the four directions of the compass, corresponding to the four wheels, so that the chariot could move in any of the four directions without turning: "When they moved,

---

74. וַעֲשׂוּי כְּרוּבִים וְתִמֹרִים בֵּין־כְּרוּב לִכְרוּב וּשְׁנַיִם פָּנִים לַכְּרוּב: **19** וּפְנֵי אָדָם אֶל־הַתִּמֹרָה מִפּוֹ **18** וּפְנֵי־כְפִיר אֶל־הַתִּמֹרָה מִפּוֹ עָשׂוּי אֶל־כָּל־הַבַּיִת סָבִיב סָבִיב: (Ezek 41:18–19)

75. וּמִתּוֹכָהּ דְּמוּת אַרְבַּע חַיּוֹת וְזֶה מַרְאֵיהֶן דְּמוּת אָדָם לָהֵנָּה: (Ezek 1:5)

76. וַיֵּרֹמּוּ הַכְּרוּבִים הִיא הַחַיָּה אֲשֶׁר רָאִיתִי בִּנְהַר־כְּבָר: (Ezek 10:15)

Are the Primaeval Narratives of Genesis 1–11 Myth? (Part 2)

they went in any of their four directions without turning as they went; but they followed in the direction which they faced, without turning as they went" (Ezek 10:11).[77]

When God instructs the craftsmen to fashion two cherubim to be placed on the lid of the ark, the face of each cherub was to face the mercy seat: "The cherubim shall have their wings spread upward, covering the mercy seat with their wings and facing one another; the faces of the cherubim are to be turned toward the mercy seat" (Exod 25:20).[78] Now it would be absurd to suppose that these cherubim had four faces as described in Ezekiel and that each of these faces would be turned in the same direction. In Ezekiel the four faces are facing the four directions of the compass. The description in Exodus indicates that each cherub had one face, and their faces were toward the mercy seat at the center of the ark.

What this means is, the cherubim referred to in the Genesis passage may not have had the characteristics described in Ezekiel. To try to make the cherubim in Genesis into creatures having human, animal, and bird characteristics simply does not do justice to the text. And why would Ezekiel's vision include these four faces? Many have tried to make a correspondence between the four faces in Ezek 1 to correspond to the themes of the four gospels—Matthew the lion, as the king of beasts: Mark the ox, the perfect servant: Luke the man: and John the eagle, symbolic of deity. However, other commentators have taken these same references in other combinations. It is unlikely that this was the association that was indicated in this vision. The four faces are probably simply indicative of the sovereignty of God. Each face represents the highest form in its kind. The lion was considered the greatest among wild animals, the ox among domestic animals, the eagle among birds, and man the highest form of created beings on the earth. The correspondence of the face of a bull/ox with the face of a cherub may indicate the ranking of a cherub in an angelic hierarchy. The imagery is designed to communicate the strength and supremacy of God. The faces point in the four directions of the compass, and the group moves in any direction without turning, both indicating God's omnipresence. The joining of the wings indicates

---

77. בְּלֶכְתָּם אֶל־אַרְבַּעַת רִבְעֵיהֶם יֵלֵכוּ לֹא יִסַּבּוּ בְּלֶכְתָּם כִּי הַמָּקוֹם אֲשֶׁר־יִפְנֶה הָרֹאשׁ אַחֲרָיו יֵלֵכוּ לֹא יִסַּבּוּ בְּלֶכְתָּם:
(Ezek 10:11)

78. וְהָיוּ הַכְּרֻבִים פֹּרְשֵׂי כְנָפַיִם לְמַעְלָה סֹכְכִים בְּכַנְפֵיהֶם עַל־הַכַּפֹּרֶת וּפְנֵיהֶם אִישׁ אֶל־אָחִיו אֶל־הַכַּפֹּרֶת יִהְיוּ פְּנֵי הַכְּרֻבִים:
(Exod 25:20)

a unity of purpose. These beings move together as one. The eyes indicate God's omniscience.

Craig asserts, "The name *cherubim* seems to be related to the *kuribu*, man-headed bulls with eagles' wings that frequently stood outside Mesopotamian temples."[79] But these associations are speculative at best, and based on the way this word is used, they do not seem to be referring to beings that have all the same characteristics. To attempt to make the reference to cherubim in Genesis into some mystical beast depicted in Mesopotamian temples is "fantastic."

Again Craig simply misses the significance of the imagery used throughout the Bible. The cherubim are placed at the entrance of the garden of Eden in order to prevent man from taking "from the tree of the life" (מֵעֵץ הַחַיִּים, mēʿēṣ haḥâyîm) and living forever. In the instructions for building the temple, God commands that the images of cherubim be woven into the curtain that separates the holy place from the most holy place. As the cherubim prevent the entrance into the garden to take of the tree of the life, so the cherubim are placed on the curtain to prevent entrance into the most holy place where is the judgment seat where God dwells above the cherubim. At the crucifixion, this curtain is torn from the top down to indicate that entrance into the presence of God is now made available to all those who eat Jesus' flesh and drink his blood. Man was driven from the garden to face physical death. Because Jesus has given access to God, man now has access to eternal life, and the ever present specter of death forces man to seek eternal life.

The Antediluvians' Life Spans

Craig has a brief discussion of the life spans of the antediluvians. He quotes from Von Rad:

> Von Rad lists some of the incredible implications: "The long lives ascribed to the patriarchs cause remarkable synchronisms and duplications. Adam lived to see the birth of Lamech, the ninth member of the genealogy; Seth lived to see the translation of Enoch and died shortly before the birth of Noah. Lamech was the first to see a dead man—Adam; Noah outlived Abraham's grandfather, Nahor, and died in Abraham's sixtieth year. Shem,

---

79. Craig, *Adam*, 119.

Are the Primaeval Narratives of Genesis 1–11 Myth? (Part 2)

Noah's son, even outlived Abraham. He was still alive when Esau and Jacob were born!"[80]

We have already shown in chapter 3 that this kind of calculation simply is not supported by the text. It is the imposition upon the biblical genealogy of the assumptions about genealogies and words by the interpreter. Once one understands the way the text presents the genealogical records, these supposed "incredible implications" disappear. Craig declares, "Commentators have found no explanation of these life spans that commends itself to most scholars."[81] However, just because most scholars have not agreed upon an explanation only proves that most scholars have not agreed upon an explanation. It does not prove that there is no explanation or that there cannot be an explanation.

And yet again Craig misses the significance of these life spans. Isaiah predicts the long life spans of those who live during the kingdom: "No longer will there be in it an infant who lives but a few days, or an old man who does not live out his days; For the youth will die at the age of one hundred and the one who does not reach the age of one hundred will be thought accursed" (Isa 65:20).[82] The word 'youth' (נַעַר, naʿar) refers to an adolescent. Isaiah is using this as a prophetic statement that once again people will live to be hundreds of years old. Before the flood judgment, ten individuals lived to be hundreds of years old. But to Noah God warns, "My Spirit will not remain [יָדוֹן, yāḏôn] in humankind indefinitely, since he also is flesh" (Gen 6:3).[83] Because man is composed of both spirit and flesh, he is mortal, and God warns that his spirit will not indefinitely remain with man. Then God says, "And will be his days one hundred and twenty years."[84] This is not referring to one's life span, but how much time is left before the judgment. After Jesus returns to judge the nations, he will establish the millennial kingdom, and once again people will live hundreds of years.

Again Craig has somehow divined, apart from any biblical evidence, what the Israelites would have thought: "The life spans of the antediluvians

---

80. Craig, *Adam*, 120.

81. Craig, *Adam*, 120.

82. לֹא־יִהְיֶה מִשָּׁם עוֹד עוּל יָמִים וְזָקֵן אֲשֶׁר לֹא־יְמַלֵּא אֶת־יָמָיו כִּי הַנַּעַר בֶּן־מֵאָה שָׁנָה יָמוּת וְהַחוֹטֶא בֶּן־מֵאָה שָׁנָה יְקֻלָּל:
(Isa 65:19)

83. (Gen 6:3): לֹא־יָדוֹן רוּחִי בָאָדָם לְעֹלָם בְּשַׁגַּם הוּא בָשָׂר

84. (Gen 6:3): וְהָיוּ יָמָיו מֵאָה וְעֶשְׂרִים שָׁנָה

would have appeared fantastic to ancient Israelites, just as they do to us. But persons in myths, even historical persons, can be made to live as long as one likes."[85] Why does Craig think that these life spans appear fantastic "to us"? Are there not many biblical commentators who do not think these life spans are "so extraordinary as to be palpably false"? If, according to Craig, the author of the Pentateuch simply made the life spans of these "historical persons" as long as he liked, this indicates that Craig has abandoned the inerrancy of the text. Moses presents these historical persons as actually having these life spans, but, according to Craig, Moses actually fabricated this information. According to Craig's measure, these numbers are palpably false if taken literally. But if the life-spans of these individuals is not intended to be taken literally even though they are presented in the text as actual genealogical records, then we can decide that any text with which we might disagree is simply not intended to be taken literally.

Noah's Flood

Craig declares that the flood story is "one of the most fantastic [therefore palpably false if taken literally] episodes in the primaeval narratives."[86] Craig reports that young earth creationists argue, "the ark would have had ample room to include members of every identified genus of terrestrial animals."[87] Craig then quotes from Hugh Ross as a rejoinder that the young earth creationists' arguments seem "to trade one implausible hypothesis for another. Animals, especially those as advanced as horses and felines, simply do not—and cannot, by any observed or postulated mechanism—evolve or diversify at such a rapid rate . . ."[88] Craig adds to this quote, ". . . so as to produce the earth's current 5.8 million land animal species after the flood."[89] But Ross' rejoinder is built on evolutionary assumptions and a misunderstanding of the amount of time following the flood. Craig and Ross assume they can simply add up the years referred to in the genealogies to calculate the number of years. But we have already shown in chapter 3 that this calculation system is incorrect. So

---

85. Craig, *Adam*, 120.
86. Craig, *Adam*, 120.
87. Craig, *Adam*, 121.
88. Craig, *Adam*, 121.
89. Craig, *Adam*, 121.

Are the Primaeval Narratives of Genesis 1–11 Myth? (Part 2) 103

neither Craig nor Ross know how much time elapsed between the flood and "earth's current 5.8 million land animal species."

In his book, *Navigating Genesis*, Hugh Ross argues, "The permanence of 'dry land' and ocean boundaries is affirmed in Job 38, Psalm 33, 104, and Proverbs 8, all passages elaborating on the creation days. Job records God's challenge, 'Who shut up the sea behind doors when it burst forth from the womb ... when I fixed limits for it and sets its doors and bars in place.' These metaphors paint a picture of permanence."[90]

The text of Job is given here:

> **8** "Or who enclosed the sea with doors when, bursting forth, it went out from the womb; **9** When I made a cloud its garment and thick darkness its swaddling band, **10** And I placed boundaries on it and set a bolt and doors, **11** And I said, 'Thus far you shall come, but no farther; and here shall your proud waves stop'? (Job 38:8–11).[91]

It is clear that neither Craig nor Ross understand the Hebrew text nor the nature of Hebrew poetry. When the sea burst forth (בְּגִיחוֹ, bĕgîḥô), then God enclosed it with doors. The verb translated "when it burst forth" has the preposition prefix בְּ (bĕ). This inseparable preposition has many uses. In this instance, the meaning is that God set the boundaries once the sea had burst forth. When did God do this? He did this on the third day of creation when he divided the waters and the dry land appeared. So, it is simply not the case that the statement in Job paints a picture of permanence. It rather paints a picture of God's creative activity. The boundaries of the sea and the appearance of dry ground were not set until the third day. To claim that Job's text speaks of permanence is a misunderstanding of the text due to a lack of understanding of Hebrew grammar.

One must also understand the nature of Hebrew poetry. Poetry is replete with figures of speech. Notice that Job's text refers to the sea bursting "from the womb," and being clothed with a cloud and being swaddled in thick darkness. God says he set its boundaries with a bolt and doors. These are all figures of speech designed to respond to Job's presumption of knowledge against God. That the boundaries of the sea were set by God does not in any way indicate that God could not remove these boundaries

---

90. Ross, *Navigating Genesis*, 145.
91. **8** וַיָּסֶךְ בִּדְלָתַיִם יָם בְּגִיחוֹ מֵרֶחֶם יֵצֵא: **9** בְּשׂוּמִי עָנָן לְבֻשׁוֹ וַעֲרָפֶל חֲתֻלָּתוֹ: **10** וָאֶשְׁבֹּר עָלָיו חֻקִּי וָאָשִׂים בְּרִיחַ וּדְלָתָיִם: **11** וָאֹמַר עַד־פֹּה תָבוֹא וְלֹא תֹסִיף וּפֹא יָשִׁית בִּגְאוֹן גַּלֶּיךָ:
(Job 38:8–11)

to produce a world-wide flood. The same misunderstanding by Ross can be seen in the other passages to which he refers.

Ross appeals to 2 Pet 3:6 to argue that the world "at that time" was not the "Roman world."

> The apostle Peter twice comments on the Genesis flood in his epistles. In 2 Peter 3:6 we read, "By water also the world of that time was deluged and destroyed." The Greek word translated "world" is kosmos, and alongside it stands the word tote, which means "at the time." By modifying kosmos with tote Peter communicates to his readers that the world of Noah is not their world, the Roman world.[92]

The immediate context of 2 Pet 3:6 is given here:

> ³ Know this first of all, that in the last days mockers will come with their mocking, following after their own lusts, ⁴ and saying, "Where is the promise of His coming? For ever since the fathers fell asleep, all continues just as it was from the beginning of creation." ⁵ For when they maintain this, it escapes their notice that aby the word of God the heavens existed long ago and the earth was formed out of water and by water, ⁶ through which the world at that time was destroyed, being flooded with water. ⁷ But by His word the present heavens and earth are being reserved for fire, kept for the day of judgment and destruction of ungodly men. ⁸ But do not let this one fact escape your notice, beloved, that with the Lord one day is like a thousand years, and a thousand years like one day (2 Pet. 3:3–8).[93]

The word translated "at that time" (*tovte, tote*) has a range of meanings, and in this context it is probably best translated "at that time." However, this does not in any way indicate that the world "at that time" was any different from the world as Peter's audience would have understood it. It is simply saying that the flood occurred over the world "at that time."

---

92. Ross, *Navigating Genesis*, 145.

93. ³τοῦτο πρῶτον γινώσκοντες ὅτι ἐλεύσονται ἐπ' ἐσχάτων τῶν ἡμερῶν [ἐν] ἐμπαιγμονῇ ἐμπαῖκται κατὰ τὰς ἰδίας ἐπιθυμίας αὐτῶν πορευόμενοι ⁴ καὶ λέγοντες, Ποῦ ἐστιν ἡ ἐπαγγελία τῆς παρουσίας αὐτοῦ; ἀφ' ἧς γὰρ οἱ πατέρες ἐκοιμήθησαν, πάντα οὕτως διαμένει ἀπ' ἀρχῆς κτίσεως. ⁵ λανθάνει γὰρ αὐτοὺς τοῦτο θέλοντας ὅτι οὐρανοὶ ἦσαν ἔκπαλαι καὶ γῆ ἐξ ὕδατος καὶ δι' ὕδατος συνεστῶσα τῷ τοῦ θεοῦ λόγῳ, ⁶ δι' ὧν ὁ τότε κόσμος ὕδατι κατακλυσθεὶς ἀπώλετο· ⁷ οἱ δὲ νῦν οὐρανοὶ καὶ ἡ γῆ τῷ αὐτῷ λόγῳ τεθησαυρισμένοι εἰσὶν πυρὶ τηρούμενοι εἰς ἡμέραν κρίσεως καὶ ἀπωλείας τῶν ἀσεβῶν ἀνθρώπων. ⁸ "Ἐν δὲ τοῦτο μὴ λανθανέτω ὑμᾶς, ἀγαπητοί, ὅτι μία ἡμέρα παρὰ κυρίῳ ὡς χίλια ἔτη καὶ χίλια ἔτη ὡς ἡμέρα μία (2 Pet 3:3–8).

Are the Primaeval Narratives of Genesis 1–11 Myth? (Part 2)

Ross is simply reading into the text his already present assumptions. Peter also goes on to say, "present heavens and earth" are reserved for fire. Peter is making a correlation between the flood and the future fire. Are we to think that if the flood was local the judgement of fire will be only local?

In fact, Ross responds to this very argument:

> Some Bible interpreters who view the flood as global in extent argue that because the coming judgment by fire, referred to in 2 Peter 3:7 will be a global event, the judgment by water mentioned in 2 Peter 3:6 must be global as well. The weakness of this argument is that Peter here is speaking not about geography but rather about people. He points out that judgment comes from God upon all the ungodly. That is the extent of it.[94]

But his response is fantastic and palpably false. The flood was global, but it was a judgment upon the people throughout the world. Like the flood, the coming fire will be upon ungodly people *throughout the world*. The correlation between the flood and the coming fire is between the people who were judged. This judgement of fire will destroy ungodly men. Will this destroy only a local group of ungodly men? Will it not destroy ungodly men throughout the whole earth as the flood destroyed ungodly men throughout the whole earth?

But Ross is not done yet. He goes on to argue,

> This comment about the flood echoes his earlier reminder, seen in 2 Peter 2:5. He wrote, "... [God] did not spare the ancient world, but preserved Noah a preacher of righteousness, with seven others, when He brought a flood upon the world of the ungodly" (NASB). In the original Greek text, the two relevant phrases are *archaiou kosmou* and *kosmo ase*. They literally mean "the ancient world" and "the world of those who were destitute of reverential awe towards God." According to Peter, God's judgment came against a world as defined by its spiritually dead people, not by geography.[95]

Again this argument is fantastic and palpably false. The very Greek words to which Ross refers refute his own argument. The text states, God "did not spare the ancient world." That pretty much includes the ancient *world*. To say this is not about geography is absolutely ridiculous. It is about the ungodly who inhabited the world. This necessarily involves the

---

94. Ross, *Navigating Genesis*, 145.
95. Ross, *Navigating Genesis*, 145–46.

geography of *the entire world*, else we must conclude that there were some ungodly in the world who were not judged. Of course it is about "spiritually dead people," but it's about spiritually dead people who inhabited the ancient world, not simply some part of it. Ross has filtered the text through his prior assumptions. He attempts to support his assertions by talking about the Greek text, but he does not understand the Greek text, nor does he seem to understand exegesis. It is not about looking up words in a dictionary. It is also about understanding grammar and syntax, and the evidence shows that Ross simply does not understand either Greek or Hebrew grammar and syntax.

Craig includes a footnote on Ross' argument:

> Ross is assuming a flood of at least ten thousand years ago. Ross's point becomes especially devastating when one realizes that on a young earth interpretation of Gen 1–11, Noah had to take about one thousand dinosaurs aboard the ark, so that the entire history of dinosaur evolution and extinction had to take place in the roughly three hundred years between the disembarkation from the ark and the birth of Abraham.[96]

Craig seems to be agreeing with Ross' assumption about the flood having occurred at least ten thousand years ago when he says, "so that the entire history of dinosaur evolution and extinction had to take place in the roughly three hundred years between the disembarkation from the ark and the birth of Abraham." This is because neither Craig nor Ross understand the nature of biblical genealogies. They simply add up numbers.

Craig appeals to modern geology and anthropology to support his claim that the biblical flood was not world wide, but these very same findings have been interpreted differently. Craig asserts, "But no such evidence exists for a worldwide deluge."[97] But in fact there are scientists whose credentials are at least equal to Ross who argue that there is indeed evidence of a worldwide deluge. Simply to make this *ex cathedra* declaration without presenting any contrary interpretations of the evidence by equally competent scientists is fantastic. Presenting and evaluating this evidence pro and con is beyond this author's expertise. Having read much of Ross' claims about the OT text, it is clear that making assertions about the Hebrew and Greek texts is beyond Ross' expertise.

---

96. Craig, *Adam*, 121n134.
97. Craig, *Adam*, 121.

In fact, once one understands the literary and textual evidence it is clear that the flood was a world wide event. The use of word אֶרֶץ ('ereṣ) can be used to refer to the whole earth. If this term can never be taken to be universal, then Gen 1:1 has nothing to say about the creation of the whole world, but only the creation of a local area. However, this is contrary to the whole testimony of the Scriptures that God created the heavens and the whole earth, a testimony that is taken from the Genesis account. Additionally, the term usually translated "world," (תֵּבֵל, tēḇēl) is never used in the Pentateuch at all. This indicates that either Moses never referred to the entire world in anything he said, or that for Moses, אֶרֶץ ('ereṣ) can be used as a universal term to refer to the whole world.

The Hebrew in Gen 8:9 states that the flood was "upon the face of the whole earth. [עַל־פְּנֵי כָל־הָאָרֶץ, 'al pĕnê ḵāl hā'āreṣ]."[98] This same terminology is used outside of the flood account in passages that clearly indicate a universal scope. In Gen 1:29 God instructs Adam that he can eat from "every herb bearing seed which is upon the face of all the earth [עַל־פְּנֵי כָל־הָאָרֶץ, 'al pĕnê ḵāl hā'āreṣ]."[99] In Gen 1:26 God created man to "rule over the fish . . . birds . . . and the cattle and over all the earth [וּבְכָל־הָאָרֶץ, ûḇḵāl hā'āreṣ]."[100] Also, in Gen 1:28 God commands the man and the woman to "Be fruitful and multiply and fill the earth [וּמִלְאוּ אֶת־הָאָרֶץ, ûmil'û 'eṯ hā'āreṣ]."[101] All these instances indicate a universal understanding of the term.

In Gen 7:19 the account states, "all the high mountains [כָּל־הֶהָרִים, kāl hehārîm haggĕḇōhîm] that were under all of the heaven [תַּחַת כָּל־הַשָּׁמָיִם, taḥaṯ kāl haššāmayim] were covered."[102] In Job 28:24[103] the

---

98. וְלֹא־מָצְאָה הַיּוֹנָה מָנוֹחַ לְכַף־רַגְלָהּ וַתָּשָׁב אֵלָיו אֶל־הַתֵּבָה כִּי־מַיִם עַל־פְּנֵי כָל־הָאָרֶץ וַיִּשְׁלַח יָדוֹ וַיִּקָּחֶהָ וַיָּבֵא אֹתָהּ אֵלָיו אֶל־הַתֵּבָה׃
(Gen 8:9)

99. וַיֹּאמֶר אֱלֹהִים הִנֵּה נָתַתִּי לָכֶם אֶת־כָּל־עֵשֶׂב זֹרֵעַ זֶרַע אֲשֶׁר עַל־פְּנֵי כָל־הָאָרֶץ וְאֶת־כָּל־הָעֵץ אֲשֶׁר־בּוֹ פְרִי־עֵץ זֹרֵעַ זָרַע לָכֶם יִהְיֶה לְאָכְלָה׃
(Gen 1:29)

100. וַיֹּאמֶר אֱלֹהִים נַעֲשֶׂה אָדָם בְּצַלְמֵנוּ כִּדְמוּתֵנוּ וְיִרְדּוּ בִדְגַת הַיָּם וּבְעוֹף הַשָּׁמַיִם וּבַבְּהֵמָה וּבְכָל־הָאָרֶץ וּבְכָל־הָרֶמֶשׂ הָרֹמֵשׂ עַל־הָאָרֶץ׃
(Gen 1:26)

101. וַיְבָרֶךְ אֹתָם אֱלֹהִים וַיֹּאמֶר לָהֶם אֱלֹהִים פְּרוּ וּרְבוּ וּמִלְאוּ אֶת־הָאָרֶץ וְכִבְשֻׁהָ וּרְדוּ בִּדְגַת הַיָּם וּבְעוֹף הַשָּׁמַיִם וּבְכָל־חַיָּה הָרֹמֶשֶׂת עַל־הָאָרֶץ׃
(Gen 1:28)

102. וְהַמַּיִם גָּבְרוּ מְאֹד מְאֹד עַל־הָאָרֶץ וַיְכֻסּוּ כָּל־הֶהָרִים הַגְּבֹהִים אֲשֶׁר־תַּחַת כָּל־הַשָּׁמָיִם׃
(Gen 7:19)

103. כִּי־הוּא לִקְצוֹת־הָאָרֶץ יַבִּיט תַּחַת כָּל־הַשָּׁמַיִם יִרְאֶה׃ (Job 28:24)

phrase "under the whole heaven [תַּחַת כָּל־הַשָּׁמָיִם, taḥaṯ kāl haššāmāyim]" is used as in indication of God's absolute sovereignty. There is also an important symbolic sense to these statements about the water covering all the high mountains. In Isaiah God declares that there will be a day of judgment upon all who exalt themselves: "12 For the Lord of hosts will have a day against everyone who is proud and lofty and against everyone who is lifted up, that he will be abased, 13 and against all the cedars of Lebanon that are lofty and lifted up, against all the oaks of Bashan, 14 against all the lofty mountains, against all the hills that are lifted up" (Isa 2:12–14).[104] God goes on to declare that his judgment would be against every high tower, recalling the Babel narrative. Without a universal flood, this symbolism is meaningless:

> The Lord of hosts will have a day against a local group who is proud and lofty and again a local group who is lifted up, that will be abased, and against a local area of the cedars of Lebanon that are lofty and lifted up, against a local group of oaks of Bashan, against a local area of lofty mountains, against all the hills in a local area that are lifted up (said God nowhere).

Additionally, the flood is an act of anti-creative judgment. As the earth was born out of water in the creation, so the earth is returned to water in the flood. This corresponds to the judgment upon the man: "For dust you are, and to dust you will return" (Gen 3:19).[105]

Craig has a brief discussion of the pros and cons of taking the biblical flood as local or global. He concludes with the observations, "What [Tremper] Longman and [John] Walton are describing [in their book *The Lost World of the Flood*] is a genre that others have identified as mytho-history, which distinguishes Gen 1–11 from Gen 12–50. This classification better explains the description of a worldwide flood than mere hyperbole."[106] But their classification of the biblical account does not "better" explain the description. They are reading back into the biblical flood account what they take to be similarities with ANE myth, which we have already shown to be questionable at best. They assume a comparison necessarily going from ANE to the biblical story, when it is more

---

104. כִּי יוֹם לַיהוָה צְבָאוֹת עַל כָּל־גֵּאֶה וָרָם וְעַל כָּל־נִשָּׂא וְשָׁפֵל׃ 13 וְעַל כָּל־אַרְזֵי הַלְּבָנוֹן 12 הָרָמִים וְהַנִּשָּׂאִים וְעַל כָּל־אַלּוֹנֵי הַבָּשָׁן׃ 14 וְעַל כָּל־הֶהָרִים הָרָמִים וְעַל כָּל־הַגְּבָעוֹת הַנִּשָּׂאוֹת׃ (Isa 2:12–14)

105. כִּי־עָפָר אַתָּה וְאֶל־עָפָר תָּשׁוּב׃ (Gen 3:19)

106. Craig, *Adam*, 128.

The Table of Nations

As is his practice, Craig makes statements based on his interpretation as if these are the only reasonable statements that can be made. He acts as if he is a one-man magisterium. He declares, "Indeed, the Table of Nations of Gen 10 is fantastic. Although the table presents the various persons and nations as descended from Noah's sons, Shem, Ham, and Japheth (Gen 10:1), the peoples listed are not necessarily connected by blood but represent eclectic groupings based on geographical, linguistic, racial, and cultural similarities."[107] How does he know that these peoples are "not necessarily connected by blood"? The biblical text presents the table of nations as peoples who have descended from Shem, Ham, and Japheth. To assert that this is not the case one must assume that the biblical author is either mistaken or misrepresenting the case. In other words, one must reject inerrancy. It is certainly true that inerrancy has been rejected by many Evangelicals, but that does not make it a closed or settled issue. Of course Craig is arguing that it is palpably false if taken literally. But why should anyone not take the text literally? One would not take the text literally if one has already decided that the text is mytho-history. But this begs the question. Craig is using his always already present conclusion as a means of reaching his conclusion.

Craig again presents the findings of modern theorists as if this is sufficient to make his claims certain: "For example, some of the peoples that modern linguists and anthropologists would classify as Semitic—that is, as sons of Shem—are listed in the table as sons of Ham instead."[108] For some reason, the findings of modern linguists and anthropologists are certainly true, while the statements of the biblical text are "fantastic." For Craig the claims of modern linguists and anthropologists seem to be beyond suspicion. The biblical text is not inerrant, but modern linguists and anthropologists seem to be. Just because some modern linguists and anthropologists would classify some of the people as Semitic does not mean that they necessarily were. Just because the names of these individuals may seem to be of Semitic origin does not mean that the persons

---

107. Craig, *Adam*, 128.
108. Craig, *Adam*, 128.

necessarily were. Even today people take names that are historically connected with ethnic groups to which they do not belong. They may take these names because they like the names, or because they like the association, or because the names are or were historically significant. To work back from names to ethnicity is dubious at best, particularly when dealing with an ancient culture.

Craig has again divined what the author must have known: "Moreover, this feature of the table is not a modern discovery; the ancient compiler would himself have been aware of how eclectic his groupings were."[109] From where does Craig get this information? The text does not say that the author was aware of any eclectic grouping. Craig is simply reading his prior assumptions into the text and thus stipulates what the author could not have failed to notice: "He could not have failed to notice that Sheba and Havilah are listed as descendants of both Ham and Shem (Gen 10:7, 28–29)."[110] He makes this assertion as if it was impossible for the people in the genealogy to have the same names even though descending from a different son of Noah. In fact, we have already shown the relations of names and the repeating of names between the descendants of Cain and the descendants of Seth in Genesis 4 and 5; for example, Lamech of Cain, Lamech of Seth. Enoch of Cain, Enoch of Seth. Once one dismisses Craig's claim about what the author "must have been aware of," it turns out that these speculations are "modern." There is no evidence from the biblical text, or from the history of mankind, that different people from different ancestors cannot have the same names. This kind of fantastic claim permeates Craig's discussions.

The Tower of Babel

Concerning the account of the tower of Babel/Babylon (בָּבֶל, Bāḇel), Craig declares, "As a result of modern linguistic studies, we know that such a sudden, unitary origin of the world's languages is palpably false."[111] Once again Craig shows that he has rejected the inerrancy of the text. What the author wrote is judged by Craig to be false. In this case Craig does not qualify his judgment with the disclaimer "if take literally." He simply declares the text to be palpably false. Craig seems not to be aware of the

---

109. Craig, *Adam*, 129.
110. Craig, *Adam*, 129
111. Craig, *Adam*, 129.

controversies and conflicts between different schools and approaches to linguistics. He writes as if modern linguistics is a monolithic group who presents a single set of conclusions to which all agree. But we have already shown that this is simply not the case. And the reader should wonder why Craig does not identify any of these linguists. Who are these modern linguists? To which tradition do they subscribe? Are the Chomskyian? Are they Saussurian? Are they Lockean? Are they postmodern linguists? Do they reject the notion that language is innate? Are they Aristotelian? Are they natural language linguists? Are they structural linguists? Are they linguistic determinists? Are they Wittgensteinian? Are they deconstructionists? In my first linguistics course, the professor and the textbook, under the influence of Franz Boas, confidently declared that the Inuit people-group had dozens of words for "snow." This is now known as the "great Eskimo vocabulary hoax." Modern linguists are not immune from errors in the interpretation of evidence. Modern linguistics is simply not composed of one single perspective, and, as in almost every other discipline, there are different conflicting interpretations of linguistic evidence. Simply to declare what "modern linguistic studies" have claimed as if this is proof of something is disingenuous.[112]

As has been shown in chapter 1 above, the name 'Shem' (שֵׁם, Šēm) is the same form as the word translated "name" (שֵׁם, šēm). There is no indication in the text that the tower was built to reestablish God's presence on earth. In fact, the orchestrators of the tower sought to build a temple at the top of a ziggurat in order to set themselves up as god or gods. This is indicated by the assertion, "and let us make for us a name." (וְנַעֲשֶׂה־לָּנוּ שֵׁם, wěna 'ăśeh lālnû šēm). This recalls Gen 4:26; "Then was begun to call upon the name of the Lord."[113] This is also significant in light of Gen 6:4: "The Nephilim were on the earth in those days (and also after this) when the sons of God were having sexual relations with the daughters of man, who gave birth to children who were the mighty men of old, the *men of the name* [אַנְשֵׁי הַשֵּׁם, 'anšê haššēm]."[114] The tower was significant as the place where one would meet with one's god or gods. When God brings

---

112. See for example, Seuren, *Western Linguistics: An Historical Introduction*; or Aarsleff, *From Locke to Saussure: Essays on the Study of Language and Intellectual History*. Or consult Frawley, *International Encyclopedia of Linguistics*, 2d ed.

113. (Gen 4:26): וּלְשֵׁת גַּם־הוּא יֻלַּד־בֵּן וַיִּקְרָא אֶת־שְׁמוֹ אֱנוֹשׁ אָז הוּחַל לִקְרֹא בְּשֵׁם יְהוָה׃

114. הַנְּפִלִים הָיוּ בָאָרֶץ בַּיָּמִים הָהֵם וְגַם אַחֲרֵי־כֵן אֲשֶׁר יָבֹאוּ בְּנֵי הָאֱלֹהִים אֶל־בְּנוֹת הָאָדָם וְיָלְדוּ לָהֶם הֵמָּה הַגִּבֹּרִים אֲשֶׁר מֵעוֹלָם אַנְשֵׁי הַשֵּׁם׃ (Gen 6:4)

Israel out of Egypt, he meets with Israel on a mountain. The mountain was indicative of the separation between God, who is high and lifted up, and the people who are below. It was symbolic of the separation that existed between God and the people. Since there were no mountains in the plain of Shinar (Gen 11:2), the people undertook to construct a mountain in which their god(s) could dwell. It was a temple for the god of their own creation. In fact, it was a temple built for themselves in which they were the unifying center for the world, in which they could exalt themselves and set themselves up to be gods.

The people were not trying to build a tower to reach God. Man cannot reach God by striving for him. Rather, God must reach down to man to bridge the gap that separates man from God. In fact, we see this very thing in Gen 28 in the case of Jacob who, having been driven out of his land by Esau, dreams of a "ladder" (סֻלָּם, sullām, "stairway") that comes down from God and connects God to Jacob. Gen 28:12 says, "... and behold, a stairway having been set up to the earth and its top touching the heavens..."[115] The ladder was set up to the earth (אַרְצָה, 'arṣāh, the final letter, ָה āh is a Directive ה indicating direction toward), not "upon" the earth; and its top was touching the heavens, not "reaching" the heavens as if the ladder went up from the earth to the heavens. Also, Gen 11:4 states, "... come now, let us build a city and a tower, and its head in the heavens..."[116] The expression "in the heavens" translates the Hebrew word בַּשָּׁמַיִם (baššāmayim). The word שָׁמַיִם (šāmayim), translated "heavens" has the prepositional prefix בְּ (ba) which means "in." The tower was supposed to be "in" the heavens, not "reaching" the heavens.

The tower builders were attempting to unite humanity under one name, theirs. God confused their language in order to force mankind to scatter and fill the earth as he had commanded. At Pentecost, the language barrier is overcome by the gift of the Holy Spirit to speak so that all could hear in their own languages. At Pentecost humanity is united under one name, the name of the God-man Jesus, Who comes down from heaven, as Paul declares, "**9** For this reason also, God highly exalted him, and bestowed on Him the name which is above every name, **10** so that at the name of Jesus every knee will bow, of those who are in heaven and on earth and under the earth, **11** and that every tongue will confess that

---

115. ... וְהִנֵּה סֻלָּם מֻצָּב אַרְצָה וְרֹאשׁוֹ מַגִּיעַ הַשָּׁמָיְמָה (Gen 28:12)

116. ... הָבָה נִבְנֶה־לָּנוּ עִיר וּמִגְדָּל וְרֹאשׁוֹ בַשָּׁמַיִם (Gen 11:4)

Jesus Christ is Lord, to the glory of God the Father" (Phil 2:9–11).[117] By treating these passages in isolation from the rest of the Bible, Craig has again missed the significance of the narrative.

The Age of the Earth

Craig opens this section with the statement: "Finally, we should be remiss if we did not mention the most fantastic element of the entire primaeval history—namely, the ostensible claim that the entire world was less than two thousand years old at the time of Abraham's birth."[118] The reader must wonder where from the biblical text does Craig get this number? It is certainly not stated anywhere in the text. Of course we know from where he gets the number. He gets if from his calculations of the ages of the individuals in the genealogies of Genesis 5. But we have already shown that this is the same error committed by James Ussher who claimed that the earth was created in 4004 BC. Craig attempts to hedge his bets by saying, "Even if we allow for gaps in the genealogies of Gen 1–11, at most a few thousand years can be reasonably interpolated."[119] But why should anyone think this to be the case? Craig declares, "The genealogy of Shem in Gen 11:10–26 is so tightly constructed by means of the ages at which fathers bore sons that generational gaps are difficult to interpolate."[120] As we have explained above, the Hebrew Bible did not use a word for 'grandson' or 'grandchild.' The word 'son' (בֵּן, bēn) was used to refer to one's immediate biological offspring, or to one's descendants. Once one understands the Hebrew language, one sees that Craig's interpretation is fantastic and palpably false. Of course Craig has adopted an evolutionary interpretation of the origin of the universe. Consequently, he thinks of the age of the earth in millions or billions of years. It is this prior assumption that leads Craig to classify the biblical account of the age of the earth as a fantastic element. In other words, his criticism does not derive from

---

117. **9** διὸ καὶ ὁ θεὸς αὐτὸν ὑπερύψωσεν καὶ ἐχαρίσατο αὐτῷ τὸ ὄνομα τὸ ὑπὲρ πᾶν ὄνομα, **10** ἵνα ἐν τῷ ὀνόματι Ἰησοῦ πᾶν γόνυ κάμψῃ ἐπουρανίων καὶ ἐπιγείων καὶ καταχθονίων **11** καὶ πᾶσα γλῶσσα ἐξομολογήσηται ὅτι κύριος Ἰησοῦς Χριστὸς εἰς δόξαν θεοῦ πατρός (Phil 2:9-11).

118. Craig, *Adam*, 130.
119. Craig, *Adam*, 130.
120. Craig, *Adam*, 130.

the biblical text, but from a prior perspective, and he judges the biblical text against his evolutionary assumptions.

Conclusion

Craig concludes this chapter, "In summation, the narratives of Gen 1–11 exhibit, sometimes dramatically, the family resemblances that mark the folklorist's genre of myth."[121] And yet that is precisely what he has not demonstrated. The errors, the misunderstanding, the misrepresentations, the one-sided claims, the misplaced reliance on the notion of family resemblances, and the repeated demonstrations of a lack of facility in the original language has undermined every one of Craig's claims. Craig does not seem to grasp the significance of the events because he seems to be unaware of the wider use of the terminology and imagery throughout the rest of the Bible. He takes events in isolation from this wider context to draw his conclusions. ANE myths simply do not evidence the prophetic nature of biblical narratives, and Craig completely misses or ignores this factor in the text. He appeals to history and linguistics without acknowledging that these disciplines include contrary and often contradictory claims and contrary interpretations of the same evidence by equally competent scholars.

But let us assume that Craig has made some valid observations. This still does not show literary dependence or literary context. All it might show is similarities. In order to conclude from his discussions that there is a literary context, one must assume that the ANE myths were produced prior to the events recorded in the biblical text, and that the biblical author employed these literary features. But that is an assumption that has not been demonstrated. It is just as reasonable to conclude that the authors of ANE myths adopted and adapted the content from oral traditions that came to be employed by the biblical authors, assuming that the content of the biblical account was composed from such sources and not from supernatural revelation.

In the previous section Craig claimed, "The fantastic elements in the narratives that we have identified have nothing to do with miracles, which we accept. Rather, they concern nonmiraculous features of the story that, if taken literally, are palpably false."[122] Why should anyone think

---

121. Craig, *Adam*, 131.
122. Craig, *Adam*, 131.

that these elements are "nonmiraculous" simply because Craig claims that they are? Does the text anywhere claim that nothing in Gen 1–11 is miraculous? Does the text anywhere claim that some of these elements are nonmiraculous? Why could not the animals on the ark be a miraculous event due to God's preservation? Why could not a world-wide flood be due to God's direct miraculous action? In order to think that none of these elements is miraculous, one would need to adopt Craig's assumptions and prejudice. If Craig believes in miracles, and there is no reason to think that he does not since he claims that he does, why arbitrarily pronounce that none of these events is miraculous? Is it necessary for the text to state that an event is miraculous in order for it to be taken as miraculous? The creation of the universe is not called a miracle in Genesis chapter 1, but can we seriously think that it was not? God created the man from the dust of the ground. Unless we believe that this is simply a fantastic element that is palpably false, can we seriously think that this was not a miracle? Craig must have a unduly narrow definition of what he calls a miracle.

Many of Craig's arguments and claims up to this point in his book lack the rigorous analysis that so many of us have come to respect and appreciate from his writings, lectures, debates, and articles. Ultimately, Craig simply has not proven his case. The most difficult aspect to accept from his evaluations is that he has abandoned the inerrancy of the text. In many places he qualifies his claim that the text is palpably false by claiming that some event or statement of the text is palpably false *if taken literally*. If the text at these points was not designed to be taken literally, then claiming that the text is palpably false only if taken literally does not deny inerrancy. But at other points he simply asserts without the qualifier that the text is palpably false. In those instances the reader might give him the benefit of the doubt and assume that he implies the qualifier. Yet his arguments in those cases do not justify the assumption of the qualifier. However, his repeated statements without the qualifier that the text includes fantastic elements that are palpably false, along with accompanying arguments, seem to leave no other conclusion possible.

5

Is Genesis 1–11 Mytho History?

Genealogies

CRAIG BEGINS THIS CHAPTER discussing the chronology of the section of Genesis which he has labeled "primaeval history." He addresses the often recognized repetition of the word תּוֹלְדֹת (tôlĕdōṯ) that introduces the various genealogical records in Genesis. He rightly rejects using this word as an indication of the structure of the book: "But here a word of caution is in order. It is repeatedly said that the *tôlədôt* formulae determine the structure of the book of Genesis. This careless statement is at best misleading and at worst grossly mistaken."[1] However, Craig has also missed the structure of Genesis: "As anyone can tell, the book of Genesis falls naturally into three parts: the primaeval history, the patriarchal narratives, and the story of Joseph and his family. The large-scale structure of Genesis is thus tripartite."[2] As is so often the case, Craig's structure is built on what he thinks are certain themes or topics. As we have shown above in chapter 2, Craig simply does not see the literary characteristics and technique of the author that signal the structure of the book. The first part of Genesis does not end at chapter 11. Dividing the book at this point disrupts the connection of Shem to Abram. Shem's genealogy begins at the end of chapter 10, is interrupted with the Babel narrative, and picked up again at Gen 11:10. The Babel narrative is integral to the

1. Craig, *Adam*, 133.
2. Craig, *Adam*, 133.

genealogy of Shem (שֵׁם, Šēm) because it focuses on the effort of the people to make a name (שֵׁם, šēm) for themselves, which serves as a contrast to the fact that God will make Abram's name (שֵׁם, šēm) great: וַאֲגַדְּלָה שְׁמֶךָ (waʾăgaddēlāh šəmekā) "... and I will make great your name." (Gen 12:2). To break the text at the end of chapter 11 loses the connection that the author is making between Shem ("name"), Babel ("make a name for ourselves"), and Abram (God will make his name great).

Craig mounts a devastating argument against the use of תּוֹלְדֹת (tôlĕḏōṯ) as indicators of the structure of the book of Genesis. From this he concludes, "What the *tôləḏôt* formulae do accomplish is to help order the primaeval narratives chronologically. Gordon Wenham calls the genealogies 'the back-bone of Genesis 1–11.'"[3] The problem with this conclusion is that, if we do not count its use in Gen 2:4, תּוֹלְדֹת (tôlĕḏōṯ) occurs twelve times throughout Genesis. It occurs only four times in the so called "primaeval history," and eight times in the remainder of Genesis. Why does the term form the backbone of Gen 1–11 and not the backbone of entire book of Genesis? Why confine its "backbone" function only to Gen 1–11. This is another instance in which Craig's prior commitment to his notion of the structure of Genesis leads him to arbitrarily ignore what does not support his assumptions. In fact, Craig points out how the genealogies move from Gen 1–11 into the patriarchal narratives: "What makes Gen 1–11 different is that the genealogies move seamlessly into the historical period of the patriarchs, where the historical interest is obvious and not in dispute."[4] That being the case, why separate Gen 1–11 from the rest of the text? We have already shown that Craig's notion of the structure of Genesis ignores and violates the literary characteristics of the book, so there is no structural reason to confine the function of the genealogies to the "primaeval history."

Craig goes on briefly to discuss the efforts of contemporary anthropologists to discover the role that genealogies play in societies, and Craig's conclusion is helpful: "However interesting this data from contemporary anthropology may be, its application to ancient Israel must be fraught with uncertainty in light of the inaccessibility of data concerning Hebrew oral traditions."[5] Craig continues, "More relevant will be comparative lit-

---

3. Craig, *Adam*, 136.
4. Craig, *Adam*, 137.
5. Craig, *Adam*, 139.

erary evidence concerning ANE genealogies."[6] Craig had pointed out the "uncertainty" of the application of the conclusions from contemporary anthropologists to biblical genealogies, and the same error would seem to apply to conclusions from ANE genealogies because of the same inaccessible data of Hebrew oral tradition. If the inaccessible data concerning Hebrew oral tradition makes the application of anthropologists' conclusion uncertain, why would a comparison to ANE genealogies be any less fraught with uncertainty? In fact, Craig seems to make this very point:

> If Wilson is right about the role of genealogical notices in the Mesopotamian king lists, then these lists are hardly comparable to the biblical genealogies, which are not incidentally but essentially genealogical. While a segmented list like the Table of Nations might be only incidentally genealogical, the linear genealogies could not even exist if the genealogical connections were removed, making them utterly different than the Mesopotamian king lists.[7]

Although Craig rejects some aspects of Wilson's claims about genealogies, he asserts,

> Still, Wilson's work reminds us that ancient genealogies were not the work of disinterested historians but can serve other ends. For example, as mentioned earlier, the segmented genealogy that constitutes the Table of Nations in Gen 10, despite its notices "sons of" and "begot," is not about blood relations but lists peoples on the basis of political, linguistic, geographical, and similar factors—and the author of Genesis knew it. It is a showcase example of Wilson's claim that segmented genealogies serve mainly domestic, political-jural, and religious purposes.[8]

Why should anyone think that the table of nations is not about blood relations. Even if it is the case that the genealogy is concerned with domestic, political-jural, and religious purposes, this does not mean it cannot also be about blood relations. In fact, the blood relations seem precisely to be the point. There is a necessary theological significance to the blood relations throughout all the genealogies of Genesis; that is, to trace the seed of the woman ultimately to Jesus (see **Figure 13**).

---

6. Craig, *Adam*, 139.
7. Craig, *Adam*, 140.
8. Craig, *Adam*, 142.

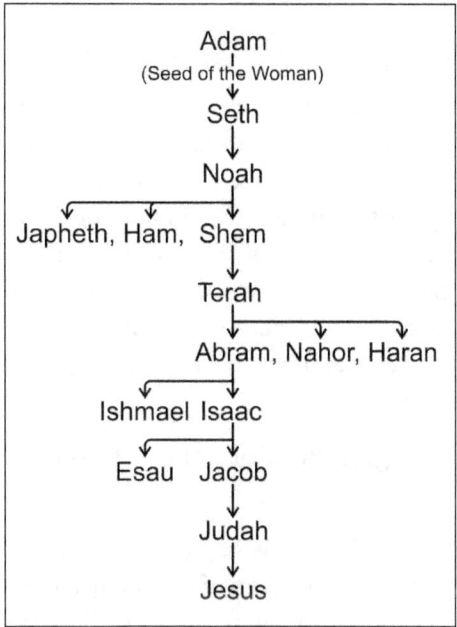

Figure: 13: Genesis Genealogies

There are important aspects to note in the genealogies:

- "This book of generations of Adam" (Gen 5:1).

Notice that the generations of Adam begin with Seth, not Cain. Cain was also a son of Adam, but neither Cain nor his descendants are part of the "generations of Adam." The genealogy of Adam through Seth ends in chapter 5 with Noah.

- "These the generations of Noah" (Gen 6:9).

Noah was a righteous man.

- "Now these the generations of the sons of Noah, Shem, Ham, and Japheth" (Gen 10:1).

Notice the order of the genealogies of the sons of Noah in chapters 10 and 11: Japheth, Ham, Shem, which is the reverse order from every previous reference to the sons of Noah.

- "These the generations of Shem" (Gen 11:10).

Shem's genealogy is last because it leads to Abram.

- "Now these the generations of Terah" (Gen 11:27).

Notice the text states that Haran became the father of Lot. This is important in the narrative relating to Abram and Lot. The text points out that Haran died, but that he was the father of Nahor's wife. These things are said to indicate that Haran was the firstborn of Terah, and Abram the youngest. As with the genealogy of Japheth, Ham, and Shem, the genealogy of Abram, Nahor, and Haran is in the reverse order of their birth. This is because Abram is the focus of the text and the most important son. The text does not claim that this is the order of their birth, so this does not violate inerrancy.

- "Now these the generations of Ishmael the son of Abraham" (Gen 25:12).

The genealogy of Ishmael is important in order to make the distinction between the promised seed of Abraham and the descendants of Ishmael. This is significant for later events in which the descendants of Ishmael become the enemies of Israel. Notice also the text specifically identifies the firstborn indicating that the names are in the order of their birth.

- "Now these the generations of Isaac the son of Abraham" (Gen 25:19).

Once again the genealogy focuses on a specific individual following the genealogy from Isaac.

- "Now these the generations of Esau, he *is* Edom" (Gen 36:1).

The significance of Esau hardly needs to be mentioned.

- "Now these the generations of Esau, the father of Edom" (Gen 36:9).
- "These the generations of Jacob" (Gen 37:2).

There are some important factors in the narratives concerning Joseph. Joseph is sold into servitude to Egypt according to God's plan. At key points through the narratives, Judah becomes the one who furthers God's plan. It is Judah who convinces the brothers to sell Joseph, which ultimately progresses God's plan. It is Judah who offers himself as a surety for Benjamin. The developing focus upon Judah is the reason for the Judah-Tamar narrative that interrupts the beginning of the Joseph narratives. The author is alerting the reader to consider Judah's role throughout the following narratives. As the Joseph narratives progress, Judah gradually becomes the focus culminating in the blessings of Jacob upon his sons. In the blessings of Jacob upon his sons given in Genesis 49, the first three sons, Reuben, Simeon, and Levi, incur curses, whereas Judah receives a blessing, and each son after Judah is blessed—the blessing comes through Judah.

By trying to show some kind of relation between biblical genealogies and ANE genealogies, Craig has completely missed the literary strategy of the author and the theological significance of the biblical genealogies.

Craig also rejects the notion that there are gaps in the genealogies:

> Do the genealogies of Gen 1–11 permit long gaps in a literal history? When the *tôlEdôt* of Adam in 5:1–32 is conjoined with the *tôlEdôt* of Shem in 11:10–26, there is a succession of descendants from Adam to Abraham that seems to permit no missing generations because of the form used throughout: "When X had lived *n* years, he became the father of Y; and when Y had lived *m* years, he became the father of Z." By stipulating the father's age at the time of his progeny's birth, gaps seem to be excluded.[9]

The text does not say, "he became the father of." The text states, וַיּוֹלֶד (wâyôled), literally, "and he brought forth." An individual can bring forth a descendant that is not his immediate biological child. However, even if the text had used the word אָב ('āb), which is usually translated "father," it does not necessarily mean the immediate biological parent. Biblical Hebrew did not use a word for "grandfather" or "grandparent." The single word אָב ('āb) served both to refer to one's immediate biological parent and to refer to an ancestor. Also, this word can be used to refer to someone who is the first in a line of those who follow in a given practice or vocation, as we might say that Ferdinand de Saussure is the father of modern linguistics. Hebrew did have a word that is often translated "ancestor." It is so translated by the NASB: "The blessings of your father Have surpassed the blessings of my ancestors [הוֹרַי, hôray]" (Gen 49:26).[10] The word translated "ancestors" is actually a participle that literally means "those who conceived me." Of course, once one goes back beyond one's immediate biological parent, it is not literally the case that one's ancestors

---

9. Craig, *Adam*, 143.
10. (Gen 49:26) בִּרְכֹת אָבִיךָ גָּבְרוּ עַל־בִּרְכֹת הוֹרַי

"conceived" one, at least not in the sense that an English speaker would take the meaning. Yet in the biblical text, one's grandfather or great grandfather, etc., can be referred to as the one "who conceived me." Also, one can refer to one's ancestor as one's father—as is said, "Abraham is our father." In fact, the word 'father' is used to refer to Moab, the son of Lot's eldest daughter, as the ancestor of the Moabites: "He is the ancestor of [אֲבִי, 'ăḇî, lit. "father of"] the Moabites to today" (NET, Gen 19:37);[11] and again, "He [Ben-Ammi] is the ancestor of [אֲבִי, 'ăḇî, lit. "father of"] the Ammonites of today" (NET, Gen 19:38).[12]

Craig appears to deal with this issue in a footnote:

> Theoretically, one could insert small gaps by interpreting "father" to mean something like "grandfather" (cf. Gen 46:12, 25; 46:16–18): "When X had lived *n* years, he became the grandfather of Y; and when Y had lived *m* years, he became the grandfather of Z." But such gaps are limited because the progenitor must still be a certain age when the descendant is born. Moreover, a few notices in the genealogies connect successors closely—e.g., Lamech's commenting on the meaning of Noah's name. This theoretical suggestion is, in any case, *ad hoc* and therefore implausible. Hamilton's suggestion that "X fathered Y" may mean "X fathered the line culminating in Y" (Victor P. Hamilton, *The Book of Genesis: Chapters 1–17*, NICOT [Grand Rapids: Eerdmans, 1990], 254) is equally implausible, since the genealogies imply that X is still alive when the line culminates in Y. One must agree with Wenham that it requires special pleading to postulate long gaps in the genealogy (Gordon J. Wenham, *Genesis j-15*, WBC 1 [Grand Rapids: Zondervan, 1987], 153).[13]

However, Craig does not seem to understand the language. It is simply not the case that "the progenitor must still be a certain age when the descendant is born." Why "must" this be the case? There is nothing in the terms used that require this to be the case. The genealogy does not use the word "father," but states that *X* brought forth *m*. The word translated "father" does not require that it mean "grandfather." As we have seen, it is used in Genesis to refer to an ancestor. When the text states that Moab was the father of the Moabites, it certainly does not require that Moab was the immediagte biological grandfather of all of the Moabites "to this

---

11. (Gen 19:37): וַתֵּלֶד הַבְּכִירָה בֵּן וַתִּקְרָא שְׁמוֹ מוֹאָב הוּא אֲבִי־מוֹאָב עַד־הַיּוֹם׃
12. (Gen 19:38): אֲבִי בְנֵי־עַמּוֹן עַד־הַיּוֹם
13. Craig, *Adam*, 144.n.31.

day." Neither is there anything in the account that requires the progenitor to be a certain age when the descendant is born. *X* is the progenitor of *m*. *X* became the progenitor of *m* at a certain age when *X* became the immediate biological parent of a child who would become the immediate biological parent of a child, who would become the immediate biological parent of a child, etc., until the *m* is born. Craig's effort to deal with this issue shows that he does not understand the language about which he is stipulating these requirements.

Craig declares *ex cathedra* that the ages of the antediluvian patriarchs is unlikely to be intended by the author to be literal:

> Moreover, the longevity of the antediluvian patriarchs seems unlikely to be intended to be literally construed. In the Sumerian King List, the antediluvian kings also have fantastically long reigns, as long as 43200 years for an individual reign, with the lengths of the reigns diminishing after the flood (see fig. 5.2). Are we seriously to think that ancient Sumerians and Babylonians took such absurdly long reigns literally?[14]

Whether or not we should think that ancient Sumerians and Babylonians took the long reigns of kings literally has nothing to do with whether we should think that Moses intended his readers to take the long lives of the patriarchs literally. How does Craig know what Moses intended? Back in chapter 4 we have discussed the significance of the long lives of the patriarchs. The text presents these ages as actual ages of these actual patriarchs. On the basis of Craig's declaration, why should anyone think that Moses intended his readers to think that he is referring to actual people who actually lived? The narrative is presented as a genealogy of these actual patriarchs who actually lived the actual long lives. There is nothing in the text that indicates that Moses did not intend these long lives to be taken as literal. Craig does not want to do that because of his prior commitment to make some connection with ANE genealogies, but the language does not support his efforts.

The significance of the long lives is also the fact that in the face of longevity, each one still died. The consequence of sin is clearly stated in Gen 2:17: "But from the tree of the knowledge, good and evil, not you will eat from it, for in a day you eat from it, to die you will die [מוֹת תָּמוּת]."[15] The expression literally translated "to die you will die" is one way Hebrew

---

14. Craig, *Adam*, 144–46.
15. (Gen 2:17): וּמֵעֵץ הַדַּעַת טוֹב וָרָע לֹא תֹאכַל מִמֶּנּוּ כִּי בְּיוֹם אֲכָלְךָ מִמֶּנּוּ מוֹת תָּמוּת

expresses an emphatic declaration: "You will most certainly die!" That this consequence followed from the couple's act of eating the fruit is again emphatically and repeatedly pressed home to the reader in the genealogy of Genesis 5 with the repeating word וַיָּמֹת (wâyāmōṯ) translated "and he died."

5 So all the days that Adam lived were nine hundred and thirty years, and he died	וַיָּמֹת.
8 So all the days of Seth were nine hundred and twelve years, and he died	וַיָּמֹת.
11 So all the days of Enosh were nine hundred and five years, and he died	וַיָּמֹת.
14 So all the days of Kenan were nine hundred and ten years, and he died	וַיָּמֹת.
17 So all the days of Mahalalel were eight hundred and ninety-five years, and he died	וַיָּמֹת.
20 So all the days of Jared were nine hundred and sixty-two years, and he died	וַיָּמֹת.
27 So all the days of Methuselah were nine hundred and sixty-nine years, and he died	וַיָּמֹת.
31 So all the days of Lamech were seven hundred and seventy-seven years, and he died	וַיָּמֹת.

The final verse of chapter 5 states, "32 Noah was five hundred years old, and Noah became the father of Shem, Ham, and Japheth."[16] It is not until Gen 9:29 that we find the same statement in the same way concerning Noah:

29 So all the days of Noah were nine hundred and fifty years, and he died וַיָּמֹת.

The sentence of death has passed upon all men, as Paul declared: "Therefore, just as through one man sin entered into the world, and death through sin, and so death spread to all men, because of which all sinned" (Rom 5:12).[17]

---

16. (Gen 2:32): וַיְהִי־נֹחַ בֶּן־חֲמֵשׁ מֵאוֹת שָׁנָה וַיּוֹלֶד נֹחַ אֶת־שֵׁם אֶת־חָם וְאֶת־יָפֶת

17. Διὰ τοῦτο ὥσπερ δι' ἑνὸς ἀνθρώπου ἡ ἁμαρτία εἰς τὸν κόσμον εἰσῆλθεν καὶ διὰ τῆς ἁμαρτίας ὁ θάνατος, καὶ οὕτως εἰς πάντας ἀνθρώπους ὁ θάνατος διῆλθεν ἐφ' ᾧ πάντες ἥμαρτον (Rom 5:12).

We have already directed attention to the fact that the genealogy of chapter 5 completely omits Cain and his descendants. These are those who are separated from God. But the genealogy of chapter 5 begins:

> ¹ This is the book of the generations of Adam. In the day when God created man, He made him ain the likeness of God. ² He created them male and female, and He blessed them and named them Man in the day when they were created. ³ When Adam had lived one hundred and thirty years, he brought forth in his likeness, according to his image, and called him Seth (Gen 5:1–3).[18]

In order to understand the reason for the long lives, we must consider some important elements of the text. (1) As we pointed out, the genealogy of Genesis 5 omits any reference to Cain and his descendants. (2) The text specifically points out that God created Adam and Eve in his image (בְּצַלְמֵנוּ, běṣalmēnû), and that Adam brought forth Seth in his likeness (בִּדְמוּתוֹ, bidmûtô) and according to his image (כְּצַלְמוֹ, kěṣalmô). (3) There is no specific statement that Cain or Able were brought forth in the image and likeness of Adam. (4) There are no references to the ages of Cain or Lamech when they brought forth children. (5) There is no statement in chapter 4 corresponding to the refrain "and he died," as in chapter 5. (6) Cain is driven from God's presence and condemned to be a wanderer (נָד, nād), yet instead of wandering, Cain goes to the land of Nod (נוֹד, nôd) and builds a city in which to live. Cain calls the city Enoch (חֲנוֹךְ, ḥănôk). Rather than wandering, Cain lives in a city. In chapter 5, Jared brings forth Enoch (חֲנוֹךְ, ḥănôk) who "walks around [וַיִּתְהַלֵּךְ, wayyithalēk, "wanders around"] with God." 7) We have already shown the comparisons of the names of the descendants of Cain and the descendants of Seth in Figure 8. These elements indicate a distinction the author is making between the line of Cain and the line of Adam through Seth. It follows that the long ages of the men in the genealogy of chapter 5 is another element of distinction that the author is making. The notion of long lives characterizes those who have not been driven from the face of God. Through the OT, the characterization of living a long and prosperous life becomes a characteristic of those who walk around with God. At the age of one hundred and twenty years, Moses, the man who did not believe God to treat him as holy in the eyes of Israel, died, and

---

18. ¹ זֶה סֵפֶר תּוֹלְדֹת אָדָם בְּיוֹם בְּרֹא אֱלֹהִים אָדָם בִּדְמוּת אֱלֹהִים עָשָׂה אֹתוֹ: ² זָכָר וּנְקֵבָה בְּרָאָם וַיְבָרֶךְ אֹתָם וַיִּקְרָא אֶת־שְׁמָם אָדָם בְּיוֹם הִבָּרְאָם: ³ וַיְחִי אָדָם שְׁלֹשִׁים וּמְאַת שָׁנָה וַיּוֹלֶד בִּדְמוּתוֹ כְּצַלְמוֹ וַיִּקְרָא אֶת־שְׁמוֹ שֵׁת:
(Gen 5:1–5)

yet the text points out, "... his eye was not dim, nor his vigor abated." (Deut 34:7).[19] The text states this because Moses did not die of old age or because he was in a physically weakened state. The implication is that Moses, the man under the law, whose faith was weakened under the law, who was forbidden from bringing the people in to the promised land, was put to death—the end of the law is death. However, three times the text of Joshua points out that Joshua was old and advanced in years; twice in 13:1 and once in 23:1:

> "Now Joshua was old and advanced in years when the LORD said to him, 'You are old and advanced in years, and very much of the land remains to be possessed'" (Josh 13:1).[20]

> "Now it came about after many days, when the LORD had given rest to Israel from all their enemies on every side, and Joshua was old, advanced in years" (Josh 23:1).[21]

Joshua, who trusted God when the people of Israel did not, the man of faith who brings the people into the land of rest, lives a long and prosperous life. Craig has completely missed these elements in his effort to make some connection between ANE and biblical genealogies.

Craig concludes this section,

> We have reason, then, to interpret the genealogies in their narrative context as evincing a historical interest but not relating straightforward history, even if we do contemplate or permit gaps in the genealogies. Mathews plausibly suggests that in general the genealogies serve the theological purpose of showing the interconnectedness of all mankind and the hope of universal blessing. Our objective is to make sense of the points adduced by Green without imagining enormous gaps in a literal historical record.[22]

---

19. (Deut 34:7) לֹא־כָהֲתָה עֵינוֹ וְלֹא־נָס לֵחֹה׃

The argument here is not that Moses was condemned, or that he was separated from God. Moses ultimately appears in the land with Christ at the mount of transfiguration. The argument here is the imagery that the author uses to contrast the end of the law and the man of faith.

20. וִיהוֹשֻׁעַ זָקֵן בָּא בַּיָּמִים וַיֹּאמֶר יְהוָה אֵלָיו אַתָּה זָקַנְתָּה בָּאתָ בַיָּמִים וְהָאָרֶץ נִשְׁאֲרָה הַרְבֵּה־מְאֹד לְרִשְׁתָּהּ׃

(Josh 13:1)

21. וַיְהִי מִיָּמִים רַבִּים אַחֲרֵי אֲשֶׁר־הֵנִיחַ יְהוָה לְיִשְׂרָאֵל מִכָּל־אֹיְבֵיהֶם מִסָּבִיב וִיהוֹשֻׁעַ זָקֵן בָּא בַּיָּמִים׃

(Josh 23:1)

22. Craig, *Adam*, 152.

As a matter of fact, Craig has not presented any persuasive arguments that would lead one to think the genealogies are not "straightforward history." Because the genealogies serve a theological purpose does not mean they cannot also be straightforward history. The resurrection of Jesus certainly has a theological purpose, but does that mean that the narratives that recount his resurrection are not straightforward history? And in fact, contrary to what Craig surmises, it is not the case that "Scholars are at a loss to find any symbolic significance in the ages themselves."[23] It is particularly problematic that Craig thinks that just because *he* and the unnamed "scholars" have not found any symbolic significance that there cannot be any. We have set forth evidence for the fact that the ages are not only the actual ages of the actual patriarchs, but also that these ages have an identifiable symbolic significance that derives from the text, namely that sin leads to death even though one lives a long and prosperous life. It is not the case that the ages do not have any symbolic significance. It is simply the case that Craig has missed this significance.

The Genre of Genesis 1–11

Craig begins this section with a brief discussion of the work of Thorkild Jacobsen. Thorkild Peter Rudolph Jacobsen (1904–1993) was a Danish historian, one of the foremost scholars on the ancient Near East, specializing in Assyriology and Sumerian literature. Craig takes issue with some of Jacobsen's assertions and conclusions, but ultimately settles on the notion that the genre of Gen 1–11 is "mytho-history." Craig says, "While the genealogies of Genesis evince an interest in history on the part of the author and his audience, it is important to keep in mind that it is a mytho-history that is being narrated. Chronological calculations become inappropriate for such a genre."[24] It is understandable that Craig believes that he has made his case, but we have seen that his conclusions and assertions are not supported by the language. He seems to be completely unaware of the literary characteristics of the text, and he imposes upon the text his prior assumption that there must be a connection between biblical narratives and ANE myth, an assumption that cannot be sustained under examination.

Again Craig asserts his position:

23. Craig, *Adam*, 149.
24. Craig, *Adam*, 153–54.

> Yet the biblical genealogies famously total to a scant 1,656 years from Adam until the flood, with another 367 years from the flood to the call of Abraham. Genesis presents a mythological history of the world that is extremely short by ancient standards, bound tightly by father-son genealogical notices that seem to contemplate no gaps of tens of thousands of years between them. We should not imagine that the genealogies contemplate the enormous leaps that would be necessary to bring them into harmony with what we know of the history of mankind; but neither should we think them to comprise purely fictitious characters. We can avoid these polar opposites by taking the brief history they relate to be a mytho-history that is not meant to be taken literally.[25]

We have already demonstrated a failure to understand the language and significance of the genealogies. The miscalculation of the years between Adam and the flood makes the same mistake made by Bishop Ussher. If we *should* think that the ages given in the biblical genealogies are fictitious, then why should we *not* think that the persons are also fictitious? Once Craig sets himself as the determiner of what is and what is not fictitious, there is no objective measure on which to base these distinctions, and whatever one wants to believe is fictitious in the Bible can be relegated to the fictitious.

---

25 Craig, *Adam*, 130–131.

6

Are Myths Believed To Be True?

As Craig acknowledges, "The question of this chapter's title is ambiguous."[1] In the first section of the chapter, titled "Comparative Anthropological Data," Craig investigates the question of the relation between truth and belief in order to clarify the question whether belief that a myth is true is expected or intended.

> By whom are myths believed to be true? Doubtless, the question concerns members of the society for which the myths are determinative, not outsiders. We have already said that it is characteristic of myths that they are objects of belief by members of the society that embraces them. But one might believe in a myth in the sense of accepting it, relying on it for determining one's values and practices, embracing it as central to one's identity as a member of one's society, without believing it to be true. No doubt some members of a society believe the myths of the society to be true. But our question is whether belief in the truth of the accepted myths is somehow expected or intended.[2]

Comparative Anthropological Data

In this first section Craig reports his research on the claims and counterclaims of anthropologists. At one point in the discussion, Craig asks,

1. Craig, *Adam*, 158.
2. Craig, *Adam*, 158.

The deeper question raised by these anthropologists is what conception (or conceptions) of truth is held by these various tribal peoples. The predicate *true* has a wide range of meanings, as is evident in such expressions as "true gold," "a true friend," "a true line," "the true path," "a true statement." Why should we think that these tribal societies' conception of truth with respect to myths is the philosopher's notion of truth as correspondence?[3]

Why indeed should these tribal societies' conceptions of truth correspond to the philosopher's notion of truth as correspondence? Consider Craig's examples of the "wide range of meanings" of "true": "true gold"—this use means that the material is actual gold, not some imitation; "a true friend"—this use means that someone relates to someone as an actual friend, not someone who is pretending to be a friend for an ulterior motive; "a true line"—this use means that the line is an actual straight line, not crooked or bent; "a true path"—this use means that one's path actually leads one to his desired goal; "a true statement"—this use means that the statement is asserting what is actually the case. It certainly seems that each one of these uses involves a correspondence between the assertion and the actual state of affairs. Why should someone *not* think that tribal societies' conception of truth corresponds to the philosopher's notion of truth as correspondence. Philosophers are not simply saying, "this is my own notion of truth." Philosophers are claiming that this is the very nature of truth whether anyone is aware of it or not. A given tribal society might not express the conception of truth in philosophical terms, but that does not mean they do not have a conception of truth that corresponds to the philosopher's proposition. If a tribal society believes that a myth is true, would that not indicate that the tribe believes that the statements of the myth are actually true, i.e., they correspond to reality, that the myth "tells it like it was"? Does Craig want his readers to think that truth is relative to what a given tribal culture thinks? Is it not the case that the correspondence view of truth is the actual nature of truth regardless of what any given culture or tribal society thinks? Tribal societies and cultures operate on the basis of a correspondence view of truth whether or not they are aware of it.

Later Craig asserts, "The fact that myths, while accepted as true and authoritative, are not necessarily taken to be literally true is evident from examples of myths that seem to be clearly metaphorical or figurative."[4] As

3. Craig, *Adam*, 160.
4. Craig, *Adam*, 161.

true as this may be, doesn't it require that the metaphorical or figurative myths are believed to communicate some literal truth? In Deuteronomy Moses declared, "The eternal God is a dwelling place, and underneath are the everlasting arms" (Deut 33:27).[5] Of course God is not a literal dwelling place nor does God have arms. Yet these metaphorical expressions are designed to communicate literal truth about God.

It makes no sense to think that anyone, even a tribal society, would take the metaphorical or figurative myths to communicate only metaphorical or figurative truths. It follows that if the literal truth that is communicated by metaphorical or figurative myths turns out to contradict the actual state of affairs, then the literal truth communicated by the metaphorical or figurative myths are literally false. Truth, whether expressed literally, metaphorically, or figuratively, must correspond to the actual state of affairs.

Craig concludes this section with an equivocation:

> The plasticity and flexibility of myths lend support to the notion that what is at stake in believing a myth is not belief in its literal truth. The different versions of the myth that are believed by contemporaneous members of the society may be logically incompatible with one another; nonetheless, a fundamental religious truth is communicated by the various versions of the myth, so it does not matter which version one relates. One does not bother to correct someone telling a different version of the myth, for it, too, expresses that fundamental truth. If myths were interpreted literalistically, they could not be changed in response to new challenges in ways that are incompatible with the earlier version. But if both versions continue to express the same fundamental truth, then they can both be regarded as absolutely true, despite their differences.[6]

Granted that someone might not believe that what is presented in the metaphor or figure is to be taken as literally true, nevertheless the one who believes the myth believes that the metaphor or figure is communicating metaphorically or figuratively a literal truth. So, someone who believes the myth believes the literal truth that the metaphor or figure is designed to communicate. Craig equivocates when he says, "what is at stake in believing a myth is not belief in its literal truth." He is saying that the believer does not believe that the myth is literally true, but that

---

5. (Deut 33:27) מְעֹנָה אֱלֹהֵי קֶדֶם וּמִתַּחַת זְרֹעֹת עוֹלָם
6. Craig, *Adam*, 165.

is not the question. The question is, does the believer believe that the metaphor or figure is communicating a literal truth that he believes to be literally true? In fact, Craig covertly reintroduces this very point when he refers to the "fundamental religious truth" that the myth is designed to communicate. So, the believer may not believe that the metaphorical or figurative statements of the myth are literally true, but he believes that the myth is communicating some fundamental, literal, religious truth. And if the myth communicates a fundamental religious claim that is literally false, then neither the myth nor the fundamental religious claim is true, and the believer believes something that is literally false.

Jesus told Nicodemus, "If I told you earthly things and you do not believe, how will you believe if I tell you heavenly things?" (John 3:12).[7] If we cannot trust the Word of God when it tells us about earthly things, whether it uses metaphor or figure—things we have the capacity to investigate and verify—how can we trust the Word of God when it tells about heavenly things—things we cannot verify—whether it uses metaphor or figure? We cannot verify heavenly things because Jesus said, "And no one has ascended into heaven, but He who descended from heaven: the Son of Man" (John 3:13).[8] The only means we have to know about heavenly things is what the Word of God tells us. And if we cannot trust what he tells us, then we have no means of knowing about heavenly things. No matter what Craig wants to call them, no matter what genre he uses to classify them, if the elements of biblical narrative, for example, ages of the patriarchs, is not actually true even though the text presents these ages as the actual ages of these actual people, then these individuals did not actually live these numbers of years, and the genealogy includes falsehoods. It is illegitimate to use what Craig speculates may have been the author's intent since the only access we have to the author's intent is the author's text. If we judge the genealogies to include exaggerations, or metaphors, or figures, whatever one wants to call them, the fact is, if these people did not actually live to be these ages, then we have judged the genealogies not to be literally true. And if the genealogies are not literally true, then what fundamental religious truth are they designed to communicate? The text presents these patriarchs and their ages as actual literal persons who

---

7. εἰ τὰ ἐπίγεια εἶπον ὑμῖν καὶ οὐ πιστεύετε, πῶς ἐὰν εἴπω ὑμῖν τὰ ἐπουράνια πιστεύσετε (John 3:12).

8. καὶ οὐδεὶς ἀναβέβηκεν εἰς τὸν οὐρανὸν εἰ μὴ ὁ ἐκ τοῦ οὐρανοῦ καταβάς, ὁ υἱὸς τοῦ ἀνθρώπου (John 3:13).

actually literally lived to these advanced ages, and Craig has no access to the author's intent apart from author's actual statements of the actual text.

Plasticity and Flexibility

From the research of scholars Craig provides a definition of the terms "plasticity" and "flexibility": "Plasticity has to do with the degree of synchronic variability of a myth, and flexibility with the degree of its diachronic variability."[9] So flexibility means that there may be different versions of a myth that develop over time. Plasticity means that there may be different versions of a myth that are related among a group in the same period of time. The point is that the myths do not need to be identical in order to relate what Craig refers to as a "fundamental religious truth."

Obviously the flexibility and plasticity cannot be without limits, or they are not communicating the same "fundamental religious truth." If one form of a myth tells the story that god X created mankind, and another version tells the story that mankind was not created but is eternal, this involves an A (created) ~A (not-created) contradiction. What fundamental religious truth might be communicated by these contradictory myths? Craig quotes Th. P. van Baaren; "changes in myth occur as a rule to prevent loss of function or total disappearance by changing it in such a way that it can be maintained."[10] But if the myth becomes so radically changed that it amounts to a different myth, then the original myth has lost its function and has totally disappeared. So, who sets the standard of measure for plasticity and flexibility? Who decides that a myth has changed so much that it is no longer the same myth? Who sets the limits on plasticity and flexibility? Craig asserts, "One does not bother to correct someone telling a different version of the myth, for it, too, expresses that fundamental truth."[11] But why should anyone think this to be accurate?

Craig's assertions flatly contradict what other scholars have reported. Paul Rhodes Eddy, who received his Ph.D. from Marquette University, is professor of biblical and theological studies at Bethel University. Gregory A. Boyd received his Ph.D. from Princeton Theological Seminary and is the senior pastor at Woodland Hills Church in St. Paul, Minnesota. In their book, *The Jesus Legend*, they show that recent scholarship has

9. Craig, *Adam*, 162–63.
10. Craig, *Adam*, 165.
11. Craig, *Adam*, 165.

demonstrated that oral cultures tend to be precise and accurate in recording and transmitting their traditions.

> Much of the extensive work done on the transmission of oral traditions over the last half century directly challenges the assumption held by previous scholars that orally oriented cultures tend to be indifferent to the distinction between historical and fictional narratives. The view of an increasing number who work within the interdisciplinary world of orality studies is that certain oral genre—namely historically oriented genre—not only can be, but *tend to be,* concerned about accurately transmitting recollections of their historical past. While "folklore is present," according to Richard Dorson, a folklorist who has been at the forefront of this discussion, "so is historical content." "Even more importantly," he continues, "so are historical attitudes of the traditions bearers."
>
> The anthropologist Patrick Pender-Cudlip makes the point even more forcefully. He argues that "oral tradente" (those entrusted with transmitting oral traditions) demonstrate as much concern to "receive and render a precise, accurate and authentic account of the past" as do modern literate historians: "Both consist of supposedly authentic narratives of past events, both explain and express truths about the present through stories about the past, and both use the present as a model for reconstructing the past. Regarded in this light, the differences between them are mainly technical."80
>
> Joseph Miller, a specialist on African history and oral tradition, goes so far as to describe "tellers of tales about the past in oral cultures" as "professional historians in the sense that they are conscious of history and evidence." Hence, he adds, "Oral historians are . . . no less conscious of the past than are historians in literate cultures." Similarly, Annikki Kaivola-Bregenhoj observes that oral peoples exhibit a capacity to determine whether a narrative performance is "a fictitious story or a report of something that really happened, something to be taken seriously or a tall story."[12]

Craig simply has not demonstrated that plasticity and flexibility are necessarily a part of myths. They may be found in some mythical traditions, but that does not demonstrate that they are a necessary part of myth *qua* myth. Why would the scholars whom Craig references have such contradictory conclusions to those referenced by Eddy and Boyd? It

---

12. Eddy and Boyd, *Jesus Legend*, 260–61.

is because Craig's scholars are no less subject to academic bias than any other scholars. As Eddy and Boyd point out, the fields of western folklorists and anthropologists "tended to be dominated by the pervasive, modern, academic assumption that nonliterate people, ancient and modern alike, are uncritical of ostensively historical stories and reports, and that a concern for reliable history is a rather recent development of the West."[13] No doubt the scholars to whom Eddy and Boyd appeal may certainly be influenced by their own biases. The point is, just because Craig quotes from certain scholars does not somehow validate his or their conclusions. Yet Craig does not even entertain contrary findings from other scholars or other research.

Of course it may be objected that Eddy and Boyd are discussing oral societies, whereas Craig is talking about the written literature of ANE myth. However, what has come to be written ANE myth was once oral tradition. In fact, Craig asserts,

> Dundee observes that there may be as many different versions of an oral myth as there are tellers of that myth. Although he contrasts oral myths with written myths, which he regards as fixed and stable, the stability of written myths is in fact only a matter of degree, as the evolution of the *Epic of Gilgamesh* so clearly demonstrates. The plasticity of myth is demonstrated by the variability of contemporaneous oral tellings of it, since that shows that the very tellers of the stories did not take them to have a rigidly fixed form; and a myth's flexibility is demonstrated by its evolution over time, its mutability and adaptability to new situations and challenges.[14]

In fact, recent scholarship has demonstrated that oral traditions do in fact tend to take rigidly fixed forms. It is certainly the case that there are myths that do not have a rigidly fixed form, but this is not a necessary characteristic of oral traditions or myths. So, even if we can classify Gen 1–11 as myth, it does not necessarily follow that the biblical narrative employs flexibility or plasticity.

---

13. Eddy and Boyd, *Jesus Legend*, 263.
14. Craig, *Adam*, 165.

Ancient Near Eastern Literary Evidence

Craig concludes that the data from anthropology "will always be of uncertain applicability to the stories told by ancient Israel,"[15] so he turns to ANE literary evidence: "literary evidence from ANE mythology will be more relevant. When we examine the myths of Mesopotamia and Egypt, we find the same use of figurative language, plasticity, and flexibility disclosed by the anthropological data."[16] In this section Craig discusses ANE, Mesopotamian, and Egyptian myths, giving much valuable information along with helpful analysis. Of course the goal here is to connect aspects of ancient myths with what Craig has identified as the "primaeval history" of Genesis.

He begins to make this connection by considering the reference to the word רָקִיעַ (rāqîaʿ) in Gen 1:6: "Then God said, 'Let there be an expanse in the midst of the waters, and let it separate the waters from the waters'" (Gen 1:6).[17] Craig rightly rejects the efforts to interpret the word by way of its supposed etymology. He argues, "The key to the meaning of rāqîaʿ as used in Gen 1 comes in verse 8: 'God called the rāqîaʿ Heaven (šāmāyim).' Šāmāyim is the word for skies. Rāqîaʿ thus denotes the sky or, expressing the notion of breadth, the skies."[18]

Craig refers to five places that he believes support his notion that רָקִיעַ (rāqîaʿ) denotes the sky or skies. We consider each of these:

"The heavens telling the glory of God; and the work of His hands declaring the expanse" (Ps 19:1).[19]

This verse uses the words הַשָּׁמַיִם (haššāmayim, "the heavens") and הָרָקִיעַ (hārāqîaʿ, "the expanse") in semantic parallelism, so they cannot be taken to be identical in meaning, but similar in meaning. This Psalm does not assert that the expanse means the skies. Craig seems to be unfamiliar with the nature of Hebrew poetry.

"Praise the LORD! Praise God in His sanctuary; Praise Him in the expanse of His might" (Ps 150:1).[20]

Most English translations of this verse are simply incorrect. The text does not say "in His mighty expanse" (NASB), or "the sky of his strength"

---

15. Craig, *Adam*, 165–66.
16. Craig, *Adam*, 166.
17. (Gen 1:6): וַיֹּאמֶר אֱלֹהִים יְהִי רָקִיעַ בְּתוֹךְ הַמָּיִם וִיהִי מַבְדִּיל בֵּין מַיִם לָמָיִם.
18. Craig, *Adam*, 166.
19. (Ps 19:1) הַשָּׁמַיִם מְסַפְּרִים כְּבוֹד־אֵל וּמַעֲשֵׂה יָדָיו מַגִּיד הָרָקִיעַ
20. (Ps 150:1) הַלְלוּ יָהּ הַלְלוּ־אֵל בְּקָדְשׁוֹ הַלְלוּהוּ בִּרְקִיעַ

(NET). The text says, "in the expanse of His might." The word בִּרְקִיעַ (birqîaʿ) is in the construct state, indicated by the morphology. The construct state of a word sets it in a genitive relation to the following word, expressing "of" in this instance. The lexical or absolute form is [רָקִיעַ, rāqîaʿ] with a *qamets* (ָ, ā) under the *resh* (ר, r). Here the word is not referring to the sky, but to God's expansive might. Craig does not seem to understand Hebrew syntax.

"Those who have insight will shine brightly like the brightness of the expanse, and those who lead the many to righteousness, like the stars forever and ever" (Dan 12:3).[21]

This verse does not even include the word "heaven." It simply says "the brightness of the expanse." It may mean "sky," but that cannot be derived from this verse.

The references in Ezek 1:22–26 and 10:1 simply refer to an expanse over the heads of the cherubim. Craig makes reference to this when he says that the word can indicate a "backdrop overhead."

Hence, the verses to which Craig refers actually do not support his notion that רָקִיעַ (rāqîaʿ) denotes "sky" or "skies."

There is also a verse to which Craig does not refer that is a problem for his definition: "Now from above the expanse [וּמִמַּעַל לָרָקִיעַ, ûmimmaʿal lārāqîaʿ] that was over [עַל, ʿal] their heads there was something resembling a throne, like lapis lazuli in appearance; and on that which resembled a throne, high up, was a figure with the appearance of a man" (Ezek 1:26).[22] If the word רָקִיעַ (rāqîaʿ) denotes the sky or skies, then are we to conclude that there is a sky above the sky? In fact, the word רָקִיעַ (rāqîaʿ) simply denotes an expanse, a wide extent, or widely spread out area.

This meaning is supported by the expression that occurs in Gen 1:14, 15, 17, and 20: בִּרְקִיעַ הַשָּׁמַיִם, "in the expanse of the heavens" (birqîaʿ haššāmayim). Since the word הַשָּׁמַיִם (haššāmayim) means "the heavens" or "the skies," if one takes בִּרְקִיעַ (birqîaʿ) to denote "in the sky of" or "in the skies of," then one is left with a meaningless repetition, "in the sky of the skies." Rather, the word רָקִיעַ (rāqîaʿ) simply refers to the expanse, the widely spread out area, in this case referring to the expansive heavens.

---

21. וְהַמַּשְׂכִּלִים יַזְהִרוּ כְּזֹהַר הָרָקִיעַ וּמַצְדִּיקֵי הָרַבִּים כַּכּוֹכָבִים לְעוֹלָם וָעֶד׃ (Dan 12:3)

22. וּמִמַּעַל לָרָקִיעַ אֲשֶׁר עַל־רֹאשָׁם כְּמַרְאֵה אֶבֶן־סַפִּיר דְּמוּת כִּסֵּא וְעַל דְּמוּת הַכִּסֵּא דְּמוּת כְּמַרְאֵה אָדָם עָלָיו מִלְמָעְלָה׃
(Ezek 1:26)

Waters Above

Some have argued that the waters above the expanse was a collection of water that surrounded the entire earth serving as a shield to sustain a temperate climate over the surface of the earth. It is argued that this collection of water fell to the earth supplying the water for the worldwide flood (see **Figure 14** below). Of course there is no evidence for such a state, and among most natural scientists it is considered implausible, but it does have the merit of accounting for the descriptions of creation of the waters above and below separated by an expanse, and the source of the flood waters.[23]

Craig argues that the waters above can be thought of as rain:

> As for the role of the rāqîaʿ in separating the waters above from the waters below, the waters above are plausibly thought to be the rain that falls from the skies. Although some scholars have alleged that ancient Israelites thought that water fell to the earth through sluice gates of some sort in the solid dome above (the so-called windows of heaven), such a wooden literalism is utterly implausible. Water falling through such an opening would appear as a destructive cataract plunging to the earth, not as rain. But in the flood story we are told, "the windows of the heavens were opened. And rain fell upon the earth forty days and forty nights" (Gen 7:11–12; cf. 8:2).[24]

Of course, there is no statement in the text that requires the waters from above to fall as one "destructive cataract plunging to the earth." We are expected to believe that God created the universe out of nothing, but God could not cause a water canopy to fall as rain rather than as a destructive downpour. Additionally, John Whitcomb has shown that referring to the waters above as rain clouds is in fact implausible:

---

23. Whitcomb argues, "If a vapor canopy of such magnitude existed from the second day of creation week to the time of the Flood, then climatic conditions must have been quite different from those we observe today. In the first place, it is probable that it never rained until the time of the Flood (cf. Hebrews 11:7—"things not seen as yet"), and that throughout the entire antediluvian age "there went up a mist from the earth, and watered the whole face of the ground" (Gen 2:5–6).

Secondly, there were no great variations in the climate in different parts of the earth because of the greenhouse effect of the vapor canopy.28 Not until after these waters fell to earth are we told of great winds (8:1), which would imply significant temperature differences between equatorial and polar regions for the first time. In these polar regions, where tropical plants and animals once lived in abundance, huge masses of snow and ice suddenly began to accumulate." Whitcomb, *The World That Perished*, 34.

24. Craig, *Adam*, 190.

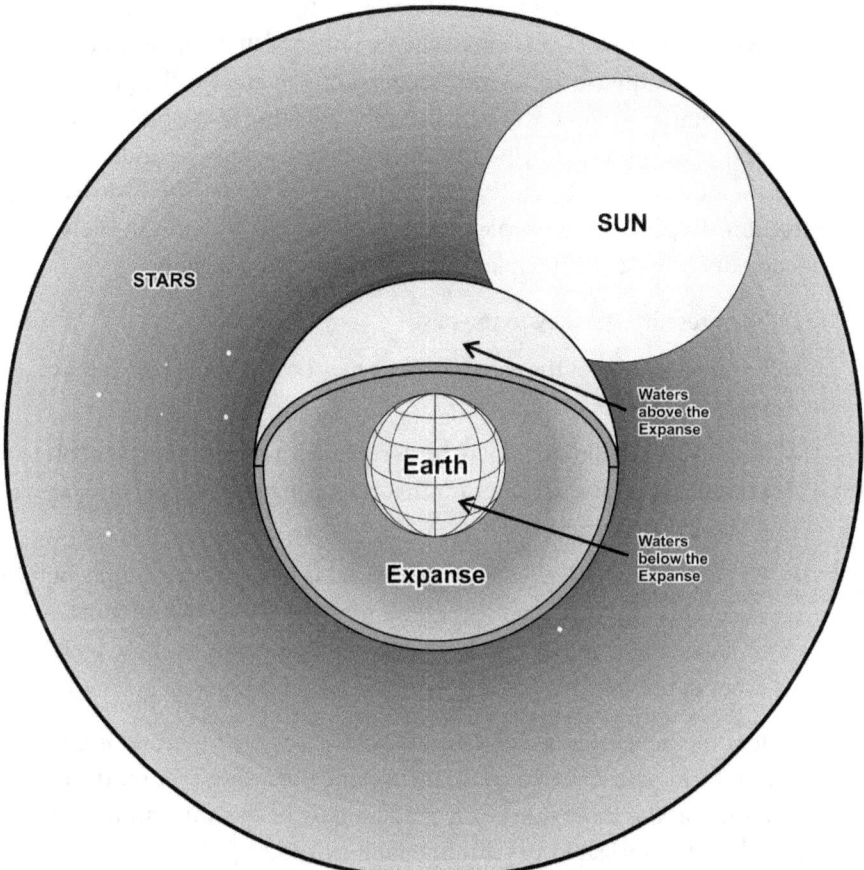

Figure 14: Waters Above and Below

Most commentators tend to interpret "the waters which were above the firmament" of Gen 1:7 simply in terms of rain clouds because of a tacit assumption that present atmospheric conditions have continued, basically unchanged, since creation. However, this concept is in serious conflict with the plain statement of Gen 7:11–12, that "the windows of heaven were opened. And the rain was upon the earth forty days and forty nights." This can refer to nothing less than the collapse of a stupendous transparent vapor canopy that existed only during the antediluvian period, for it required *six weeks* for this water to pour down upon the earth. By contrast, if all the water vapor and clouds in the present atmosphere were precipitated to earth, the rain would last only a few hours and would produce an average depth of less than two inches.[25]

---

25. Whitcomb, *World that Perished*, 33–34.

The proposal that the waters above refer to the rain is entirely implausible, and Craig's claims about the meaning of רָקִיעַ (rāqîaʿ) do not stand up to scrutiny. In fact, Craig seems subtly to employ the principle of uniformitarianism in order to explain the meaning of the biblical text. Uniformitarianism is the belief that ancient history must be understood in terms of the absolute uniformity of nature such that the historian's present is the grid through which one accepts or rejects claims in ancient documents. The basic principles of uniformitarianism include:

- The present is the key to the past.
- Former changes of the earth's surface may be explained by reference to causes now in action.
- The history of the earth may be deciphered in terms of present observations, on the assumption that physical and chemical laws are invariant with time.
- Not only are physical laws uniform, that is invariant with time, but the events of the geologic past have proceeded at an approximately uniform rate, and have involved the same processes as those which occur at present.[26]

It is the belief that natural events have always followed an immutable, uniform pattern. As a consequence one must interpret on the assumption that the Bible must be a product only of the uniform natural, cultural, and historical forces throughout history.

Uniformitarianism was developed in the discipline of geology by James Hutton (1726–97), a Scottish geologist, chemist, naturalist, and originator of one of the fundamental principles of geology. Hutton argued that in order for geology to become a science it need not only be an empirical theory *unencumbered by divine interference*. As Hutton says in one place,

> I flatter myself, that when the Chevalier de Dolomieu, who has employed his uncommon talents in examining and elucidating the effects of fire in the bowels of those burning mountains, shall consider and examine the effects of time upon the surface of the earth, he will be ready to adopt my opinion, that there is no occasion to have recourse to any unknown cause, in explaining appearances which are every where to be found, although not

---

26. Song and An, "Critique of the Principle of Uniformitarianism," 76.

always attended with such remarkable circumstances as those with which his labours have enriched natural history.[27]

In his book, *Principles of Geology: Being an Inquiry How Far the Former Changes of the Earth's Surface are Referable to Causes Now in Operation*, Sir Charles Lyell, (1797–1875), also a Scottish geologist, developed Hutton's theory into what is known today as uniformitarianism:

> The establishment, from time to time, of numerous points of identification, drew at length from geologists a reluctant admission, that there was more correspondence between the physical constitution of the globe, and more uniformity in the laws regulating the changes of its surface, from the most remote eras to the present, than they at first imagined. If, in this state of the science, they still despaired of reconciling every class of geological phenomena to the operations of ordinary causes, even by straining analogy to the utmost limits of credibility, we might have expected, at least, that the balance of probability would now have been presumed to incline towards the identity of the causes. But, after repeated experience of the failure of attempts to speculate on different classes of geological phenomena, as belonging to a distinct order of things, each new sect persevered systematically in the principles adopted by their predecessors. They invariably began, as each new problem presented itself, whether relating to the animate or inanimate world, to assume in their theories, that the economy of nature was formerly governed by rules for the most part independent of those now established. Whether they endeavored to account for the origin of certain igneous rocks, or to explain the forces which elevated hills or excavated valleys, or the causes which led to the extinction of certain races of animals, they first presupposed an original and dissimilar order of nature; and when at length they approximated, or entirely came round to an opposite opinion, it was always with the feeling, that they conceded what they were justified *à priori* in deeming improbable. In a word, the same men who, as natural philosophers, would have been most incredulous respecting any extraordinary deviations from the known course of nature, if reported to have happened *in their own time*, were equally disposed, as geologists, to expect the proofs of such deviations at every period of the past.[28]

Uniformitarianism actually commits the fallacy of *petitio principii*, or Begging the Question. This fallacy is committed when

---

27. Hutton, *Theory of the Earth*, 510–11.
28. Lyell, *Principles of Geology*, 1.124–25.

the conclusion is smuggled into the evidence that is purported to provide reasons for the conclusion. Ho Jang Song and Hui Soo An have shown that, "Although uniformitarianism is widely recognized as the basic principle upon which the structure of historical geology has been erected, a closer investigation on the basis of present scientific knowledge and the philosophy of science reveals some of its invalid aspects."[29]

Steven Boyd and Andrew A. Snelling give a helpful characterization of uniformitarianism with reference to the Genesis flood:

> The turning point in relation to the overthrow of the Genesis Flood has (sic) having any relevance to geology was the work of James Hutton (1788, 1795) and Charles Lyell (1830–833). By 1850 the rout was complete. The ruling paradigm in geology had become uniformitarianism, the belief in the uniformity of natural processes in space and time, or the present is the key to past, as being the *only* tool for interpreting the earth's past history. If there had been a Genesis Flood, it must have been tranquil or local, as it apparently left no evidence and was therefore irrelevant to the earth sciences.[30]

Although Craig subtly employs a uniformitarian assumption, he attempts to overthrow the notion of a worldwide flood by appeal to ANE myth.

Plasticity and Flexibility of Ancient Near Eastern Myths

Craig presents analyses and arguments to show that ANE myths were not intended to be taken literally: "All this has been said with respect to the metaphoricalness of many ANE myths. Not only does the metaphorical and figurative language of ANE myths support a nonliteral reading of such myths, but their plasticity and flexibility also indicate that they are not best interpreted literally."[31] Throughout this section Craig provides some interesting analysis of the plasticity and flexibility of ANE myths. He concludes this section, "The language of myth is figurative and therefore need not be taken literally."[32] Of course, Craig wants to show that, since

---

29. Song and An, "Critique of the Principle of Uniformitarianism," 75.
30. Boyd and Snelling, "Profit of the Venture," 21.
31. Craig, *Adam*, 191.
32. Craig, *Adam*, 198.

ANE myths were not intended to be taken literally, then the narrative of Gen 1–11 should likewise be taken as metaphorical. He attempts to do this in the next section.

Application to Genesis 1–11

Craig begins with the guarded statement, "If Gen 1–11 functions as mytho-history, then these chapters need not be read literalistically."[33] Craig stipulates, "Some of the accounts, such as the origin and fall of man, are clearly metaphorical or figurative in nature, featuring as they do a humanoid deity incompatible with the transcendent God of the creation story. Others, as we have seen, would be fantastic, even to the author himself, if taken literally."[34] We have already shown in chapter 5 that Craig does not understand the language of the fall narrative. God is not depicted as a humanoid deity. Rather, the description depicts God as the judge coming to hold the couple accountable for their actions. The text does not present God as walking around in the garden. In fact, the text presents the scene as a literal storm, a sign of God's coming to judge. The descriptions are designed to show the separation that exists between God and the couple.

However, even if we take the description as depicting a humanoid deity, we see the same kind of depictions in other places in the Pentateuch. Genesis 32 describes Jacob wrestling with a man (אִישׁ, 'îš): "24 Then Jacob was left alone, and a man wrestled with him until daybreak. 25 When he saw that he had not prevailed against him, he touched the socket of his thigh; so the socket of Jacob's thigh was dislocated while he wrestled with him" (Gen 32:24–25).[35] The next morning Jacob builds an altar and calls it פְּנִיאֵל, (pĕnî'ēl), because he says, "I have seen God face to face, yet my life has been preserved" (Gen 32:30; H31).[36] The man with whom Jacob wrestled was an appearance of the pre-incarnate Christ in the form of a man.

---

33. Craig, *Adam*, 198.
34. Craig, *Adam*, 198.
35. 25 וַיִּוָּתֵר יַעֲקֹב לְבַדּוֹ וַיֵּאָבֵק אִישׁ עִמּוֹ עַד עֲלוֹת הַשָּׁחַר׃ 26 וַיַּרְא כִּי לֹא יָכֹל לוֹ וַיִּגַּע בְּכַף־יְרֵכוֹ וַתֵּקַע כַּף־יֶרֶךְ יַעֲקֹב בְּהֵאָבְקוֹ עִמּוֹ׃
(Gen H32:25–26)
36. (Gen 32:30 H31): כִּי־רָאִיתִי אֱלֹהִים פָּנִים אֶל־פָּנִים וַתִּנָּצֵל נַפְשִׁי׃

On Mt. Sinai God appeared in a cloud, yet the elders could look up toward the cloud and see God's feet: "⁹ Then Moses went up with Aaron, Nadab and Abihu, and seventy of the elders of Israel, ¹⁰ and they saw the God of Israel; and under His feet [רַגְלָיו, raglāyw] there appeared to be a pavement of sapphire, as clear as the sky itself" (Exod 24:9–10)."[37] These are all figures of speech. But what Craig is attempting to do is to extrapolate from these figures to the conclusion that the account is itself a metaphor or figure and not to be taken as a literal event. On this basis should we conclude that the account of Jacob is only a metaphor, or that the giving of Torah on Sinai is a metaphor? Of course, Craig would argue that the account of the appearance of God in the garden is part of the primaeval, mytho-history, and therefore the entire account should be taken as metaphor. But he has not proven this to be the case.

But it does not follow that because aspects of the account are figurative that the entire account is therefore not to be taken literally. Do we not use figurative expressions to describe events that actually, literally occurred? In a car race, does not the winner often say to the loser, "You ate my dust"? This figurative expression is used to describe an actual event, and the use of figurative language does not mean that event should not be taken literally. Craig has conflated the use of figurative language with myth. Craig has still failed to make the case that Gen 1–11 is mytho-history. In fact, the method Craig is using is to identify the various metaphorical elements of the text of Gen 1–11, compare them with what he takes to be similarities with ANE literary evidence, and conclude that Gen 1–11 is mytho-history and therefore not to be taken literally. But this line of reasoning is faulty. Similarities do not constitute identity. It is illegitimate to conclude that because Genesis includes metaphors and figures, and ANE literature includes what seem to be similar metaphors and figures, that they must be the same kind of literature, i.e., genre.

Craig questions the validity of the tradition-historical analyses of the flood account, but he goes on to assert, "On the other hand, the *prima facie* inconsistencies between the order of events in the creation account and the account of the creation of mankind suggest that the pentateuchal author would not have been overly concerned about relating events in a somewhat different order, so long as the central theological truths are

---

37. ⁹ וַיַּעַל מֹשֶׁה וְאַהֲרֹן נָדָב וַאֲבִיהוּא וְשִׁבְעִים מִזִּקְנֵי יִשְׂרָאֵל: ¹⁰ וַיִּרְאוּ אֵת אֱלֹהֵי יִשְׂרָאֵל וְתַחַת רַגְלָיו כְּמַעֲשֵׂה לִבְנַת הַסַּפִּיר וּכְעֶצֶם הַשָּׁמַיִם לָטֹהַר:
(Exod 24:9–10)

faithfully expressed."[38] But we have already shown that what Craig takes to be inconsistencies in the order of events in the creation account stems from his lack of understanding the basic grammar and syntax of the language. Since there are no inconsistencies between the order of events in the creation account, it does not follow that the author was not overly concerned about relating events in a somewhat different order. Additionally, relating things in a different order is not necessarily an inconsistency if the author does not stipulate that different arrangements were each in the correct order. Many events in life occur simultaneously, but an author cannot report them simultaneously. The author must report one event and then another. When an author reports events that actually occurred simultaneously, he might report them in different places in different orders. But if the author does not claim that each of the orders was the actual order in which the events occurred, it is not an inconsistency. Craig is reading into the text what he wants to find there. He is relying only on English translations, and he does not seem to understand the underlying Hebrew grammar and syntax. As a result, Craig cannot recognize his own inconsistencies.

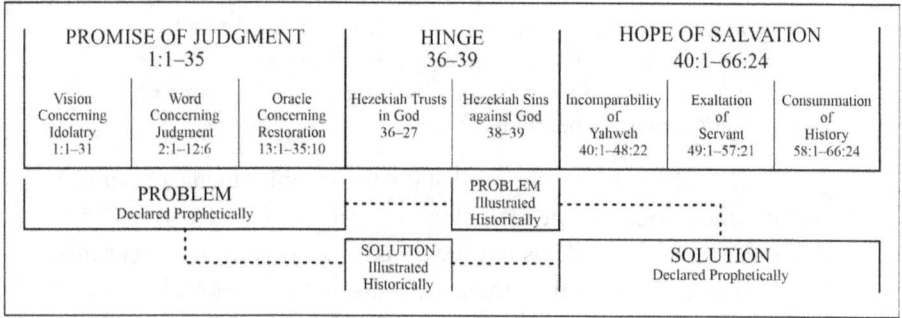

Figure 15: Thematic Structure of Isaiah

Take for example the historical accounts contained in the book of Isaiah, chapters 36–39. The events reported in chapters 36 and 37 actually happened after the events reported in chapters 38–39. We know this to be the case because of extra-biblical historical records. However, Isaiah does not claim that he has reported these events in the order in which they actually occurred. Isaiah has arranged the material in thematic order (see **Figure 15** above).

---

38. Craig, *Adam*, 199.

It is characteristic of biblical authors to arrange material in thematic order. If an author does not claim that a given order is *the* actual order in which the events occurred, then different orders that are arranged thematically are not inconsistencies. Craig's claim about the order of events in the creation account is simply wrong.

In a footnote Craig argues against the notion that the appearance of God in Gen 2–3 is a theophany:

> The anthropomorphic descriptions of God in chaps. 2–3 are not plausibly taken to be a theophany of God in human form, such as we have in God's appearance to Abraham in Gen 18, as suggested by John D. Currid, "Theistic Evolution Is Incompatible with the Teachings of the Old Testament," in *Theistic Evolution: A Scientific, Philosophical, and Theological Critique*, ed. J. P. Moreland et al. (Wheaton: Crossway, 2017), 858. For (1) the language of theophany is missing from chaps. 2–3, in contrast to Gen 18, which begins, "And the Lord appeared to him by the oaks of Mamre, as he sat at the door of his tent in the heat of the day. He lifted up his eyes and looked, and behold, three men stood in front of him" (vv. 1–2). And (2), crucially, God is described anthropomorphically in chaps. 2–3 even when *not* appearing to Adam, as in the story of God's fashioning Adam from the dust of the earth and breathing into his nostrils the breath of life, or as in the story of God's building Eve from Adam's rib while Adam is unconscious.[39]

First, we have already shown that the theophanic language is in fact present in the account of God searching for Adam in the garden. As we have shown above, Jeffrey Niehaus has presented a convincing argument that the appearance of God in the garden is the first of the series of theophanic appearances. Craig simply does not know the Hebrew language.

Second, that God is described anthropomorphically when creating Adam and when taking a rib from his side does not indicate that the appearance of God in the garden cannot be a theophany. That is simply a category mistake. God can be described anthropomorphically when appearing in a theophany and when not appearing in a theophany. Anthropomorphic language does not require either the presence of a theophany nor does it require the absence of one. In fact, the description, "They heard the sound of the LORD God going back and forth in the garden in the wind of the storm" is quite comparable to the statement in Gen 18:1,

---

39. Craig, *Adam*, 199.

"And the Lord appeared to him . . ." Craig has simply read into the text what he wants to find there.

Again Craig completely misses the significance of the events described in the text. He asserts, "When God takes one of the sleeping Adam's ribs, closes up the flesh, and builds a woman out of it, the story sounds like a physical surgery that God performs on Adam followed by his building a woman out of the extracted body part."[40] In chapter 5 we have already considered the theological significance of the imagery in this description, an aspect that Craig completely misses.

Craig asserts, "Similarly, given God's bodily presence in the garden, the conversations between God and the protagonists in the story of the fall read like a dialogue between persons physically present to one another."[41] God spoke to Moses as one would speak to a friend: "The LORD would speak to Moses face to face, the way a person speaks to a friend. Then Moses would return to the camp, but his servant, Joshua son of Nun, a young man, did not leave the tent" (Exod 33:11).[42] God knew Moses face to face: "Since that time no prophet has risen in Israel like Moses, whom the LORD knew face to face [פָּנִים אֶל־פָּנִים, pānîm ʾel pānîm]" (Deut 34:10).[43] That the garden narrative presents God as engaging in a dialogue between persons physically present to one another does not qualify this as mytho-history. Are we to think that God *could not* talk to Adam, Eve, the serpent, or Moses as if physically present? It is in fact Craig's characterizations that are "incompatible with the transcendent God of the creation story." Again Craig is conflating figures of speech with myth.

Craig declares, "Moreover, we have seen that many features of these stories are fantastic—that is to say, palpably false if taken literally. Previously, we used this fact as an earmark to identify narratives as myths. But now we limit our consideration to features of the narrative that the author himself would have plausibly thought fantastic."[44] From where does Craig get the information about the biblical author plausibly thinking that these features were fantastic? There is nothing in the biblical text that indicates

---

40. Craig, *Adam*, 199–200.

41. Craig, *Adam*, 200.

42. וְדִבֶּר יְהוָה אֶל־מֹשֶׁה פָּנִים אֶל־פָּנִים כַּאֲשֶׁר יְדַבֵּר אִישׁ אֶל־רֵעֵהוּ וְשָׁב אֶל־הַמַּחֲנֶה וּמְשָׁרְתוֹ יְהוֹשֻׁעַ בִּן־נוּן נַעַר לֹא יָמִישׁ מִתּוֹךְ הָאֹהֶל׃
(Exod 33:11)

43. וְלֹא־קָם נָבִיא עוֹד בְּיִשְׂרָאֵל כְּמֹשֶׁה אֲשֶׁר יְדָעוֹ יְהוָה פָּנִים אֶל־פָּנִים (Deut 34:10)

44. Craig, *Adam*, 200.

this or even implies this. Craig is imposing his own conclusion on the biblical authors. This is particularly illegitimate since we have demonstrated that not one of the features Craig claims to be fantastic has been convincingly demonstrated to be fantastic. Craig builds on suppositions, built on speculations, built on assumptions which he now takes to be fact.

Craig claims, "In light of chapter 1's affirmation that God had separated the waters above from the waters below, it is hard to believe that the author thought that there was ever a time when the earth was devoid of rain."[45] Just because it is hard for Craig to believe that the author thought that there was ever a time when the earth was devoid of rain does not show that it is hard to believe in itself. Craig's assertion is predicated on his interpretation that the waters above are rain, a view that is wildly implausible. Why should anyone think that the biblical author did not think that there was a time when there was no rain? In fact, the text specifically states that there was a time when there was no rain:

> "⁵ Now no shrub of the field had yet grown on the earth, and no plant of the field had yet sprouted. Because the LORD God had not caused it to rain on the earth, and there was no man to cultivate the ground, ⁶ springs would well up from the earth and water the whole surface of the ground." (Gen 2:5–6).[46]

Of course, again we must deal with the pesky and annoying matter of the Hebrew text. Most English translations lead the reader to suppose that the reason the shrubs and plants had not begun to sprout is because God had not caused rain nor was there a man to cultivate the ground. But this is not what this verse is saying. The verse is saying that the shrubs and plants had not begun to sprout, and because (כִּי, kî) God had not caused rain to fall, nor was there a man to cultivate the ground, springs would well up to water the earth so that the shrubs and plants would begin to grow and sprout. In other words, the reason springs would go up to water the ground is because God had not caused the rain to fall and because there was not man to cultivate the ground. One can understand why it is hard for Craig to believe this, given his unacknowledged commitment to uniformitarianism and his lack of facility in the Hebrew text.

---

45. Craig, *Adam*, 200.

46. ⁵ וְכֹל שִׂיחַ הַשָּׂדֶה טֶרֶם יִהְיֶה בָאָרֶץ וְכָל־עֵשֶׂב הַשָּׂדֶה טֶרֶם יִצְמָח כִּי לֹא הִמְטִיר יְהוָה אֱלֹהִים עַל־הָאָרֶץ וְאָדָם אַיִן לַעֲבֹד אֶת־הָאֲדָמָה: ⁶ וְאֵד יַעֲלֶה מִן־הָאָרֶץ וְהִשְׁקָה אֶת־כָּל־פְּנֵי־הָאֲדָמָה: (Gen 2:5–6)

Craig continues, "Just as the waters below took the form of seas and rivers and springs, so the waters above took the form of rain. So an earth replete with seas and rivers and springs, but without rain, seems fantastic, even for an ancient Israelite, given his knowledge of the water cycle."[47] Of course the seas and rivers is not a problem since, according to the text, the springs would well up and water the whole surface of the ground (כָּל־פְּנֵי־הָאֲדָמָה, kāl pĕnê hā'ăḏāmāh, lit. "all the face of the ground"). And we have already shown that to identify the waters above as rain is wildly implausible.

Again Craig supposes he knows what the biblical author would have thought to be fantastic: "In addition, the idea of an arboretum containing trees bearing fruit that, if eaten, would confer immortality or yield sudden knowledge of good and evil must have seemed fantastic to the pentateuchal author."[48] We have already shown that Craig's lack of facility in the language has led him to the incorrect conclusion that the fruit of the tree would yield "sudden knowledge of good and evil." But why would the biblical author think it fantastic that eating the fruit of the tree of life would confer immortality? Is not God capable of doing this? Craig reminds his reader, "Recall that we are not dealing here with miraculous fruit, as if God would, on the occasion of eating, supernaturally impose on the eater immortality or knowledge of good and evil against God's will."[49] Ignoring again Craig's misunderstanding of the tree of the knowledge, good and evil, as we have shown back in chapter 1, why should anyone think that the fruit of the tree of life imparting life would not be a miraculous act of God? As we have already pointed out the tree of life is referred to in Revelation as imparting life:

> He who has an ear, let him hear what the Spirit says to the churches. To him who overcomes, I will grant to eat of the tree of life which is in the Paradise of God (Rev 2:7).[50]
>
> ¹ Then he showed me a river of the water of life, clear as crystal, coming from the throne of God and of the Lamb, ² in the middle of its street. On either side of the river was the tree of life [ξύλον ζωῆς, xulon zōēs], bearing twelve kinds of fruit, yielding its fruit

---

47. Craig, *Adam*, 200.
48. Craig, *Adam*, 200.
49. Craig, *Adam*, 200.
50. ὁ ἔχων οὖς ἀκουσάτω τί τὸ πνεῦμα λέγει ταῖς ἐκκλησίαις. τῷ νικῶντι δώσω αὐτῷ φαγεῖν ἐκ τοῦ ξύλου τῆς ζωῆς, ὅ ἐστιν ἐν τῷ παραδείσῳ τοῦ θεοῦ (Rev. 2:7).

150　A Critique of William Lane Craig's *In Quest of the Historical Adam*

> every month; and the leaves of the tree were for the healing of the nations (Rev 22:1-2).[51]

> Blessed are those who awash their robes, so that they may have the right to the tree of life, and may center by the gates into the city (Rev 22:14).[52]

Figure 16: Plate 163

Of course Craig would respond that he is saying that these figures and metaphors are fantastic and palpably false if taken literally. It certainly may be the case that the references to the tree of life in Revelation are symbolic of the life that one gains by being born again, but that something can be symbolic does not preclude it also being actually historical. The biblical author seems to have a better grasp of the transcendent God than does Craig. But it does not follow that these symbolic expressions do not refer to some literal thing or person. Just because something is symbolic does not mean it cannot also be literal. Again Craig is conflating

---

51. ¹ καὶ ἔδειξέν μοι ποταμὸν ὕδατος ζωῆς λαμπρὸν ὡς κρύσταλλον, ἐκπορευόμενον ἐκ τοῦ θρόνου τοῦ θεοῦ καὶ τοῦ ἀρνιου. ² ἐν μέσῳ τῆς πλατείας αὐτῆς καὶ τοῦ ποταμοῦ ἐντεῦθεν καὶ ἐκεῖθεν ξύλον ζωῆς ποιοῦν καρποὺς δώδεκα, κατὰ μῆνα ἕκαστον ἀποδιδοῦν τὸν καρπὸν αὐτοῦ, καὶ τὰ φύλλα τοῦ ξύλου εἰς θεραπείαν τῶν ἐθνῶν (Rev. 22:1-2).

52. Μακάριοι οἱ πλύνοντες τὰς στολὰς αὐτῶν, ἵνα ἔσται ἡ ἐξουσία αὐτῶν ἐπὶ τὸ ξύλον τῆς ζωῆς καὶ τοῖς πυλῶσιν εἰσέλθωσιν εἰς τὴν πόλιν (Rev 22:14).

figure and symbolism with myth. Babylon was an actual city that actually existed in the actual ancient near east. Babylon housed one of the wonders of the ancient world, the hanging gardens. The Euphrates river flowed through the city. The description is designed to connect Babyon with Eden. Yet Babylon is also symbolic of the false Eden; the place on this world that offers life, but inside are dead men's bones. Remember that the name 'Babel' is the same name translated "Babylon." Babel/Babylon is the place where mankind attempted to set themselves to be god(s). In Eden, the tree of life was an actually existing tree that is also symbolic of life that comes to those who trust and obey God. The tree of the knowledge, good and evil, was an actual tree that was also symbolic of separation from God to all those who seek to be independent from God's authority, to become as God. Craig is completely unaware of this imagery and the significance of these places and events.

Figure 17: Plate 165

Craig again reveals his lack of understanding the narrative relating to the serpent:

> Then there is the notorious snake in the garden. He makes for a great character in the story, conniving, sinister, opposed to God, perhaps a symbol of evil, but not plausibly a literal reptile such as one might encounter in one's own garden, for the pentateuchal

author knew that snakes neither talk nor are intelligent agents. Again, the snake's personality and speech cannot be attributed to the miraculous activity of God, lest God become the author of the fall.[53]

Craig does not seem to grasp the significance of the biblical imagery. The word נָחָשׁ (nāḥāš) can certainly be used to refer to what we think of as a snake, but it has other uses also, as we have shown. Simply because the word is used to refer to a snake does not mean that it must always refer to a snake. Craig has committed the fallacy that James Barr called, "illegitimate totality transfer." It is an instance of a Platonic view of language; a meaning of a word exists such that every occurrence of the word participates in that meaning, and the meaning is transferred into every context in which the word occurs. Whatever form the נָחָשׁ (nāḥāš) took prior to the curse, he is cursed by God so that the description resembles snake: "Cursed are you more than all cattle, and more than every beast of the field; on your belly you will go, and dust you will eat all the days of your life; (Gen 3:14).[54] However, the curse does not say that the נָחָשׁ (nāḥāš) was a snake or was turned into a snake. Snakes as we know them cannot converse with humans so as to deceive them. Snakes as we know them do not eat dust. A snake would not have been able to understand the curse that was being pronounced upon it. The seed of the נָחָשׁ (nāḥāš) is cursed, and the snake becomes a symbol of the cursed נָחָשׁ (nāḥāš). But because the imagery of a snake is a symbol does not mean that the נָחָשׁ (nāḥāš) was not an actually existing entity of some sort.

Craig declares the cheribum to be fantasy and symbol:

> When God drives Adam and Eve from the garden and posts cherubim and a flashing sword at its entrance to block their reentry, this is doubtless not intended to be literal, since cherubim were regarded as creatures of fantasy and symbol. It is not as though the author thought—what realism requires—that the cherubim remained at the entrance of the garden for years on end until it was either overgrown with weeds or swept away by the flood.[55]

---

53. Craig, *Adam*, 200.

54. וַיֹּאמֶר יְהוָה אֱלֹהִים אֶל־הַנָּחָשׁ כִּי עָשִׂיתָ זֹּאת אָרוּר אַתָּה מִכָּל־הַבְּהֵמָה וּמִכֹּל חַיַּת הַשָּׂדֶה עַל־גְּחֹנְךָ תֵלֵךְ וְעָפָר תֹּאכַל כָּל־יְמֵי חַיֶּיךָ׃
(Gen 3:14)

55. Craig, *Adam*, 201.

Craig takes the biblical cherubim to have been "composed of a lion's body, a bird's wings, and a man's head" and "were not thought to be real beings but fantasies." Craig gets this information from Nahum M. Sarna. However, Sarna's attempt to equate biblical cherubim with the beings referred to in Genesis fails. Sarna argues, "The name [cherubim] would appear to be connected with the *kuribu*, the Akkadian term often applied to the composite figures—man-headed bulls with eagles' wings—that frequently stood outside Mesopotamian temples. These are highly reminiscent of the descriptions of Ezekiel 1:6–11 and 10:14."[56] However, the composite figures that stood outside Mesopotamian temples do not at all fit the description of the cherubim in Ezekiel. In Ezekiel's vision there were four living beings, each having human form, each with four faces and four wings. Each being had four faces; the face of a man, the face of a lion, the face of a bull, and the face of an eagle. Craig references two plates from James B. Pritchard's text, *The Ancient Near East: An Anthology of Texts and Pictures*, plates 163 and 165 (see **Figure 16** and **Figure 17** above).[57] Neither one of these resemble the cherubim as they are described in the biblical text.

Even if it can be demonstrated beyond speculation that the Hebrew word כְּרוּב (kĕrûḇ) is connected with the Akkadian word *kuribu*, it does not necessarily follow that the Hebrew word would have the same meaning or referential significance as the Akkadian word. The Hebrew word נָחָשׁ (nāḥāš, "serpent") may be connected to the Aramaic word נְחָשׁ (nāḥāš), which means "bronze," but it does not follow that the Hebrew word means "bronze." The English word "nice" came from Latin through an Old French word that meant "silly, simple." According to the *Concise Oxford English Dictionary*, "The word **nice** entered Middle English in the sense 'stupid,' from Latin *nescius*, meaning 'ignorant.'"[58] Simply because words may be historically connected does not mean that the words necessarily have the same meaning or the same connotation or denotation.

There is nothing in the Old Testament that indicates that the people of Israel thought of the cherubim as "creatures of fantasy and symbol." Also, the fact that some entity can be a symbol does not mean that it must also be a fantasy. Particularly in the book of Isaiah, Babylon becomes a symbol of the false Eden, but it was also an actual city that existed in the

---

56. Sarna, *Genesis*, 375.

57. Pritchard, ed., *Ancient Near East*, 158

58. *Concise Oxford English Dictionary* (2004), s.v. "nice."

ancient world. The serpent becomes a symbol of Satan, but serpents are also actually existing creatures. Craig is reading into the biblical text what he has taken from ANE myth.

Central Truths

Craig constructs a list of what he takes to be "some of the central truths expressed in the primaeval history:"

1. God is one, a personal, transcendent Creator of all physical reality, perfectly good and worthy of worship.
2. God has designed the physical world and is the ultimate source of its structure and life-forms.
3. Man is the pinnacle of the physical creation, a personal, if finite, agent like God, and therefore uniquely capable of all Earth's creatures of knowing God.
4. Mankind is gendered, man and woman being of equal value, with marriage given to mankind for procreation and mutuality, the wife being a helper to her husband.
5. Work is good, a sacred assignment by God to mankind to steward the earth and its creatures.
6. Human exploration and discovery of the workings of nature are a natural outgrowth of mans' capacities, rather than divine bestowals without human initiative and effort.
7. Mankind is to set apart one day per week as sacred and for refreshment from work.
8. Man and woman alike have freely chosen to disobey God, suffering alienation from God and spiritual death as their just desert, condemned to a life of hardship and suffering during this mortal existence.
9. Human sin is agglomerative and self-destructive, resulting in God's just judgment.
10. Despite human rebellion against God, God's original purpose to bless all mankind remains intact, as he graciously finds a way to work his will despite human defiance.[59]

59. Craig, *Adam*, 201–2.

There is a serious problem with these "truths." If the "primaeval history" is not intended to be taken literally, then none of the events recorded or the words reported actually, literally occurred the way they are presented in the text. Since they are about things that did not actually occur, then why should anyone believe that these "truths" are actually telling us anything that is actually true? These are just stories, like Aesop's fables or ANE myths. If we can glean these "truths" from the myths of Gen 1–11, then should we likewise glean "truths" from ANE myths, or Aesop's fables? Readers may glean morals from stories—"the moral of the story is . . ."—but that does not mean that these morals tell us anything that is necessarily true. Since the creation account is not to be taken literally, then the text is not telling us anything about God actually creating the universe. It also follows that any place in the Bible in which an author appeals to the creation account is based on a text that is not literally true. It seems to follow, then, that a biblical author's appeal to an account that is not based in any actual, literal events would tend to undermine the validity and the truth of the author's own assertions.

Let us consider these points.

1. "God is one, a personal, transcendent Creator of all physical reality, perfectly good and worthy of worship." Of course one can get this truth from other parts of the Bible. So, we have this mythological story about Elohim creating the heavens and the earth. It is not intended to be taken literally, so what are we to take from this account? Assume for the sake of argument that we have not learned about God from other parts of the Bible. Since the creation account is not to be taken literally, then the account is simply a story, but it doesn't teach me anything that I should think is literally true about God any more than what ANE myth presents should be taken to be literally true about the gods depicted in them. And remember, Jesus said that if we cannot trust him, that is, his word, about earthly matters, then how can we believe him, that is, his word, when it tells us about God? So, Craig's "truth" does not literally come from Gen 1. If the text is not telling us about an actual, literal Adam, then why should we take it to be telling us about an actual, literal God? He is reading into this mythological story his already assumed theology, and he continues to conflate metaphor and figure with myth.

2. "God has designed the physical world and is the ultimate source of its structure and life-forms." If the creation account is not to be taken literally, then it does not tell us that God actually did design the physical world or that he is its ultimate source. Once again, these truths can be found in

other parts of Scripture. Craig is in fact taking what he has learned from other parts of Scripture and imposing it upon the Genesis account, an account that he says should not be taken literally.

3. "Man is the pinnacle of the physical creation, a personal, if finite, agent like God, and therefore uniquely capable of all Earth's creatures of knowing God." That man is the pinnacle of the physical creation is certainly true, but to take this as a literal truth from a text that is not intended to be taken literally means that this truth must be imposed upon the creation account on the basis of truth that is taught somewhere else.

4. "Mankind is gendered, man and woman being of equal value, with marriage given to mankind for procreation and mutuality, the wife being a helper to her husband." Once again this truth is expressed in other parts of Scripture. If this is not intended to be taken literally, then Craig is simply reading back into the Genesis account this truth that is expressed elsewhere. Additionally, we will show in chapter 7 that Craig has misunderstood and misrepresented the relation of Eve as "helper to her husband."

5. "Work is good, a sacred assignment by God to mankind to steward the earth and its creatures." This is likewise not to be taken literally, but the story seems to be saying something quite different from Craig's "truth."

> [17] Then to Adam He said, "Because you have listened to the voice of your wife, and have eaten from the tree about which I commanded you, saying, 'You shall not eat from it'; cursed is the ground because of you; in toil you will eat of it all the days of your life. [18] "Both thorns and thistles it shall grow for you; and you will eat the plants of the field; [19] By the sweat of your face you will eat bread, till you return to the ground, because from it you were taken; for you are dust, and to dust you shall return" (Gen 3:17–19).[60]

It certainly seems to tell us that working the ground is part of the curse. In fact, a case has been made that the text of Gen 2:15 is not talking about work at all: "Then the LORD God took the man and put him into the garden of Eden to cultivate it and keep it" (NASB).[61] The word

---

60. [17] וּלְאָדָם אָמַר כִּי־שָׁמַעְתָּ לְקוֹל אִשְׁתֶּךָ וַתֹּאכַל מִן־הָעֵץ אֲשֶׁר צִוִּיתִיךָ לֵאמֹר לֹא תֹאכַל מִמֶּנּוּ אֲרוּרָה הָאֲדָמָה בַּעֲבוּרֶךָ בְּעִצָּבוֹן תֹּאכֲלֶנָּה כֹּל יְמֵי חַיֶּיךָ׃ [18] וְקוֹץ וְדַרְדַּר תַּצְמִיחַ לָךְ וְאָכַלְתָּ אֶת־עֵשֶׂב הַשָּׂדֶה׃ [19] בְּזֵעַת אַפֶּיךָ תֹּאכַל לֶחֶם עַד שׁוּבְךָ אֶל־הָאֲדָמָה כִּי מִמֶּנָּה לֻקָּחְתָּ כִּי־עָפָר אַתָּה וְאֶל־עָפָר תָּשׁוּב׃

(Gen 3:17–19)

61. (Gen 2:15): וַיִּקַּח יְהוָה אֱלֹהִים אֶת־הָאָדָם וַיַּנִּחֵהוּ בְגַן־עֵדֶן לְעָבְדָהּ וּלְשָׁמְרָהּ׃

translated "and put him" is from the root נוח (nuḥ). In the text it is a Hiphil form of the verb נוּחַ (nûaḥ), which literally means "to cause to rest." God has done the work, and he causes the man to rest in the garden. John Currid and John Sailhamer have made a significant case that the text should not be translated "to work it and to keep it":

> Many modern translations render the end of this verse as, 'to cultivate it and keep it' (NASB), or a similar expression. The problem is that the ending **'it'** (used twice) is feminine in Hebrew, and the **'garden'** to which the pronoun is assumed to refer is masculine. There is no agreement between the noun and the ending. It is better, therefore, to understand the two verbs as infinitives without endings, which would give the reading: **'to serve and to obey'**.
>
> The verb **'to serve'** is found throughout the Pentateuch to indicate man's service to God (e.g., Exod. 8:1, 20; 9:1, 13). **'To obey'** is also employed of man's keeping God's Word (17:9; 18:19). And when the two words appear together in the Torah they reflect the worship of God. At the very core of the book of Deuteronomy, for instance, Moses asks the question: what does God require of Israel? He answers: 'To serve Yahweh your God with all your heart and with all your soul and to obey Yahweh's commands' (10:12–13).
>
> The upshot is that Adam was placed in the garden to worship God by serving him and obeying him.[62]

The word "garden" is not feminine. It is masculine. The word "garden" is the head of the word "Eden." This is like, "the city of Charlotte," where the word "city" is the head of the word "Charlotte." The head word always dictates the gender of the word of which it is the head, even if the head noun is not present in a particular expression. So, since "garden" is masculine, the name "Eden" will always be masculine even without the head noun being present. The word "garden" is classified as an umnarked gender. An unmarked gender means that there is no morphological indicator to specify gender. For example, the word סוּס (sûs) is the Hebrew word for "horse." It is lexically masculine and unmarked. To make the feminine form, a feminine ending is added to the unmarked form, סוּסָה (sûsāh), meaning "mare." Very few unmarked nouns in the Hebrew Bible are actually feminine; אֶרֶץ ('ereṣ "earth") being one. We know it is feminine because its Aramaic cognate, אֲרַע ('ăra') is feminine. We know

---

62. Currid, *Genesis 1:1–25:18*, 106–7. See also, Sailhamer, *Pentateuch as Narrative*, 101ff.

that the word "garden" (גַּן, gan) is masculine because its Syriac cognate, ܦܪܕܝܣܐ (prdys'), is masculine (Syriac and Aramaic are sister languages).[63] In fact, the Syriac word is used in the Peshitta to translate the Hebrew word "garden." As Currid points out, the English pronouns "it" are used to translate the Hebrew pronominal suffixes on the two infinitives. Since the pronominal suffixes are feminine, and the words "garden" and "Eden" are masculine, the pronouns cannot be referring to either the garden or Eden.

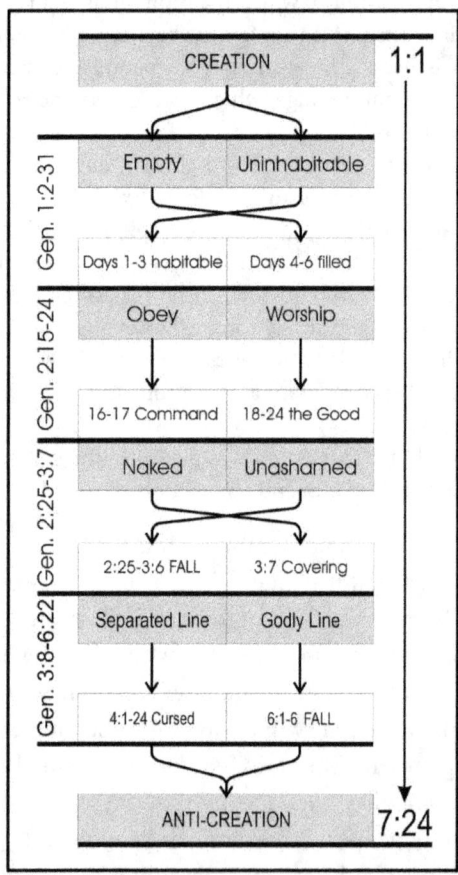

Figure 18: Flow in Genesis 1–7

The translation proposed by Currid fits well with Moses' literary structure to which we have referred earlier. In the creation account, the text refers to two states, "uninhabitable and empty" (תֹהוּ וָבֹהוּ, ṯōhû

63. See SSL, s.v. "ܦܪܕܝܣܐ."

wābōhû). The six days are directed at these two states. The first three days make the earth habitable, and the final three days fill it up. Moses uses the same structure beginning in 2:15. God causes the man to rest in the garden to serve/worship and to obey him. Verses 16–17 give the commands that the man is set in the garden to obey. Beginning in verse 18 the man worships God by trusting God to provide the good that man lacks. Whether or not one agrees with Currid's argument and translation, the text is not as straightforward as Craig would have his readers think, and his conclusions are not supported by the syntax of the text.

This literary structure also fits into the flow of Genesis 1–7 as depicted in **Figure 18**. And this flow shows again the fact that the structure of the Pentateuch the way Clines and Craig present it violates the literary structure. The movement is from creation out of water to judgment with water. As a judgment on his rebellion, the man returns to the dust from which he came, so the earth returns to water from which it came as the judgement upon mankind's rebellion. Craig simply does not understand the literary characteristics of the text.

6. "Human exploration and discovery of the workings of nature are a natural outgrowth of mans' capacities, rather than divine bestowals without human initiative and effort." This point is clearly derived from material not literally contained in the "primaeval narrative."

7. "Mankind is to set apart one day per week as sacred and for refreshment from work." Interestingly, there is no statement in the text that mankind is to set apart one day per week as sacred and for refreshment from work. The text states, "² By the seventh day God completed His work which He had done, and He rested on the seventh day from all His work which He had done. ³ Then God blessed the seventh day and sanctified it, because in it He rested from all His work which God had created and made" (Gen 2:2–3).[64] God set apart the seventh day because He ceased and rested from his work. There is no reference after the fall to man being given rest from his toil until Gen 5:29: "Now he [Lamech] called his name Noah, saying, 'This one will give us rest [יְנַחֲמֵנוּ, ye"nah\ a"meμnuÆ] from our work and from the toil of our hands arising from the ground which the LORD has cursed'" (Gen 5:29).[65] In fact, there is

---

64. ² וַיְכַל אֱלֹהִים בַּיּוֹם הַשְּׁבִיעִיהש מְלַאכְתּוֹ אֲשֶׁר עָשָׂה וַיִּשְׁבֹּת בַּיּוֹם הַשְּׁבִיעִי מִכָּל־מְלַאכְתּוֹ אֲשֶׁר עָשָׂה: ³ וַיְבָרֶךְ אֱלֹהִים אֶת־יוֹם הַשְּׁבִיעִי וַיְקַדֵּשׁ אֹתוֹ כִּי בוֹ שָׁבַת מִכָּל־מְלַאכְתּוֹ אֲשֶׁר־בָּרָא אֱלֹהִים לַעֲשׂוֹת:
(Gen 2:2–3)

65. וַיִּקְרָא אֶת־שְׁמוֹ נֹחַ לֵאמֹר זֶה יְנַחֲמֵנוּ מִמַּעֲשֵׂנוּ וּמֵעִצְּבוֹן יָדֵינוּ מִן־הָאֲדָמָה אֲשֶׁר אֵרְרָהּ יְהוָה
(Gen 5:29)

nothing said about keeping the Sabbath until it is commanded in Exodus: "Remember the Sabbath day, to keep it holy" (Exod 20:8).[66] Again Craig misses the significance of the text. The Sabbath day is to be remembered because God rested from his work. The Sabbath is an object lesson. God does the work, and we rest in his completed work. We do not work in order to gain rest. Craig is not getting point 7 from Genesis. He is importing this into the text from his prior theological belief.

8. "Man and woman alike have freely chosen to disobey God, suffering alienation from God and spiritual death as their just desert, condemned to a life of hardship and suffering during this mortal existence." But if this is not intended to be taken literally, then on what basis is anyone to think that this is literally true? If there was no actual, historical Adam and Eve, then the story is only that—a story, a myth. We can learn from the New Testament that we are sinful and condemned, but the Genesis story does not literally tell us that.

9. "Human sin is agglomerative and self-destructive, resulting in God's just judgment." This point is particularly problematic for Craig's argument. Either the Genesis narrative tells us that sin actually entered the world by the acts of Adam and Eve, or it does not. Since Craig rejects the notion that all sinned in Adam, as we will discuss in chapter 7, then the account of the fall does not tell us anything about human sin and righteous judgment except in the case only of these two individuals who are not to be taken as literal. Consequently, we must learn about human sin and just judgment from other parts of Scripture. Of course it could be argued that the Genesis account is symbolic of human sin and just judgment. However, it remains that we must learn about human sin and just judgment from other parts of Scripture in order for the Genesis account to have an identifiable symbolism.

10. "Despite human rebellion against God, God's original purpose to bless all mankind remains intact, as he graciously finds a way to work his will despite human defiance." Again this truth must be discovered in other parts of Scripture and read back into the "primaeval history."

One important aspect of Craig's list of truths expressed in the "primaeval history" is how Craig arbitrarily chooses to take some aspects as literal and others as not to be taken literally. If we are not to take the account of Adam and Eve literally, then why should we take the gendered nature of humanity literally? What hermeneutical principle does Craig

---

66. (Exod 20:8): זָכוֹר אֶת־יוֹם הַשַּׁבָּת לְקַדְּשׁוֹ

employ to shift from taking some aspects as literal and others as not to be taken literally? Of course Craig argues that even ANE myths express some literal truths. But, in an ANE myth, how does Craig know which parts are to be taken as true and literal and which are not? This judgment cannot be made on the basis of the myths alone. In order to know what parts of an ANE myth express truths one must evaluate the claims of the myth by reference to actual, literal historical information. If the Genesis narratives are not to be taken literally, Craig is actually reading back into the Genesis account the truths that are taught elsewhere as if they came from the "primaeval history." And it does not work to claim that the Genesis narratives are symbolic stores about these truths since to identify the symbolism of the stories they must be related to some literal truth that is communicated in other parts of Scripture.

Summary and Conclusion

Craig concludes this chapter, "Genesis 1–11 exhibits quite a number of the family resemblances characteristic of myths, especially the prominent and abundant presence of etiological motifs. At the same time, the chapters' interest in history, most evident in their genealogical notices that chronologically order the narratives, reveals that we are dealing here, not with pure myth, but with a sort of mytho-history."[67] But just because Craig thinks that the genealogies show the author's interest in history does not prove that this is the case. It is arbitrary for Craig to take some parts as myth and take other parts as mytho-history. Do not ANE myths contain genealogies? Are not some of these genealogies clearly not to be taken literally? So if we are not to take literally the genealogies of Genesis, then how do they show an interest in history? Craig simply selects what he wants to take as myth and what he wants to take as showing an interest in history, but he offers no objective verification of the accuracy of his selections.

---

67. Craig, *Adam*, 202.

7

Adam in the New Testament

CRAIG BEGINS THIS CHAPTER by quoting what he takes to be the "principal texts" that have to do with Adam: Luke 3:23, 38; Matt 19:4–6; Acts 17:26; 1 Cor 11:8–9; 15:21–22; 15:45–49; 2 Cor 11:3; Rom 5:12–21; 1 Tim 2:12–14.¹ Adam is referred to by name nine times in the NT: Luke 3:38; 1 Cor 15:22; 45; Rom 5:14; 1 Tim 2:13, 14; Jude 14. It is curious, but perhaps not significant, that Craig omits Jude 14 from his list of "principal texts." Jude 14–15 states,

> "**14** It was also about these men that Enoch, in the seventh generation from Adam, prophesied, saying, 'Behold, the Lord came with many thousands of His holy ones, **15** to execute judgment upon all, and to convict all the ungodly of all their ungodly deeds which they have done in an ungodly way, and of all the harsh things which ungodly sinners have spoken against Him'" (Jude 14–15).²

Jude is quoting from 1 En 1:9. It certainly seems to be the case that Jude took both Enoch and Adam to be actual individuals who lived at the time the Genesis narrative depicts. But this is certainly not decisive. It is understandable why Craig would not think this passage to be a primary text.

1. Craig, *Adam*, 204–6.
2. **14** Προεφήτευσεν δὲ καὶ τούτοις ἕβδομος ἀπὸ Ἀδὰμ Ἐνὼχ λέγων, Ἰδοὺ ἦλθεν κύριος ἐν ἁγίαις μυριάσιν αὐτοῦ **15** ποιῆσαι κρίσιν κατὰ πάνων καὶ ἐλέγξαι πᾶσαν ψυχὴν περὶ πάντων τῶν ἔργων ἀσεβείας αὐτῶν ὧν ἠσέβησαν καὶ περὶ πάντων τῶν σκληρῶν ὧν ἐλάλησαν κατ' αὐτοῦ ἁμαρτωλοὶ ἀσεβεῖς (Jude 14–15).

The Literary and the Historical Adam

Craig first makes a distinction between truth and truth-in-a-story:

> This distinction implies a further distinction between *truth* and *truth-in-a-story*. A statement S is true iff S states what is the case. A statement S is true-in-a-story iff it is found in or implied by that story. So if I say, for example, that Gilgamesh slew the Bull of Heaven, my statement, though *true-in-the-Epic-of-Gilgamesh*, is false. Truth-in-a-story does not, however, preclude truth. In the *Epic of Gilgamesh* are, or are implied, statements, such as "Gilgamesh was an ancient Sumerian king," that are both true-in-the-epic as well as true. So the relevant question for us is whether the above NT passages are intended to assert truths or merely truths-in-the-stories-of-Genesis.[3]

But Craig has omitted an important aspect of this distinction. In the first instance, an interpreter of the *Epic of Gilgamesh* says, "Gilgamesh slew the Bull of Heaven," and if that is what the story describes, then the interpreter has asserted what is true in the story. However, when it comes to saying, "In a book by *X*, *X* claims that *Y* performed an action," the interpreter must discover whether *X* is making a truth-in-the-story claim, or making a truth-claim

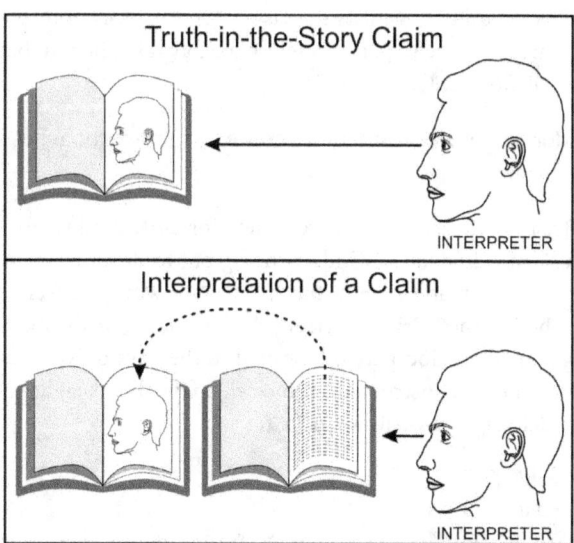

Figure 19: Claims about Claims

3. Craig, *Adam*, 207.

As Craig says, "the relevant question for us is whether the above NT passages are intended to assert truths or merely truths-in-the-stories-of-Genesis." But that is not the whole question. One must also ask whether the interpreter has correctly interpreted the statements that the NT authors make about other texts, and this interpretation must take into consideration the interpreter's philosophical, theological, and literary presuppositions. In the case of Craig, we have already shown his prior assumptions about the relation of ANE myth to biblical narrative, his lack of facility in the Hebrew text, his neglect of the literary aspects of the text, and his failure to deal with the theological significance of the text, so he comes to the NT text with these prior assumptions—assumptions we have shown to be faulty at best—and this will unavoidably influence his determination of whether the NT author is making a truth-in-the-story statement or a truth claim.

Next Craig makes a distinction between assertoric and illustrative use of a text: "Using a text illustratively is using the text merely to provide an illustration, real or imagined, of the point that the author is trying to assert."[4]

> A paradigmatic example of this situation seems to be 1 Pet 3:19–20: following his death, Christ "went and preached to the spirits in prison, who formerly did not obey, when God's patience waited in the days of Noah, during the building of the ark." Who are these spirits in prison? On the basis of texts like 2 Pet 2:4 and Jude 6–7, one might plausibly take them to be the "sons of God" of Gen 6:1–4.[5]

In order to get the immediate context, the text of 1 Pet 3:18–20 is given here:

> **18** Because Christ also suffered once for sins, the just for the unjust, to bring you to God, by being put to death in the flesh but by being made alive in the spirit. **19** In which he went and preached to the spirits in prison, **20** after they were disobedient long ago when God patiently waited in the days of Noah as an ark was being constructed. In the ark a few, that is eight souls, were delivered through water (1 Pet 3:18–20).[6]

4. Craig, *Adam*, 207.
5. Craig, *Adam*, 208.
6. **18** ὅτι καὶ Χριστὸς ἅπαξ περὶ ἁμαρτιῶν ἔπαθεν, δίκαιος ὑπὲρ ἀδίκων, ἵνα ὑμᾶς προσαγάγῃ τῷ θεῷ θανατωθεὶς μὲν σαρκὶ ζῳοποιηθεὶς δὲ πνεύματι· **19** ἐν ᾧ καὶ τοῖς ἐν φυλακῇ πνεύμασιν πορευθεὶς ἐκήρυξεν, **20** ἀπειθήσασίν ποτε ὅτε ἀπεξεδέχετο ἡ τοῦ θεοῦ μακροθυμία ἐν ἡμέραις Νῶε κατασκευαζομένης κιβωτοῦ εἰς ἣν ὀλίγοι, τοῦτ' ἔστιν ὀκτὼ ψυχαί, διεσώθησαν δι' ὕδατος (1 Pet 3:18–20).

Speculations about who these spirits are is a misunderstanding of the passage. Peter is not saying that after Jesus died he went to preach to spirits in prison. Peter is saying that through Noah and in the Spirit, Jesus preached to the spirits that are now in prison. Verse 20 specifically refers to these persons who "at that time" (ποτε, pote) were disobedient "in the days of Noah" (ἐν ἡμέραις Νῶε, en hēmerais Nōe).[7] Craig acknowledges this when he says,

> The modifying clause "who formerly did not obey, when God's patience waited in the days of Noah, during the building of the ark" is a much more suitable description for Noah's contemporaries than for the angels of Gen 6:1–4, who are not said to have disobeyed God, tried God's patience, or sinned during the building of the ark, as Noah's contemporaries are implied to have done.[8]

But Craig makes the very common error of thinking that the "sons of God" (בְּנֵי־הָאֱלֹהִים, běnê hā'ĕlōhîm) in Gen 6:2 refers to angels. There is, of course, a long-standing debate over the reference of the expression, which also involves the question of the reference of the Nephilim (הַנְּפִלִים, hannĕphilîm). The word נְפִלִים (nĕphilîm) is the participial form of the verb נָפַל (nāphal, "he fell") and simply means "fallen ones." The translation "giants" is an imposition of the use of the word in Numbers 13: "There also we saw the Nephilim (the sons of Anak are part of the Nephilim); and we became like grasshoppers in our own sight, and so we were in their sight" (Num 13:33).[9] Interpreters took the estimate of the men appearing as grasshoppers to indicate that the Nephilim were giants. However, it was simply designed to indicate that the spies saw themselves as helpless in their sight. As Craig pointed out, "But it is plausible that the pentateuchal author regards the spies' report as exaggeration inspired by cowardice ('we seemed to ourselves like grasshoppers, and so we seemed to them')."[10] Even in that assertion Craig cannot seem to get the text right. He says, ". . . the Anakim are said by Israelite spies to be descended from

---

7. Clement of Alexandria asserted, "Wherefore the Lord preached the Gospel to those in Hades": Διόπερ ὁ Κύριος εὐηγγελίσατο καὶ τοῖς ἐν ᾅδου. Clement of Alexandria, "Stromata, or Miscellanies," VI.6.35–36.

8. Craig, *Adam*, 208.

9. וְשָׁם רָאִינוּ אֶת־הַנְּפִילִים בְּנֵי עֲנָק מִן־הַנְּפִלִים וַנְּהִי בְעֵינֵינוּ כַּחֲגָבִים וְכֵן הָיִינוּ בְּעֵינֵיהֶם׃ (Num 13:33)

10. Craig, *Adam*, 125.

the Nephilim."[11] The text states that the sons of Anak were "from the Nephilim [מִן־הַנְּפִלִים, min hannĕphilîm]." The text does not say they were "descended" from the Nephilim, and since the word 'Nephilim' simply means "fallen ones," the sons of Anak were certainly from those who are "fallen ones." In other words, they are from the same kind that existed before the flood.

Craig takes the text of 2 Peter to highlight the distinction between the assertoric and the illustrative. He concludes this section:

> These distinctions are not drawn in order to weasel out of commitments on the part of NT authors to the truth of the Genesis stories and, hence, to the historical Adam. Rather, they are important in our treatment of many NT passages, which, if interpreted assertorically, would be unfounded in the OT and sometimes plausibly false. Intriguingly, as mentioned above, some of these passages involve the citation of pseudepigraphal and mythological texts to whose truth we should not wish to be committed. These texts seem to be used illustratively by NT authors, just as we use illustrations drawn from Greco-Roman mythology without thinking to commit ourselves thereby to their historicity.[12]

But again Craig has omitted an important aspect of his conclusion. The reason one would not think to commit himself to the historicity of the Greco-Roman mythology is because, independent of the texts of these mythologies, one can judge the truth or falsity of the Greco-Roman myths against reality. Craig is not simply relating the NT texts to the OT text. Rather, he is judging whether the NT texts are assertoric or illustrative on the basis of his prior commitment to his belief that the "primaeval history" is mytho-history. It is important that Craig says, "if interpreted assertorically." In other words, Craig is deciding on whether the NT text is assertoric based on his interpretations, and his interpretations involve his prior assumptions and commitments. It is not simply a matter of comparing the NT texts with the OT texts. Additionally, interpretations necessarily involve an understanding of the original language, its lexicology, grammar, and syntax.

---

11. Craig, *Adam*, 125.
12. Craig, *Adam*, 209–10.

New Testament Authors' Use of Extrabiblical Literary Figures

In this section Craig considers the use of extra-biblical literary figures by NT authors. He begins with a passage from 2 Peter, providing the following translation:

> For if God did not spare the angels when they sinned, but cast them into hell and committed them to pits of nether gloom to be kept until the judgment; if he did not spare the ancient world, but preserved Noah, a herald of righteousness, with seven other persons, when he brought a flood upon the world of the ungodly; if by turning the cities of Sodom and Gomorrah to ashes he condemned them to extinction and made them an example to those who were to be ungodly; and if he rescued righteous Lot, greatly distressed by the licentiousness of the wicked (for by what that righteous man saw and heard as he lived among them, he was vexed in his righteous soul day after day with their lawless deeds), then the Lord knows how to rescue the godly from trial, and to keep the unrighteous under punishment until the day of judgment, and especially those who indulge in the lust of defiling passion and despise authority. (2 Pet 2:4–10)[13]

Craig points out that Peter "includes information that is not included in or implied by Genesis."[14] Concerning this passage, Craig states, "In the first of these illustrations we find a reference to the sons of God of Gen 6:1–4, interpreted now as angels, and their punishment."[15] Of course when one actually reads the text it is easy to see that nowhere does Peter

---

13. Ibid., 210. The Greek text of these verses is given here: ⁴ Εἰ γὰρ ὁ θεὸς ἀγγέλων ἁμαρτησάντων οὐκ ἐφείσατο ἀλλὰ σειραῖς ζόφου ταρταρώσας παρέδωκεν εἰς κρίσιν τηρουμένους, ⁵ καὶ ἀρχαίου κόσμου οὐκ ἐφείσατο ἀλλὰ ὄγδοον Νῶε δικαιοσύνης κήρυκα ἐφύλαξεν κατακλυσμὸν κόσμῳ ἀσεβῶν ἐπάξας, ⁶ καὶ πόλεις Σοδόμων καὶ Γομόρρας τεφρώσας [καταστροφῇ] κατέκρινεν ὑπόδειγμα μελλόντων ἀσεβέ[σ]ιν τεθεικώς, ⁷ καὶ δίκαιον Λὼτ καταπονούμενον ὑπὸ τῆς τῶν ἀθέσμων ἐν ἀσελγείᾳ ἀναστροφῆς ἐρρύσατο· ⁸ βλέμματι γὰρ καὶ ἀκοῇ ὁ δίκαιος ἐγκατοικῶν ἐν αὐτοῖς ἡμέραν ἐξ ἡμέρας ψυχὴν δικαίαν ἀνόμοις ἔργοις ἐβασάνιζεν· ⁹ οἶδεν κύριος εὐσεβεῖς ἐκ πειρασμοῦ ῥύεσθαι, ἀδίκους δὲ εἰς ἡμέραν κρίσεως κολαζομένους τηρεῖν, ¹⁰ μάλιστα δὲ τοὺς ὀπίσω σαρκὸς ἐν ἐπιθυμίᾳ μιασμοῦ πορευομένους καὶ κυριότητος καταφρονοῦντας. Τολμηταὶ αὐθάδεις, δόξας οὐ τρέμουσιν βλασφημοῦντες, ¹¹ ὅπου ἄγγελοι ἰσχύϊ καὶ δυνάμει μείζοντες ὄντες οὐ φέρουσιν κατ' αὐτῶν παρὰ κυρίου βλάσφημον κρίσιν (2 Pet. 2:4–11). Verse 11 is added on the basis of the punctuation of the UBS 5th edition and the Nestle-Aland 28th edition of the Greek text.

14. Craig, *Adam*, 210.

15. Craig, *Adam*, 211.

say that the sons of God in Genesis 6 are interpreted as angels. In fact, Peter does not even use the phrase "sons of God." Peter states that God did not spare the angels when they sinned. Peter is not talking about angels sinning in the time of Noah, but that angels sinned by leaving their first estate. Craig appeals to Jude 6–7, but he also misinterprets these verses. The text states,

> ⁵ Now I desire to remind you, though you know all things once for all, that the Lord, after saving a people out of the land of Egypt, subsequently destroyed those who did not believe. ⁶ And angels who did not keep their own domain, but abandoned their proper abode, He has kept in eternal bonds under darkness for the judgment of the great day, ⁷ just as Sodom and Gomorrah and the cities around them, since they in the same way as these indulged in gross immorality and went after strange flesh, are exhibited as an example in undergoing the punishment of eternal fire (Jude 5–7).[16]

These verses do not say anything about "the sons of God" or about the days of Noah. To connect these statements with the events in Genesis 6 is nothing less than eisegesis. Earlier Craig asserted that the angels of Genesis 6, "... are not said to have disobeyed God, tried God's patience, or sinned during the building of the ark, as Noah's contemporaries are implied to have done."[17] If the angels did not disobey or try God's patience or sin during the building of the ark, then why would Peter refer to these angels as having sinned? Of course, Craig argues that they did not sin "during the building of the ark." However, later he refers to statements from 1 Enoch:

> *First Enoch*, however, later quoted explicitly by Jude, states that these angels, having "left the high, holy, and eternal heaven" (12.4; 15.3) that was "their dwelling" (15.7) in their lust for human women (chaps. 6–10), have now been bound "underneath the rocks of the ground until the day of their judgment and of their consummation, until the eternal judgment is concluded" (10.12).[18]

---

16. ⁵ ὑπομνῆσαι δὲ ὑμᾶς βούλομαι, εἰδότας [ὑμᾶς] πάντα ὅτι [ὁ] κύριος ἅπαξ λαὸν ἐκ γῆς Αἰγύπτου σώσας τὸ δεύτερον τοὺς μὴ πιστεύσαντας ἀπώλεσεν, ⁶ ἀγγέλους τε τοὺς μὴ τηρήσαντας τὴν ἑαυτῶν ἀρχὴν ἀλλὰ ἀπολιπόντας τὸ ἴδιον οἰκητήριον εἰς κρίσιν μεγάλης ἡμέρας δεσμοῖς ἀϊδίοις ὑπὸ ζόφον τετήρηκεν, ⁷ ὡς Σόδομα καὶ Γόμορρα καὶ αἱ περὶ αὐτὰς πόλεις τὸν ὅμοιον τρόπον τούτοις ἐκπορνεύσασαι καὶ ἀπελθοῦσαι ὀπίσω σαρκὸς ἑτέρας, πρόκεινται δεῖγμα πυρὸς αἰωνίου δίκην ὑπέχουσαι (Jude 5–7).

17. Craig, *Adam*, 208.

18. Craig, *Adam*, 211.

If, following Enoch, these angels left heaven in their lust for human women, then they sinned prior to Noah beginning to build the ark. If the sons of God are the angels who left heaven in their lust for human women, then the text *does* in fact say that the angels disobeyed God, tried his patience, and sinned before the beginning of the building of the ark. If we take the sons of God in Genesis to have been these angels, then Craig is either wrong in his interpretation that these angels did not disobey God, or he is wrong that the sons of God are angels. And simply because Jude quoted from 1 Enoch in one place does not mean that he is connecting the sons of God in Genesis 6 with angels. It is disingenuous to make the comment, "later quoted explicitly by Jude," since the single sentence Jude quotes is not about whether the sons of God in Genesis 6 is about angels.

It is important to understand the text of Jude: "And angels who did not keep their own domain . . ." (Jude 6 NASB). The text states, ἀγγέλους τε τοὺς μὴ τηρήσαντας τὴν ἑαυτῶν ἀρχὴν (aggelous te tous mē tērēsantas tēn heautōn archēn). The word translated "domain" in the NASB, and "proper domain" in the NET, is ἀρχὴν (archēn). According to BDAG, it is most frequently used to indicate "beginning, origin."[19] This is not a reference to the angels not keeping their beginning by burning in their lust for human women. This is referring to the position in which these angels began, namely, heaven. Even if we think that these angels left heaven because they burned in their lust for human women, the text of Jude does not say this. It simply says, they did not keep their ἀρχὴν (archēn, "beginning or origin"), and Jude does not say what motivated them to do this. To take Jude's statement as saying they left their beginning because of their lust is reading into the text what it does not say. It is assuming what must be proven.

It also should strike the reader of Genesis to be curious that, if the sons of God are angels, and if the mating with human women brought forth the Nephilim, then the angels are ultimately responsible for the evil that plagues the earth. Yet the text of Genesis says nothing about the angels being held responsible for the evil, nor does it say anything about God judging the angels for their actions. Neither the assertions of Enoch nor those of Craig derive from the text of Genesis 6. Even Craig acknowledges that these details are "not part of the canonical sons of God."[20] But

---

19. BDAG, s.v. "ἀρχή."
20. Craig, *Adam*, 212.

if the angels are responsible for this evil by intermarrying with human women, why does God judge the humans and not the angels?

A serious problem that plagues the claim that the sons of God are angels is the nature of angels. Angels are not physical creatures, not material beings. "Angels belong to the class of spirit beings, that is, they are generally understood as immaterial and incorporeal beings. They certainly do not have a material, fleshy body such as humans have. This follows from the fact that (1) angels are described in Hebrews 1:14 as 'all ministering spirits,' and (2) demons, if assumed to be fallen angels, are called 'evil spirits' (Luke 8:2) and 'unclean spirits' (Luke 11:24, 26)."[21] Thomas Aquinas argues that angels are separated substances that do not have material bodies:

> I answer that, the angels have not bodies naturally united to them. For whatever belongs to any nature as an accident is not found universally in that nature: thus, for instance, to have wings, because it is not of the essence of an animal, does not belong to every animal. Now since to understand is not the act of a body, nor of any corporeal energy, as will be shown later, it follows that to have a body united to it is not of the nature of an intellectual substance, as such; but it is accidental to some intellectual substance on account of something else . . . Consequently not all intellectual substances are united to bodies; but some are quite separated from bodies, and these we call angels.[22]

Angels are composed of fully actualized form and existence. They have no materiality. Although angels may have appeared in physical form and acted upon material entities, and may interact with material beings, they do not have physical bodies by which they could have sexual relations with human women.

Of course there is also the problem since Jesus said, "For in the resurrection they neither marry nor are given in marriage, but are like angels

---

21. Dickason, *Angels, Elect and Evil*, 33.

22. Aquinatis, *Pars Prima Summae Theologiae*, Ia.51.1. "Respondeo dicendum quod angeli non habent corpora sibi naturaliter unita. Quod enim accidit alicui naturae, non invenitur universaliter in natura illa: sicut habere alas, quia non est de ratione animalis, non convenit omni animali. Cum autem intelligere non sit actus corporis nec alcuius virtutis corporeae, ut infra patebit, habere corpus unitum non est de ratione substantiae intellectualis inquantum huiusmodi, sed accidit alicui substantiae intellectuali proper aliquid aliud; . . . Non igitur omnes substantiae intellectuales sunt unitae corporibus; sed aliquae sunt a corporibus separatae. Et has dicimus angelos." Translated by Fathers of the English Dominican Province.

of God in heaven" (Matt 22:30).²³ Jesus is certainly not talking about angels not going through a marriage ceremony. He is talking about angels not being united to women, that is, not having sexual relations. Taking Enoch's statements, quoted explicitly by Craig, the angels left heaven and burned in their lust for human women. So, before they burned, they were angels of God in heaven. But, as angels of God in heaven, they could not have sexual relations, so why would they burn in lust for human women? However, if they left heaven and became fallen angels before they burned in their lust for human women, then the fall was not the event in Genesis 6, but a prior abandonment of heaven. That being the case, then neither Peter nor Jude are referring to Genesis 6, but rather to a previous event in which these angels rebelled against God and left heaven, their ἀρχήν (archēn). Craig is wrong on all accounts. Also, if they fell before burning in their lust for human women, then they would certainly not be called "sons of God," so the sons of God in Genesis 6 cannot be angels.

Besides the fact that there has been a centuries-long debate about who the sons of God were and to whom the term "Nephilim" refers, there simply is no statement in Genesis 6 that the sons of God were angels. This is an interpretation that Craig has imposed upon the text of Genesis 6, and now Craig imposes it upon 2 Peter and Jude.

Craig next discusses Peter's use of the word ταρταρόω (tartaroō) in 2 Pet 2:4: "For if God did not spare angels when they sinned, but cast them into hell and committed them to pits of darkness, reserved for judgment;"²⁴ Craig says, "Intriguingly, the word in 2 Pet 2:4 for 'cast into hell' is tartaroō, referring to Tartarus, the realm in Greek mythology lower than even Hades."²⁵ According to the *New International Dictionary of New Testament Theology and Exegesis* (NIDNTTE), the word Τάρταρος (Tartaros) was associated with Jewish apocalyptic:

> The term Τάρταρος does not occur in the NT, and the vb. ταρταρόω only in 2 Pet 2:4, which reflects the Jewish apocalyptic view of Tartarus as the place where the disobedient angels were sent after they rebelled against the Lord (the close par[allel] in Jude 6 does not use the vb.). This place, however, is not identified as the actual place of punishment for these angels. Rather, they

---

23. ἐν γὰρ τῇ ἀναστάσει οὔτε γαμοῦσιν οὔτε γαμίζονται, ἀλλ' ὡς ἄγγελοι θεοῦ ἐν τῷ οὐρανῷ εἰσιν (Matt 22:30).

24. Εἰ γὰρ ὁ θεὸς ἀγγέλων ἁμαρτηρσάντων οὐκ ἐφείσατο, ἀλλὰ σειραῖς ζόφου ταρταρώσας παρέδωκεν εἰς κρίσιν τηρουμένους (2 Pet 2:4).

25. Craig, *Adam*, 212.

are being "held" there temporarily as prisoners until judgment is meted out on them (but it is not clear whether a distinction with Gehenna is thereby intended). Through this imprisonment, presumably, God limits their ability to wreak havoc on the earth.[26]

Craig gives the following footnote to his statement: "See BDAG, s.v. 'ταρταρόω,' for references. The verbal forms were almost always used with reference to the Greek myths."[27] Notice that Craig provides no support for the claim that the verbal forms were almost always used with reference to the Greek myths. In fact, the quote from NIDNTTE above points out that the verb form in 2 Pet. 2:4 reflects the Jewish apocalyptic view of Tartarus, not the Greek myth. And the entry in BDAG does not support Craig's claim either:

> ταρταρόω (Τάρταρος 'the Netherworld') 1 aor. ἐταρτάρωσα (Acusilaus Hist. [V B.C.]: 2 Fgm. 8 Jac. I p. 50; Lydus, Men. 4, 158 p. 174, 26 W.; cp. Sext. Emp., Pyrrh. Hypot. 3, 24, 210 ὁ Ζεὺς τὸν Κρόνον κατεταρτάρωσεν [this compound several times in Ps.—Apollod.: 1, 1, 4; 1, 2, 1, 2; 1, 2, 3]. Tartarus, thought of by the Greeks as a subterranean place lower than Hades where divine punishment was meted out, and so regarded in Israelite apocalyptic as well: Job 41:24; En 20:2; Philo, Exs. 152; Jos., C. Ap. 2, 240; SibOr 2, 302; 4, 186) **hold captive in Tartarus** 2 Pt 2:4.—DELG s.v. Τάρταρος. M-M.[28]

This unsupported claim is also very curious since the verb ταρταρόω (tartaroō) occurs nowhere else in the NT. Even if it were true that the verbal form "almost always" referred to the Greek myth, this does not prove that it is so used by Peter. Since the noun Τάρταρος (Tartaros) is used in Jewish apocalyptic, see for example Job 41:24,[29] why would the verb form in 2 Peter suddenly not reflect Jewish apocalyptic. Here Craig is reading into the sources as well as the text what he needs them to say to support his speculations.

Craig goes on to assert, "We thus have in 2 Peter and Jude an expansion of the canonical narrative of the sons of God mating with women

---

26. Moisés Silva, ed., *New International Dictionary of New Testament Theology and Exegesis*, s.v. "tartarovw."

27. Craig, *Adam*, 212.n12.

28. BDAG, s.v. "ταρταρόω." Emphasis in original.

29. τὸν δὲ τάρταρον τῆς ἀβύσσου ὥσπερ αἰχμάλωτον, ἐλογίσατο ἄβυσσον εἰς περίπατον (Job 41:24: ZJ).

2 Peter 2:5

Next Craig assaults 2 Pet. 2:5: "The second illustration in 2 Peter's list concerns Noah, who is said to have been 'a herald of righteousness' (2:5). But in Gen 6–9 Noah is not presented as a proclaimer (kēryx) of righteousness."[31] The text is given here: "and did not spare the ancient world, but preserved Noah, a herald of righteousness, with seven others, when He brought a flood upon the world of the ungodly;" (2 Pet 2:5).[32] The word translated "preacher" in the NASB (κήρυκα, kēruka) can refer to a herald as someone whose life proclaims righteousness even if he does not orally preach it. Even though the words are different in the *Septuaginta* from Peter's text, we find such a notion in the Psalms: "The heavens are declaring the glory of God; the expanse is announcing His handiwork" (Ps 19:1 in the English Bible, Ps. 18:1 in the *Septuaginta*).[33] Of course neither the heavens nor the expanse communicate orally. They communicate God's glory by virtue of being his handiwork. In fact, Gen 6:9 states, "Noah was a righteous man; he was blameless among his generation. Noah walked around with God" (Gen 6:9).[34] The verb translated "walked around" is a Hithpael. As Waltke and O'Connor put it, "On balance, the *Hithpael* probably denotes iterative or frequentative aspect . . ."[35] The word indicates that Noah walked around with God among his generation (בְּדֹרֹתָיו, bĕdōrōṯāyô). The word is not simply saying that Noah "walked with God" in some merely spiritual sense. It is saying that Noah actually walked around with God. This same expression is used to refer to Enoch, who walked around ("wandered around") with God in contrast to Cain who was condemned to wander but settled in Nod. It does not take much of a leap to conclude that Noah heralded righteousness by his life

---

30. Craig, *Adam*, 208.

31. Craig, *Adam*, 213.

32. καὶ ἀρχαίου κόσμου οὐκ ἐφείσατο, ἀλλὰ ὄγδοον Νῶε δικαιοσύνης κήρυκα ἐφύλαξεν, κατακλυσμὸν κόσμῳ ἀσεβῶν ἐπάξας (2 Pet 2:5).

33. Οἱ οὐρανοὶ διηγοῦνται δόξαν θεοῦ, ποίησιν δὲ χειρῶν αὐτοῦ ἀναγγέλει τὸ στερέωμα· Rahlfs, *Psalmi Cum Odis*, vol. X, *Vetus Testamentum Graecum*, Ps 18:2a–b.

34. (Gen 6:9): נֹחַ אִישׁ צַדִּיק תָּמִים הָיָה בְּדֹרֹתָיו אֶת־הָאֱלֹהִים הִתְהַלֶּךְ־נֹחַ

35. Waltke and O'Connor, *Introduction to Biblical Hebrew Syntax*, 428.

and by his speech as he walked around with God. Again, Craig just does not understand the Hebrew text.

Craig asserts, "Contrary, perhaps, to popular impression, Noah is not said to preach to the masses facing imminent destruction, vainly urging them to repent, but goes silently about his work."[36] But the text does not say Noah "goes silently about his work." So, Craig wants to argue that the text of Genesis does not say that Noah was a preacher of righteousness, and then he wants to argue that the text indicates that Noah silently did his work, which the text does not say. If the text does not say he was a preacher of righteousness, it also does not say he silently did his work. He argues one point on the fact that the text does *not* say something, and he argues another point even though the text does not say what he claims it says. In fact, the text of Genesis indicates that Noah did proclaim righteousness as he walked around with God, if not by speech, certainly by his life.

Craig goes on to argue, "The author of 2 Peter seems to draw on a similar Jewish tradition in his characterization of Noah. Being a herald of righteousness is not part of the literary Noah of Genesis but of the literary Noah of Jewish tradition, which 2 Peter exploits for illustrative purposes."[37] But Craig is reading into the text what it does not say, and he ignores what the text does in fact say. Peter's statement that Noah was a herald of righteousness is a valid inference from what the text does say, but Craig's statement is not a valid inference from what the text does not say.

Craig next discusses another statement in 2 Peter:

> The third and fourth illustrations in 2 Peter's list refer to God's judgment on Sodom and Gomorrah in Gen 19 and, rather surprisingly, to the "righteous Lot, greatly distressed by the licentiousness of the wicked (for by what that righteous man saw and heard as he lived among them, he was vexed in his righteous soul day after day with their lawless deeds)" (2:7–8). Such a description of Lot's character hardly seems apt from the narrative of Gen 19.[38]

The text of 2 Peter is given here:

> **7** and if he rescued Lot, a righteous man in anguish over the debauched lifestyle of lawless men, **8** (for while he lived among

---

36. Craig, *Adam*, 213.
37. Craig, *Adam*, 213.
38. Craig, *Adam*, 213–14.

them day after day, that righteous man was tormented in his righteous soul by the lawless deeds he saw and heard) (2 Pet. 2:7–8).[39]

Again Craig's argument is faulty. What in the text indicates that Lot's character was less than righteous? There is nothing in the text that states this. One begins to wonder whether Craig actually read these passages. The text of Gen 19:1–3 is given here:

> [1] Now the two angels came to Sodom in the evening as Lot was sitting in the gate of Sodom. When Lot saw them, he rose to meet them and bowed down with his face to the ground. [2] And he said, "Now behold, my lords, please turn aside into your servant's house, and spend the night, and wash your feet; then you may rise early and go on your way." They said however, "No, but we shall spend the night in the square." [3] Yet he urged them strongly, so they turned aside to him and entered his house; and he prepared a feast for them, and baked unleavened bread, and they ate (Gen 19:1–3).[40]

Lot's invitation to the angels to come to spend the night in his house was part of the practice of hospitality in this ancient culture. However, when the angels say they would spend the night in the square, Lot "strongly" urged them to come into his house. The word translated "strongly" (מְאֹד, mĕʾōd) indicates that he impressed upon them with power. Why would Lot do this? Lot urged them strongly because he knew the character of the people, and Lot knew what would happen to them if they remained in the square. When the men of the city came to demand that the angels be brought out to them, Lot urged, "Please, my brothers, do not act wickedly" (Gen 19:7). The word translated "act wickedly" is the Hiphil form of the root רעע (rʿʿ). It means, "do or cause evil." Lot is urging them not to do this evil.

Craig completely ignores the statements of the men in verse 9: "But they said, 'Stand aside.' Furthermore, they said, 'This one came in as an

---

39. [7] καὶ δίκαιον Λὼτ καταπονούμενον ὑπὸ τῆς τῶν ἀθέσμων ἐν ἀσελγείᾳ ἀναστροφῆς ἐρρύσατο· [8] βλέμματι γὰρ καὶ ἀκοῇ ὁ δίκαιος ἐγκατοικῶν ἐν αὐτοῖς ἡμέραν ἐξ ἡμέρας ψυχὴν δικαίαν ἀνόμοις ἔργοις ἐβασάνιζεν (2 Pet 2:7-8).

40. [1] וַיָּבֹאוּ שְׁנֵי הַמַּלְאָכִים סְדֹמָה בָּעֶרֶב וְלוֹט יֹשֵׁב בְּשַׁעַר־סְדֹם וַיַּרְא־לוֹט וַיָּקָם לִקְרָאתָם וַיִּשְׁתַּחוּ אַפַּיִם אָרְצָה: [2] וַיֹּאמֶר הִנֶּה נָּא־אֲדֹנַי סוּרוּ נָא אֶל־בֵּית עַבְדְּכֶם וְלִינוּ וְרַחֲצוּ רַגְלֵיכֶם וְהִשְׁכַּמְתֶּם וַהֲלַכְתֶּם לְדַרְכְּכֶם וַיֹּאמְרוּ לֹּא כִּי בָרְחוֹב נָלִין: [3] וַיִּפְצַר־בָּם מְאֹד וַיָּסֻרוּ אֵלָיו וַיָּבֹאוּ אֶל־בֵּיתוֹ וַיַּעַשׂ לָהֶם מִשְׁתֶּה וּמַצּוֹת אָפָה וַיֹּאכֵלוּ:
(Gen 19:1-3)

alien, and already he is acting like a judge; now we will treat you worse than them.' So they pressed hard against Lot and came near to break the door" (Gen 19:9).[41] As a judge, Lot is condemning their actions as evil. Lot was certainly more righteous than the men at his door. It is not difficult to infer from these verses that Lot knew the evil character of the men, and he identified their plans as evil. There is no doubt that Lot had personal failings, but there is nothing in the text that would lead the reader to think that he was not a righteous man. David was considered a righteous man although he took another man's wife and orchestrated that man's death. Craig does not seem to be any more adept at Greek than at Hebrew. The word that is used in 2 Pet 2:7 is δίκαιος (*dikaios*), which, according to BDAG, means "pert[aining] to being in accordance with high standards of rectitude, *upright, just, fair*."[42] Peter is not claiming that Lot was a perfectly righteous man, but that he was an upright man who was "in anguish over the debauched lifestyle of disgraceful [ἀθέσμων, *athesmōn*] men" (2 Pet 2:7b).

Even the fact that Lot offers his daughters indicates Lot's uprightness because he abides by the law of hospitality, as Roland de Vaux explains:

> The guest is sacred: the honour of providing for him is disputed, but generally falls to the sheikh. The stranger can avail himself of this hospitality for three days, and even after leaving he has a right to protection for a given time. This time varies from tribe to tribe: among some it is 'until the salt he has eaten has left his stomach' . . . Both Lot and the old man of Gibeah are ready to sacrifice the honour of their daughters in order to protect their guests, and the reason is stated in both cases: it is simply because the latter have come under their roof (Gn 19:8; Jg 19: 23).[43]

Concerning Lot, Craig concludes, "As for the idea that Lot was distressed day after day by the people's lawlessness, that either reflects a tradition that has not survived or is purely the product of the author's imagination."[44] However, once one actually studies the texts, it becomes clear that the inferences drawn by Peter grow out of the text of Genesis.

On the basis of his interpretations of the various texts, Craig states,

---

41. וַיֹּאמְרוּ גֶּשׁ־הָלְאָה וַיֹּאמְרוּ הָאֶחָד בָּא־לָגוּר וַיִּשְׁפֹּט שָׁפוֹט עַתָּה נָרַע לְךָ מֵהֶם וַיִּפְצְרוּ בָאִישׁ בְּלוֹט מְאֹד וַיִּגְּשׁוּ לִשְׁבֹּר הַדָּלֶת׃ (Gen 19:9)

42. BDAG, s.v. "δίκαιος."

43. de Vaux, *Social Institutions*, 10

44. Craig, *Adam*, 214.

The conclusion to be drawn from these examples is not that the expansions of the canonical text are historical (or unhistorical) but rather that we are not committed to their historicity simply in virtue of an NT author's relating them. For the use of these incidents is illustrative, and the aptness of the illustration with respect to the point being made does not depend on the illustration's historicity.[45]

Besides the fact that Craig has misunderstood and mishandled each of these texts, Craig simply concludes that his interpretations are the only interpretations possible and that, since he interprets these texts as being illustrative, then we are not committed to their historicity. But because these texts are illustrative does not mean that they are not also assertoric. These categories are not mutually exclusive. The statements made by Peter in each case are presented as statements about the actual state of affairs, and they have illustrative value because they were actual events. Craig's conclusion simply does not follow, and his interpretations are at best faulty.

Craig claims, "The only plausible exception to this conclusion is perhaps 1 Pet 3:19, which does seem to assert Christ's preaching to the spirits in prison, though even this passage is set forth by the author as an illustration of bearing suffering for doing right."[46] Again, just because Peter is using this as an illustration does not mean that it is not something that Peter is presenting as an assertion. In fact, if the things Peter discusses did not actually occur, then their supposed illustrative value is diminished. If Christ did not actually preach in the Spirit to those in the time of Noah whose spirits are now in prison, then we can take it or leave it as an illustration. The illustration is not binding anymore than is the claim that Gilgamesh slew the Bull of Heaven.

But when one actually considers the texts, there is no grammatical, rhetorical, or literary difference that determines one statement to be illustrative only and another to be illustrative and assertoric. Take for example the verbs and participles in 2 Pet 2:1, 2, 4, and 5. The chart in **Figure 20** shows these verbs and participles.

---

45. Craig, *Adam*, 214.
46. Craig, *Adam*, 214.

v.	Verb or Verbal	Parsing					
1	Ἐγένοτο	3rd Person	Plural	Aorist	Middle	Indicative	
	ἔσονται	3rd Person	Plural	Future	Middle	Indicative	
	παρεισάξουσιν	3rd Person	Plural	Future	Active	Indicative	
2	ἐξακολουθήσουσιν	3rd Person	Plural	Future	Active	Indicative	
	βλασφημηθήσεται	3rd Person	Singular	Future	Passive	Indicative	
	ἐμπορεύσονται	3rd Person	Plural	Future	Middle	Indicative	
4	ἁμαρτησάντων	Masculine	Plural	Genitive	Aorist	Active	Participle
	ἐφείσατο	3rd Person	Singular	Aorist	Middle	Indicative	
	παρέσωκεν	3rd Person	Singular	Aorist	Active	Indicative	
	τηρουμένους	Masculine	Plural	Accusative	Present	Passive	Participle
5	ἐφείσατο	3rd Person	Singular	Aorist	Middle	Indicative	
	ἐφύλαξεν	3rd Person	Singular	Aorist	Active	Indicative	
	ἐπάξας	Masculine	Singular	Nominative	Aorist	Active	Participle

Figure 20: Verbs and Verbals in 2 Peter 2

There are no subjunctives or optatives that would indicate that some statements are presented as assertoric and others as only illustrative. In fact, there are no subjunctives or optatives in 2 Peter. Why take the statements in verses 1 and 2 as assertoric and the statements in verses 4 and 5 as only illustrative? The determination is not on the basis of the grammar or syntax of the verses, so it must be some factor outside of these statements themselves. In this case it must be on the basis of the texts to which Peter is referring that one decides whether the statement is assertoric or only illustrative. Craig's determination is based on his interpretation of the texts involved, and since we have already shown that he has misinterpreted, misunderstood, mishandled, and misrepresented the texts to which Peter is referring, his determinations that these texts are only illustrative and not also assertoric is faulty at best.

Craig continues,

> On other occasions we have, not merely expansions of canonical narratives, but wholesale importation of extrabiblical material for illustrative purposes. For example, in condemning the false teachers of his day, Jude contrasts them negatively to the archangel Michael in his dispute with the devil over Moses's body: "But when the archangel Michael, contending with the devil, disputed about the body of Moses, he did not presume to pronounce

a reviling judgment upon him, but said, 'The Lord rebuke you.' But these men revile whatever they do not understand, and by those things that they know by instinct as irrational animals do, they are destroyed" (Jude 9–10).[47]

Again, just because material is used for illustrative purposes does not mean it cannot also be talking about events that actually occurred. Jude says nothing about this being only illustrative. He presents this in a straightforward manner as if he believed these events actually occurred in real space-time history. Even if it is the case that Jude is presenting this as only illustrative and not also assertoric so that the reader is not committed to the historicity of the event described, it does not follow that other passages are also only illustrative and not also assertoric. Each passage must be taken in its own context. One must then ask, is Craig's statement about Jude only illustrative and not also assertoric? How can one know if Craig is merely using Jude as an illustration so that his reader is not committed to the historicity of Jude or what Jude wrote? Of course we can go to the text of Jude and discover that what Craig has referred to as the words of Jude are in fact historical. Jude actually wrote this. So, in order to decide whether Craig's text is assertoric or only illustrative, one can verify the historicity of what he has reported.

Jude seems to be presenting his text as if these events actually occurred, which is why they have illustrative value. In order to discover whether Jude is using the OT texts as only illustrative or illustrative and also assertoric one needs to go to those OT passages and discover whether they were recounting actual historical persons and events. We have already seen that Craig has misunderstood and mishandled the OT texts, so his conclusion that Jude's use of these texts is only illustrative and not also assertoric is predicated on his faulty interpretation of the OT texts, and therefore his conclusion about Jude's text is faulty.

Craig provides a very helpful discussion of the possible source of Jude's story. Craig concludes, "However we reconstruct the story and its evolution within Christian tradition, what is clear is that Jude is citing extrabiblical legends about the burial of Moses to illustrate his point about

---

47. Craig, *Adam*, 214–15. The Greek text is included here: **9** ὁ δὲ Μιχαὴλ ὁ ἀρχάγγελος, ὅτε τῷ διαβόλῳ διακρινόμενος διελέγετο περὶ τοῦ Μωϋσέως σώματος, οὐκ ἐτόλμησεν κρίσιν ἐπενεγκεῖν βλασφημίας ἀλλὰ εἶπεν, Ἐπιτιμήσαι σοι κύριος. **10** οὗτοι δὲ ὅσα μὲν οὐκ οἴδασιν βλασφημοῦσιν, ὅσα δὲ φυσικῶς ὡς τὰ ἄλογα ζῷα ἐπίστανται, ἐν τούτοις φθείρονται (Jude 9–10).

false teachers."[48] By Craig's own account, the source of Jude's story has been lost: "Unfortunately, the extant version of this treatise, known only from a single, incomplete, sixth-century manuscript, does not include the story."[49] Since Jude's source is lost, how does Craig know that it is a legend? It is certainly extrabiblical, but that does not make it a legend, if by the word 'legend' one means a story that is not historical. Since we do not know Jude's source, for Craig to claim therefore that it is a legend, that is, not historical, is speculation at best and does not support his conclusions about Jude.

Craig discusses how Richard J. Bauckham has attempted to reconstruct the story, but the fact is, the source of Jude's story is lost, and one can only assume, based on the testimony of Origen, that it came from the "apocryphal book *The Assumption of Moses*."[50] So, since we do not know Jude's actual source, for Craig to conclude that Jude is citing a legend is illegitimate. Craig does not know whether Jude got this story from some pseudepigraphical book or from divine revelation. Again Craig jumps to unsupported conclusions because they fit his assumption. Consequently, Jude's account does not function for Craig as an example of material that is only illustrative.

Next Craig completely changes direction: "After providing various further examples to illustrate the danger and fate of false teachers, Jude then proceeds to actually quote *1 Enoch* as though it were authentic."[51] Why does Craig think that Jude is presenting this "as though it were authentic"? If Craig interprets Jude's quote of 1 Enoch as if Jude believes it to be authentic, why does not Craig think that Peter is presenting his sources as if he, Peter, thinks they are authentic? Craig's argument is that if an author is using material in only an illustrative sense, then the reader is not committed to the historicity of the author's source. But if Jude and Peter present their material as if they believe it is authentic, then the reader is in fact committed to accepting or rejecting the historicity of the material. According to Craig's position, either the author is presenting his material as illustrative and not necessarily presenting it as assertoric, or he is presenting it as authentic and therefore assertoric. But this is a false dilemma.

48. Craig, *Adam*, 216.
49. Craig, *Adam*, 215.
50. Craig, *Adam*, 215.
51. Craig, *Adam*, 216.

Craig then argues, "Indeed, Jude is one of the textual witnesses used to establish the text of 1 Enoch 1.9. Jude cites the author of 1 Enoch, a pseudepigraphal book from 400–200 BC, as though he were identical to the Enoch of the antediluvian primaeval history."[52] But again Craig has misrepresented the situation. Nowhere does Jude say that the statement made by Enoch the seventh from Adam is the same individual who composed *1 Enoch*. It is important that Craig does not provide the entire quote from Jude. The text states, "¹⁴ It was also about these men that Enoch, in the seventh generation from Adam, prophesied, saying, "Behold, the Lord came with many thousands of His holy ones, ¹⁵ to execute judgment upon all, and to convict all the ungodly of all their ungodly deeds which they have done in an ungodly way, and of all the harsh things which ungodly sinners have spoken against Him" (Jude 14–15).[53] What Jude says is that Enoch, the seventh from Adam, made this prophecy. He does not claim that Enoch who made the statement is the same individual who composed 1 Enoch. In fact, the passage Jude quotes is from the section titled "The Parable of Enoch," and it begins, "The words of the blessing of Enoch, just as he blessed the elect righteous, who will be living in the day of tribulation, when all the wicked and godless are to be removed."[54] So, "The Parable of Enoch" begins with a reference to the blessing of Enoch. Although the book is titled 1 Enoch, there is no attribution of authorship. It is assumed that Enoch was the author, but that has not been established. According to James H. Charlesworth, it is not even clear in what language it was originally written:

> Some scholars believe that the original language of 1 Enoch is Hebrew; others, however, think that it is Aramaic; still others contend that the book, like Daniel, was composed partly in Hebrew and partly in Aramaic. Recently there have been attempts either to counter or to substantiate entirely the Aramaic origin of the Ethiopic text. Neither theory provides wholly convincing arguments which may be accepted without reservation.[55]

52. Craig, *Adam*, 217.

53. ¹⁴ Προεφήτευσεν δὲ καὶ τούτοις ἕβδομος ἀπὸ Ἀδὰμ Ἐνὼχ λέγων, Ἰδοὺ ἦλθεν κύρους ἐν ἁγίαις μυριάσιν αὐτοῦ ¹⁵ ποιῆσαι κρίσιν κατὰ πάντων καὶ ἐλέγξαι πᾶσαν ψυχὴν περὶ πάντων τῶν ἔργων ἀσεβείας αὐτῶν ὧν ἠσέβησαν καὶ περὶ πάτων τῶν σκληρῶν ὧν ἐλάησαν κατ' αὐτοῦ ἁμαρτωλοὶ ἀσεβεῖς (Jude 14–15).

54. I.1. Λόγος ευλογίας Ἐνωχ, καθὼς εὐλόγησεν ἐκλεκτοὺς δικαίους οἵτινες ἔσονται εἰς ἡμέραν ἀνάγκης ἐξᾶραι πάντας τοὺς ἐχθρούς, καὶ σωθήσονται δίκαιοι. R. H. Charles, "Book of Enoch or 1 Enoch," I.1.273.

55. Charlesworth, "Introduction," in "1 (Ethiopic Apocalypse of) Enoch," 6.

Craig discusses the arguments of Guy Waters concerning Jude's quote. Waters argues,

> One may cogently argue that *1 Enoch* preserves some authentic statements of the historical Enoch, the seventh from Adam, without attributing the whole of *1 Enoch* to the historical Enoch. That Jude identifies Enoch with a precise genealogical marker and quotes him in the train of a host of historical Old Testament references (Jude 5–11) indicates Jude's understanding of Enoch in Jude 14–15 as a historical person. That Enoch is said to be "the seventh from Adam" furthermore requires the conclusion that Jude understood Adam to be no less a historical person than Enoch. Versteeg rightly notes, "When [Jude] calls Enoch 'the seventh from Adam,' he sees a specific historical distance between Enoch and Adam." Jude makes this statement because he regards the narratives about both Adam and Enoch in Genesis 1–5 as historically accurate.[56]

Craig's response to the claims of Waters is designed to miss the point:

> There are two claims made in Waters's "more plausible" suggestion: first, that Jude personally believed that the words cited from *1 Enoch* were a historically accurate, authentic utterance of the antediluvian Enoch, and second, that Enoch's words were, in God's providence, preserved in *1 Enoch*. The first claim is irrelevant and the second desperate. As we have seen, an author using a text illustratively may or may not believe in the factuality of the illustration, and the utility of the illustration is independent of the author's personal belief. So if Jude is using *1 Enoch* illustratively, as seems plausible, his personal beliefs about Enoch's historicity are irrelevant. The further suggestion that an oral tradition emanating from the antediluvian Enoch has been preserved over thousands of years to reach the ears of the author of *1 Enoch* can hardly be said to be plausible.[57]

First Craig asserts that Waters' first claim is "irrelevant." One wonders how the clam that Jude believed that Enoch was an actual historical person could be irrelevant since this is the very point of contention. In fact, earlier Craig himself stated, "Jude then proceeds to actually quote

---

56. Waters, "Theistic Evolution is Incompatible with the Teachings of the New Testament," 892.

57. Craig, *Adam*, 217–18.

1 Enoch as though it were authentic."[58] What Craig wants to argue is that Jude is using the quote illustratively which does not commit him to thinking that this was a quote from an actual person named *Enoch*. That being the case, how could Craig then claim that Waters' claim is irrelevant? By labeling it as irrelevant Craig does not have to deal with it. He has effectively missed the point.

Craig claims that Waters' second claim is "desperate." Again this misses the point. Waters claims that "Jude regarded these words as a historically accurate, authentic utterance of the prophet Enoch, an utterance that, in the providence of God, was preserved in *1 Enoch*."[59] Waters' claim is no more "desperate" than Craig's. In fact, Waters is speaking to precisely the same point, whether Jude's claim should be taken as only illustrative, or whether it should be taken as assertoric and illustrative. One can only surmise that Craig thinks Waters' argument is desperate because Waters refers to divine providence. Since an appeal to divine providence is not an explanation in terms of natural causes, it seems to Craig to be punting to God. But for a Christian who believes in divine providence, the possibility of divine providence is a reality, no matter how desperate it may sound to a naturalistic scientist.

But Craig claims, "an author using a text illustratively may or may not believe in the factuality of the illustration." But this is the very point at issue, that is, whether the statement of Jude should be taken as only illustrative or as assertoric and illustrative. This is the very point that Waters is addressing, i.e., whether Jude believed the quote to be authentic, that is, Jude's statement is assertoric and illustrative, or whether Jude was using this statement in only an illustrative sense, therefore not committed to whether it was authentic or not. Again, Craig avoids the issue simply by asserting his position. But he has not proven his position. Simply because Craig takes Jude's use to be only illustrative does not resolve the problem.

Craig also refers to John Walton's claim. According to Walton, taking Jude's statement as a literary fact, "yes this is how the story goes," rather than an historical fact "is the path typically followed in the interpretation of Jude 14: 'Enoch, the seventh from Adam, prophesied about them.' Even very conservative interpreters consider this a reflection of a literary truth, not a historical truth. None of them seriously considers the Enoch from the book of Genesis to be the author of the intertestamental book of

---

58. Craig, *Adam*, 216.
59. Waters, "Theistic Evolution," 891.

Enoch."⁶⁰ But this is a *non sequitur*. Just because Jude takes the statement of Enoch the seventh from Adam to be an historical fact does not commit Jude to the belief that the book of Enoch was written by the historical Enoch of Genesis. A reader can take as historical fact what Craig says about what Waters claims Walton says without being committed to the belief that Craig believes that Walton wrote Waters' book. The reader can take Jude's statement about what Enoch said without Jude being committed to the belief that the historical Enoch wrote the book of 1 Enoch.

For Craig to assert that Jude cites this portion of 1 Enoch "as though he were identical to the Enoch of the antediluvian primaeval history" is an illegitimate inference and is reading into the text what it does not say. Jude quotes this statement from "The Parable of Enoch" as if Jude believes that Enoch the seventh from Adam actually made this prophecy, but he does not say that he thinks that the compiler of 1 Enoch is identical with the Enoch of the antediluvian primaeval history. Craig and Walton have made an invalid and illegitimate inference from Jude's quote.

2 Timothy 3:8

Next Craig aims at Paul's statement in 2 Tim 3:8:

> Another fascinating example comes from 2 Tim 3:8. Warning against religious hypocrites, the author (Paul?) says, "As Jannes and Jambres opposed Moses, so these men also oppose the truth, men of corrupt mind and counterfeit faith." These personages do not appear in the OT but are widely known in Jewish folklore as the unnamed magicians in Pharaoh's court who opposed Moses (Exod 7:11, 22).⁶¹

Craig has an informative and helpful discussion of the traditions surrounding the names Jannes and Jambres. Craig refers to the two passages in Exodus that refer to the sorcerers who stood against Moses:

> "Then Pharaoh also called for the wise men and the sorcerers, and they also, the magicians of Egypt, did the same with their secret arts" (Exod 7:11).⁶²

---

60. Walton and Wright, *Lost World of Adam and Eve*, 100.

61. Craig, *Adam*, 218. The text of 2 Tim 3:8 is given here: ὅν τρόπον δὲ Ἰάννης καὶ Ἰαμβρῆς ἀντέστησαν Μωϋσεῖ, οὕτως καὶ οὗτοι ἀνθίστανται τῇ ἀληθείᾳ, ἄνθρωποι κατεφθαρμένοι τὸν νοῦν, ἀδόκιμοι περὶ τὴν πίστιν (2 Tim. 3:8).

62. וַיִּקְרָא גַם־פַּרְעֹה לַחֲכָמִים וְלַמְכַשְּׁפִים וַיַּעֲשׂוּ גַם־הֵם חַרְטֻמֵּי מִצְרַיִם בְּלַהֲטֵיהֶם כֵּן׃ (Exod 7:11)

"But the magicians of Egypt did the same with their secret arts; and Pharaoh's heart was hardened, and he did not listen to them, as the LORD had said" (Exod. 7:22).[63]

Granting the tradition that developed with reference to these individuals, one wonders why Craig never addresses the most important question, "How do you know that these were not actually their names?" Just because, as Craig points out, "A bewildering variety of contradictory traditions concerning Jannes and Jambres grew up in Judaism,"[64] does not prove that these were not really their names. It never seems to occur to Craig that Paul may have had information about these individuals which has simply been lost to history. Because of the tradition, Craig just assumes that these were not their real names. But bewildering and contradictory traditions have grown up concerning many things about which we have come to learn the historical actuality.

1 Corinthians 10:4

Finally, Craig discusses Paul's statement in 1 Corinthians:

> Finally, we have Paul's allusion in 1 Cor 10:4 to the rock which accompanied the ancient Israelites through their wilderness wanderings: "All drank the same supernatural drink. For they drank from the supernatural Rock which followed them, and the Rock was Christ." Commentators commonly see a reference here to a Jewish legend based on Num 21:16–18 concerning a miraculous well, shaped like a rock, that continually supplied Israel with water in the desert.[65]

The text of 1 Cor 10:1–4 is given here: "**1** For I do not want you to be unaware, brethren, that our fathers were all under the cloud and all passed through the sea; **2** and all were baptized into Moses in the cloud and in the sea; **3** and all ate the same spiritual food; **4** and all drank the same spiritual drink, for they were drinking from a spiritual rock which followed them; and the rock was Christ" (1 Cor 10:1–4).[66] Again Craig

---

63. וַיַּעֲשׂוּ־כֵן חַרְטֻמֵּי מִצְרַיִם בְּלָטֵיהֶם וַיֶּחֱזַק לֵב־פַּרְעֹה וְלֹא־שָׁמַע אֲלֵהֶם כַּאֲשֶׁר דִּבֶּר יְהוָה׃ (Exod 7:22)

64. Craig, *Adam*, 219.

65. Craig, *Adam*, 220.

66. **¹** Οὐ θέλω γὰρ ὑμᾶς ἀγνοεῖν, ἀδελφοί, ὅτι οἱ πατέρες ἡμῶν πάντες ὑπὸ τὴν νεφέλην ἦσαν καὶ πάντες διὰ τῆς θαλάσσης διῆλθον **²** καὶ πάντες εἰς τὸν Μωϋσῆν ἐβαπτίσθησαν

gives an interesting discussion of a possible pre-Christian tradition, and he concludes, "Paul picks up this extracanonical tradition in order to identify the Rock in the story as Christ, who sustained Israel throughout its sojourn in the wilderness, just as he can elsewhere say, 'Hagar is Mt. Sinai in Arabia' (Gal 4:25)." Craig is making the same mistake here that he made throughout his treatment of the Old Testament. Similarity of design does not necessarily mean identity of origin. Just because there may be a similarity between the tradition and the statement of Paul does not prove that Paul "picks up this extracanonical tradition." This is an illegitimate jump on Craig's part.

Craig concludes this section,

> On the basis of these examples, we can see how naive it is to argue that because some NT author refers to a literary figure, whether found in the OT or outside it, therefore that figure is asserted to be a historical person, much less is a historical person. We need to pay close attention to the context in order to determine whether the NT author does not merely believe in the historicity of the person referred to but is asserting his historicity, rather than referring to the figure illustratively. Again, use of a literary figure illustratively does not imply that the figure is unhistorical; it simply short-circuits overly easy proofs of historicity.[67]

However, at every step we have shown that Craig's assertions are at best only his interpretations and in many instances the imposition of his own assumptions upon the text. His lack of facility in the languages has led him to misunderstand and misrepresent the texts. Not one of Craig's claims about texts being only illustrative has been demonstrated to be the case, except to his own satisfaction. In each case it is only a matter of Craig's choice, none of which actually derives from any of the texts with which he deals. Of course, what does Craig mean by "overly easy proofs of historicity," and who makes that determination? Craig has simply not proven his case. Rather, he has engaged in overly easy "proofs" of illustrative use, and the determination is made by the texts that he misunderstands.

ἐν τῇ νεφέλῃ καὶ ἐν τῇ θαλάσσῃ ³ καὶ πάντες τὸ αὐτὸ πνευματικὸν βρῶμα ἔφαγον ⁴ καὶ πάντες τὸ αὐτὸ πνευματικὸν ἔπιον πόμα· ἔπινον γὰρ ἐκ πνευματικῆς ἀκολουθούσης πέτρας, ἡ πέτρα δὲ ἦν ὁ Χριστός (1 Cor 10:1–4).

67. Craig, *Adam*, 220–21.

New Testament Authors' Use of the Literary Adam

Plausibly Illustrative Uses

In this section Craig takes his claims about illustrative uses and applies them to statements in the NT about Adam. He begins with the teaching of Jesus in Matt 19:4-5:

> So returning to our list of texts concerning Adam in the NT, we find that some of them plausibly do not go beyond the literary figure of Adam in Genesis. The statements of our Lord concerning Adam in Matt 19:4-5 are plausibly illustrative. He begins by drawing attention to the literary Adam: "Have you not read . . . ?" He then cites Gen 1:27, "male and female he created them," and weds this statement with Gen 2:24, "Therefore a man leaves his father and his mother and cleaves to his wife, and they become one flesh." This forms the basis for his teaching on divorce. Jesus is exegeting the story of Adam and Eve to discern its implications for marriage and divorce, not asserting its historicity.[68]

The text of Matthew is given here:

> [4] And He answered and said, "Have you not read that He who created them from the beginning made them male and female, [5] and said, 'for this reason a man shall leave his father and mother and be joined to his wife, and he two shall become one flesh'? [6] So they are no longer two, but one flesh. What therefore God has joined together, let no man separate" (Matt. 19:4-6).[69]

Now why would Craig state that Jesus is not asserting historicity? Does he conclude this because Jesus said "Have you not read"? That is a very dubious conclusion to draw from that simple statement. If the events to which Jesus is referring are not historical, then what binding authority does the story have? This would be the same as if Jesus said, "Have you not read that Gilgamesh slew the Bull of heaven?" Perhaps a fine story, but the fact that such a thing never happened, it offers no authority on which to base one's beliefs or actions. The whole reason Jesus refers to

---

68. Craig, *Adam*, 221.

69. [4] ὁ δὲ ἀποκριθεὶς εἶπεν, Οὐκ ἀνέγνωτε ὅτε ὁ κτίσας ἀπ' ἀρχῆς ἄρσεν καὶ θῆλυ ἐποίησεν αὐτούς; [5] καὶ εἶπεν, Ἕνεκα τούτου καταλείψει ἄνθρωπος τὸν πατέρα καὶ τὴν μητέρα καὶ κολληθήσεται τῇ γυναικὶ αὐτοῦ, καὶ ἔσονται οἱ δύο εἰς σάρκα μίαν. [6] ὥστε οὐκέτι εἰσὶν δύο ἀλλὰ σάρξ μία. ὃ οὖν ὁ θεὸς συνέζευξεν ἄνθρωπος μὴ χωριζέτω (Matt 19:4-6).

this event is because God actually did declare these things as binding. But what God declared is binding not only for this culture, but for all of mankind throughout history.

And which part of Jesus' statement should we not take as Jesus asserting its historicity? Should we not take it as an historical fact that God created them male and female? Even if Jesus is not talking about Adam and Eve only, it must still be true that God created mankind, both male and female and that these male and female beings were actual historical persons. So, since it is an historical fact that God created mankind, both male and female, Craig is just picking out what he wants to support his assumption. "Oh, well, that part is historical, but not the part about Adam and Eve." Craig is cherry-picking details and ignoring the context to create the illusion that Jesus is not asserting or assuming historicity.

Why cannot an exegesis of a story also be an assertion about its historicity or at least an assumption about its historicity? No doubt there are instances in which the exegesis of a story is not an assertion or an assumption of historicity, but that is not necessarily the case. This must be proven, not simply asserted. Jesus' statements come across as if he assumes that his audience assumes the historicity of the account. Did God actually say the things to which Jesus refers? Jesus assumes that his audience believes that God actually said these things. And if these things are not true, then what is their binding authority? Did God actually join together male and female? Why take some parts as historical fact and not other parts.

But in fact, Jesus is not exegeting the story. He is in fact reporting what the text of Genesis says and then stating inferences that derive from the statements of the text. But reporting the story and drawing inferences is not exegesis. Exegesis involves bringing out the meaning of the text. This certainly may include drawing inferences, but drawing inferences from a story does not amount to exegesis.

Since the text states that the male and female become one flesh, it follows from this that the two are no longer two, but one flesh. It follows from this that what God has joined together no man should separate. But if God did not actually do this or say this, then it does not matter whether a man separates. The binding authority for not separating is because God actually, historically did this and said this about actual historical persons. The binding force of what Jesus is saying derives from the historical facts. To claim that Jesus is not asserting historicity is simply false. By assuming its historicity, Jesus is asserting its historicity.

This is true even if someone makes the statement, "Have you not read that Gilgamesh slew the Bull of Heaven," and then draws some inference from this that is supposed to be authoritatively binding upon our behavior. To this we can simply respond, "That never happened! Gilgamesh never slew the Bull of Heaven because there has never been such a beast, and these events never occurred. Therefore, I am not bound by any supposed authority over my behavior on the basis of an event that never happened." But because it is an historical fact that God did this and said this, I am bound to obey God.

Craig does the same thing with another of Jesus' statements:

> Similarly, Jesus's statement that "the blood of all the prophets, shed from the foundation of the world, may be required of this generation, from the blood of Abel to the blood of Zechariah" (Luke 11:50–51) is a paradigmatic case of the use of literary figures. Commentators have often remarked that what is surveyed here is not the history of the world but the history of the OT canon. Jesus is talking about the literary history of the OT and the literary bookends of it.[70]

It is revealing that Craig does not provide the entire quote from Jesus. The entire statement is given here:

> **50** so that the blood of all the prophets, shed since the foundation of the world, may be charged against this generation, **51** from the blood of Abel to the blood of Zechariah, who was killed between the altar and the house of God; yes, I tell you, it shall be charged against this generation (Luke 11:50–51).[71]

No doubt Jesus is referring to the literary aspects of the text, but why cannot he also be talking about actual history? Is Craig now claiming that there never was an Abel or Zechariah, that there never were any prophets, that none of these events actually occurred? Craig conveniently omits Jesus' final statement: "yes, I tell you, it shall be charged against this generation." The word translated "charged" is ἐκζητηθήσεται (*ekzētēthēsetai*). According to BDAG, the word indicates fixing blame: "**to look for in expectation of fixing blame,** *look for, seek,* in the judicial sense *charge*

---

70. Craig, *Adam*, 222.
71. **50** ἵνα ἐκζητηθῇ τὸ αἷμα πάντων τῶν προφητῶν τὸ ἐκκεχυμένον ἀπὸ καταβολῆς κόσμου ἀπὸ τῆς γενεᾶς ταύτης, **51** ἀπὸ αἵματος Ἄβελ ἕως αἵματος Ζαχαρίου τοῦ ἀπολομένου μεταξὺ τοῦ θυσιαστηρίου καὶ τοῦ οἴκου· ναὶ λέγω ὑμῖν, ἐκζητηθήσεται ἀπὸ τῆς γενεᾶς ταύτης (Luke 11:50–51).

(*to, with*) τὸ αἷμα (Gen 9:5; 42:22; 2 Km 4:11; Ezk 3:18; Job 4:21 v.1.) ἀπό τινος **Lk 11:50f**; Pol 2:1."[72] If Jesus is not talking about actual history, then what will be charged against this generation? If these events did not actually occur, then no blood was actually shed, and no guilt is actually incurred, and there is no blame. In his mishandling of the text, Craig must omit Jesus' final statement because it undermines his claim. This is called selective reporting.

Craig attempts to use the Greek text to support his point:

> Another clear example of illustrative usage is 2 Cor 11:3: "I am afraid that as the serpent deceived Eve by his cunning, your thoughts will be led astray from a sincere and pure devotion to Christ." Here the use of "as" (hōs) shows that Paul is drawing a comparison. He uses the story of the fall as an illustrative analogy to the dangerous situation of the Christians in Corinth. The historicity of the story is neither germane nor asserted.

There is no question that the particle ὡς (hōs) is being used as a comparative, but this fact actually undermines Craig's claim. If the serpent did not actually deceive Eve by his cunning, then the comparison has lost its force. If there was no serpent, no Eve, no deception, then of what is Paul warning them? Just as (ὡς, hōs) this actually happened to Eve, it could actually happen to you. If it did not actually happen to Eve, then what are we concerned about?

Paul uses the same kind of construction in 2 Cor 1:7:

> "and our hope for you is firmly grounded, knowing that as [ὡς, hōs] you are sharers of our sufferings, so also you are sharers of our comfort" (2 Cor 1:7).[73]

Using Craig's reasoning we should conclude that Paul did not actually suffer. He is just using a story as an illustrative analogy. To claim that the particle ὡς (hōs) indicates that Paul is using a comparison only as an illustrative analogy betrays Craig's lack of understanding of Greek. The particle ὡς (hōs) can be used as a comparative irrespective of whether the events compared actually occurred or not. Craig's claim that Paul is using an illustrative analogy is not determined by the presence to the particle. It is determined by Craig's assumptions and his interpretative choice. To appeal to the Greek particle as if this indicates an illustrative analogy is

---

72. BDAG, s.v. "ἐκζητέω." Emphasis in original.
73. Καὶ ἡ ἐλπὶς ἡμῶν βεβαία ὑπὲρ ὑμῶν εἰδότες ὅτι ὡς κοινωνοί ἐστε τῶν παθημάτων, οὕτως καὶ τῆς παρακλήσεως (2 Cor 1:7).

disingenuous at best. It comes across as an attempt to lead the reader to think that Craig's interpretation derives from the Greek text, which it absolutely does not.

Craig refers to other instances which he takes to be "less clear." Craig refers to 1 Corinthians again: "Similarly, his statement 'For man was not made from woman, but woman from man. Neither was man created for woman, but woman for man' (1 Cor 11:8–9) can be plausibly taken as purely literary. Paul is here summarizing what the story says, how Eve was created as Adam's helper, and basing his teaching on his exegesis of that story."[74] There is no argument that Paul is exegeting the story, but his appeal is not to his exegesis but to the actual events that actually occurred. If these events did not actually occur, then Paul's exegesis is so much beating the air.

In a footnote to his brief comments on Paul's statements in 1 Tim 2:13–14, Craig takes issue to some observations made by D. A. Carson. Carson argued,

> What must be pointed out is that Paul's argument has no force if it is taken to be a mere illustration drawn from mythological sources. Even in the highest sense of "myth," in which the "myth" somehow pictures general truths, it is not obvious what general truths are being expounded. Is it an obvious general truth that males were created before females? Or that females are intrinsically more susceptible to deception? Some might wish to argue along such lines, I suppose; but such argument is becoming increasingly difficult (to say the least) in the contemporary climate. In fact, Paul can be so unbending on the restrictions he lays down in this passage ("I do not permit," v. 12) precisely because his appeal is to history made known through revelation. If there were no Adam and Eve at the head of the race, no fall, no creation narratives as recorded in Gen 1–3, Paul's argument would simply not hold up: its basis would have been destroyed. (D. A. Carson, "Adam in the Epistles of Paul," in *In the Beginning . . . : A Symposium on the Bible and Creation*, ed. N. M. de S. Cameron [Glasgow: Biblical Creation Society, 1980], 38).[75]

Craig's objection is that Carson's argument is weak:

> Whether we think that Paul is speaking of the literary Adam or the historical Adam, the claim that Paul's *argument* depends

---

74. Craig, *Adam*, 222–23.
75. Quoted in Craig, *Adam*, 222–23.n33.

crucially on the historicity of Adam and Eve is weak. What his argument depends crucially on is the authority of the Hebrew myths of Eve's creation and transgression. As we have seen, myths are sacred narratives for the societies that embrace them and are therefore determinative for them. By exegeting those stories Paul is able, in his mind, to extract some specific applications of those myths for the behavior of women in the churches. A good example of such authoritative use of a text in moral teaching is 1 Cor 6:16–18: "Do you not know that he who joins himself to a prostitute becomes one body with her? For, as it is written, 'The two shall become one flesh.' But he who is united to the Lord becomes one spirit with him. Shun immorality." One can envision, analogously, an ancient Mesopotamian saying, "We must labor in the fields, for when Mami created man, she said, 'I have imposed your toil on man.'" Carson is entirely off-point in thinking that there must be some "general truths" such as he suggests expressed by the Genesis stories. Similarly, Beall is off-point in defending a literal interpretation of the Pauline passages on the grounds that Paul "uses the specific details of the account" (Todd Beall, "Reading Genesis 1–2: A Literal Approach," in Charles, *Reading Genesis 1–2*, 53). See Longman's retort: "I am not sure why he thinks a figurative approach would only be making broad conceptual claims to make their points" (Tremper Longman III, "Responses to Chapter Two," in Charles, *Reading Genesis 1–2*, 67). Of course, NT authors refer to the details of the stories to make their theological and ethical points, whose validity is independent of the historicity of the stories.[76]

Notice Craig's initial objection: "What his [Paul's] argument depends crucially on is the authority of the Hebrew myths of Eve's creation and transgression." Craig has assumed his position in order to object to Carson's argument. But whether the account of Eve's creation is a Hebrew myth is the very point at issue. For Craig simply to assume that his position is the correct one does not at all show that Carson's argument is weak. In fact, it is Craig's argument that is weak since his argument stands only on his prior assumptions. And we have already shown that every one of Craig's arguments about the so called "primaeval history" have miserably failed to demonstrate his assumptions to be accurate.

Basically Craig has not even addressed Carson's argument. Craig interjects a red herring argument as if this has anything to do with the issue: "One can envision, analogously, an ancient Mesopotamian saying,

76. Craig, *Adam*, 222–23.n33.

'We must labor in the fields, for when Mami created man, she said, 'I have imposed your toil on man.'"[77] This interjection completely misses the point. Those to whom the Mesopotamian is speaking would submit to the authority precisely because they believed that the statement was true. However, the statement by an ancient Mesopotamian would not have any actual binding authority precisely because it is false. One can envision, analogously, a contemporary Christian saying, "We must reject the existence of God and Christianity because William Lane Craig said, 'I have proven to you that these things are false.'" But no Christian would do this precisely because William Lane Craig would never have said such a thing. They would reject this injunction as having any binding authority precisely because it is false. Craig fails to deal with the real issue.

Craig concludes his argument by simply asserting his position as if it is incontestable: "Of course, NT authors refer to the details of the stories to make their theological and ethical points, whose validity is independent of the historicity of the stories." But Craig has completely ignored the issue by merely asserting his position as if this constitutes some substantive evidence against Carson.

Plausibly Assertoric Uses

In this section Craig proposes to consider various passages that seem to be assertoric rather than only illustrative. He identifies several Pauline passages, and he then states, "In treating these theologically rich passages, we shall not attempt in this brief compass to unpack them thoroughly but shall restrict our attention to their implications for the issue of the historical Adam."[78] By taking this step Craig has effectively stacked the argument against any objections. It is the thorough "unpacking," the exegesis, of these passages that must be considered in deciding whether they are referring to an historical Adam. By deciding that he will not thoroughly unpack these passages he has effectively giving himself the option to cherry-pick what he wants to consider and what he chooses not to consider, to ignore the context, and to give the illusion his interpretation is accurate. With this kind of treatment he can make his argument sound convincing even though a thorough unpacking might go against his conclusions. He is effectively drawing his conclusions on partial evidence.

77. Craig, *Adam*, 223.n33.
78. Craig, *Adam*, 224.

1 Corinthians 15:21-22, 45-46

The first passages he addresses are 1 Cor 15:21-22, 45-46. These texts are given here:

> **20** But now Christ has been raised from the dead, the first fruits of those who are asleep. **21** For since by a man came death, by a man also came the resurrection of the dead. **22** For as in Adam all die, so also in Christ all will be made alive. **23** But each in his own order: Christ the first fruits, after that those who are Christ's at His coming, **24** then comes the end, when He hands over the kingdom to the God and Father, when He has abolished call rule and all authority and power. **25** For He must reign until He has put all His enemies under His feet. **26** The last enemy that will be abolished is death **27** For He has put all things in subjection under His feet. But when He says, "All things are put in subjection," it is evident that He is excepted who put all things in subjection to Him. **28** When all things are subjected to Him, then the Son Himself also will be subjected to the One who subjected all things to Him, so that God may be all in all (1 Cor 15:20-28).[79]

> **42** So also is the resurrection of the dead. It is sown a perishable body, it is raised can imperishable body; **43** it is sown in dishonor, it is raised in glory; it is sown in weakness, it is raised in power; **44** it is sown a natural body, it is raised a spiritual body. If there is a natural body, there is also a spiritual body. **45** So also it is written, "The first man, Adam, became a living soul." The last Adam became a life-giving spirit. **46** However, the spiritual is not first, but the natural; then the spiritual. **47** The first man is from the earth, earthy; the second man is from heaven. 48 As is the earthy, so also are those who are earthy; and as is the heavenly, so also are those who are heavenly. **49** Just as we have

---

79. **20** Νυνὶ δὲ Χριστὸς ἐγήερται ἐκ νεκρῶν ἀπαρχὴ τῶν κεκοιμημένων. **21** ἐπειδὴ γὰρ δι' ἀνθρώπου θάνατος, καὶ δι' ἀνθρώπου ἀνάστασις νεκρῶν. **22** ὥσπερ γὰρ ἐν τῷ Ἀδὰμ πάντες ἀποθνῄσκουσιν, οὕτως καὶ ἐν τῷ Χριστῷ πάντες ζωοποιηθήσονται. **23** ἕκαστος δὲ ἐν τῷ ἰδίῳ τάγματι· ἀπαρχὴ Χριστός, ἔπειτα οἱ τοῦ Χριστοῦ ἐν τῇ παρουσίᾳ αὐτοῦ, **24** εἶτα τὸ τέλος, ὅταν παραδιδῷ τὴν βασιλείαν τῷ θεῷ καὶ πατρί, ὅταν καταργήσῃ πᾶσαν ἀρχὴν καὶ πᾶσαν ἐξουσίαν καὶ δύναμιν. **25** δεῖ γὰρ αὐτὸν βασιλεύειν ἄχρι οὗ θῇ πάντας τοὺς ἐχθροὺς ὑπὸ τοὺς πόδας αὐτοῦ. **26** ἔσχατος ἐχθρὸς καταργεῖται ὁ θάνατος· **27** πάντα γὰρ ὑπέταξεν ὑπὸ τοὺς πόδας αὐτοῦ. ὅταν δὲ εἴπῃ ὅτι πάντα ὑποτέτακται, δῆλον ὅτι ἐκτὸς τοῦ ὑποτάξαντος αὐτῷ τὰ πάντα. **28** ὅταν δὲ ὑποταγῇ αὐτῷ τὰ πάντα, τότε [καὶ] αὐτὸς ὁ υἱὸς ὁ υἱὸς ὑποταγήσεται τῷ ὑποτάξαντι αὐτῷ τὰ πάντα, ἵνα ᾖ ὁ θεὸς [τὰ] πάντα ἐν πᾶσιν (1 Cor 15:20-28).

borne the image of the earthy, we will also bear the image of the heavenly (1 Cor 15:42-49).[80]

Craig's first observation is, "Paul's expression 'Thus it is written,' followed by his paraphrase of Gen 2:7 in vv. 45-46, directs our attention immediately to the Genesis narrative."[81] Once again Craig reveals his lack of facility in the biblical languages. Paul's statement is not a paraphrase. It is an exact quote of the statement in Gen 2:7.

לְנֶפֶשׁ חַיָּה (lĕnepheš ḥāyāh) "into a soul living" BHS
εἰς ψυχὴν ζῶσαν (eis psuchēn zōsan) "into a living soul," LXX
εἰς ψυχὴν ζῶσαν (eis psuchēn zōsan) "into a living soul," GNT

The rest of the verses are not a paraphrase of Genesis either. The part that comes from Gen 2:7 is the statement "into a living soul," which is an exact quote of the LXX.[82]

Craig's next observation is, "There is little in the ensuing paragraph that takes us beyond the literary character who appears in Gen 2."[83] What seems to have become Craig's *modus operandi* is to state a conclusion before he has presented any argument or evidence. Simply to assert that there is nothing that takes us beyond the literary character is an unsubstantiated assertion. In fact, this is the very point at issue, but Craig assumes his conclusion as evidence for his argument. This is called begging the question.

Next Craig says, "In saying that we all bear the image of the one made of dust, Paul may not be saying anything more than that we are all like the man described in the story. Each of us has a natural body (*sōma psychikon*), made of dust, and therefore mortal."[84] But if Adam was not an actual historical person with a natural body, made of dust, and mortal,

---

80. [42] Οὕτως καὶ ἡ ἀνάστασις τῶν νεκρῶν. σπείρεται ἐν φθορᾷ, ἐγείρεται ἐν ἀφθαρσίᾳ· [43] σπείρεται ἐν ἀτιμίᾳ, ἐγείρεται ἐν δόξῃ· σπείρεται ἐν ἀσθενείᾳ, ἐγείρεται ἐν δυνάμει· [44] σπείρεται σῶμα ψυχικόν, ἐγείρεται σῶμα πνευματικόν. εἰ ἔστιν σῶμα ψυχικόν, ἔστιν καὶ πνευματικόν. [45] οὕτως καὶ γέγραπται, Ἐγένετο ὁ πρῶτος ἄνθρωπος Ἀδὰμ εἰς ψυχὴν ζῶσαν, ὁ ἔσχατος Ἀδὰμ εἰς πνεῦμα ζωοποιοῦν. [46] ἀλλ᾽ οὐ πρῶτον τὸ πνευματικὸν ἀλλὰ τὸ ψυχικόν, ἔπειτα τὸ πνευματικόν. [47] ὁ πρῶτος ἄνθρωπος ἐκ γῆς χοϊκός, ὁ δεύτερος ἄνθρωπος ἐξ οὐρανοῦ. [48] οἷος ὁ χοϊκός, τοιοῦτοι καὶ οἱ χοϊκοί, καὶ οἷος ὁ ἐπουράνιος, τοιοῦτοι καὶ οἱ ἐπουράνιοι· [49] καὶ καθὼς ἐφορέσαμεν τὴν εἰκόνα τοῦ χοϊκοῦ, φορέσομεν καὶ τὴν εἰκόνα τοῦ ἐπουρανίου (1 Cor 15:42-49).

81. Craig, *Adam*, 224.

82. We are using the designation LXX as a non-exact designation. See Karen H. Jobes and Moisés Silva, *Invitation to the Septuagint*.

83. Craig, *Adam*, 224.

84. Craig, *Adam*, 225.

then we have borne the image of someone who did not actually exist. Paul does not say, "We are like the man in the story who is depicted as a person with a natural body, made of dust, and mortal." Paul says, "And just as we have borne the image of the earthy, we will also bear the image of the heavenly" (1 Cor 15:49).[85] Since Paul declared that the one—bearing the image of the earthly—is "just as" (καθὼς, *kathōs*) the other—bearing the image of the heavenly, if we believe that we will actually bear the image of the heavenly as real, actual redeemed people, and if the heavenly image is the image of an actual historical Christ, then the image of the earthly is of an actual historical Adam. If the earthly is only a literary figure, then the other must also be only a literary figure: "Just as we bore the image of a literary figure, so also we will bear the image of another literary figure." The force of the adverb καθὼς (kathōs) is stated in BDAG: "of comparison, just as . . . of extent or degree to which, as, to the degree that."[86] If the earthy is only a literary figure, then bearing the image of the heavenly is "just as" bearing the image of a fictional character. Paul uses this same construction in 1 Cor 10:6: "Now these things happened as examples for us, so that we would not crave evil things just as [καθὼς, kathōs] they also craved."[87] They actually did crave evil things and we ought not to crave evil things just as they did.

Of course Craig could respond that we have missed his point. His point is that just as we have borne the image of a mortal human being, so we will bear the image of an immortal heavenly being, but the mortal human being whose image we have borne is not an historical Adam. But in order to understand the text this way one must already assume that Adam is merely a literary figure. But it is illegitimate to assume what must be proven, and Craig has not proven that Adam is only a literary figure. Rather, this only his interpretation. It is not proof or evidence.

Craig seems to be denying that human beings have a spirit and that the spiritual will not be borne until the resurrection: "But it is not the case that in the story after the physical 'then the spiritual' is created. True, God breathes into the earthly man the divine breath so that the man becomes a living being (*psychēn zōsan*), but that belongs still to the natural (*to psychikon*), not to the spiritual (*to pneumatikon*). We shall have to wait until

---

85. καὶ καθὼς ἐφορέσαμεν τὴν εἰκόνα τοῦ χοϊκοῦ, φορέσομεν καὶ τὴν εἰκόνα τοῦ ἐπουρανίου (1 Cor 15:49).

86. BDAG, s.v. "καθώς."

87. Ταῦτα δὲ τύποι ἡμῶν ἐγενήθησαν, εἰς τὸ μὴ εἶναι ἡμᾶς ἐπιθυμητὰς κακῶν, καθὼς κἀκεῖνοι ἐπεθύμησαν (1 Cor 10:6).

Christ's resurrection for the spiritual to appear (1 Cor 15:23)." So, is Craig saying that there is no spiritual aspect to man until the resurrection? I think that is *not* what he is saying or even implying. But if the spiritual aspect of man is not given to man when man is created, then when does he get it? And, if man gets the spiritual at creation, then the creation account does in fact describe the physical first—from the dust of the ground—and the spiritual after—breathing into man's nostrils the breath of life so that the man becomes a living soul. There is no other instance in the creation account in which the text states that God breathed into something other than the man he created. Man is unique in that he not only has physical life, but he also has a spirit. In fact, Job refers to this fact: "For as long as life is in me, and the breath [וְרוּחַ, wĕrûaḥ] of God is in my nostrils"; (Job 27:3).[88] Job specifically uses the word רוּחַ (rûaḥ), "spirit."

It is also important to notice Craig's statement, "True, God breathes into the earthly man the divine breath so that the man becomes a living being . . ." Craig does not say, "True, the story depicts God breathing into the earthly man the divine breath." Here Craig is saying that this event actually occurred in history. But I thought Paul was referring to these passages only as literary figures for the purpose of illustration. If Craig is referring to this event only as a literary illustration, then this event did not actually occur, and one must wonder what Craig's point is and what it proves? Craig's point counts on the fact that this event actually occurred. Unless God actually breathed into an actual man an actual breath so that the actual man actually became an actual living being, then Craig's point is moot. Again, Craig is cherry-picking what he needs to support his assumptions.

And Craig's appeal to 1 Cor 15:23 does not support his assertion. In the passage from 20–28 Paul is talking about those who have died: "But now Christ has been raised from the dead, the first fruits of those who are asleep" (1 Cor 15:20).[89] Paul is not talking about the creation of man. Paul is talking about the death of man and the resurrection from the dead. This passage has nothing to do with Craig's point about the physical first and then the spiritual.

Craig concedes that Paul may be referring to an historical Adam, but he goes on to argue,

---

88. (Job 27:3):כִּי־כָל־עוֹד נִשְׁמָתִי בִי וְרוּחַ אֱלוֹהַּ בְּאַפִּי

89. Νυνὶ δὲ Χριστὸς ἐγήγερται ἐκ νεκρῶν, ἀπαρχὴ τῶν κεκοιμημένων (1 Cor 15:20).

Ultimately, whether Paul is using Adam more than just illustratively in 1 Cor 15:45-46 is apt to depend on what he meant by his earlier statement "As in Adam all die, so also in Christ shall all be made alive" (15:22). An illustrative reference to the literary Adam would suffice for the statement "As by a man came death, by a man has come also the resurrection of the dead" (15:21), for the protasis of this sentence does not clearly move outside the Genesis narrative, although the apodosis is external to the narrative.[90]

Verses 21-22 are given here:

²¹ For since through man death, also through man resurrection of dead. ²² For as in the Adam all die, so also in the Christ all will be made alive.[91]

In fact, a reference to an Adam that is only a literary figure does not suffice for the statement. This is indicated by the Greek text. First, the text does not say "by a man came death." Rather, the text states, "through man death." Greek does not have an indefinite article, so to add one into the text is an interpretive choice. Second, the text does not say "in Adam all die." The text states, "in the Adam [ἐν τῷ Ἀδάμ, *en tō Adam*] all die." Greek does have a definite article, and it is used here. Paul is not talking about some non-historical personage. He is talking about *the* Adam. This is supported by the parallel expression "in the Christ [ἐν τῷ Χριστῷ, *en toō Christō*] all will be made alive." There is a parallelism between "the Adam" and "the Christ" that shows that the Adam must be as much a historical person as the Christ. There is also a parallelism between verses 21 and 22 that supports the fact that Adam must be an historical person since Christ is an historical person (see **Figure 21**).

v. 21	ἐπειδὴ γάρ for since	δι' through	ἀνθρώπου man	θάνατος	death
	καὶ also	δι' through	ἀνθρώπου man	ἀνάστασις νεκρῶν	resurrection of dead
v. 22	ὥσπερ just as	ἐν in	τῷ Ἀδάμ the Adam	πάντες ἀποθνῄσκουσιν	all die
	οὕτως καὶ thus also	ἐν in	τῷ Χριστῷ the Christ	πάντες ζωοποιηθήσονται	all will be made alive

Figure 21: Adam and Christ Parallel

90. Craig, *Adam*, 225.

91. ²¹ ἐπειδὴ γάρ δι' ἀνθρώπου θάνατος, καὶ δι' ἀνθρώπου ἀνάστασις νεκρῶν. ²² ὥσπερ γὰρ ἐν τῷ Ἀδὰμ πάντες ἀποθνῄσκουσιν, οὕτως καὶ ἐν τῷ Χριστῷ πάντες ζωοποιηθήσονται (1 Cor 15:21-22).

To deny that "the Adam" was an historical person necessarily involves the denial that "the Christ" is an historical person. This is reinforced by Paul's use of ὥσπερ (*hōsper*, "just as") and οὕτως καὶ (*houtōs kai*, "thus also").

Craig goes on to argue,

> His statement "in Adam all die" may look like a truth asserted external to the narrative, since it does not seem to be part of the literary Adam of Genesis that in him all die. But if Paul is talking about physical death, not spiritual death, then mortality does seem to belong to the literary Adam. It is important to note that while Rom 5 contrasts spiritual death and condemnation in Adam with justification and righteousness in Christ, here in 1 Cor 15 the contrast is not forensic but physical: in Adam all persons die physically, but in Christ we shall someday enjoy resurrection life. The concern here is with immortality, not righteousness and salvation.[92]

But to claim that this is not about righteousness and salvation is patently absurd. How does one obtain the resurrection from the dead? Only by righteousness and salvation. In order to assert that this is not about righteousness and salvation one must cherry-pick details and completely ignore the context.

> ¹ Now I make known to you, brethren, the gospel which I preached to you, which also you received, in which also you stand, ² by which also you are saved, if you hold fast the word which I preached to you, unless you believed in vain. ³ For I delivered to you as of first importance what I also received, that Christ died for our sins according to the Scriptures, ⁴ and that He was buried, and that He was raised on the third day according to the Scriptures (1 Cor 15:1-4).[93]
>
> ¹² Now if Christ is preached, that He has been raised from the dead, how do some among you say that there is no resurrection of the dead? ¹³ But if there is no resurrection of the dead, not even Christ has been raised; ¹⁴ and if Christ has not been raised,

---

92. Craig, *Adam*, 225.

93. ¹ Γνωρίζω δὲ ὑμῖν, ἀδελφοί, τὸ εὐαγγέλιον ὃ εὐηγγελισάμην ὑμῖν, ὃ καὶ παρελάβετε, ἐν ᾧ καὶ ἑστήκατε, ² δι' οὗ καὶ σῴζεσθε, τίνι λόγῳ εὐηγγελισάμην ὑμῖν εἰ κατέχετε, ἐκτὸς εἰ μὴ εἰκῇ ἐπιστεύσατε. ³ παρέδωκα γὰρ ὑμῖν ἐν πρώτοις, ὃ καὶ παρέλαβον, ὅτι Χριστὸς ἀπέθανεν ὑπὲρ τῶν ἁμαρτιῶν ἡμῶν κατὰ τὰς γραφὰς ⁴ καὶ ὅτι ἐτάφη καὶ ὅτι ἐγήγερται τῇ ἡμέρᾳ τῇ τρίτῃ κατὰ τὰς γραφὰς (1 Cor 15:1-4).

then our preaching is vain, your faith also is vain. ¹⁵ Moreover we are even found to be false witnesses of God, because we testified against God that He raised Christ, whom He did not raise, if in fact the dead are not raised. ¹⁶ For if the dead are not raised, not even Christ has been raised; ¹⁷ and if Christ has not been raised, your faith is worthless; you are still in your sins. ¹⁸ Then those also who have fallen asleep in Christ have perished. ¹⁹ If we have hoped in Christ in this life only, we are of all men most to be pitied (1 Cor 15:12–19).[94]

The whole point is that the resurrection of the dead is the Gospel of salvation by grace through faith. If there is no resurrection from the dead, then there is no righteousness—"you are still in your sins"—and there is no life after death. If there is no resurrection of the dead, then there is no Gospel of salvation, and our faith is vain. How can this not be about righteousness and salvation?

Craig's argument gets even more bizarre:

> In 1 Cor 15 Paul associates human mortality with the creation of Adam, not with his fall. Adam is created with a *sōma psychikon*; he does not obtain one by sinning. Paul implies that physical mortality is the natural human condition. In saying that in Adam all die, Paul may be saying that in virtue of sharing a common human nature with Adam we share in his natural mortality. If the creation of Adam from the dirt is a figurative way of recounting how mortal man came to be, then the claim that we, too, are mortal does not depend on the historicity of the narrative, just on our sharing a similar constitution to the man described in the story. Paul may draw the inference of human mortality on the basis of the literary Adam alone, though it is difficult to exclude that his argument may go beyond the boundaries of the literary Adam to touch the historical Adam.[95]

---

94. ¹² Εἰ δὲ Χριστὸ κηρύσσεται ὅτι ἐκ νεκτῶν ἐγήγερται, πῶς λέγουσιν ἐν ὑμῖν τινες ὅτι ἀνάστασις νεκρῶν οὐκ ἔστιν; ¹³ εἰ δὲ ἀνάστασις νεκρῶν οὐκ ἔστιν, οὐδὲ Χριστὸς ἐγήγερται· ¹⁴ εἰ δὲ Χριστὸς οὐκ ἐγήγερται, κενὸν ἄρα [καὶ] τὸ κήρυγμα ἡμῶν, κενὴ καὶ ἡ πίστις ὑμῶν· ¹⁵ εὑρισκόμεθα δὲ καὶ ψευδομάρτυρες τοῦ θεοῦ, ὅτι ἐμαρτυρήσαμεν κατὰ τοῦ θεοῦ ὅτι ἤγειρεν τὸν Χριστόν, ὃν οὐκ ἤγειρεν εἴπερ ἄρα νεκροὶ οὐκ ἐγείρονται. ¹⁶ εἰ γὰρ νεκροὶ οὐκ ἐγείρονται, οὐδὲ Χριστὸς ἐγήγερται· ¹⁷ εἰ δὲ Χριστὸς οὐκ ἐγήγερται, ματαία ἡ πίστις ὑμῶν, ἔτι ἐστὲ ἐν ταῖς ἁμαρτίαις ὑμῶν, ¹⁸ ἄρα καὶ οἱ κοιμηθέντες ἐν Χριστῷ ἀπώλοντο. ¹⁹ εἰ ἐν τῇ ζωῇ ταύτῃ ἐν Χριστῷ ἠλπικότες ἐσμὲν μόνον ἐλεεινότεροι πάντων ἀνθρώπων ἐσμέν (1 Cor 15:12–19).

95. Craig, *Adam*, 225–26.

Craig has introduced a contradiction in Paul's teaching. If in 1 Corinthians Paul is saying that death is part of the common human nature, then this flatly contradicts what Paul says in Romans: "Therefore, just as through one man sin entered into the world, and death through sin, and so death spread to all men, because of which all sinned" (Rom 5:12).[96] Death spread to all men because of sin, not because of a common human nature. Paul does not say "and spiritual death passed upon all men." He simply states, "so death spread to all men." Craig discusses this passage in the next section.

Romans 5:12–21

Since Craig will be discussing only parts of this passage, the context is given here:

> 12 Therefore, just as through one man sin entered into the world, and bdeath through sin, and cso death spread to all men, because all sinned— 13 for until the Law sin was in the world, but sin is not imputed when there is no law. 14 Nevertheless death reigned from Adam until Moses, even over those who had not sinned in the likeness of the offense of Adam, who is a type of Him who was to come. 15 But the free gift is not like the transgression. For if by the transgression of the one the many died, much more did the grace of God and the gift by the grace of the one Man, Jesus Christ, abound to the many. 16 The gift is not like that which came through the one who sinned; for on the one hand the judgment arose from one transgression resulting in condemnation, but on the other hand the free gift arose from many transgressions resulting in justification. 17 For if by the transgression of the one, death reigned through the one, much more those who receive the abundance of grace and of the gift of righteousness will reign in life through the One, Jesus Christ. 18 So then as through one transgression there resulted condemnation to all men, even so through one act of righteousness there resulted justification of life to all men. 19 For as through the one man's disobedience the many were made sinners, even so through the obedience of the One the many will be made righteous. 20 The Law came in so that the transgression would increase; but where sin increased, grace abounded all the more,

---

96. Διὰ τοῦτο ὥσπερ δι' ἑνὸς ἀνθρώπου ἡ ἁμαρτία εἰς τὸν κόσμον εἰσῆλθεν καὶ διὰ τῆς ἁμαρτίας ὁ θάνατος, καὶ οὕτως εἰς πάντας ἀνθρώπους ὁ θάνατος διῆλθεν ἐφ' ᾧ πάντες ἥμαρτον (Rom 5:12).

²¹ so that, as sin reigned in death, even so grace would reign through righteousness to eternal life through Jesus Christ our Lord (Rom 5:12–21).⁹⁷

Craig has a brief discussion of Douglas Moo's questions and assertions about the relation of Adam's sin and the fact that all have sinned in Adam. Craig points out that Moo refers to 4 Ezra as an indication of the notion of corporate solidarity of the Jewish world.

> One last point inclines Moo toward such a reading of Paul—namely, the conception of corporate solidarity popular in the Jewish world of Paul's day. The Jewish text that comes closest to Paul's teaching, he thinks, is *4 Ezra* 7:118 : "O Adam, what have you done? For though it was you who sinned, the fall was not yours alone, but ours also who are your descendants." For Paul, Adam was both a historical figure and the corporate figure whose sin could be regarded as the sin of all his descendants.⁹⁸

However, it is not necessary to appeal to 4 Ezra since the notion of corporate solidarity is clearly demonstrated in the OT. In the case of Achan, his sin impacted the entire nation such that they were defeated by the defenders of Ai. When Joshua fell on his face and cried out to the LORD, God responded: "¹⁰ So the LORD said to Joshua, 'Rise up! Why is it that you have fallen on your face? ¹¹ Israel has sinned, and they have also transgressed My covenant which I commanded them. And they have even taken some of the things under the ban and have both stolen and

---

97. ¹² Διὰ τοῦτο ὥσπερ δι' ἑνὸς ἀνθρώπου ἡ ἁμαρτία εἰς τὸν κόσμον εἰσῆλθεν καὶ διὰ τῆς ἁμαρτίας ὁ θάνατος, καὶ οὕτως εἰς πάντας ἀνθρώπους ὁ θάνατος διῆλθεν, ἐφ' ᾧ πάντες ἥμαρτον· ¹³ ἄχρι γὰρ νόμου ἁμαρτία ἦν ἐν κόσμῳ, ἁμαρτία δὲ οὐκ ἐλλογεῖται μὴ ὄντος νόμου, ¹⁴ ἀλλὰ ἐβασίλευσεν ὁ θάνατος ἀπὸ Ἀδὰμ μέχρι Μωϋσέως καὶ ἐπὶ τοὺς μὴ ἁμαρτήσαντες ἐπὶ τῷ ὁμοιώματι τῆς παραβάσεως Ἀδάμ ὅς ἐστιν τύπος τοῦ μέλλοντος. ¹⁵ Ἀλλ' οὐχ ὡς τὸ παράπτωμα, οὕτως καὶ τὸ χάρισμα· εἰ γὰρ γῷ τοῦ ἑνὸ παραπτώματι οἱ πολλοὶ ἀπέθανον, πολλῷ μᾶλλον ἡ χάρις τοῦ θεοῦ καὶ ἡ δωρεὰ ἐν χάριτι τῇ τοῦ ἑνὸς ἀνθρώπου Ἰησοῦ Χριστοῦ εἰς τοὺς πολλοὺς ἐπερίσσευσεν. ¹⁶ καὶ οὐχ ὡς δι' ἑνὸς ἁμαρτήσαντος τὸ δώρημα· τὸ μὲν γὰρ κρίμα ἐξ ἑνὸς εἰς κατάριμα, τὸ δὲ χάρισμα ἐκ πολλῶν παραπτωμάτων εἰς δικαίωμα. ¹⁷ εἰ γὰρ τῷ τοῦ ἑνὸς παραπτώματι ὁ θάνατος ἐβασίλευσεν διὰ τοῦ ἑνός, πολλῷ μᾶλλον οἱ τὴν περισσείαν τῆς ζωῆ βασιλεύσουσιν διὰ τοῦ ἑνὸς Ἰησοῦ Χριστοῦ. ¹⁸ Ἄρα οὖν ὡς δι' ἑνὸς παραπτώματος εἰς πάντας ἀνθρώπους εἰς δικαίωσιν ζωῆς· ¹⁹ ὥσπερ γὰρ διὰ τῆς παρακοῆς τοῦ ἑνὸς ἀνθρώπου ἁμαρτωλοὶ κατεστάθησαν οἱ πολλοί, οὕτως καὶ διὰ τῆς ὑπακοῆς τοῦ ἑνὸς δίκαιοι κατασταθήσονται οἱ πολλοί. ²⁰ νόμος δὲ παρεισῆλθεν, ἵνα πλεονάσῃ τὸ παράπτωμα· οὗ δὲ ἐπλεόνασεν ἡ ἁμαρτία, ὑπερεπερίσσευσεν ἡ χάρις, ²¹ ἵνα ὥσπερ ἐβασίλευσεν ἡ ἁμαρτία ἐν τῷ θανάτῳ, οὕτως καὶ ἡ χάρις βασιλεύσῃ διὰ δικαιοσύνης εἰς ζωὴν αἰώνιον διὰ Ἰησοῦ Χριστοῦ τοῦ κυρίου ἡμῶν (Rom 5:12–21).

98. Craig, *Adam*, 228.

deceived. Moreover, they have also put them among their own things" (Josh. 7:10–11).⁹⁹ Notice that God says, "Israel has sinned [חָטָא יִשְׂרָאֵל, ḥāṭā' yiśrā'ēl], and also *they* have transgressed [עָבְרוּ, 'āḇrû] My covenant which I commanded them." Also, God declares, "And also *they* have taken [לָקְחוּ, lāqḥû] some of the things under the ban . . ." But only Achan did this, yet Achan's act is imputed to all Israel, and all Israel suffers for Achan's sin.

Craig provides a quote from Douglas Moo, but Craig does not give the entire quote:

> Many interpreters and scientists are convinced that we are no longer able to posit a single human, or human pair, as the ancestor(s) of the entire human race; see, e.g., Schneider, "Recent Genetic Science"; Giberson and Collins, *Language of Science and Faith*, 206–14. Many are also convinced that the biblical accounts do not require a single "Adam" as the original human (see, e.g., C. Hays and Herring, "Adam and the Fall," 24–54; Lamoureux, "No Historical Adam," 37–65; , *Evolution of Adam*). However, the effects of Adam's act *in history* (universal sinfulness and death) would seem to demand an Adam who sinned *in history*. I might, for instance, compare or contrast Aslan (from *Chronicles of Narnia*) with Christ to make a general theological point (as Aslan died for Edmund on the stone table, Christ dies for us on the cross), but my listeners would be quite confused if I claimed that the White Witch introduced into our world a condition that Christ has saved us from. And the confusion would be quite natural: I would be positing events in our history caused by, respectively, a fictional character and a real character. Adam, as Paul makes clear, functions on the same historical plane as Moses, the law, and Christ (of whom he is the "type"). For arguments supporting the need to posit a historical Adam in faithfulness to biblical teaching, see, e.g., Carson, "Adam in Epistles of Paul," 28–43; C. Collins, "Adam and Eve"; and on the scientific evidence, see D. Alexander, *Creation or Evolution?*; Rana and Ross, *Who Was Adam?*¹⁰⁰

The quote is from a footnote in Moo's text, but Craig does not quote Moo's statement to which the footnote is attached: "For Paul, Adam, like

---

99. **10** וַיֹּאמֶר יְהוָה אֶל־יְהוֹשֻׁעַ קֻם לָךְ לָמָּה זֶּה אַתָּה נֹפֵל עַל־פָּנֶיךָ: **11** חָטָא יִשְׂרָאֵל וְגַם עָבְרוּ אֶת־בְּרִיתִי אֲשֶׁר צִוִּיתִי אוֹתָם וְגַם לָקְחוּ מִן־הַחֵרֶם וְגַם גָּנְבוּ וְגַם כִּחֲשׁוּ וְגַם שָׂמוּ בִכְלֵיהֶם: (Josh 7:10–11)

100. Moo, *Letter to the Romans*, 355.n196.

Christ, was both a historical figure and a corporate figure, whose sin could be regarded at the same time as the sin of all his descendants."[101]

In the footnote to Moo's quote, Craig argues,

> Although it is often asserted that typology alone is sufficient to establish a purported historical connection between the type and the antitype (e.g., Ellis, *Paul's Use of the Old Testament*, 127), such a claim is both conceptually and biblically flawed. Conceptually, it is perfectly possible to draw a comparison between a literary figure and a historical person as pattern/model and instance (Dunn, *Romans 1–8*, 289: "An act of mythic history can be paralleled to an act in living history without the point of comparison being lost"). Biblically, Jude and 2 Peter present illustrations, not just from the OT but from Jewish folklore, that serve as types of the false teachers (Bauckham, *Jude, 2 Peter*, 47, 256).[102]

The problem here is that Craig does not understand what typology is. Typology is not simply a comparison. Take, for example, the following definitions:

> Typology and the typological method have been part of the church's exegesis and hermeneutics from the very beginning. Obviously this is due to the influence of the NT and it is attested by the writings of the Apostolic Fathers and the pictures in the catacombs. So far as we can tell, Paul was the first to use the Greek word τύπος (adj. τυπικός) as a term for the prefiguring of the future in prior history. God dealt in a typical way (τυπικῶς) with Israel in the wilderness, in a manner that is a pattern for his dealing with the church in the last days. The fortunes of Israel are types (τύποι) of the experiences of the church (1 Cor 10:11, 6; cf. Rom 5:14) ... For typological interpretation, however, the reality of the things described is indispensable. The typical meaning is not really a different or higher meaning, but a different or higher use of the same meaning that is comprehended in type and antitype.[103]

> A type is a person, object, or fact, really existing in some past time, which, because of a divine intent based upon some actual resemblance to some other person, object, or fact, showed what

---

101. Moo, *Letter to the Romans*, 355.
102. Craig, *Adam*, 229.n48.
103. Goppelt, *Typos*, 4–5, 13.

was to be, in some respect, the nature or the character of this second person, object, or fact.[104]

A type is an Old Testament institution, event, person, object, or ceremony which has reality and purpose in Biblical history, but which also by divine design foreshadows something yet to be revealed.[105]

A type is an institution, historical event or person, ordained by God, which effectively prefigures some truth connected with Christianity.[106]

Types are historical realities (persons, events, or institutions) which by God's appointment embody, and therefore exhibit, the same truths, principles, and relationships as the corresponding New Testament realities.[107]

A type may be defined as an Old Testament person, event, or thing having historical reality and designed by God to prefigure (foreshadow) in a preparatory way a real person, event, or thing so designated in the New Testament and that corresponds to and fulfills (heightens) the type.[108]

A biblical *type*, by contrast [with a *symbol*], is like a shadow cast on the pages of earlier literature, which presents a limited account of a truth, the full embodiment of which is amplified in a later revelation. A type invariably points forward in time to its antitype. Types are rooted in history yet are prophetic in nature. Their basic ideas lie in their earthly and human correspondence to a heavenly and divine reality. Genuine OT types are not concerned with unessential similarities between type and antitype (counterpart). They are realities (persons, events, things) of the OT, which later are shown by inspired writers to have a corresponding spiritual reality superceding the historical fact.[109]

Typology differs from direct prophecy in that the latter texts are forward-looking and directly predict the New Testament event, while typology is indirect and analogously relates the old Testament event to the New Testament event. The early Christians

---

104. Burnham, *Elements of Biblical Hermeneutics*, 4.
105. Campbell, "Interpretation of Types, 250.
106. Fritsch, "Biblical Typology," 214.
107. Stek, "Biblical Typology Yesterday and Today," 138.
108. Zuck, *Basic Bible Interpretation*, 176.
109. Murdoch, "Interpretation of Symbols, Types, Allegories, and Parables," 209.

(like the Jews) saw all of salvation history (God working out his plan of salvation in human history) as a single continuous event. Therefore events in the past are linked to those in the present, so that God's mighty deeds like the exodus or the return from exile foreshadow the experiences of God's present community, the church.[110]

Typological understanding of Scripture makes use of the doctrine latent in the history God has brought to pass. It does so in older to understand the Bible more comprehensively. It presupposes that there are important points of analogy between what took place long ago and what takes place today, These comparable features of disparate times bridge the centuries. They are enduring. At the same time they repeat themselves in certain respects. They are, in a word, "typical." Typological understanding also presupposes that God brought about the recording of what took place long ago in order to furnish later generations with information that transcends mere reminiscence. That is, he wished to point the way for subsequent generations.[111]

The older conception (mostly represented by authors before the 1950s) views typology in terms of divinely preordained and predictive prefigurations. The more recent consensus describes typology in terms of historical correspondences retrospectively recognized within the consistent redemptive activity of God.[112]

Each one of these definitions asserts the historicity of the OT events and persons as a necessary ingredient for typology. And definitions could be multiplied. It is certainly true that not all scholars hold to the necessity of the historicity of the type, and many definitions from these scholars could be given, yet Daniel Treier points out that the necessity of the historicity of the antetype is the view of the NT authors: "Neither do all scholars accept the historicity of the types, so approaches to salvation history affect discussions about what would count as evidence for typological hermeneutics. For the moment, whatever modern convictions might be, we must admit that the NT authors took the precedents of the canonical salvation history to anticipate patterns of further divine action."[113] Treier goes on to explain:

---

110. Osborne, *Hermeneutical Spiral*, 328.
111. Maier, *Biblical Hermeneutics*, 85.
112. Davidson, *Typology in Scripture*, 94.
113. Treier, "Typology," 824.

> For there is an interrelationship between patterns of divine action we extrapolate typologically, and patterns of human response we should or should not emulate figurally. That we should expect, since NT "typology"—while deploying a pattern of interpretation with precursors in the OT itself—is fundamentally a Christ-centered development, and in him the divine and human connect. Both particular OT persons and Israel the people of God anticipate Christ by being divine action with a human vocation; OT events and institutions likewise foreshadow his work.[114]

If Craig wants to define typology differently, he can certainly do that, but this basically amounts to defining his position into existence. It is certainly possible to draw a comparison between a literary figure and an historical person as pattern/model and instance, but there are many kinds of comparisons. Typology is a specific kind of comparison. We have already shown that Craig's interpretations of 2 Peter and Jude are simply wrong. It is Craig's view of typology that is conceptually and biblically flawed.

Craig poses the question:

> The question is, indeed, how to relate v. 12cd, "As sin came into the world through one man and death through sin, and so death spread to all men because all men sinned," to v. 18a, "One man's trespass led to condemnation for all men." Moo rightly insists that some explanation is needed for why "people so consistently turn from good to evil of all kinds." No one thinks that every person sins by sheer coincidence. Moo says, "Paul affirms in this passage that human solidarity in the sin of Adam is the explanation—and whether we explain this solidarity in terms of sinning in and with Adam or because of a corrupt nature inherited from him does not matter at this point."[115]

---

114. Treier, "Typology," 824.
115. Craig, *Adam*, 230.

208   A Critique of William Lane Craig's *In Quest of the Historical Adam*

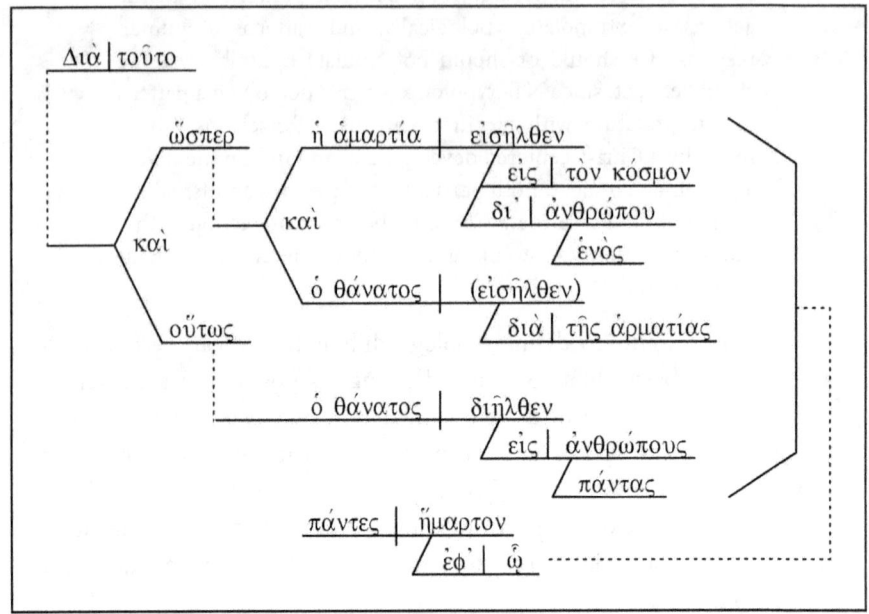

Figure 22: Rom 5:12 Diagram: Greek

To deal with this question, it will be necessary first to examine Rom 5:12.

> "Because of this, just as through one man the sin entered into the world, and through the sin the death, and so unto all men the death spread, because of which all sinned" (Rom 5:12).[116]

For purposes of illustration, a diagram of the Greek text of Rom 5:12 is given in **Figure 22**, and a diagram of the English translation is given in below in **Figure 23**.

---

116. Διὰ τοῦτο ὥσπερ δι' ἑνὸς ἀνθρώπου ἡ ἁμαρτία εἰς τὸν κόσμον εἰσῆλθεν καὶ διὰ τῆς ἁμαρτίας ὁ θάνατος, καὶ οὕτως εἰς πάντας ἀνθρώπους ὁ θάνατος διῆλθεν ἐφ' ᾧ πάντες ἥμαρτον (Rom 5:12).

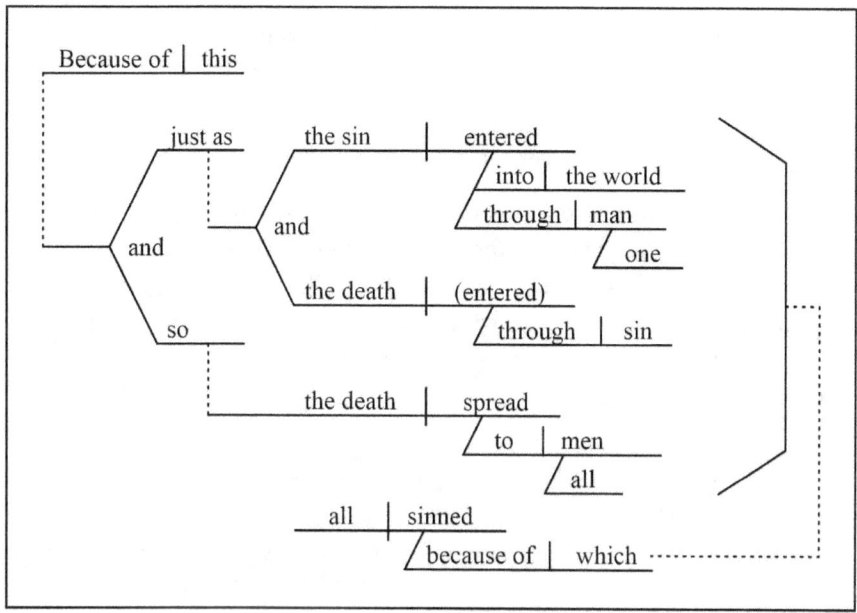

Figure 23: Rom 5:12 Diagram: English

First, it must be noted that the text does not say "because all sinned." The text literally states, "upon which all sinned [ἐφ' ᾧ πάντες ἥμαρτον, *eph hō pantes hēmarton*]." The expression ἐφ' ᾧ (*eph hō*) can be taken to indicate a cause, "because of which." In fact, later Crag points out, "Most commentators construe *eph' hō* as a causal conjunction, 'because,' and take 'all men sinned' to refer to people's own individual acts of sin."[117] In fact, ἐπί[118] (*epi*) is not a conjunction. It is a preposition followed by a relative pronoun. The relative pronoun ᾧ (*hō*) is neuter, not masculine. As a neuter relative pronoun, "this" (ᾧ, *hō*) cannot be referring to "the death" (ὁ θάνατος, *ho thanatos*) since it is masculine, and it cannot be referring to "the sin" (ἡ ἁμαρτία, *hē hamartia*) because it is feminine, and it cannot be referring to "all men" because "men" (ἀνθρώπους, *anthrōpous*) is masculine. So, if we take this as a causal statement, it should be translated "on the basis of which," as Daniel Wallace notes: "Ἐπί A.2. With Dative. c. Cause: *on the basis of*,"[119] or

---

117. Craig, *Adam*, 232.

118. When ἐπί precedes a word beginning with a vowel and rough breathing, in this case ᾧ, the *iota* elides and the *pi* aspirates to a *phi* (ἐφ').

119. Wallace, *Greek Grammar Beyond the Basics*, 376.

"because of which." The reference of the relative pronoun ᾧ (hō) is the entire previous section, as indicated in the diagrams.

Paul used the same kind of construction in Eph 2:8:

> "For by grace you have been saved through faith; and that not of yourselves, it is the gift of God;" (Eph 2:8).[120]

The demonstrative pronoun translated "this" (τοῦτο, touto) is neuter. It cannot be referring to "the grace" (τῇ χάριτι, tē chariti) or to "faith" (πίστεως, pisteōs) since both are feminine. The neuter, demonstrative pronoun is referring to the previous statement, "for by grace you are having been saved through faith" (see **Figure 24**).

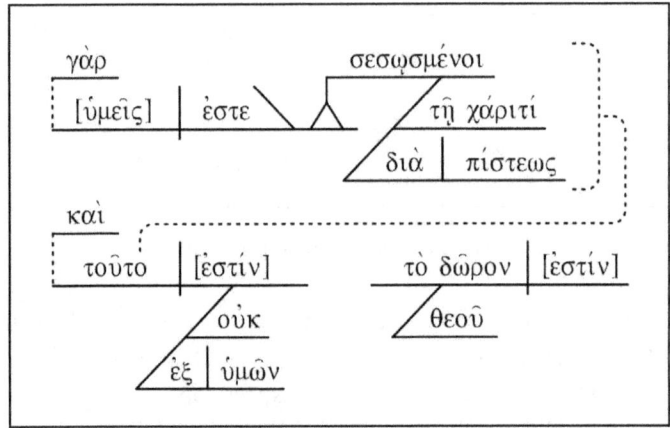

Figure 24: Eph. 2:8 Diagram

Second, it cannot be saying what Craig claims it is saying: "So Adam was the floodgate through which sin and death entered the world, and death then spread to all men because each one sinned in his own turn."[121] When death passed upon all, all had not yet sinned since all were not in existence when death passed upon all. Whether or not one takes Adam to be only a literary person, Paul is undeniably referring to the Genesis account when death passed upon all men. Paul cannot be saying that death passed upon each man as he sinned in his own turn since that is contrary to the Genesis account to which Paul is referring, and it is contrary to the syntax

---

120. τῇ γὰρ χάριτί ἐστε σεσῳσμένοι διὰ πίστεως καὶ τοῦτο οὐκ ἐξ ὑμῶν, θεοῦ τὸ δῶρον· (Eph 2:8).

121. Craig, *Adam*, 232.

of Rom 5:12. The text is saying, through one man sin entered the world and death through sin, death spread to all men, and on the basis of this/because of this all sinned. It is because of the sin of one man that sin entered the world and death by sin which made all men sinners. This means either that all men sinned in Adam, or that all men sin because of what the one man did, or it means both. Additionally, if death passed upon all men because all men sin in their own turn, then this leaves the death of new born children unexplained? Why do infants die who have not sinned?

Craig could certainly respond, "Well infants die because humans are mortal by their common nature." But this does not work. According to Craig's position, death passed on all because all men sinned in their own turn. So, since an infant has not sinned in his own turn, then, according to Craig's position, death has not passed upon the infant. Again Craig could respond, "We are talking about spiritual death, not physical death," to which we respond next.

Third, "the death" (ὁ θάνατος, ho thanatos) cannot be a reference only to physical death. The statement in Genesis is, "but from the tree of the knowledge, good and evil, you shall not eat, for in the day [בְּיוֹם, bĕyôm] that you eat from it you will certainly die" (Gen 2:17).[122] But Adam did not physically die the day he ate from the fruit of the tree. According to Gen 5:5, Adam lived to be nine hundred and thirty years old. The physical death is a sign of the spiritual death that occurred on that day. So, since Paul is referring to this event, it cannot be the case that Paul is talking only about physical death. The resurrection is not merely a physical resurrection. It is also a spiritual resurrection. We are spiritually raised from the dead when we are born again. We are physically raised at the time of the resurrection of those who have fallen asleep. As Paul explained, first the natural then the spiritual, after this the spiritual then the natural.

Next it will be necessary to consider the event recounted in Genesis. There is no doubt that the text describes the sin of Adam and Eve as disobeying God's command not to eat from the tree of the knowledge, good and evil. Also, the text specifically states that Eve saw "the tree was good for food, and that it was a delight to the eyes, and that the tree was desirable to make one wise" (Gen 3:6).[123] The motivation for this act was that Eve desired to be "as God knowing good and evil" (כֵּאלֹהִים יֹדְעֵי טוֹב

---

122. (Gen 2:17): וּמֵעֵץ הַדַּעַת טוֹב וָרָע לֹא תֹאכַל מִמֶּנּוּ כִּי בְּיוֹם אֲכָלְךָ מִמֶּנּוּ מוֹת תָּמוּת׃

In the translation, the word "the" is added because definite articles were regularly omitted from prepositional phrases.

123. (Gen 3:6) כִּי טוֹב הָעֵץ לְמַאֲכָל וְכִי תַאֲוָה־הוּא לָעֵינַיִם וְנֶחְמָד הָעֵץ לְהַשְׂכִּיל

וָרָע, kē'lōhîm yōd'ê ṭôḇ wārā'), having the freedom and wisdom to make these decisions for themselves. In the creation account, seven times the text states, "And God saw that good" (וַיַּרְא אֱלֹהִים כִּי־טוֹב, wayar' 'ĕlōhîm kî ṭôḇ). God is the one who determines what is good, but Eve desired that they become gods, able to decide for themselves what is good.

Craig asserts, "Now it is crucial that we understand that the first proffered explanation [by Moo] of our solidarity with Adam (sinning in and with Adam) in fact does nothing to explain why people consistently sin, for imputation is purely a legal or forensic notion that has no effect whatever on a person's moral character."[124] However, once one understands the text it is clear that the motivation for sin can simply be the desire to have the freedom and independence to decide for oneself what is good and evil; "I want the freedom to make these decisions for myself." This certainly goes a long way to account for why people consistently sin. It also explains why people do things that are sinful even though they may not realize these things are sinful. Acts of sin are not always motivated by malicious intent.

On the basis of his understanding of the nature of imputation, Craig argues, "Such forensic transactions cannot explain why people consistently turn from good to evil. Just as the pardon of a condemned criminal does not make him suddenly a virtuous person but simply no longer legally guilty, so also the imputation of legal guilt does not transform the moral character of an otherwise blameless person."[125] But Craig simply ignores the text to draw his conclusion. Before the fall, the text states, "And the man and his wife were both naked and were not put to shame" (Gen 2:25).[126] After the fall, the couple cover their nakedness: "Then the eyes of both of them were opened, and they knew that they were naked; and they sewed fig leaves together and made themselves loin coverings" (Gen 3:7).[127] Something in their moral character was changed. Before the fall they were not put to shame by their nakedness. After the fall they are morally cognizant of their shame of nakedness, and they are morally cognizant of their guilt before God. The fall did in fact change their moral character. It also changed their moral awareness. Also, just because Craig does not know how to explain why people consistently turn from good to evil does not mean there is no explanation why.

124. Craig, *Adam*, 230.
125. Craig, *Adam*, 230.
126. (Gen 2:25) וַיִּהְיוּ שְׁנֵיהֶם עֲרוּמִּים הָאָדָם וְאִשְׁתּוֹ וְלֹא יִתְבֹּשָׁשׁוּ
127. (Gen 3:7) וַתִּפָּקַחְנָה עֵינֵי שְׁנֵיהֶם וַיֵּדְעוּ כִּי עֵירֻמִּם הֵם וַיִּתְפְּרוּ עֲלֵה תְאֵנָה וַיַּעֲשׂוּ לָהֶם חֲגֹרֹת

Craig agrees with Moo that the belief in a corrupt nature is not taught in Rom 5:12–21 and that the tendency to sin explained by "our inherent self-seeking animal nature in combination with the web of corruption in which we are born and raised."[128] Craig quotes Christopher M. Hays and Stephen Lane Herring concerning an alternative explanation for human sin: "Even if one did not believe that Adam's fall was the source of human concupiscence, one could quite easily provide an alternative account of the doctrine, saying, for example, that humans have an evolutionary biological propensity to selfishness that is reinforced and quickened by our society, psychology and spiritual estate."[129] Craig goes on to quote Daryl Domning as an expansion on Hays and Herring:

> The overt selfish acts that, in humans, demonstrate the reality of original sin by manifesting it as actual sin do indeed owe their universality among humans to natural descent from a common ancestor. However, this ancestor must be placed not at the origin of the human race but at the origin of life itself. Yet these overt acts did not acquire their sinful character until the evolution of human intelligence allowed them to be performed by morally responsible beings.
>
> We all sin because we have all inherited—from the very first living things on earth—a powerful tendency to act selfishly, no matter the cost to others. Free will enables us to override this tendency, but only sporadically and with great effort; we more readily opt for self. This tendency in all of us is what our tradition calls "the stain of original sin.[130]

Before the fall, Eve sought to take the freedom to decide what is good. However, when God confronted Eve, she responded, "The serpent deceived me, and I ate" (Gen 3:13).[131] Lest anyone think that this was only an excuse, in the curse upon the serpent God declares, "Because you did this, cursed are you more than all cattle, and more than every beast of the field; on your belly you will go, and dust you will eat all the days of your life;" (Gen 3:14).[132] The serpent did in fact deceive Eve. Now, if the "propensity to selfishness" and the "powerful tendency to act selfishly, no

---

128. Craig, *Adam*, 231.
129. Hays and Herring, "Adam and the Fall," 53; quoted in Craig, *Adam*, 231.
130. Domning, "Evolution, Evil and Original Sin,"; quoted in Craig, *Adam*, 231.
131. הַנָּחָשׁ הִשִּׁיאַנִי וָאֹכֵל (Gen 3:13)
132. כִּי עָשִׂיתָ זֹּאת אָרוּר אַתָּה מִכָּל־הַבְּהֵמָה וּמִכֹּל חַיַּת הַשָּׂדֶה עַל־גְּחֹנְךָ תֵלֵךְ וְעָפָר תֹּאכַל כָּל־יְמֵי חַיֶּיךָ:
(Gen 3:14)

matter the cost to others" is evil, then this approach requires that God created evil because he created man with these evil tendencies. Also, if God created life with a "powerful tendency to act selfishly, no matter the cost to others," then why are we held responsible for the fact that we were created this way? This alternative not only requires God to be the creator of evil, but it also requires that God is responsible for our sin.

Craig asserts, "Such a natural biological tendency toward survival and hence selfishness, coupled with a morally corrupt environment, suffices to explain why all have sinned."[133] But this does not explain sin. In the Genesis account there was no "morally corrupt environment" for Adam and Eve. Although this may explain why people sin after the fall, it does not explain why Adam and Eve sinned. If there was a morally corrupt environment for Adam and Eve, then Craig has only pushed the question back so it becomes necessary for him to explain from where this morally corrupt environment came. Did it come as a result of the sin of one man prior to Adam? How did this morally corrupt environment come about? Did God create the world as a morally corrupt environment? Craig fails to address these problems with his claim about a morally corrupt environment. And we have already demonstrated that Craig's interpretation of Rom 5:12 is simply incorrect. He does not seem to understand the syntax of the verse. Additionally, Craig's alternative seems to leave unexplained such statements as, "Enoch walked with God; and he was not, for God took him" (Gen 5:24),[134] and "Noah was a righteous man, blameless in his time; Noah walked around with God" (Gen 6:9), and the many other such ascriptions.[135]

Craig argues that verses 18–19 should be understood in light of verse 12 rather than, as Moo, understanding verse 12 in light of verses 18–19. Verses 18–19 are given here:

> "**18** So then as through one transgression there resulted condemnation to all men, even so through one bact of righteousness there resulted justification of life to all men. **19** For as through the one man's disobedience the many were made sinners, even so through the obedience of the One the many will be made righteous" (Rom 5:18–19).[136]

---

133. Craig, *Adam*, 232.
134. (Gen 5:24): וַיִּתְהַלֵּךְ חֲנוֹךְ אֶת־הָאֱלֹהִים וְאֵינֶנּוּ כִּי־לָקַח אֹתוֹ אֱלֹהִים׃
135. (Gen 6:9): נֹחַ אִישׁ צַדִּיק תָּמִים הָיָה בְּדֹרֹתָיו אֶת־הָאֱלֹהִים הִתְהַלֶּךְ־נֹחַ׃
136. **18** Ἄρα οὖν ὡς δι' ἑνὸς παραπτώματος εἰς πάντας ἀνθρώπους εἰς κατάκριμα, οὕτως καὶ δι' ἑνὸς δικαιώματος εἰς πάντας ἀνθρώπους εἰς δικαίωσιν ζωῆς· **19** ὥσπερ γὰρ διὰ τῆς

Of course, this argument is moot since we have shown that Craig's interpretation of verse 12 is wrong.

Craig then makes the inexplicable claim, "That Adam is singled out instead of Eve is as plausibly an expression of Jewish patriarchy (she was, after all, Adam's 'helper') as an affirmation of Adam's federal headship of the human race."[137] Craig does not understand the Hebrew text. The text states,

> Then the LORD God said, "It is not good for the man to be alone; I will make him a עֵזֶר [ʿēzer] suitable for him (Gen 2:18).[138]

The word translated "helper" does not necessarily indicate an inferior. It is used in Exod. 18:4 to refer to God:

> The other was named Eliezer, for he said, "The God of my father was my help [בְּעֶזְרִי, bĕʿezrî], and delivered me from the sword of Pharaoh" (Exod. 18:4).[139]

Additionally, the word translated "suitable for him" (כְּנֶגְדּוֹ, kĕnegdô) literally means "corresponding to him," not inferior to him. Again, Craig does not understand the Hebrew text. The reason the eyes are said to be opened after Adam ate is because the couple as one flesh sinned.

Next Craig attempts to deal with Paul's statement in verse 13. Verses 13–14 are given here:

> **13** For until the Law sin was in the world, but sin is not imputed when there is no law. **14** Nevertheless death reigned from Adam until Moses, even over those who had not sinned ain the likeness of the offense of Adam, who is a type of Him who was to come" (Rom 5:13–14).[140]

Craig argues,

> It is generally agreed that in v. 13 Paul interrupts his train of thought with a possible objection—namely, even if people lied

---

παρακοῆς τοῦ ἑνὸς ἀνθρώπου ἁμαρτωλοὶ κατεστάθησαν οἱ πολλοί, οὕτως καὶ διὰ τῆς ὑπακοῆς τοῦ ἑνὸς δίκαιοι κατασταθήσονται οἱ πολλοί (Rom 5:18-19).

137. Craig, *Adam*, 233.

138. (Gen 2:18): וַיֹּאמֶר יְהוָה אֱלֹהִים לֹא־טוֹב הֱיוֹת הָאָדָם לְבַדּוֹ אֶעֱשֶׂה־לּוֹ עֵזֶר כְּנֶגְדּוֹ

139. (Exod 18:4): וְשֵׁם הָאֶחָד אֱלִיעֶזֶר כִּי־אֱלֹהֵי אָבִי בְּעֶזְרִי וַיַּצִּלֵנִי מֵחֶרֶב פַּרְעֹה

140. **13** ἄχρι γὰρ νόμου ἁμαρτία ἦν ἐν κόσμῳ, ἁμαρτία δὲ οὐκ ἐλλογεῖται μὴ ὄντος νόμου, **14** ἀλλὰ ἐβασίλευσεν ὁ θάνατος ἀπὸ Ἀδὰμ μέχρι Μωϋσέως καὶ ἐπὶ τοὺς μὴ ἁμαρτήσαντας ἐπὶ τῷ ὁμοιώματι τῆς παραβάσεως Ἀδὰμ ὅς ἐστιν τύπος τοῦ μέλλοντος (Rom 5:13-14).

and stole and murdered and so on prior to the giving of the Mosaic law, how could such acts count as sin, since they had not been forbidden? Such an objection seems to arise from Paul's own theology, for he has just said, "Where there is no law there is no transgression" (Rom 4:15). The objection is a profound one, which still occupies Christian ethicists today. On a typical divine command theory of ethics, moral values are rooted in God's nature and our moral duties in his commands. The question arises, then, concerning acts that are objectively evil, since they are incompatible with the divine nature, but which have not been forbidden to certain persons at various times and places in history and therefore are not wrong for them. Such acts are morally *bad* but not morally *wrong*. Someone engaged in such acts is therefore evil but blameless, since he contravenes no moral duty. Such persons therefore cannot be justly punished for their acts, since they have done nothing wrong, but nevertheless find themselves alienated from God by their evil character. Paul seems to envision just such persons living between the time of Adam and Moses.[141]

Following this brief discussion, Craig asserts, "Unfortunately, Paul's thinking about this problem is not as clear as we might wish."[142] Again, just because it is not clear to Craig does not mean it is not clear in itself. The word translated "imputed" is ἐλλογεῖται (*ellogeitai*), which, according to BDAG means, "to charge to the account of someone."[143] In fact, it is used this way in Philemon 18: "But if he has wronged you in any way or owes you anything, charge that to my account;"[144] But if sin is not charged to someone's account where there is no law, how could death reign from Adam to Moses? Because all sinned in Adam. Paul is not raising an objection to his previous statement. Rather, he is clarifying and reinforcing it. Because of the fact that through one man the sin entered into the world, and the death through the sin, and the death spread to all men, so death reigned from Adam to Moses even though individual sins were not charged to the account of individuals. It is because all men sinned in Adam. This argues decisively against Craig's interpretation that death passed upon all men because all men sinned in their own turn. Craig's interpretation cannot be correct according to Paul's argument.

141. Craig, *Adam*, 234.
142. Craig, *Adam*, 234.
143. BDAG, s.v. "ἐλλογέω."
144. Εἰ δέ τι ἠδίκησέν σε ἢ ὀφείλει, τοῦτο ἐμοὶ ἐλλόγα· (Phlm 18).

For Craig to assert, "Such acts are morally *bad* but not morally *wrong*. Someone engaged in such acts is therefore evil but blameless, since he contravenes no moral duty,"[145] and "Paul seems willing to countenance the existence of people who lived between the times of Adam and Moses who were evildoers but not wrongdoers; that is to say, they were morally evil but not accountable"[146] is not only absurd but theological indefensible. How can someone engage in evil acts, be an evil doer, and morally evil but not be "wrongdoers"? Isn't "wrong" part of what it means to do evil? And if these individuals engage in evil acts, are evil doers, and are morally evil, how can they be blameless?

Craig goes on to argue, "Paul asserts that death nevertheless reigned over such people. So saying [*sic*] seems to require an implicit differentiation between death as a *consequence* of sin and death as a *penalty* for sin. Since the relevant persons are not accountable, death cannot be their just desert—that is, the punishment that justice requires. Rather, death would have to be a consequence of their sin."[147] But Paul has just argued the opposite point. Death entered because of sin. In fact, when God confronts Adam he says, "By the sweat of your face you will eat bread, till you return to the ground, because from it you were taken; for you are dust, and to dust you shall return" (Gen 3:19).[148] The pronouncement of physical death is part of the curse. Craig is making a distinction without a difference. Whether Craig wants to call death a consequence or a punishment, it enters into the world because of the sin of Adam. In fact, Craig's distinction between consequence and punishment enters into his text because of his wrong interpretation of the biblical text.

Craig declares, "It would be outlandish to think that each person is born physically immortal and then by sinning brings physical mortality on himself."[149] But why is this outlandish? It is considered outlandish for Craig because his interpretations are wrong. The text declares that death enters because of sin. The text does not make a distinction between spiritual and physical death. In fact, as we have seen above, the genealogy of Genesis 5 brings home the fact that physical death is as much a

---

145. Craig, *Adam*, 234.

146. Craig, *Adam*, 235.

147. Craig, *Adam*, 235.

148. בְּזֵעַת אַפֶּיךָ תֹּאכַל לֶחֶם עַד שׁוּבְךָ אֶל־הָאֲדָמָה כִּי מִמֶּנָּה לֻקָּחְתָּ כִּי־עָפָר אַתָּה וְאֶל־עָפָר תָּשׁוּב: (Gen 3:19)

149. Craig, *Adam*, 235.

consequence/penalty of sin as is spiritual death. In fact, it is outlandish to think that God created mankind to die.

God did not create man to die. He created man and woman to be his representatives on earth, to multiply and fill the earth, to expand the boarders of Eden to cover the whole earth, and to show forth the glory of God. Craig claims, "Although we might think that physical death is the result of Adam's sin, Paul does not affirm this."[150] But this is patently false. In Rom 5:12 Paul declares specifically that death entered into the world through sin. Paul does not say "Only spiritual death entered into the world through sin." The Genesis account affirms this.

Craig argues, "If Adam and Eve were naturally immortal, moreover, then why have a tree of life in the garden at all? It would serve no physical purpose in paradise. The tree serves to rejuvenate its eater physically, not spiritually, hence the concern in Gen 3:22 about fallen man's eating from the tree and living forever (NB not his being spiritually regenerated)."[151]

First of all, it is absurd for someone to think that just because he does not know the reason why, that there cannot be a reason why. There are many things in life concerning which we do not know the reason why, but it does not follow that there is no reason why, nor does it follow that something cannot be a fact simply because we do not know the reason why. Such an argument comes across as both absurd and arrogant. We have already dealt with the significance of the tree of life—the "why"—in chapter 6.

Second, there is no statement or assertion in the Genesis account before the fall that man needed to eat from the tree of life in order to live forever. The tree is simply identified three times, once before the fall in Gen 2:9, and twice after the fall in Gen 3:22 and 24:

> Out of the ground the LORD God caused to grow every tree that is pleasing to the sight and good for food; the tree of life also in the midst of the garden, and the tree of the knowledge of good and evil (Gen 2:9)."[152]

> Then the LORD God said, "Behold, the man has become like one of Us, to know good and evil; and now, he might stretch

---

150. Craig, *Adam*, 235.

151. Craig, *Adam*, 236.

152. וַיַּצְמַח יְהוָה אֱלֹהִים מִן־הָאֲדָמָה כָּל־עֵץ נֶחְמָד לְמַרְאֶה וְטוֹב לְמַאֲכָל וְעֵץ הַחַיִּים בְּתוֹךְ הַגָּן וְעֵץ הַדַּעַת טוֹב וָרָע:
(Gen 2:9)

out his hand, and take also from the tree of life, and eat, and live forever"—(Gen 3:22).[153]

So He drove the man out; and at the beast of the garden of Eden He stationed the cherubim and the flaming sword which turned every direction to guard the way to the tree of life (Gen 3:24).[154]

God drives the couple out of the Eden and sets the cherubim to guard the entrance to the tree of life to prevent man from eating from the tree and living forever. This must be a reference to physical death since it cannot be the case that at physical death a person ceases to exist. The author of Hebrews declares, "And inasmuch as it is appointed for men to die once and after this, judgment" (Heb 9:27).[155] It is not until after the fall that there is any reference to eating from the tree of life and living forever. Because death entered the world, it became necessary for the couple to eat from the tree of life in order physically to live forever, which God prevented by driving the couple from Eden.

Third, Craig has argued that Paul's teaching in 1 Cor 15 is concerning physical death. Yet Paul declared, "The last enemy that will be abolished is death" (1 Cor 15:26).[156] If physical death is an enemy that will be abolished, then it is outlandish to think that God created man to die, or that physical death is part of "a common human nature with Adam we share in his natural mortality."[157] And it will not work for Craig to argue that physical death became an enemy after the fall. If physical death is supposed to be part of a common human nature with Adam, then it follows that man's common human nature has been changed and corrupted, and part of man's common human nature with Adam has become an enemy that will be abolished. But Craig has argued that physical death is part of *our* common human nature with Adam, not part of the fall. So, either God created our common human nature as an enemy, or physical death and spiritual death entered because of sin as Paul declared.

153. וַיֹּאמֶר יְהוָה אֱלֹהִים הֵן הָאָדָם הָיָה כְּאַחַד מִמֶּנּוּ לָדַעַת טוֹב וָרָע וְעַתָּה פֶּן־יִשְׁלַח יָדוֹ וְלָקַח גַּם מֵעֵץ הַחַיִּים וְאָכַל וָחַי לְעֹלָם:
(Gen 3:22)

154. וַיְגָרֶשׁ אֶת־הָאָדָם וַיַּשְׁכֵּן מִקֶּדֶם לְגַן־עֵדֶן אֶת־הַכְּרֻבִים וְאֵת לַהַט הַחֶרֶב הַמִּתְהַפֶּכֶת לִשְׁמֹר אֶת־דֶּרֶךְ עֵץ הַחַיִּים:
(Gen 3:24)

155. καὶ καθ' ὅσον ἀπόκειται τοῖς ἀνθρώποις ἅπαξ ἀποθανεῖν, μετὰ δὲ τοῦτο κρίσις (Heb 9:27).

156. ἔσχατος ἐχθρὸς καταργεῖται ὁ θάνατος (1 Cor 15:26).

157. Craig, *Adam*, 226.

As we have already established, the creation account depicts God subduing and filling, and he commissions the couple to fill and subdue. They are created in order to imitate God, and by imitating God, showing forth his glory. But death does not show forth the glory of the eternal, never dying God. To claim that God created Adam and Eve as mortal human beings destined to die is contrary to the commission to manifest God's glory. God is life. But death, physical or spiritual, is contrary to God's glory.

Craig argues for a diachronic understanding of Rom 5:12–21:

> In the remainder of Rom 5:12–21, then, Paul is, on this view, describing how the sin of Adam unleashes the power that results in all persons' sinning, with the result that they are condemned to spiritual death. When Paul says, "The judgment following one trespass brought condemnation," we may take that to refer to God's swift judgment on Adam's sin; but when he thinks of the result of Adam's sin, he says, "One man's trespass led to condemnation for all men," since all men sinned. Paul would be confused if he thought that the judgment following Adam's one trespass involved the condemnation of all people, since nonexistent persons cannot be condemned.[158]

We have already shown that Craig's interpretation of Rom 5:12 cannot be correct, because of both the syntax of the verse and Paul's own subsequent arguments. Craig asserts, "nonexistent persons cannot be condemned." But this is precisely the problem with Craig's argument. If nonexistent persons cannot be condemned, then neither have nonexistent persons sinned. Yet Paul specifically asserts "all sinned [πάντες ἥμαρτον, *pantes hemarton*]." It is important that the word translated "sinned" is in the Aorist tense. According to Buist Fanning, the aorist aspect does not include a diachronic meaning:

> According to this approach, the aorist is a viewpoint aspect (see section 1.2.1), in that it reflects the speaker's or writer's focus or *perspective* on the occurrence and not the actional character of the occurrence itself (duration-momentariness, process-event, etc.). Nor does it give the speaker's *portrayal* of the actional character (i.e. 'viewed as an event,' 'viewed as momentary'). Instead the aorist presents an occurrence *in summary, viewed as a whole from the outside, without regard for the internal make-up of the occurrence.* This 'external, summarizing' viewpoint

---

158. Craig, *Adam*, 238.

concerning the occurrence is what is invariant in the meaning of the aorist itself.[159]

In other words, for Craig to take the statement "all sinned" as a diachronic expression is contrary to the verbal aspect of the Aroist tense and, as Fanning asserts, "the aorist itself does not bear these meanings."[160] So, when Craig claims, "Perhaps the greatest objection to this diachronic view of the effect of Adam's sin is that the parallelism with Christ's atoning death seems to become rather loose," this is false. The greatest objection to Craig's diachronic view is the syntax of the Greek NT.

Craig attempts to argue that his interpretation does not fall victim to the claim that the parallelism with Christ's atoning death becomes "rather loose:"

> Perhaps the greatest objection to this diachronic view of the effect of Adam's sin is that the parallelism with Christ's atoning death seems to become rather loose. For in Christ's case, we do not seem to have his act of obedience leading over time to justification and life for all. Rather, all are made righteous and alive in his act of obedience. But, in fact, the doctrine of the imputation of our sins to Christ and of his righteousness to us (found elsewhere in Paul) does not appear in this passage any more than does the imputation of Adam's sin to us.[161]

Craig seems to want to separate Paul's teaching into incommensurable compartments. Are we to think that because Paul's doctrine is not specifically present in a given text that it is therefore irrelevant to this text? Whether or not Paul's doctrine of imputation of our sins to Christ and his righteousness to us is found in a particular passage does not forbid that doctrine from being assumed in all Paul's teaching. And we have already shown that Craig's diachronic interpretation is contrary to the verbal aspect of NT Greek.

Craig attempts to argue that Paul's statement in Rom 1:17 should also be interpreted in a diachronic sense:

> For he says, "Those who receive the abundance of grace and the free gift of righteousness will reign in life through the one man Jesus Christ," a process that is ongoing throughout history as people are born, come to hear the gospel, and embrace it.

---

159. Fanning, *Verbal Aspect in New Testament Greek*, 97. Emphasis in original.
160. Fanning, *Verbal Aspect in New Testament Greek*, 97–98.
161. Craig, *Adam*, 238.

So "by one man's obedience many will be made righteous," and "one man's act of righteousness leads to acquittal and life for all men." We seem to have here the same sort of diachronic impact of Christ's atoning death as we have in the case of Adam's sin, making them surprisingly parallel.

But Craig has made an assumption that he has not demonstrated. Craig takes Paul's statement "will reign in life" (ἐν ζωῇ βασιλεύσουσιν, en zōē basileusousin) as referring to this life that the righteous live prior to death and resurrection. But this is not the case. Paul is not talking about reigning in this life. He is talking about reigning with Christ, as he states in 2 Timothy: "If we endure, we will also reign with Him; if we deny Him, He also will deny us;" (2 Tim 2:12).[162] The verb used in the Romans passage is βασιλεύσουσιν (basileusousin) from βασιλεύω (basileuō). The verb used in 2 Timothy is συμβασιλεύσομεν (sumbasileusomen), from συμβασιλεύω (sumbasileuō). The verb is the same in the two passages, only the verb in 2 Timothy adds the prepositional prefix συν (sun)[163] to indicate reigning together. Paul never uses the word βασιλεύω (basileuō) to refer to reigning in this life. Craig has read into the text the meaning he needs it to have in order to support his claim, but he has not understood the language or the syntax.

Craig concludes this chapter saying, "The several references by NT authors to mythological or pseudepigraphal figures caution us to avoid overly easy proofs of OT historicity on the basis of NT citations."[164] Actually, Craig's treatment should caution us against making declarations without understanding the lexicology, grammar, and syntax of the text, eisegesis, and building conclusions on suppositions that are grounded on assumptions that have not been proven. Finally, Craig admits, "Adam is regarded by Paul as a historical person whose actions affected the course of history . . . still it remains the case that Adam's sin is, in Paul's thinking, in some sense the fount of the sin and spiritual death that beset our world, which suffices for the affirmation of a historical Adam."[165] Although Craig acknowledges that Paul regards Adam as an historical figure, ultimately Craig concludes that the quest for an historical Adam is inconclusive.

---

162. εἰ ὑπομένομεν, καὶ συμβασιλεύσομεν· εἰ ἀρνησόμεθα, κἀκεῖνος ἀρνήσεται ἡμᾶς· (2 Tim 2:12).

163. The final letter ν changes to μ when followed by a labial.

164. Craig, *Adam*, 241.

165. Craig, *Adam*, 242.

8

Scientific and Philosophical Preliminaries

CRAIG BEGINS THIS CHAPTER with the following pronouncement: "If the biblical Adam is, or was, a historical person who actually lived, then the obvious question arises: When did he live? Given the mythical nature of the primaeval history of Gen 1–11, it is to modern science that we must turn in the attempt to answer this question."[1] It is certainly understandable that an author would build on what he believes he has established. Since we have shown that Craig has in fact not demonstrated, except to his own satisfaction, that Gen 1–11 is mythical, it seems to follow that we do not need to turn to modern science to attempt to answer the question of whether Adam was an historical person. Craig goes on to point out that modern science does not address itself to the existence or non-existence of Adam of the Genesis account, yet Craig states, "Nevertheless, contemporary scientists are vitally interested in a question that is empirically equivalent to our question—namely, when did human beings first appear in the evolutionary process?"[2] Of course, this assumes that the evolutionary process actually occurred. It would seem important, then, that Craig first prove that the evolutionary process is an historical fact before using the evolutionary process to investigate the question of the historical Adam, or any other historical figure of the past. Unfortunately for his readers, Craig simply assumes the fact of the evolutionary process

1. Craig, *Adam*, 245.
2. Craig, *Adam*, 245.

without addressing whether it is even true. On the basis of his unproven assumption that the evolutionary process is an historical fact, Craig launches his investigation.

Since the discussion beginning with the heading, "Timescales," deals with matters outside of my area, I will not be able to address Craig's claims and arguments on the level of modern science. Suffice it to say that the debate about evolution is not primarily a scientific debate. It is a philosophical debate. Empirical data do not come with tags that provide interpretations and meanings of the data. The data must be interpreted by the scientist from his own interpretive gird and world view, and adjudicating between interpretive girds and world views is a philosophical exercise, not a scientific one. Additionally, evolution is not universally accepted among practicing scientists. According to Edgar Harold Andrews, an English physicist and engineer, and Emeritus Professor of Materials at Queen Mary, University of London,

> Here and there, however, and apart from Christians who reject evolution on biblical and theological grounds, there are to be found scientists of various disciplines who recognize that many aspects of the theory offend the canons of rigorous science. They see that many of the so-called facts of evolution arise from carefully selected evidence and depend upon preconceived interpretations of the observations. They recognize that the mechanisms by which the evolution of life and biological species is said to have occurred are, at best, unproven hypotheses and, at worst, contradictions of the experimental facts ... We must therefore recognize evolutionary theory for what it is, a philosophy (indeed, for some, a religion) and not basically a scientific discipline at all; only then shall we appreciate both its impact on our minds and attitudes and its decidedly unscientific character.[3]

What Is It to Be Human?

That evolution in particular, and modern science in general, is principally a matter of a prior philosophical commitment is ably demonstrated by Craig in the opening statements of this section:

> We have seen that it would be rash to assume that organisms classified as *Homo* are *ipso facto* human beings. Rather, we need

---

3. Andrews, *Evolution Scientific*, 1, 3.

to specify certain conditions that are jointly sufficient for humanity. There is, in fact, a noteworthy consensus among scientists as to what these conditions are. We are, after all, familiar with ourselves as human beings and therefore know what a paradigmatic human being is like.[4]

The question, "What is it to be human?" is not a scientific question. It is a philosophical and theological question. Consequently, any "noteworthy consensus" among scientists is not the result of scientific investigation, but is rather a product of philosophical speculation. As Anton Pegis wrote, "The human soul, which is a spiritual substance *as* the form of matter, is an intellectual creature destined by nature for a historical existence, for an incarnate and therefore temporal duration, in order to express and to realize the intellectuality proper to it ... He cannot be examined with laboratory tools, though scientists can tell us a great many things about him."[5]

Edward Feser makes a similar claim:

> The proper approach to the study of the mind, in the dualist's view, is via metaphysics rather than physics, and philosophy rather than natural science. For since, in the dualist's view, the arguments for dualism show that the mind is non-physical, they thereby show also that it is only via inquiry other than scientific inquiry that we are going to understand its nature, if we are going to understand it at all.[6]

By "dualist" view, Feser is referring to the fact that the human person is composed of the incorporeal and the corporeal, soul and body.

Jacques Maritain points out that philosophy stands in judgment over other sciences:

> 1.) All science is its master, in the sense that it has the necessary and sufficient means to establish the truth in its field, and that no one is justified in denying the truths thus established.
>
> But it can happen that a science, or rather a scientist, accidentally gets it wrong in his own field. In this case the science in question can undoubtedly judge and rectify itself, but it is clear that a higher science is also founded to judge it and to rectify it, supposing that the committed error comes up against one of its truths and thus falls under its light. Now philosophy and

---

4. Craig, *Adam*, 257.
5. Pegis, *Origins of the Thomistic Notion of Man*, 52.
6. Feser, *Philosophy of Mind*, 207.

> above all philosophy par excellence or metaphysics is the highest science. So it is up to it to JUDGE all other human sciences, in the sense that it condemns as false any scientific proposition incompatible with its own truths.[7]

J. P. Moreland pointed out, "Science cannot be practiced in thin air; it is based on many assumptions, each with its challenges. And the business of stating, criticizing, and defending its assumptions is not scientific but philosophical."[8] He also produced a chart in which he lists some of the first-order and second-order questions in philosophy of mind. He divided these questions into the categories, "Ontological," "Epistemological," "Semantic," and "Methodological. Commenting on this chart, Moreland states, "These are the sorts of questions that form the warp and woof of philosophy of mind. Please read the list carefully. It becomes evident, as we shall see, that *these are in no way scientific questions; they are philosophical to the core* and nicely illustrate the autonomy of philosophy thesis."[9] The question, "What is a human person?" as Moreland points out, is not a scientific question, but is a philosophical question. Craig's turn to science is a turn to an area that is not capable to answering the question.

Sufficient Conditions for Humanness

In this section Craig sets out what he takes to be some of the sufficient conditions for humanness. He begins with the observation, "We know, for example, that any putative human being must be anatomically similar to ourselves. While a self-conscious, rational extraterrestrial (or even chimpanzee) would be a person, he would not be a *human* person."[10] This

---

7. Maritain, *Introduction Générale a las Philosophie*, 71. "1.) Toute science est maîtresse chez elle, en ce sens qu'elle a les moyens nécessaires et suffisants d'établir la vérité dans son domaine, et que personne n'est fondé à nier les vérités ainsi établies.

Mais il peut arriver qu'une science ou plutôt qu'un savant *se trompe* par accident dans son propre domaine. En ce cas la science en question peut sans doute se juger et se rectifier elle-même, mais il est clair qu'une science plus élevée est fondée aussi à la juger et à la rectifier, à supposer que l'erreur commise vienne heurter quelqu'une de ses vérités et tomber ainsi sous sa lumière. Or la philosophie et avant tout la philosophie par excellence ou métaphysique est la science la plus élevée. Donc il lui appartient de JUGER toutes les autres sciences humaines, en ce sens qu'elle condamne comme fausse toute proposition scientifique incompatible avec ses propres vérités."

8. Moreland, *Scientism and Secularism*, 55.

9. Moreland, *Scientism and Secularism*, 120. Emphasis added.

10. Craig, *Adam*, 257.

observation is, obviously, a philosophical conclusion, not a conclusion based on the findings of natural science. Why should we assume that in order for any being to qualify has being human that this being must be "anatomically similar to ourselves"? Craig has simply stipulated that anatomical similarity is part of what constitutes a paradigmatic example of humanness: "On the basis of our paradigmatic examples of humans, we can delineate certain features that, given sufficient anatomical similarity, are sufficient (if not necessary) for human personhood."[11] I am not objecting to this criterion. Rather I am pointing out that this is not a scientific criterion. It is a philosophical one.

Craig quotes anthropologists Sally McBrearty and Alison Brooks who have composed a list of four characteristics of modern human behavior:

- abstract thinking, the ability to act with reference to abstract concepts not limited in time or space
- planning depth, the ability to formulate strategies on the basis of past experience and to act on them in a group context
- behavioral, economic, and technological innovativeness
- symbolic behavior, the ability to represent objects, people, and abstract concepts with arbitrary symbols, vocal or visual, and to reify such symbols in cultural practice[12]

Craig goes on to point out, "It is worth pausing to underline the fact that McBrearty and Brooks are not offering anatomical conditions for biological humanness but philosophical conditions for human personhood."[13] Unfortunately Craig does not tell us from what philosophical perspective these authors come, nor are we told why the list is confined to these characteristics only. Nevertheless, Craig's point about the philosophical aspects of the work of these authors shows that they derive these particular characteristics on the basis of a philosophical perspective, not merely on the basis of the principles and methods of modern, natural science.

Craig goes on to assert, "Although some glimmerings of some of these behaviors, such as behavioral and technological innovativeness, might appear among nonhuman animals, they will pale next to the degree

---

11. Craig, *Adam*, 258.
12. Craig, *Adam*, 258.
13. Craig, *Adam*, 259.

to which they are found among modern humans, and the combination of all four behaviors would remain unprecedented."[14] It appears, then, that the difference between modern humans and nonhuman animals is simply a matter of degree, not kind.

However, there is a qualitative difference between humans and animals. John Deely points out that there is in fact a qualitative difference between all species:

> First of all, it is no longer possible to participate intelligently in this discussion without taking account of the fact that there are qualitative differences in the communication systems of all biological species or forms. Not only the human species, but, it would seem, every species exhibits species-specific modalities of apprehension and consequent communication. So the question of whether human understanding differs qualitatively or only quantitatively from the cognition of other animals becomes to a large extent moot. Every cognitive organism belongs to one or another species, and every cognitive species is distinguished by apprehensive modalities peculiar to itself.[15]

This qualitative difference indicates a difference not merely in degree, but in kind. Mortimer Adler explains these:

> Two things differ in degree when, with respect to a certain property that they have in common, one has more of it and the other less. In geometry, two triangles differ in degree with respect to their area if one is larger and the other smaller. In the physical world, two runways on an airfield differ in degree if one is longer, the other shorter.
>
> Two things differ in kind when one of them has characteristics or properties not possessed by the other. In geometry, a triangle and a circle differ in kind by virtue of the fact that one figure has angles and the other has none. In the physical world, invertebrates and vertebrates differ in kind. The latter have backbones lacked by the former.[16]

Adler goes on to show that there is not merely a difference in degree between humans and animals, but there is a difference in kind:

> While thought is present in both man and the higher animals, animal thought is perceptual thought; only human thought is

14. Craig, *Adam*, 259.
15. Deely, *What Distinguishes Human Understanding?* 5.
16. Adler, *Intellect*, 25.

> conceptual. While motivating appetites or desires are present in both man and other animals, only man has an intellectual appetite, a will that is able to make free choices.[17]

> Only human beings live with the awareness of death and with the certain knowledge that they are going die.
> Only human beings use their minds to become artists, scientists, historians, philosophers, priests, teachers, lawyers, physicians, engineers, accountants, inventors, traders, bankers, and statesmen.
> Only among human beings is there a distinction between those who behave ethically and those who are knaves, scoundrels, villains, and criminals.
> Only among human beings is there any distinction between those who have mental health and those who suffer mental disease or have mental disabilities of one sort or another.
> Only in the sphere of human life are there such institutions as schools, libraries, hospitals, churches, temples, factories, theaters, museums, prisons, cemeteries, and so on.[18]

After a lengthy discussion concerning the claims that animals have intellect, George Klubertanz concludes,

> Hence, there is no proof that animals possess an intellect, and some very strong indications that they do not possess such a power. Activities which would be unequivocal proofs for intellect, such that they could not be interpreted in any other way, are: the use of a real language; the invention of tools of a kind which involve more than merely spatial relations; learning by independent originality; appreciation of beauty, morality, and so forth; freedom of choice; culture, and a progress in it. None of these are had by animals; in some instances (freedom as contrasted with uniformity and specificity of response), their activities are directly contrary to activities which imply the possession of intellect.
> To sum up this section, we conclude that there is no proof that animals possess an intellect, and there is positive proof that they do not.[19]

Craig concludes, "Human beings, in the full sense of organisms anatomically similar to ourselves and capable of abstract thought; deep

---

17. Adler, *Intellect*, 28.
18. Adler, *Intellect*, 38.
19. Klubertanz, *Philosophy of Human Nature*, 155.

planning; behavioral, economic, and technological innovativeness; and symbolic behavior, therefore originated on this planet sometime between the Lower and Middle Palaeolithic (or ESA and MSA)."[20] The Lower and Middle Palaeolithic period supposedly spanned from about three hundred thousand to thirty thousand years ago. One problem that arises in these proposals is the assumption that there were no beings having these characteristics prior to these dates whose remains just have not survived. It is possible that there were beings who would meet Craig's criteria the remains of whose existence have simply been lost. Additionally it must be pointed out that empirical evidence does not come with tags explaining how the evidence should be interpreted. Empirical evidence must the interpreted by the observer, and interpretation necessarily involves one's philosophical perspective.

Having shown that there is a difference in kind between humans and animals, Craig's claim about the origin of human beings amounts only to showing that the earliest empirical evidence suggests that there were human beings at the time indicated. It does not show that humans originated on this planet at this time since empirical evidence of earlier humans may simply have been lost. Additionally, the empirical evidence does not show the cause of the origin of the human species. It cannot be the case that animals are the cause of humans. The error assumes that the semen of one species can generate something different than that species. An ape cannot produce a man. This error is what Michael Chaberek explains as "attributing too much to secondary causes":

> The objection says that the primary cause can act upon the secondary cause in an instrumental manner, so that the power of the instrument is exceeded by the first cause (as when a man writes with a pen). Yet, a chalk, or a pen, is designed for writing, as much as a chisel is designed for sculpting. Thus, even though a pen cannot write by itself, its nature is such that it is used for writing. In evolution, however, the very tool (a natural biological process) is not fitting for production of the effect, which would be a new species. It would be like writing with a pot of water or sculpting rock with a plastic knife. The impossibility of obtaining the effect by the primary cause while using inadequate and disproportional tools is not due to the lack of power on the part of the primary cause, but due to the lack of power and suitability on the part of the secondary cause. The same problem pertains to saying that not one or two causes (such as random mutations

---

20. Craig, *Adam*, 264.

and natural selection), but a set or a number of causes generate the supposed evolutionary effect. In fact, it does not matter how many causes there are, but whether they are suitable to produce a particular type of effect or not. Multiplication of causes does not make them more suitable. Similarly, in designing a machine, ten uneducated people cannot make up for a counsel of one engineer, and it does not matter whether there are ten or a thousand tinkerers if none of them has the appropriate knowledge.[21]

And it will not work to claim that the human species developed on the basis of random mutation of DNA. As Stephen Meyer has demonstrated,

> Recent experiments on proteins performed by Douglas Axxe and others, however, have shown in a precise quantitative way that functional genetic sequences (and their corresponding proteins) are indeed too rare to be accounted for by the neo-Darwinian mechanism of natural selection sifting through random genetic mutation. The "space" or number of possible arrangements are simply too vast, and the available time to search by undirected mutation too short for their to have been a realistic chance of producing even one new gene or protein by undirected mutation and selection in the time allowed for most evolutionary transitions.[22]

Thus far, Craig has not shown that evolution can account for the origin of humans. Chapters 9 through 11 investigate additional aspects of empirical evidence for the origin of humans. Much of this information is interesting and informative. Evaluating this evidence in terms of the disciplines and sciences involved is outside of my area. However, it is nevertheless the case that all of this empirical evidence must be interpreted by the scientist, and this interpretation necessarily involves the philosophical perspective of the interpreter, and Craig has yet either to present the philosophical perspective or justify it as an adequate basis for his conclusions. Additionally, none of the evidence presented addresses the question of the necessary and sufficient cause of the origin of the human species. To claim that the human species developed from a (or some) non-human species is an argument to something (humanness) from nothing (nonhumanness). But nothing cannot produce something.

---

21. Chaberek, *Aquinas and Evolution*, 69.

22. Meyer, "Neo-Darwinism and the Origin of Biological Form and Information," 105–6.

9

Locating the Historical Adam

IN THIS CHAPTER CRAIG presents various interpretations of the fossil record in an attempt to develop a modified genealogical tree to show the time of the divergence between Neanderthals and Homo Sapiens (see **Figure 25**).[1] However, things are not as straightforward as Craig presents them. Casey Luskin has shown that the fossil record does not document the evolutionary development of modern humans from ape-like species.

> The standard evolutionary view of human origins—generally accepted by theistic evolutionists—holds that our species, *Homo sapiens*, evolved from ape-like species through apparently unguided evolutionary processes like natural selection and random mutation. Theistic evolutionists and other evolutionary scientists often claim the fossil evidence for this Darwinian evolution of humans from ape-like creatures is incontrovertible. But their viewpoint is not supported by the fossil evidence. Hominin fossils generally fall into one of two groups: ape-like species and human-like species, with a large, unbridged gap between them. Virtually the entire hominin fossil record is marked by fragmented fossils, especially the early hominins, which do not document precursors to humans. Around 3 to 4 million years ago, the australopithecines appear, but they were generally ape-like and also appear in an abrupt manner. When our genus *Homo* appears, it also does so in an abrupt fashion, without clear evidence of a transition from previous ape-like hominins. Major members of

---

1. Craig, *Adam*, 332.

Homo are very similar to modern humans, and their differences amount to small-scale microevolutionary changes. The archaeological record shows an "explosion" of human creativity about thirty to forty thousand years ago. Despite the claims of evolutionary paleoanthropologists and the media hype surrounding many hominin fossils, the fragmented hominin fossil record does not document the evolution of humans from ape-like precursors, and the appearance of humans in the fossil record is anything but a gradual Darwinian evolutionary process.[2]

Craig proposes that Adam may have been a member of the hominin family dubbed *Homo heidelbergensis*, an extinct species or subspecies of archaic humans who supposedly existed during the Middle Pleistocene age, about 781,000 to 126,000 years ago. Craig proposes, "Adam, then, may be plausibly identified as a member of *Homo heidelbergensis*, living perhaps >750 kya [kya = thousand years ago]. He could even have lived in the Near East in the biblical site of the Garden of Eden—though vastly earlier than usually thought, of course. His descendants migrated southward into Africa, where they gave rise to *Homo sapiens*, and westward into Europe, where they evolved into Neanderthals/Denisovans."[3]

Craig concludes this chapter with the assertion, "Adam and Eve may therefore be plausibly identified as members of *Homo heidelbergensis* and as the founding pair at the root of all human species."[4] It is curious that in this closing statement Craig would refer to "*the* founding pair." Earlier Craig referred to Adam and Eve as "*a* founding pair of the human race belonging to the species *Homo heidelbergensis*." After the claims and arguments that he made concerning the existence of *Homo heidelbergensis* as a hominin group, it makes no sense for Craig actually to be asserting in his conclusion that Adam and Eve were "the founding pair." It is clear from his arguments that, if there were an actual Adam and Eve, they would have been one pair among the population of individuals grouped under the classification *Homo heidelbergensis*. Although it may seem that Craig is asserting the actual historical existence of Adam and Eve, this pair is certainly not the pair depicted in the Genesis account. In the Genesis account, Adam is created from the dust of the ground. He did not evolve from prior beings. Adam and Eve are depicted as the first humans.

2. Luskin, "Missing Transitions: Human Origins and the Fossil Record," 437–38.
3. Craig, *Adam*, 336.
4. Craig, *Adam*, 359.

They were not part of a group or community of like beings. Genesis does not depict Adam and Eve as a species or subspecies of archaic humans.

Additionally, the notion that Adam and Eve were part of a group of humanoid beings undermines the notion that all humans sin in their own turn. If Adam and Eve were the pair by which sin and death entered into the world, and if Adam and Eve were a part of this group of humanoid beings, then it remains possible that those of this group of humanoid beings who did not sin could produce descendants who do not sin in their own turn. This introduces the possibility that not all humans are sinners. Rather, only those who are descendants of Adam and Eve are sinners. Everyone else is okay and not in need of salvation by grace through faith, and Paul's statement that all sin is simply false.

10

Putting It All Together

IN THIS FINAL CHAPTER, Craig discusses the debates about the image of God in man, about body-soul dualism, and about the relation of Adam and Eve to their supposed contemporaries. In the opening paragraph of this chapter, Craig acknowledges that the biblically faithful Christian is obliged "to affirm the historicity of Adam and Eve."[1] Of course the Adam and Eve that Craig describes is almost unrecognizable to a "biblically faithful Christian." Craig's Adam and Eve are the products of an evolutionary development at which point there was some sort of "radical transition effected in the founding pair that lifted them to the human level [that] plausibly involved both biological and spiritual renovation, perhaps divinely caused."[2] This description is diametrically opposed to the biblical account in which God formed Adam from the dust and breathed into his nostrils the breath of life, and he formed Eve from the rib he took from Adam's side.

The diametric opposition of the biblical account to Craig's description would certainly not be taken by him as a substantive argument against his position since he believes he as demonstrated that "it is plausible to regard these chapters [Gen 1–11] as a Hebrew mytho-history that serves as a universal foundational charter for the election and identity of

---

1. Craig, *Adam*, 363.
2. Craig, *Adam*, 376.

Israel over against its neighbors," and that "these narratives need not be read as literal history."[3]

He concludes this chapter with the following observations:

> Despite the inconclusiveness of the quest, we have managed to narrow the window of opportunity considerably as to Adam's place in history. Adam plausibly lived sometime between around 1 mya to 750 kya, a conclusion consistent with the evidence of population genetics. The *terminus ad quern* will probably be pushed back with further palaeontological and archaeological discoveries. We may also expect clarification of the place of *Homo heidelbergensis* through palaeoproteomic analysis of the remains of this species. The name serves at least as a useful placeholder for that large-brained human species that was ancestral to *Homo sapiens* and our various sister species of the human family. We can live with uncertainty. For though we now see through a glass darkly, we shall one day see face to face (1 Cor 13:12). In the meantime, we await new discoveries with excitement and anticipation.[4]

But has he accomplished what he thinks he has? Let us summarize what Craig has actually accomplished.

What Hath Craig Wrought?

Chapter 1: What Is at Stake?

In this first chapter, Craig discusses what is at stake, the structure of the Pentateuch, and the relation of biblical narrative to ANE myths.

What is at Stake?

In the first section of chapter 1, Craig argues that Christian doctrine does not require a doctrine of original sin.

- Craig's claim that the doctrine is not taught in the NT is wildly implausible.
- Craig's appeal to various passages do not support his claim because he misinterprets them.

---

3. Craig, *Adam*, 363.
4. Craig, *Adam*, 380.

- Craig's notion of "getting along" is nonsensical.
- Craig attempts to prejudice the reader by stating his conclusions as fact before presenting any evidence to support these conclusions.
- Craig's appeal to 1 Cor 15:3 does not support his assertion.
- Craig tends to misrepresent and misunderstand his opponents' views.
- Craig has demonstrated a lack of facility in Hebrew lexicology, grammar, and syntax that leads him to make assertions that cannot be supported by the text.

We have not shown, nor have we attempted to show, that Christian theology requires a doctrine of original sin. As a result of the analysis, what we have shown is that Craig has not made his case that Christian doctrine does not require a doctrine of original sin. There are a multitude of commentators and theologians who have argued that the NT does teach the doctrine of original sin and that this doctrine is a necessary part of orthodox Christian theology. Craig has failed to interact with any of these arguments, commentators, or theologians.

Structure of the Pentateuch

In this section Craig argues that Gen 1–11 constitutes a distinct thematic unit that is set off from the remainder of the Pentateuch, and that this unit should be taken as Hebrew mytho-history.

- The structure of the Pentateuch as Craig, following Clines, depicts it violates the literary structure of the text.
- The literary characteristics of the text provide a completely different structural arrangement of the Pentateuch that is supported by the objective characteristics of the text, not the subject judgments about themes and topics.
- Dividing Genesis at chapter 11 disrupts the continuity of the genealogy of Shem as it leads into the narratives about Abram.
- Craig's lack of facility in Hebrew lexicology, grammar, and syntax has led him to misunderstand and misrepresent the structure of the Pentateuch.

- The relation of literary imagery throughout the OT and into the NT supports the literary structure and features, and the meaning and imagery that is used by the author of Genesis.

Because Craig has either ignored or is unaware of the literary characteristics of the text, he has adopted a structure of the Pentateuch that does not reflect the author's literary strategy. Because Craig is not adequately familiar with the language, he has adopted a structure that cannot be supported. Gen 1–11 is not either thematically or structurally distinct from the rest of the Pentateuch. The first major section of Genesis ends at 7:24, not at the end of Genesis 11. A new major section begins with the declaration in 8:1, "And God remembered Noah" at which point the creation imagery begins to be repeated.

In Relation to ANE Mythology

Because of the supposed similarity of themes between ANE myth and biblical narrative, Craig assumes that this indicates a literary context in which the Bible is constructed. Craig assumes that the movement is always from ANE myth to biblical narrative because he believes that the content of ANE myths predates the content of biblical narratives.

- Neither Craig nor OT scholars have proven that ANE myth forms a literary context by which one should understand biblical narrative.
- The similarities between ANE myth and biblical narrative can be explained because both texts are dealing with perennial questions of origin, life and death, creation, the nature of God or gods, etc.
- These very same themes are dealt with by authors throughout the history of mankind.
- Supposed similarity of design does not necessarily mean identity of origin.
- In order to prove literary context much more evidence must be presented than has presently been given by OT scholars.
- Craig has misunderstood the theme of the Pentateuch.

Craig has not grasped the theme of the Pentateuch, which is salvation by grace through faith, a theme that is not found in ANE myth, and it is the differences that make the difference.

Chapter 2: The Nature of Myth

In this chapter, Craig employs Wittgenstein's method of family resemblances to argue that biblical narrative of Gen 1–11 has sufficient similarity to ANE myths to be understood against this literary context. On the basis of this method, Craig sets forth 10 characteristics of myths in order to apply these characteristics to his interpretation of the biblical text.

Family Resemblances

Wittgenstein's notion of family resemblances is arbitrary and illegitimate and does not provide a sufficient method for comparing ANE myth to biblical narrative.

- The notion of family resemblances is arbitrary.
- The notion of family resemblances is predicated on Wittgenstein's always, already present assumptions about language and meaning.
- Craig's use of family resemblances is inadequate as a method of comparison between ANE myth and biblical narrative because it is predicated on Craig's always, already present assumptions about the relation between ANE literature and biblical narrative.
- Both Wittgenstein's and Craig's use of family resemblances begs the question and assumes what must be proven.
- Craig's appeal to Burridge's characterization of the Gospels as Greco-Roman biography begs the question and is illegitimate.
- The classification of the Gospels as Greco-Roman biography has been demonstrated to be wrong, and it entails a rejection of inerrancy.

Characteristics of Myth

Craig sets out ten characteristics of myths that he will compare to the narratives of Gen 1–11 to discover family resemblances. However, there is no reason to think that any of the characteristics are legitimate, nor is there any reason to think that these are the only characteristics that should be counted.

- Particular characteristics are predetermined by Craig's assumptions of what constitutes a myth.
- Since Craig's list is a construct of his own assumptions, the list is not developed from the myths themselves.
- Craig has already settled on a class of myths as paradigmatic, but these are arbitrarily chosen.
- Because the list of characteristics are pre-determined by Craig's assumptions, his list suffers from vicious circularity.
- Since Craig's list is a construct of his own assumptions, there is no reason why someone could not add to the list.
- An eleventh characteristic that can be added to the list is that all myths are false.
- Since this eleventh characteristic can be added to the list, the biblical narratives of Gen 1–11 cannot be classified as myth without rejecting inerrancy.
- Once one rejects inerrancy, one can simply stipulate which narratives are false and which are true depending upon the interpreter's preferences.

Craig never sets out a number of characteristics or a percentage of characteristics that the biblical narratives must have in order to be classified as myths. Should the biblical narratives be considered myths if they reflect only one or two of the characteristics? Must the biblical narratives reflect more than 50% of the characteristics? Additionally, the characteristics that are set out in the list are not specific enough to distinguish myths from any kind of literature that anyone has ever composed or handed down throughout the history of mankind.

Chapter 3: Are the Primaeval Narratives of Genesis 1–11 Myth? (Part 1)

In this and the following chapters Craig attempts to specify the characteristics set forth in the previous chapter and to compare them with the narratives of Gen 1–11 in order to show that the biblical narratives can and should be classified as myth.

1. Narrative

In this section Craig compares ANE myth with biblical narratives. He refers to content of Gen 1–11 as recording "primaeval events" and to Gen 1–11 as "primaeval history." However, the literary structure of Genesis sets off only Gen 1:1–7:24 as constituting what might be called "primaeval history."

- Craig's lack of facility in Hebrew leads him to misunderstand and misrepresent the genealogical record of Genesis 5.
- Craig's calculation of at least one thousand, nine hundred and forty-eight years from Gen 1 to the call of Abraham makes the same mistake made by Bishop James Ussher who calculated the date of creation at 4004 BC.
- Craig's lack of facility in Hebrew prevents him from understanding the literary and linguistic relation between the account of the descendants of Cain, in Gen 4, and the descendants of Seth, in Gen 5, which provides the rationale for including these particular names in the Gen 5 genealogy.
- The most that is accomplished in this section is to show that Gen 1–11 contains narrative. This is hardly enough to qualify as myth.
- Craig has not sufficiently defined the notion of ANE narrative to show that biblical narrative should be considered in that literary context.

2. Traditional Narratives

In this section Craig discusses the various critical approaches to Genesis in an effort to show that Gen 1–11 is composed of traditional stories in conformity with Craig's second characteristic of myth.

- Craig almost completely ignores the fatal problems with the critical approach.
- Craig's appeals to OT scholars does not help his argument. Most OT scholars are heavily influenced by critical philosophy, which undermines the methodology as an objective study of the text.
- Craig completely ignores the OT scholars who have rejected the critical approach.

- Just because a majority of OT scholars have not "entirely" rejected the conclusions of critical analysis does not prove that the critical approach is a reasonable or even a reliable approach. Truth is not determined by majority vote, and OT scholars are as susceptible to prejudice and unstated and unanalyzed assumptions as anyone else.
- Craig completely ignores the fact that the critical methodology entails the rejection of inerrancy, the rejection of divine inspiration, the assumed historical and literary priority of extra-biblical pseudonymous works, and the assumed and discredited evolutionary paradigm as an explanation of the religious development of Israel.
- Craig completely ignores the fatal problems with the dating of Deuteronomy and how this undermines the whole dating methodology of the critical approach.

Craig has not sufficiently circumscribed the notion of "traditional narratives" so as to show that the narratives of Gen 1–11 should fall into the class of myth.

3. Sacred Narrative

In this brief section Craig argues that the narratives of Gen 1–11 are sacred in conformity with his third characteristic of myth. His opening claim that Gen 1–11 is uncontroversially sacred is certainly uncontroversial. However, it is also certainly uncontroversial that the Qur'an is sacred to those who believe it. It is also certainly true that many thousands of religious texts are considered sacred by believers. Again, this characteristic is so broad that it is meaningless as a characteristic by which one can classify Gen 1–11 as myth.

4. Belief

In this brief section Craig argues that the narratives of Gen 1–11 were to be believed by Israelite society. Again, this is an uncontroversial claim, but it is also so broad that it is ultimately meaningless. Many thousands of religious texts throughout the history of mankind have been produced to be believed by the societies to which they were and are directed. Also, many thousands of philosophical texts have been produced to be believed by members of different societies, but they hardly qualify as literary myth.

5. Deities

In this section Craig argues that, like myth, deities are important characters in the Genesis primaeval history. However, biblical narrative does not fit this category since "deities" are not important characters in the Genesis primaeval history. Gen 1–11 presents only one God, not deities. And God is not depicted as "an important character" in the narrative. God is depicted as the only Creator of all that has come to be.

- Craig claims that a story about deity is a story about deities. This is patently false. A story about only one God is a story about only one God, not "deities."
- Craig's appeal to quantificational logic is irrelevant in this case because the Bible claims that God is the only God.
- For Craig to refer to God as "a deity" is already to beg the question.
- For Craig to refer to God as "a deity" is already to assume that God is a species in the genus "deity." But this is false. Even if God were the only individual in the genus "deity" it would nevertheless be false.
- As is declared in Isaiah, God cannot be compared to anything or anyone. There is no god besides God.
- Craig's appeal to Bumba does not support his claim since Bumba cannot be compared to God. Bumba is depicted as a temporal being existing in space.

If we take Craig as simply claiming that some myths present one god or many gods, the characteristic is so broad that it is meaningless. For many thousands of texts god or gods are important characters. In fact, in Craig's own book deities are important characters, but I do not think Craig would agree that his book should be classed as ANE myth.

6. Primaeval Narratives

Craig begins this section by pointing out that Gen 1–11 in set in the primaeval age. If this simply means, as Craig indicates, that the narrative goes back to the beginning of the world, then this claim is uncontroversial. But again, this characteristic is so broad that it could be applied to myths and philosophies and histories. Yet the narratives of Gen 1–11 are radically different from any of Craig's paradigmatic cases of myth. The biblical material simply does not equate with myth.

In this chapter Craig's effort to equate the Genesis narratives with the characteristics of myth simply is not successful. Either the characteristics are so broad that they can be applied to almost any kind of literature in the history of mankind, or the difference between biblical narratives and myth are so radical that the characteristic does not apply. Out of the six characteristics discussed, not one has shown that Gen 1–11 should be classed as myth or that everything that has been written in the history of mankind could be classed as myth. How many of the characteristics must equate with biblical narrative in order to classify it as myth? Already six out of ten characteristics have proven not to equate with the biblical narratives of Gen 1–11.

Chapter 4: Are the Primaeval Narratives of Genesis 1–11 Myth? (Part 2)

In this chapter Craig continues his comparison between the Gen 1–11 narratives and the remaining characteristics set forth in chapter 2.

7. Etiology

In this section Craig soundly refutes that claim of many OT scholars that the author of Genesis has borrowed from ANE myth, or that there is a causal dependence of biblical narrative on ANE myth. Craig identifies two pitfalls that one must avoid in attempting to make a connection between biblical narrative and ANE myth; (1) neglecting context, (2) overgeneralization or abstraction. Yet these are the very pitfalls into which Craig falls in his effort to connect Gen 1–11 with ANE myth.

Craig discusses the following topics in this section: origin of the world, origin of humanity, natural phenomena, cultural practices, and religious cult. In each one of the categories Craig neglects the theological and literary context in which the biblical narrative recounts these events. The context in which these categories are presented in the biblical narratives are so radically different from ANE myth that the two are incommensurable, except in such a broad since that they deal with themes that have been the subjects of all religious literature throughout the history of mankind. Craig also so overgeneralizes the content of the biblical narrative that the comparison is meaningless.

8. Ritual

In this brief section Craig acknowledges that the Gen 1–11 narratives do not compare with the eighth characteristic of myth.

9. Correspondences

In this brief section Craig acknowledges that the Gen 1–11 narratives do not compare with the correspondences between deities and nature that are depicted in myth.

10. Fantastic and Inconsistent Elements

In this final section on the relation of Craig's ten characteristics of myth to biblical narratives, Craig divides his discussion into two main categories each having subcategories. Under the subheading "Inconsistencies," he considers anthropomorphisms and narrative inconsistencies. Under the subheading "Fantastic Elements," he discusses six-day creation, vegetarianism, the snake, the trees of life and of the knowledge of good and evil, the rivers of Eden, the cherubim, the antediluvians' life spans, Noah's flood, the Table of Nations, the Tower of Babel, and the age of the earth.

Under these subheadings, Craig attempts to show that the biblical narratives of Gen 1–11 contain fantastic and inconsistent elements. Each of these discussions revisits arguments and claims that have been made against the biblical text since there were critics. Yet Craig has not advanced any of these charges from what has been claimed by a multitude of others, and not one of Craig's discussions has established either inconsistencies or contradictions. What Craig holds to be "fantastic" elements are principally due to the fact that he does not understand the original language, or he misses the theological and literary significance of these events. Craig has not demonstrated that the biblical narratives of Gen 1–11 have any fantastic or inconsistent elements.

Craig has not shown that his characteristics of myth can be so applied to the biblical narratives of Gen 1–11 that they should be classified as mytho-history. Except for the tenth characteristic, the characteristics of myth are not specific enough to make a distinction between myths and all kinds of literature. The characteristics are so general and open ended that they are ultimately meaningless in classifying any literature as myth, or they qualify all literature as myth. The tenth characteristic, though specific enough, does not apply to the biblical narratives.

Chapter 5: Is Genesis 1–11 Mytho History?

In a word: No!

Genealogies

By trying to show some kind of relation between biblical genealogies and ANE genealogies, Craig has completely missed the literary strategy of the author and the theological significance of the biblical genealogies. Again his lack of facility in the original language leads him to conclusions that cannot be supported by the text.

The Genre of Genesis 1–11

Craig does not deal with the fact that genre does not determine meaning, and his inability to deal with the original language surfaces again.

Chapter 6: Are Myths Believed to Be True?

In this chapter Craig deals with several topics: comparative anthropological data, ancient Near Eastern literary evidence, plasticity and flexibility of ancient Near Eastern myths, and application to Gen 1–11.

Comparative Anthropological Data

Although the information in this section may be interesting, Craig presents a one-sided interpretation of the anthropological data. His effort to make a distinction between truth as correspondence and truth as might be conceived by tribal societies fails. Craig equivocates on the notion of truth, which undermines his claim. He either ignores or is unaware of recent anthropological data that shows that oral traditions do tend to have fixed traditions that do not tolerate alteration.

Ancient Near Eastern Literary Evidence

In this section, Craig's efforts to compare the biblical narrative to ANE literary evidence fails because Craig does not understand Hebrew lexicology, grammar, or syntax.

- Craig misunderstands and misrepresents the notion of the expanse as this is used in the Genesis account.
- Craig subtly employs a form of uniformitarianism in which he imposes on the biblical account his contemporary notions of the waters above and below as described in the creation account.
- His explanation of the waters above as rain is wildly implausible.

Plasticity and Flexibility of Ancient Near Eastern Myths

Craig's notions of plasticity and flexibility contradict recent scholarship about oral traditions.

Application to Genesis 1–11

- Because he does not understand Hebrew, he is led to conclusions about the depictions of God that cannot be supported by the text.
- His attempts to build on the claim that there are inconsistencies in the creation accounts of Gen 1 and 2 is based on his failure to understand the language.
- His failure to deal with the original language leads him to unsupportable conclusions about God confronting Adam in the garden, about the tree of life, and about the serpent.
- Craig does not seem to understand the literary aspects of the text which are important in interpretation.
- Craig continues to conflate figure and metaphor with myth leading him to conclude that since the biblical text uses figures and

metaphors that it must be classified as myth since ANE myth uses figures and metaphors.

Chapter 7: Adam in the New Testament

In this chapter Craig introduces a distinction between truth and truth-in-a-story. He discusses several NT passages by which he attempts to show that the NT authors' references to Adam are only illustrative and not assertoric.

- Craig's treatment of 2 Peter and Jude cannot be sustained by the language.
- Neither 2 Peter nor Jude are talking about Gen 6.
- Craig's effort to connect Tartarus to Greek myth fails because Peter uses it in the context of Jewish apocalyptic, not Greek myth.
- In every one of the passages Craig discusses, he does not understand the original language, he reads into the text what it does not say, and he does not understand what the text does say.
- Craig does not understand the nature of typology as this is employed by the NT authors.
- Craig's treatment of Rom 5:12 cannot be supported by the grammar and syntax of the Greek.

Chapter 8: Scientific and Philosophical Preliminaries

In this chapter Craig attempts to deal with the question of what is it to be human.

- Craig addresses this question by an appeal to natural science.
- This approach is fallacious since this is a philosophical question and not a question of natural science.
- Craig appeals to evolution in attempt to show that Adam and Eve may have descended from non-human entities.

- The appeal to evolution to account for the existence of Adam and Eve is to claim that something (humanness) derived from nothing (non-humanness).

Chapter 9: Locating the Historical Adam

In this chapter Craig argues that Adam and Eve may have been a part of the group dubbed *Homo heidelbergensis*.

- Besides the fact that the theory of the evolution of the human species from non-human entities is fraught with devastating and ultimately insurmountable problems, the scenario sketched by Craig is certainly contradictory to the biblical account.
- An author is certainly free to decide the view he wishes to endorse, but an author is not free to claim that his view is a Christian view if it contradicts the biblical account.
- If sin and death entered through the founding pair, and if the founding pair were a part of a humanoid group, then sin did not enter the world through others in the group.
- If sin did not enter the world through others in the group, then they could have had descendants that do not sin in their own turn.
- Consequently, it is possible that there are descendants of those others who are not sinners and not in need of salvation by grace through faith.
- If there are descendants of others who are not sinners, then it is not true that all sinned. Only the descendants of Adam and Eve sin.

Conclusion

It is important in this conclusion to make some critical observations. First, nowhere in his text does Craig specifically define what he means by "literary context." To some degree this notion emerges in his list of ten characteristics of myths and as he investigates aspects of biblical narrative in relation to ANE myths. It would have been helpful if he had offered a definition or description or an explanation of his own understanding of what constitutes literary context. Second, Craig's first characteristic of myth is that myths are narratives. However, it cannot be the case that Craig is simply arguing that biblical narratives and ANE narratives have similar literary characteristics, or that they used similar modes of expression, or similar wording. If these are what constitute literary context, then the point is trivial. Third, Craig is not arguing simply that biblical authors and ANE authors employed similar literary characteristics. He is arguing for the more substantial claim that ANE myth provides the conceptual context in which the author of Gen 1–11 composed his narratives. His point is, the similarity of literature indicates the conceptual context in which the biblical narratives are composed. However, similarity of literature cannot establish conceptual context. Craig must already assume a conceptual context. Fourth, the conceptual content of ANE myths cannot be compared to the conceptual content of the biblical narrative. That is one reason Craig must appeal to the Bumba myth. In terms of conceptual content, biblical narratives are unique among the writings of ancient cultures. Indeed, the Bible is unique among all writings of mankind, and YHWH Elohim is unique among all the portrayals of gods in all the literary contexts of the world.

At the end of his final chapter, Craig states that his quest has not led to a conclusion about the historical Adam: "Given the incompleteness of the data and the provisionality of science, the quest of the historical Adam will doubtless never be concluded in our lifetime—or in anyone's lifetime, for that matter."[5] It is particularly problematic that Craig actually believes that because his quest is inconclusive that the question of the historical Adam is necessarily inconclusive in itself and must be taken as inconclusive for everyone. Craig has declared *ex cathedra* what must be true about the quest for the historical Adam, and he expects all to grant *nihil obstat* to his pronouncements. However, Craig might not have intended that his arguments and conclusions should be taken literally, because, if taken literally, they are palpably false.

---

5. Craig, *Adam*, 380.

Bibliography

Aarsleff, Hans. *From Locke to Saussure: Essays on the Study of Language and Intellectual History*. Minneapolis, MN: University of Minnesota Press, 1982.
Adler, Mortimer J. *Intellect: Mind over Matter*. New York: Macmillan, 1990.
Aland, Barbara, et al., eds. *The Greek New Testament*, 5th ed. Stuttgart: United Bible Societies, 2014.
———. *Novum Testamentum Graece*, 28th ed. Stuttgart: Deutsche Bibelgesellschaft, 2012.
Allis, Oswald T. *The Five Books of Moses*. Phillipsburg, NJ: Presbyterian and Reformed, 1974.
Andrews, E. H. *Is Evolution Scientific?* Welwyn Herts, UK: Evangelical, 1977.
Aquinatis, Sancti Thomas. *Pars Prima Summae Theologiae*. Tomus Quintus, *Opera Omnia*. Romae: Typographia Polyglotta, 1882.
Arndt, William, Frederick W. Danker, Walter Bauer, and F. Wilbur Gingrich. *A Greek-English Lexicon of the New Testament and Other Early Christian Literature*. Chicago: University of Chicago Press, 2000.
Astruc, Jean. *Conjectures sur les mémoires originaux dont il paroit que Moyse s'est servi pour composer le livre de la Génèse. Avec des remarques qui appuient ou qui éclaircissent ces conjectures*. Bruxelles: Chez Fricx, Imprimeur de Sa Majesté, vis-à-vis l'Eglise de la Madelaine, 1753.
Augustine of Hippo. *The City of God, Books VIII–XVI*. Edited by Hermigild Dressler. Translated by Gerald G. Walsh and Grace Monahan. Vol. 14, *The Fathers of the Church*. Washington, DC: The Catholic University of America Press, 1952.
Augustini, Sancti Aurelii. *Civitate Dei*. Paris: Apud gaume Fratres, Bibliopolas, 1888.
Biblia Hebraica Stuttgartensia. Stuttgart: Deutsche Bibelstiftung, 1977.
Boyd, Steven, and Andrew A. Snelling. "The Profit of the Venture: The Significance of Flood Chronology." In *Grappling with the Chronology of the Genesis Flood*, edited by Steven W. Boyd and Andrew A. Snelling, 13–25. Green Forest, Arizona: Master, 2014.

Burnham, Sylvester. *The Elements of Biblical Hermeneutics*. Hamilton, New York: Publican, 1916.

Burridge, Richard A. *What Are the Gospels? A Comparison with Graeco-Roman Biography*. 2nd ed. Waco, TX: Baylor University Press, 2018.

Campbell, Donald K. "The Interpretation of Types." *Bibliotheca Sacra* 112 (1955): 248–55.

Carabine, Deirdre. *The Unknown God: Negative Theology in the Platonic Tradition Plato to Eriugena*. Eugene, OR: Wipf and Stock, 1995.

Carpenter, J. Estlin, and G. Harford-Battersby. "Introduction and Tabular Appendices." In *The Hexateuch According to the Revised Version, vol. 1*, 183–221. London: Longmans, Green, and Company, 1900.

Cassuto, Umberto. *The Documentary Hypothesis and the Composition of the Pentateuch*. Translated by Israel Abrahams. Jerusalem: Magnes, 1983.

Chaberek, Michael. *Aquinas and Evolution: Why St. Thomas's Teaching on the Origins is Incompatible with Evolutionary Theory*. n.p.: Chartwell, 2019.

Charles, R. H. *The Book of Enoch or 1 Enoch: Gizeh Greek Fragment of Enoch*. Oxford: Clarendon, 1912.

Charlesworth, James H. "1 (Ethiopic Apocalypse of) Enoch." In *The Old Testament Pseudepigrapha: Apocalyptic Literature and Testaments*, edited by James H. Charlesworth, 5–89. New York: Doubleday, 1983.

Clement of Alexandria. "The Stromata, or Miscellanies." In *Patrologia Graeca*, edited by J. P. Migne, Vol. IX. Paris: J. P. Migne, 1857.

Clines, David J. A. *On the Way to the Postmodern: Old Testament Essays, 1967–1998*. Sheffield: Sheffield Academic, 1998.

Craig, William Lane. "Anti-Platonism." In *Beyond the Control of God? Six Views on the Problem of God and Abstract Objects*, edited by Paul M. Gould, 113–41. New York: Bloomsbury Academic, 2014.

———. *In Quest of the Historical Adam: A Biblical and Scientific Exploration*. Grand Rapids: Eerdmans, 2021.

Currid, John D. *Genesis 1:1—25:18*. Vol. 1. Webster, NY: Evangelical Press, 2003.

Davidson, Richard M. *Typology in Scripture: A study of hermeneutical tupos structures*. Berrien Springs, MI: Andrews University Press, 1981.

de Vaux, Roland. *Social Institutions, Vol. 1. Ancient Israel*. New York: McGraw-Hill, 1965.

Deely, John. *What Distinguishes Human Understanding?* South Bend, IN: St. Augustine's, 2002.

Dickason, C. Fred. *Angels, Elect and Evil*. Chicago: Moody, 1975.

Domning, Daryl P. "Evolution, Evil and Original Sin." *America*, November 12, 2001. http://americamagazine.org/issue/350/article/evolution-evil-and-original-sin.

Eddy, Paul Rhodes, and Gregory A. Boyd. *The Jesus Legend: A Case for the Historical Reliability of the Synoptic Tradition*. Grand Rapids: Baker Academic, 2007.

Enns, Paul P. *The Moody Handbook of Theology*. Chicago: Moody, 1989.

Epiphanii. "Adversus Octoginta Hæreses." In *Patrologia Graeca*, edited by J. P. Migne, Vol. XLI. Paris: J. P. Migne, 1863.

Fanning, Buist M. *Verbal Aspect in New Testament Greek*. Oxford: Clarendon, 1990.

Feser, Edward. *Philosophy of Mind*. Oxford: Oneworld, 2005.

Fogelin, Robert J. *Wittgenstein*. 2nd ed. Edited by Ted Honderich. London: Routledge, 1995.

Frawley, William J., ed. *International Encyclopedia of Linguistics*, 2nd ed. Oxford: Oxford University Press, 2003.
Fritsch, Charles T. "Biblical Typology." *Bibliotheca Sacra* 104 (1947): 214–22.
Glock, Hans-Johann. *What Is Analytic Philosophy?* Cambridge: Cambridge University Press, 2008.
Goppelt, Leonhard. *Typos: The Typological Interpretation of the Old Testament in the New*. Translated by Donald H. Madvig. Grand Rapids: Eerdmans, 1982.
Gould, Paul M. ed. *Beyond the Control of God? Six Views on the Problem of God and Abstract Objects*. New York: Bloomsbury Academic, 2014.
Hacker, P. M. S. *Wittgenstein's Place in Twentieth-century Analytic Philosophy*. Oxford: Blackwell, 1996.
Harrison, R. K. *Introduction to the Old Testament*. Grand Rapids: Eerdmans, 1969.
Hays, Christopher M., and Stephen Lane Herring. "Adam and the Fall." In *Evangelical Faith and the Challenge of Historical Criticism,* edited by Christopher M. Hays and Christopher B. Ansberry, 25–54. Grand Rapids: Baker Academic, 2013.
Howe, Thomas A. "Does Genre Determine Meaning?" *Christian Apologetics Journal* 6.1 (2007): 1–19.
Hutton, James. *Theory of the Earth, with Proofs and Illustrations*. Edinburgh: Cadell, Junior, and Davies, 1795.
Jobes, Karen H., and Moisés Silva. *Invitation to the Septuagint*, 2nd ed. Grand Rapids: Baker Academic, 2015.
Joseph, Ziegler, ed. *Iob*. Vol. XI, 4, *Vetus Testamentum Graecum. Auctoritate Academiae Scientiarum Gottingensis Editum*. Göttingen: Vandenhoeck and Ruprecht, 1982.
Kahane, Howard. *Logic and Philosophy: A Modern Introduction*. Belmont, CA: Wadsworth, 1973.
Kirk, G. S., J. E. Raven, and M. Schofield. *The Presocratic Philosophers: A Critical History with a Selection of Texts*, 2nd ed. Cambridge: Cambridge University Press, 1983.
Klubertanz, George P. *The Philosophy of Human Nature*. New York: Appleton-Century-Crofts, 1953.
Koehler, Ludwig, Walter Baumgartner, M. E. J. Richardson, and Johann Jakob Stamm. *The Hebrew and Aramaic Lexicon of the Old Testament*. Leiden: Brill, 1994–2000.
Leiden Peshitta. Leiden: Peshitta Institute Leiden, 2008.
Licona, Michael. *The Resurrection of Jesus: A New Historiographical Approach*. Downers Grove: IVP Academic, 2010.
Lowe, E. J. "Nominalism." In *The Oxford Companion to Philosophy*, edited by Ted Honderich, 624. Oxford: Oxford University Press, 1995. 624.
Luskin, Casey. "Missing Transitions: Human Origins and the Fossil Record." In *Theistic Evolution: A Scientific, Philosophical, and Theological Critique*, edited by J. P. Moreland, 437–73. Wheaton, IL: Crossway, 2017.
Lyell, Charles. *Principles of Geology: Being an Inquiry How Far the Former Changes of the Earth's Surface are Referable to Causes Now in Operation*, 3nd ed. London: John Murray, 1835.
Lyotard, Jean-François. *La Condition Postmoderne: Rapport Sur Le Savoir*. Paris: Les Éditions De Minuit, 1979.
Machen, J. Gresham. *The Origin of Paul's Religion*. New York: Macmillan, 1923.
Maier, Gerhard. *Biblical Hermeneutics*. Translated by Robert W. Yarbrough. Wheaton, IL: Crossway, 1994.
Maritain, Jacques. *Introduction Générale a las Philosophie*. Vol. 1, Éléments de Philosophie, 6th ed. Paris: Pierre Téqui, Libraire-Éditeur, 1921.

McGrew, Lydia. *Review of Michael Licona's Why Are There Differences in the Gospels?* Matthews, NC: Bastion, 2019.

———. *The Mirror or the Mask: Liberating the Gospels From Literary Devices.* Tampa, FL: DeWard, 2019.

Meyer, Stephen C. "Neo-Darwinism and the Origin of Biological Form and Information." In *Theistic Evolution: A Scientific, Philosophical, and Theological Critique*, edited by J. P. Moreland, 105–37. Wheaton, IL: Crossway, 2017.

Modrak, Deborah K. W. *Aristotle's Theory of Language and Meaning.* Cambridge: Cambridge University Press 2001.

Moo, Douglas J. *The Letter to the Romans*, 2nd ed. Grand Rapids: Eerdmans, 2018.

Moreland, J. P. "Postmodernism and the Intelligent Design Movement." *Philosophia Christi* 2.1 (1999): 97–101.

———. "Truth, Contemporary Philosophy and the Postmodern Turn." *Journal of the Evangelical Theological Society* 48 (2005): 77–88.

———. *Scientism and Secularism: Learning to Respond to a Dangerous Ideology.* Wheaton, IL: Crossway, 2018.

Moreland, J. P., and William Lane Craig. *Philosophical Foundations for a Christian Worldview.* Downers Grove, IL: InterVarsity, 2003.

Moreland, J. P., ed. *Theistic Evolution: A Scientific, Philosophical, and Theological Critique.* Wheaton, IL: Crossway, 2017.

Murdoch, W. G. C. "Interpretation of Symbols, Types, Allegories, and Parables." In *A Symposium on Biblical Hermeneutics*, edited by Gordon M. Hyde, 209–23. Washington, D.C.: Review and Herald, 1974.

Nahum M. *Genesis: The JPS Torah Commentary* tyvarb. Philadelphia: The Jewish Publication Society, 1989.

Nash, Ronald H. *Christianity and the Hellenistic World.* Grand Rapids: Zondervan, 1984.

Niehaus, Jeffrey J. *God at Sinai.* Grand Rapids: Zondervan, 1995.

Osborne, Grant R. *The Hermeneutical Spiral: A Comprehensive Introduction to Biblical Interpretation*, 2nd ed. Downers Grove, IL: IVP Academic, 2006.

Parvish, Samuel. *An Enquiry into the Jewish and Christian Revelation.* London: T. Cox, 1746.

Payne, Smith, R. *A Compendious Syriac Dictionary: Founded upon the Thesaurus Syriacus of R. Payne Smith.* Oxford: Oxford University Press, 1902.

Pegis, Anton C. *At the Origins of the Thomistic Notion of Man.* New York: Macmillan, 1962.

Pritchard, James B., ed., *The Ancient Near East: An Anthology of Texts and Pictures.* Princeton: Princeton University Press, 1958.

Rahlfs, Alfred. *Psalmi Cum Odis.* Vol. X, *Vetus Testamentum Graecum. Auctoritate Academiae Scientiarum Gottingensis Editum.* Göttingen: Vandenhoeck and Ruprecht, 1979.

Ross, Hugh. *Navigating Genesis: A Scientist's Journey through Genesis 1–11.* Covina, CA: Reasons to Believe, 2014.

Sailhamer, John H. *Genesis Unbound: A Provocative New Look at the Creation Account.* Colorado Springs, CO: Dawson, 2011.

———. *The Meaning of the Pentateuch: Revelation, Composition, and Interpretation.* Downers Grove, IL: IVP Academic, 2009.

———. *The Pentateuch as Narrative: A Biblical-Theological Commentary.* Grand Rapids: Zondervan, 1992.

Sarna, Nahum M. *Genesis: The JPS Torah Commentary* tyvarb. Philadelphia: The Jewish Publication Society, 1989.
Seuren, Pieter A. M. *Western Linguistics: An Historical Introduction*. Malden, MA: Blackwell, 1998.
Silva, Moisés, ed., *New International Dictionary of New Testament Theology and Exegesis*. Grand Rapids: Zondervan, 2014.
Smith, J. Payne, ed. *A Compendious Syriac Dictionary: Founded upon the Thesaurus Syriacus of R. Payne Smith*. Oxford: Clarendon, 1990.
Soanes, Catherine, and Angus Stevenson, eds. *Concise Oxford English Dictionary*. Oxford: Oxford University Press, 2004.
Sokoloff, Michael. *A Syriac Lexicon: A Translation from the Latin, Correction, Expansion, and Update of C. Brockelmann's Lexicon Syriacum*. Winona Lake, IN: Eisenbrauns, 2009.
Song, Ho Jang, and Hui Soo An. "The Critique of the Principle of Uniformitarianism and the Analysis of High School Earth Science Textbooks." *SNU Journal of Education Research* 6 (1996): 75–93.
Stek, John H. "Biblical Typology Yesterday and Today." *Calvin Theological Journal* 5 (1970): 133–62.
Tertullian. "De Testimonio Animae." In *Libri Apologetici*. Pars I, *Tertulliani Opera*. Edited by E. F. Leopold, 178–85. Lipsiae: Sumtibus et Typis Bernh. Tauchnitz, 1839.
Thomas, D. Winton, ed., "The Epic of Creation." In *Documents from Old Testament Times*, translated by D. Winton Thomas, 3–16. New York: Harper and Row, 1958.
Treier, Daniel J. "Typology." In *Dictionary for Theological Interpretation of the Bible*, edited by Kevin J. Vanhoozer, 823–27. Grand Rapids: Baker Academic, 2005.
Ussher, James. *The Annals of the World*. London: E. Tyler and G. Bedell, 1658.
Wallace, Daniel B. *Greek Grammar Beyond the Basics: An Exegetical Syntax of the New Testament*. Grand Rapids: Zondervan, 1996.
Waltke, Bruce K., and Michael Patrick O'Connor. *An Introduction to Biblical Hebrew Syntax*. Winona Lake, IN: Eisenbrauns, 1990.
Walton, John H., and N. T. Wright. *The Lost World of Adam and Eve: Genesis 2—3 and the Human Origins Debate*. Downers Grove, IL: IVP Academic, 2015.
Waters, Guy Prentiss. "Theistic Evolution is Incompatible with the Teachings of the New Testament." In *Theistic Evolution: A Scientific, Philosophical, and Theological Critique*, edited by J. P. Moreland, et al. Wheaton, IL: Crossway, 2017.
Wellhausen, Julius. *Prolegomena zur Geschichte Israels*. Berlin: Druck und Verlag von Georg Reimer, 1899.
Wenham, Gordon J. "The Date of Deuteronomy: Linch-Pin of Old Testament Criticism." *Themelios* 10.3 (1985): 15–18.
Wevers, John William, ed. *Deuteronomium*. Vol. III, 2. *Vetus Testamentum Graecum. Auctoritate Academiae Scientiarum Gottingensis Editum*. Göttingen: Vandenhoeck and Ruprecht, 2006.
Whitcomb, John C., Jr. *The World That Perished*. Grand Rapids: Baker, 1973.
Whybray, R. Norman. *Introduction to the Pentateuch*. Grand Rapids: Eerdmans, 1995.
Wittgensetin, Ludwig. *Philosophical Investigations*. 2nd ed. Translated by G. E. M. Anscombe. Oxford: Blackwell, 1997.
Xenophanes of Kolophon. "Fragments of Xenophanes." In *The First Philosophers of Greece*. Translated by Arthur Fairbanks. London: Kegan Paul, Trench, Trübner & Company, 1898.

Ziegler, Joseph, ed., *Iob*, Vol. XI, 4, *Vetus Testamentum Graecum. Auctoritate Academiae Scientiarum Gottingensis Editum*. Göttingen: Vandenhoeck and Ruprecht, 1982.

Ziegler, Joseph, ed. *Ezechiel*. Vol. XVI, 1. *Vetus Testamentum Graecum. Auctoritate Academiae Scientiarum Gottingensis Editum*. Göttingen: Vandenhoeck & Ruprecht, 2006.

Zuck, Roy B. *Basic Bible Interpretation: A Practical Guide to Discovering Biblical Truth*. Colorado Springs, CO: Victor, 1991.

Index

OLD TESTAMENT

Genesis

	27, 51, 99, 107, 116, 117, 118, 127, 128, 160, 169, 174, 211, 214, 218, 238
1	7, 21, 69, 70, 74, 77, 78, 79, 84, 85, 115, 148, 241, 247
1:1	7, 69, 69n8, 107
1:1—7:24	21, 65, 241
1:2	16, 17, 19, 22, 23, 81, 81n42
1:2—2:4a	7
1:2–31	158
1:3	17
1–3	191
1:3–5	83
1:3–29	17
1–5	182
1:6	17, 136, 136n17
1:6–8	83, 84, 85n46
1:7	139
1–7	158, 159
1:8	136
1:9	17, 22
1:9ff	16
1–11	xv, xvi, 11, 12, 14, 21, 27–30, 34, 44, 46, 47, 50, 65, 67, 68, 72–74, 85, 106, 108, 113, 117, 121, 127, 135, 143, 144, 155, 161, 223, 235, 237–47, 250
1:11	17
1:14	137
1:14–19	83
1:15	137
1:17	137
1:20–23	83
1:24–31	83
1:26	107, 107n100
1:27	187
1:28	19, 107, 107n101
1:29	107, 107n99
2	63, 70, 71, 74, 77, 79, 94, 195, 247
2:2–3	159, 159n64
2–3	146
2:4	69, 117

Genesis (cont.)

2:5–6	77, 77n35, 138n23, 148, 148n46
2:6	77
2:7	195
2:7 LXX	195
2:8	8, 8n11, 17
2:9	218, 218n152
2:10–14	95, 95n69
2:15	17, 156, 156n61, 159
2:15–24	158
2:16–17	158, 159
2:17	123, 123n15, 211, 211n122
2:18	159, 215, 215n138
2:18–24	158
2:19	77, 77n36, 79n37
2:19–20	71
2:20	71, 71n12
2:21	71, 71n13
2:24	187
2:25	212, 212n126
2:25—3:6	158
2:25—3:7	158
2:32	124n16
3	72, 73, 86
3:1	87
3:5	90, 90n57
3:6	90, 211, 211n123
3:7	7, 158, 212, 212n127
3:8	75, 75n29
3:8—6:22	158
3:13	213, 213n131
3:14	72, 72n20, 72n21, 152, 152n54, 213, 213n132
3:17	72, 72n18
3:17–19	156, 156n60
3:19	108, 108n105, 217, 217n148
3:22	90, 90n58, 93, 93n66, 218, 219, 219n153
3:24	218, 219, 219n154
4	110, 241
4:1–24	158
4:20–21	49, 49n4
4:26	23, 80, 111, 111n113
5	17, 48, 49, 110, 113, 119, 125, 241
5:1	119
5:1–3	125
5:1–5	125n18
5:1–32	121
5:5	124, 211
5:6–8	48, 48n3
5:8	124
5:11	124
5:14	124
5:17	124
5:20	124
5:24	214, 214n134
5:27	124
5:29	85, 86, 86n49, 159, 159n65
5:31	124
5:32	124
6	168, 169, 171, 248
6:1–4	164, 165, 167
6:1–6	158
6:2	165
6:3	101, 101n83, 101n84
6:4	111, 111n114
6:5	17
6:9	119
6–9	173
6:9	173, 173n34, 214, 214n135
6:10	21
6:11	17
6:17	21
6:18–20	21
7	23
7:1–3	21
7:11–12	138, 139
7:19	107, 107n102
7:19–20	21
7:21–24	21
7:24	17, 238
8:1	17, 21, 22, 23, 65, 138n23, 238
8:2	138

8:3	21, 84
8:4–5	21
8:7	21–22
8:8–12	17
8:9	107, 107n98
8:11	17
8:14	17
8:15–17	21
8:20	17, 22
8:21	22
8:21a	22n35
9:5	190
9:8–10	21
9:11–17	21
9:18	21
9:19	21
9:20	17
9:29	124
10	23, 109, 116, 118, 119
10:1	109, 119
10:2–19	24
10:7	110
10:20–30	24
10:28–29	110
10:31–32	24
11	23, 116, 117, 119, 237, 238
11:1–9	24
11:2	112
11:4	112, 112n116
11:10	116, 119
11:10–26	113, 121
11:10–32	24
11:27	120
12:1ff	24
12:2	117
12:3	9
12:3a	9
12:8	23, 80, 80n39
12–50	108
15:6	32
17:9	157
18	146
18:1	146
18:1–2	146
18:19	157
19	174
19:1–3	175, 175n40
19:7	175
19:8	176
19:9	176, 176n41
19:37	122n11
19:37 NET	122
19:38	122n12
19:38 NET	122
22:17	9
22:18	9
25:12	120
25:19	120
26:4	9, 31
26:5	31, 31n47
28	112
28:12	112, 112n115
28:14	9
32	143
32:20 H31	143n36
32:24–25	143
32:25–26 H	143n35
32:30 H31	143
36:1	120
37:2	120
42:22	190
46:12, 25	122
46:16–18	122
46:25	122
49:1	14
49:17	86, 86n50
49:26	121, 121n10

Exodus

1:1–22	25
1:9	24, 26
1:11–12	26
1:11–14	17
2:1—15:21	25
2:23–25	17
4:1	87
4:31	32
6:3	80
7:9	87
7:11	184, 184n62
7:22	184, 185, 185n63
8:1	157
8:20	157
9:1	157
9:7	24

Exodus (*cont.*)

9:13	157
11–14	26
13:5	17
14:1–22	17
14:21	17
14:22	17
15–21	26
16:4–34	25
16:35	25
16—Numbers 21	24, 25
17:1–7	25
17:8–13	25
17:14–16	25
18:4	215, 215n139
19	17
19—Numbers 10	25
20:8	160, 160n66
20:11	22, 22n36
22	26
24:9–10	144, 144n37
25:20	99, 99n78
33:11	147, 147n42

Numbers

11:4–34	25
13	165
13:33	165, 165n9
14:11	32, 32n49
14:21–22	25
20:1–12	25
20:12	32, 32n48
20:23–29	25
21:1–16	25
21:6	87, 88, 88n55
21:6 LXX	88n55
21:16–18	185
22:1—24:25	25
22:2	26
22:3	24, 26
22:6	24, 26
22:17	24, 25
22:41—23:12	26
22:41—24:25	26
23:13–26	26
23:27—24:25	26
24:14	14
25:1—36:13	25

33:52	58, 58n18

Deuteronomy

	55, 57, 58, 59, 60
1:32	32, 32n50
2:18	70n11
2:29	70, 70n10
4:30	14
9:23–24	32, 32n51
10:12–13	157
12:5–14	55–56, 56n15
12:10	17
12:13–14	58, 58n19
13:21	17
29:8	91n61
29:9 (H8)	90, 91
31:28–29	14
32:11	16, 16n30, 17, 22, 23
32:28	91, 91n63
32:29	91, 91n62
33:27	131, 131n5
34:7	126, 126n19
34:10	147, 147n43

Joshua

	57
7:10–11	203, 203n99
13:1	126, 126n20
23:1	126, 126n21

Judges

	57
19:23	176

Ruth

2:12	74, 75, 75n27

2 Kings

	57
4:11	190
19:19	61, 61n25
23	57

Job

4:21	190

26:13	87
27:3	197, 197n88
28:24	107, 107n103
38	103
38:8–11	103, 103n91
41:24	172
41:24 ZJ	172n29

Psalms

18:1 LXX	173
18:2a–b	173n33
19:1	136, 136n19, 173
33	103
90	70
90:2	70, 70n9
104	103
119:119	3, 3n4
150:1	136, 136n20

Proverbs

	29
8	103

Isaiah

1:1–31	145
1:1–35	145
2:1—12:6	145
2:12–14	108, 108n104
5:2	17
6:2	87
13:1—35:10	145
14:29	88
14:39	87
30:6	87
36	145
36–27	145
36–39	145
37	145
38–39	145
40:1—48:22	145
40:1—66:24	145
40:18	63, 63n33
41	15
41:21–23	15, 15n28
44:6	61, 61n26
45:5	61, 61n27
46:5	63, 63n34
46:9–10	15, 15n29
49:1—57:21	145
58:1—66:24	145
65:19	101n82
65:20	101

Jeremiah

	57

Ezekiel

	57, 99
1	98, 99
1:5	98, 98n75
1:6–11	153
1:22–26	137
1:26	137n22
3:18	190
10	97, 98
10:1	137
10:11	99, 99n77
10:14	97, 97n73, 153
10:15	98, 98n76
29:3	87, 88n51
29:3 ZE	88n51
36:25	18
37:5	18, 18n33
41	98
41:18–19	98, 98n74

Daniel

	181
2	21
12:3	137, 137n21

Amos

9:3	87

ANCIENT NEAR EASTERN TEXTS

Atra-Hasis (Akkadian epic)	29

Enki and Ninmah

24–37	62–63

Enuma Elish	65–66
Epic of Gilgamesh	29, 135, 163
Eridu Genesis	29

DEUTEROCANONIAL BOOKS

1 Enoch

	181, 182, 184
1–5	183
1.9	162, 181
10.12	168
12.4	168
15.3	168
15.7	168
20:2	172

4 Ezra

7:118	202

PSEUDEPIGRAPHA (OLD TESTAMENT)

The Assumption of Moses

	180

ANCIENT JEWISH WRITERS

Josephus

Contra Apionem

2, 240	172

Philo

Exposition of the Law

152	172

NEW TESTAMENT

Matthew

	38, 99
3:16	23
19:4–5	187
19:4–6	162, 187, 187n69
22:30	171, 171n23
24	19
24:37–41	19, 19n34

Mark

	38, 99

Luke

	99
3:23, 38	162
3:38	162
11:24	170
11:26	170
11:50–51	189, 189n71
11:50f	190

John

	38, 99
3:5	18, 18n31
3:10	18
3:12	132, 132n7
3:13	132, 132n8
5:44	61, 61n29
6:53–56	92, 92n65

Acts

17:26	162

Romans

1:17	221
3:23–24	5
4:15	216
5	199
5:12	73, 124, 124n17, 201n96, 208m116, 208, 209, 211, 214, 215, 218, 220, 248
5:12–21	162, 201–2, 202n97, 213, 220
5:13	215
5:13–14	215, 215n140
5:14	162, 204
5:18–19	214
15:4	71, 71n14

Index

1 Corinthians

	185, 191
6:16–18	192
10:1–4	185, 186n66
10:4	185–86
10:6	196, 196n87, 204
10:11	204
11:8–9	162, 191
13:12	236
15	199, 200, 219
15:1–4	199, 199n93
15:3	1, 2, 2n2, 237
15:12–19	200, 200n94
15:20	197, 197n89
15:20–28	194, 194n79, 197
15:21	198
15:21–22	162, 198, 198n91
15:21–22, 45–46	194
15:22	198
15:22, 45	162
15:23	197
15:26	219, 219n156
15:42–49	195, 195n80
15:45	162
15:45–46	194, 195, 198
15:45–49	162
15:49	196, 196n85

2 Corinthians

| 1:7 | 190, 190n73 |
| 11:3 | 162, 190 |

Galatians

| 4:25 | 186 |

Ephesians

| 2:8 | 210, 210n120 |

Philippians

| 2:9–11 | 113, 113n117 |

1 Timothy

| 1:17 | 61, 61n28 |

2:12	191
2:12–14	162
2:13, 14	162
2:13–14	191
2:14	162

2 Timothy

	222
2:12	222, 222n162
3:8	184–85, 184n61

Philemon

| 18 | 216, 216n144 |

Hebrews

1:14	170
5:13–14	92, 92n64
9:27	219, 219n155
11:7	138n23

1 Peter

3:18–20	164, 164n6
3:19	177
3:19–20	164
3:20	165

2 Peter

	166, 167, 171, 172, 174, 204, 248
2:1	177, 178
2:2	177, 178
2:4	164, 171, 171n24, 172, 177, 178
2:4–10	167
2:4–11	167n13
2:5	173–84, 173n32, 177, 178
2:5 NASB	105
2:7–8	174, 175, 175n39
2:7b	176
3:3–8	104, 104n93
3:6	104, 105
3:7	105

Jude

	169, 171, 172, 179, 204, 248
5–7	168, 168n16
5–11	182
6 NASB	169
6–7	164, 168
9–10	179, 179n47
14	162
14–15	162, 162n2, 181, 181n53, 182

Revelation

2:7	149, 149n50
5:12	73n24
12:3	88, 88n53
12:9	73, 73n22, 87, 88, 88n54
22:1–2	93, 93n67, 150, 150n51
22:5	81, 81n41
22:14	150, 150n52

EARLY CHRISTIAN WRITINGS

Aquinas
Pars Prima Summae Theologiae

Ia.51.1	170n22

Augustine
City of God

VIII–XVI, 537–38	
	3n4
XVI.27.700	3n4

Clement of Alexandria
"Stromata, or Miscellanies"

VI.6.35–36	165n7

Epiphanius	51

Adversus Octoginta Haereses

I.2.292	51n6

Origen	180

Tertullian
"De Testimonio Animae"

3.181	2n3

GRECO-ROMAN LITERATURE

Aristotle	10, 10n16

Homer
Illiad

	51

Isocrates	38
Nepos	38

Plato

Timaeus	43
Protagoras	43
Satyrus	38

Sibylline Oracles

2, 302	172
4, 186	172

Xenophon of Kolophon

	38, 42, 43

Fragments of Xenophanes

66–67	42n23

www.ingramcontent.com/pod-product-compliance
Lightning Source LLC
Chambersburg PA
CBHW071243230426
43668CB00011B/1568